A Purchasing Manager's Guide to Strategic Proactive Procurement

David N. Burt, Ph.D.

NAPM Professor of Supply Management and Marketing,
School of Business Administration,
University of San Diego

Richard L. Pinkerton, Ph.D., C.P.M.

Professor of Marketing and Logistics,
The Sid Craig School of Business,
California State University, Fresno

amacom

American Management Association

New York • Boston • Chicago • Kansas City • San Francisco • Washington, D.C.
Brussels • Mexico City • Tokyo • Toronto

Library of Congress Cataloging-in-Publication Data

Burt, David N.
   A purchasing manager's guide to strategic proactive procurement/
David N. Burt, Richard L. Pinkerton.
     p. cm.
   Includes bibliographical references and index.
   ISBN 0-8144-0288-7
   1. Industrial procurement.   2. Purchasing.   I. Pinkerton, Richard
L. II. Title.
   HD39.5.B857   1996
   658.7'2—dc20   95-44558
                                                       CIP

Printing number

10   9   8

To Lamar Lee, Jr., Gayton Germane, and Bob Davis,
all former members of Stanford University's great School of Business,
and mentors of David N. Burt

To William P. Stilwell, J. Howard Westing, Harland E. Samson, and
Isadore V. Fine, all professors emeriti, The University of Wisconsin,
Madison, and the superb teachers of Richard L. Pinkerton

Contents

of estimates; price increases; cost within a strategic supply alliance; target costing; summary.

materials handler to buyer and then take a place at the product development table. The topics at these meetings are simply too technical and too complex, and most of the team possesses university-level technical and business training. Dear Old Betty and Good Old Fred are out of place; they have little credibility, little to contribute, and little respect from the other members. They simply cannot add value. This is one reason some forward-thinking companies have separated strategic procurement planning from day-to-day buying: one procurement group designs, develops, implements, and ensures the optimal functioning of the procurement process and another group executes the plan.

It is our hope that this book will provide renewed stimulation to move from reactive-passive purchasing to proactive procurement, a move almost guaranteed to reduce material costs by 10% per year, reduce the cost of converting purchased materials, virtually eliminate incoming quality problems, and reduce time-to-market. We define *proactive procurement* as the process of professionally and aggressively adding value during the four stages required for effective procurement: (1) the determination of what to buy; (2) the identification and development of the appropriate relationship with the desired source of supply; (3) obtaining the lowest all-in or total cost associated with purchasing and converting the required material or service; and (4) ensuring that the required material or service is received in the quality required on time and that relations with preferred suppliers are used to ensure these suppliers' availability for future procurements. Proactive procurement requires the development and implementation of an integrated procurement system as described in Chapter 1. It takes years for new concepts such as agricultural improvements regarding crop rotation and other high-yield payoff techniques to be embraced. Our experience has been that only a handful of U. S. firms have actually progressed from reactive purchasing to proactive procurement. Many firms go through the motions of progressing to proactive procurement: they attend only one or two training seminars and "think" that real change has occurred when, in fact, business goes on as usual. Thus, even though many of Burt's concepts first appeared in 1984, this book is needed to rekindle the fire so that American business can regain its competitive edge through the contributions of a proactive approach to procurement.

The 1990s are the years of the *revitalization* of industry. Managers everywhere recognize the need to increase profits or, in some cases, to become profitable once again. They know that productivity must increase. They know that to compete in the world marketplace, they must improve the quality of their firms' products, reduce cycle time, and lower costs.

There are abundant responses to the challenge of industrial revitalization: total quality management (TQM); just-in-time (JIT); reengineering; lean manufacturing; the list seems endless. But the simplest and quickest solution all too frequently is overlooked. It can be exciting, provocative, and challenging. Its impact can exceed all the benefits of the foregoing techniques. It is called *proactive procurement*. Ironically, it is a prerequisite for success with all of these techniques.

The procurement of material and services cuts across organizational boundaries. The process includes activities in Marketing, Design and Manufacturing, Engineering, Operations, Production Planning, Quality Assurance, Inventory Control, Purchasing, and Finance. Integration of the procurement activities per-

Preface

Much has happened in procurement circles since David N. Burt's book *Proactive Procurement* was published in 1984. We like to think *Proactive Procurement* had at least a small part in focusing attention on the importance of procurement in containing costs, improving quality, increasing productivity, shortening concept to customer delivery times, and strengthening the integration of materials management into the total operations of an organization. *A Purchasing Manager's Guide to Strategic Proactive Procurement* retains the visionary topics of *Proactive Procurement* while adding the very latest and, indeed, future procurement methods for effective purchasing in the twenty-first century.

A great many trade books addressing an organization's relations with its suppliers have appeared recently. Perhaps the most advanced is the *American Keiretsu* by Burt and Michael Doyle (Homewood, Ill.: Business One Irwin, 1993). Whether these books stress early supplier involvement, partnerships, alliances, strategic procurement, or supply management, all these themes require and expressly state the need for the procurement process to be a "value adder." The integrated procurement system (or IPS) as first described in *Proactive Procurement* adds value to the firm's operations. The heart of the IPS is the cross-functional procurement team composed of representatives of Design Engineering, Manufacturing Engineering, Purchasing, Manufacturing, Quality Control, key suppliers, Marketing, and, when relevant, Finance. This integrated procurement system preceded the horizontal corporation by some 10 years, and in some ways, it prepared the way for this approach to organization and management.

The other major action prescribed in Burt's 1984 work was the growing practice of beginning the procurement emphasis at the design stage while contracting or outsourcing maintenance, repairs, and operating supplies (MRO) and basic raw materials under long-term systems contracts and blanket orders with one or two suppliers. Management is slowly recognizing that the major procurement effort must be strategic and play a key role at the product-service concept development stage. At this stage, quality is designed in, cost is designed out, and the time required to bring a new product to market is reduced.

The foregoing changes also dictate the need for more professionally trained personnel in the purchasing or procurement function, now called *supply management* or *sourcing* by a few forward-thinking firms. Gone are the days when an individual could simply progress through on-the-job-training from secretary or formed by these departments results in a synergism, a situation in which the whole is greater than the sum of its parts. This type of integration and the resulting synergism take place in many settings: manufacturing, service and construction firms, not-for-profit organizations, and government. The net result for all is greatly increased profitability, productivity, and quality.

Proactive procurement requires that all members of the procurement system—whether forecasters in Marketing, designers and cost estimators in Engineering, planners and inventory managers, quality assurance personnel, the purchasing staff, and others—recognize their role in value-added procurement. In reactive purchasing, the purchasing department becomes involved in the procurement process only on receipt of a requisition for materials, supplies, or services and functions in a non-value-adding mode.

Often at least 60% of a product's or service's cost is in the form of purchased supplies, equipment, materials, and services. On average, 50% of a firm's quality problems can be tracked back to purchased materials. The amount of time required to bring new products to market successfully can be reduced by 25% and more through the successful early involvement of Purchasing and preferred suppliers during the new product development process. Thus, it is easy to see that procurement has more impact on the bottom line than any other process required to make the firm viable.

The concepts of proactive procurement and the integrated procurement systems have been embraced by several authors since the publication of *Proactive Procurement* in 1984. A very popular trade book, *Reverse Marketing: The New Buyer-Supplier Relationship*, by Leenders and Blenkhorn in 1988 urges "the purchaser take the initiative in making the proposal" for supply objectives.[1] In 1986, Witt described the virtues of looking at the entire logistical pipeline as "Logistics Early Involvement (LEI)."[2] All three approaches require the implementation of IPS and a proactive approach to procurement and IPSs. By the way, as far back as 1981, Victor H. Pooler and David J. Porter were using the term *proactive* purchasing.[3]

Successful integration of the system leading to proactive procurement requires dedication, qualified managers and subordinates, an understanding of sound procurement techniques by all involved, and a can-do attitude.

This book is an outgrowth of more than 60 years of experience as practitioners, professors, and students of procurement. It is based on the belief that proactive procurement is the key to greatly improved profits, productivity, and product quality.

Although written for the purchasing manager, *A Purchasing Manager's Guide to Strategic Proactive Procurement* has considerable relevance for top management. The understanding and support of senior management will greatly facilitate implementation of the recommended improvements.

This book outlines and discusses the steps required to gain the benefits of proactive procurement. Over 50 specific problems that frequently block effective procurement are identified together with suggestions for avoiding or overcoming them. The book is written with the objective of aiding busy managers in their efforts to ensure the successful survival and increase the profitability of their organizations.

This book will aid you in many ways. It will:

- Create an awareness of the benefits resulting from implementation of an integrated procurement system.
- Show you how to develop and sell your integrated system, including advice on how to overcome resistance to the required changes.
- Provide understanding of the *key* procurement activities so that *all* individuals involved in procurement understand their responsibilities and those of their counterparts.
- Identify and address over 50 problems or problem areas that result in ineffective procurement.
- Identify six points in the engineering design process at which purchasing can make a contribution to the profitability and success of the new product.
- Describe how the procurement system can improve the quality of your firm's products.
- Show how to integrate engineering into the procurement system.
- Portray the cost implications of alternate approaches to describing requirements and show how to conduct procurement research systematically.
- Describe professional sourcing procedures.
- Show how to improve purchasing lead time and how to live with material requirements planning.
- Provide insight into the conflicting forces that should be considered when developing inventory policies.
- Tell when make-or-buy analyses should be conducted and discuss the issues that should be considered.
- Explore pricing theory and practice including how to fight price increases with the Zero Base Pricing™ approach.
- Identify the basis of cost analysis including target costs, cost drivers, and cost containment.
- Discuss issues to consider when dealing with potential suppliers in foreign countries and list several critical cultural nuances to consider in such dealings.
- Describe the keys to successful win-win negotiations in concise and understandable language and discuss the role of nonpurchasing members of the negotiating team.
- Tell how to develop and implement profit contributing value engineering and analysis programs.
- Explain all facets of TQM and how to ensure timely delivery of the prescribed quality.
- Describe the benefits resulting from purchasing's involvement in the corporate planning process.
- Tell how to develop a strategic material plan and detailed tactical plans.
- Describe the benefits from purchaser-supplier collaboration and long-term relations.
- Show how to develop and manage competent suppliers.
- Show how to minimize the impact of material shortages.
- Describe the basics of team building.

- Bring you up to date on the latest thinking from the best of the current literature.
- And much more!

Notes

1. Michiel R. Leenders and David L. Blenkhorn, *Reverse Marketing: The New Buyer-Supplier Relationship* (New York: The Free Press, 1988).
2. Phillip R. Witt, *Cost Competitive Products: Managing Product Concept to Marketplace Reality* (Reston, Va.: Reston Publishing, 1986).
3. Victor H. Pooler and David J. Porter, "Purchasing's Elusive Conceptual Home," *Journal of Purchasing and Materials Management* (Summer 1981), p. 16.

Acknowledgments

Many people have contributed directly or indirectly to the development of this book. Burt's first and greatest teachers were two people who "worked for me" in his first two purchasing offices during the 1950s: Dick Curtis and Ed Williams. Many people in academia have played significant roles in the development of our understanding of business activities: George W. Zinke and Ruben A. Zubrow of the University of Colorado; Clyde Johnson and Norman Maier at the University of Michigan; and Bob Davis, Gayton F. Germane, the late Lamar Lee, Jr., and Steve Wheelwright at Stanford University. Colleagues during Burt's days in Dayton—Joe Boyett, Dean Martin, Frank Stickney, Ted Thompson, and Bob Trimble—played key roles in the development of our philosophy and insight into the procurement process. Steve Achtenhagen, Mel Kline, Bill Little, Jack and Cathy Bergquist, and the late Ed Cochran and Gail Murray all provided guidance and inspiration as the project developed and grew.

Many individuals in industry have provided assistance: Ralph Dixon of Hughes Aircraft provided invaluable input and counsel; Richard Y. Moss II of Hewlett-Packard, who developed the charts describing the engineering design process depicted in Chapter 2, and Evelyn Szabo of Megateck were both the source of great assistance. In addition, others in industry gave freely of their time: Nick Alex of NCR; Richard Baribault and his staff at Alcoa; Tony Dereczo of Rohr Industries; the late Kenneth Gay and Bob Peterson of Rockwell International; Brian Robertson of Apple Computer, Inc.; James M. Hill of Raytheon; Bill Lambert of Boeing; Gordon Olson, Malcolm Smith, Don Taylor, and John Veterren of Hewlett-Packard; Kevin C. Beidelman, and Gary Lenik of Newport Corp.; Bob Paul of Lockheed; Myron Schwartz of Memorix; The Sea Ray Corporation; Bob Reynolds of McDonnell Douglas; Andrew Scanlon of Hobart; James Walz of General Electric; D. C. Weinstein and Larry Michael of Westinghouse; John Kelsey and Dick West of the Ford Motor Company; Anthony P. Marino of Saint Agnes Hospital in Fresno, Calif.; Dick Erskine of the Bechtel group; John Zech of Kaiser Engineering; Harry Wright of FMC; and one of Burt's other coauthors, Michael F. Doyle, formerly of The Ford Motor Company and Motorola and now president of Doyle and Associates.

Deans James Burns and Robert O'Neil of the University of San Diego provided both support and encouragement. The word processing staff at California

State University—Fresno, The Sid Craig School of Business, including Marcia D. Martin, Lorna E. Lewis, and Kathy Uchiyama provided invaluable manuscript preparation. Sharon Burt provided scholarly advice, counsel, Exhibit 3-1, and much encouragement. Finally, Linda Vail, Secretary of Marketing and Logistics at California State University—Fresno, Sid Craig School of Business, helped on many details.

1

Benefits of the Integrated Procurement System

It is Saturday afternoon, September 6. Ted Jones, purchasing manager for the Eagle Manufacturing Company, is in his office reviewing his life at Eagle. Since becoming the head of Purchasing, Ted has been struggling with one crisis after another while trying to placate Operations, Plant Maintenance, and seemingly half the management team (and their secretaries). Although only 35, Ted feels like 60 (his wife thinks he's starting to act like 60, too). Eagle is expecting a great deal for the money it is paying Ted.

In the two years since taking over the department, Ted has put together a great team of buyers, expediters, and support staff. Their work is tops . . . they are all professionals. But morale is becoming a problem. On Friday, Bill Wilson, Ted's senior buyer, submitted his resignation. Bill decided to take a job with a handsome salary increase at Cable Manufacturers of America. He said, "If I'm going to get ulcers, I might as well be paid for them!"

Ted looks at the August performance data for the office: 743 transactions, 91% with delivery dates on or before specified, 87% of supplies and material purchases at or within 5% of target price, 9% late deliveries, and a 5% rejection rate of materials and supplies received. Compared with previous months' activity, the trends look good, but there is still room for improvement. Ted feels that his department could have a much greater impact on the firm's profitability if only he could generate more cooperation with the other departments. He also realizes that a better training program will bring along some of his own people a bit faster.

Ted thinks about some of the "big ones" that happened in August. Maintenance submitted a purchase request for a new robot on August 29. According to the estimates supplied, the machine would cost $4.4 million. It was to be delivered and operational in seven months. Only one source of supply was able to meet the delivery date. Ted wonders how much extra money the lack of lead time had cost.

Tim Raines, vice president of Operations, held Ted's feet to the coals in the weekly staff meeting on August 7. Operations had run out of parts that week. The vice president of Marketing, Ron Hankins, helped to apply the coals. In retrospect, Ted is puzzled over the hopscotch communication patterns between Operations, Material Control, Marketing, and his own office.

Tim jumped Ted on August 14, again during the staff meeting, saying that quality on the incoming parts was causing major production problems. Ted tried to explain the greater attrition rate inherent in new supplier production processes, but Tim was not convinced.

In fairness, not all his problems are with Operations, Ted thinks during his Saturday afternoon reverie. The president's secretary called twice to say that the janitorial services contractor had not washed the windows properly. Ted mentioned that poorly described, unenforceable specifications were part of the problem. But the secretary was just trying to do her job in seeing that somebody else's job was done right . . . she didn't know about the "contractual provisions."

Mary Jacobs, head of Administration, had been complaining to Ted on a daily basis about the new brand of reproduction paper: The quality of reproduction was down and the paper was constantly jamming the machine. The resulting downtime was reducing productivity and increasing frustration in her people. Ted pointed out that Finance had reduced funds available for supplies by 20%, which consequently had forced some sacrifice in quality.

Yesterday, John McCauly, an experienced buyer and normally as cool as a cucumber, had exploded when Ted asked how everything was going. John had replied, "Those blankety, blank estimators. This morning, I was negotiating with Fenwick Electronics for that robot. The maintenance department's estimate was $4.4 million. Fenwick proposed $5.8 million. You know that because of time, they were already in a sole-source position. Imagine my reaction when I learned that our 4.4 million 'estimate' was not an estimate at all but merely the amount budgeted for that machine last year! I had no basis for developing a realistic negotiating objective. I literally had to throw myself on the mercy of Fenwick's marketing manager."

Bringing his thoughts back to the present, Ted decides there just has to be a better way.

Extreme? Perhaps. Perhaps not. All managers have experienced many of Ted's problems. There is a way of avoiding most of them, and, in turn helping the purchasing department to make a greater contribution to profitability. That way is proactive procurement. And you can and should be responsible for making it happen.

Total quality management (TQM), just-in-time (JIT) manufacturing, simultaneous engineering, strategic cost management, flexible manufacturing, the virtual corporation, the protection of core competencies, value chain management, activity-based costing (ABC), and reduced time to market all have one thing in common: For the utmost success, the organization must have a well-designed, well-managed supply management system! And the designer and manager of this system is the vice president of Procurement.

The Integrated Procurement System

Procurement is the systematic process of deciding what, when, and how much to purchase; the act of purchasing it; and the process of ensuring that what is required is received on time in the quantity and quality specified. Procurement is much broader than purchasing, involving activities that take place in many departments.

The quantity, quality, and cost of purchased items affect the quality of the firm's product, the ability to produce it, productivity, and, most important, the firm's profitability. Determining what to buy does not begin when the purchase requisition is written but, rather, during the development of the product. Early involvement of Purchasing can avoid these common situations:

* New product introduction delays, a deadly error in this age of intensive global competition
* Overbuying, based on excessive specifications
* Underbuying based on traditional overfocus on price (price myopia vs. a focus on total cost), resulting in scrap, process yield losses, rework, time delays, and final customer rejection
* The purchase of large amounts of materials at quantity discounts causing needlessly high inventory carrying costs
* Manufacturing downtime due to stock outages because of inventory reductions
* Use of slower modes of transportation to save transportation dollars, resulting in large inventory carrying costs and/or manufacturing downtime
* The purchase of individual components without regard to the economies of modular packages (buying pieces instead of systems) and neglecting the ease of assemblability

Organizations exercise the best control over the cost and quality of purchased goods and services only when appropriate members of the various departments involved in the procurement process operate as an interdependent, integrated system. When this happens, a synergism takes place with the result that the integrated efforts become greater than the sum of the individual efforts. Conversely, uncoordinated action by one department's representative may optimize the success of that department but cause undesirable results in another, to the detriment of the organization as a whole. For example, incorporation of extremely high tolerances may make a product of great technical excellence but one that is too costly to survive in the marketplace. The purchase of large quantities of materials or supplies may mean lower unit prices through quantity discounts, but there will be increased inventory carrying costs. Conversely, inventories may be reduced in an effort to lower carrying costs, causing downtime in manufacturing due to stock outages, more frequent purchases at higher unit costs, or both. Slower modes of transportation may save shipping dollars but lead to larger inventories or downtimes in manufacturing.

Proactive procurement results in implementation of an integrated procurement system (IPS). With proactive procurement, all members of the procurement system—whether forecasters in Marketing, designers and cost estimators in Engineering, production planners and inventory managers, quality assurance personnel, the purchasing staff, and others—recognize their role in the IPS. And they cooperate in making the organization more profitable through more effective procurement. With this proactive approach, representatives of the purchasing department are involved (frequently with one or more preferred suppliers) in the requirements process in which they provide input on the commercial and technical implications of alternative materials, equipment, and services. The purchasing department takes the initiative in developing and managing the system and making savings happen. In reactive purchasing, the purchasing department becomes involved in the procurement process only on receipt of a requisition for materials, supplies, or services. (In some unfortunate cases, purchasing is not involved until even later.) An integrated procurement system is the key to increased profits and productivity and is the quickest way to quality improvement. The many interfaces and interdependencies of the IPS are shown in the IPS diamond, Exhibit 1-1, and are discussed throughout this book.

During the design stage of a product's development, incorporating the "right" material to be purchased significantly reduces material expenditures. Here are three examples of how this was done with Purchasing's help.

1. A manufacturer found that a zinc alloy was an acceptable alternative to a high-leaded tin-bronze casting alloy under consideration. The zinc alloy cost half the price of the tin-bronze alternative.
2. Another manufacturer found that a synthetic insulation material was far superior to asbestos in the production of high-temperature hose lines. The synthetic material cost one third as much as the asbestos and avoided the latter's hazards.
3. An appliance manufacturer found molded plastic knobs to be suitable alternatives to machined metal knobs, at a savings of 85%.

Market share, prices, and profits are all favorably affected by attention to quality. Today, *quality and reduced time to market have replaced price as the key to increased market share and profit margins.* Procuring the right quality materials frequently is the quickest and easiest way to improve the quality of the final product. Procuring the right quality materials is far more likely to occur when a firm uses a proactive approach to procurement than the traditional reactive approach.

A recent famous case of unilateral purchasing decision making involved the enormous price pressure by Ignacio Lopez, GM's former corporate purchasing chief. Lopez restored a focus on low price versus total cost at GM with, according to *Business Week,* the following results:

> But already, the Lopez system is causing problems. At the company's Arlington (Tex.) plant, an ill-fitting ashtray from a new, sub par supplier caused a six-week shutdown of Buick Roadmaster production. At another plant, GM managers had to go begging for help from a supplier that Lopez had rejected in favor of one that bid 5% less. Trouble was, half the low bidder's parts flunked quality tests. So within four days, the other supplier geared up to make parts that were flown to GM by charter plane. 'My guess is that their 5% savings turned into a 15% loss,' the second supplier says.[1]

Exhibit 1-1. The many interfaces of the IPS.

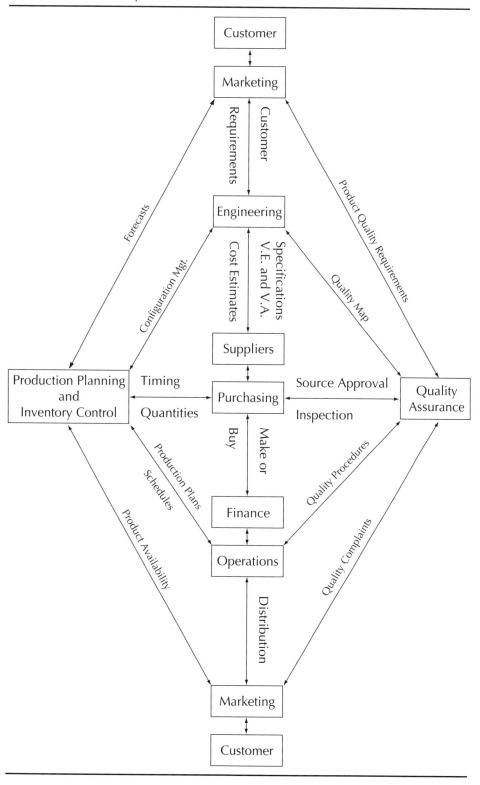

Here are five classic examples of procurement success stories:

1. An electronics manufacturer was able to reduce rework and warranty expenses by more than 50% through consideration of supplier quality capabilities during the design process.
2. A truck manufacturer reduced field failure and warranty expenses by 45% by specifying a more appropriate level of quality for purchased components during the redesign of a truck line.
3. An electronics manufacturer converted from using his own custom-designed specifications to commercial standards, realizing savings in excess of 10%.
4. Using performance specifications to describe the anticipated function of capital equipment allowed an organization to solicit competitive prices at significant savings.
5. Use of the correct method of specifying construction services reduced a manufacturer's expenditures in this unique area by 63%.

The Make-or-Buy Question

The make-or-buy (often referred to as "outsourcing") analysis is an extremely important activity in procurement and a major profit contributor. The decision to make or to buy is one of the most challenging and critical issues to confront management. The make-or-buy issue is becoming increasingly critical to a company's profitability—even survival—as it focuses on its competencies and outsources other activities. Great amounts of money are wasted making goods and providing services that could be purchased more economically, and great amounts of money are wasted buying those things that properly should be made by the firm. Chapter 7 covers this topic in detail.

Cost Savings

Expenditures for goods and services can be reduced significantly. For example, the right degree of competition, proper execution of negotiations, and implementation of sound value analysis engineering and analysis programs all can produce reduced expenditures. Additional savings result from selection and effective management of the right source—one that provides the right level of service, one that is dependable to the point where inventory can be reduced safely, and one that provides the specified level of quality. Unfortunately, the *savings that can be achieved by a reactive purchasing department generally are constrained by activities that have taken place before purchasing becomes involved in the procurement.*

The very survival of the organization may be affected by the presence or absence of a viable strategic material plan. Under the myopic approach of traditional reactive purchasing, the company may awaken one day to a world in which sources of supply capable of meeting its requirements are fully occupied supplying the company's competitors and are unavailable. *Proactive procurement includes strategic supply management as a key responsibility and, as discussed in Chapter 15, helps to avoid such situations.*

Materials Selection

The implementation of an integrated proactive approach to procurement can significantly affect productivity. For example, many of the quality problems encountered in manufacturing are the result of defective purchased materials. In fact, it is estimated that approximately 50% of a firm's quality problems can be attributed to purchased materials. The common sources of these quality problems are inefficiencies in the procurement system: incorrect specifications, inadequate regard for producibility by the suppliers, selection of the wrong source, failure of the designer at the purchasing firm or the supplying firm to use design of experiments (DOE) to develop a robust design, failure to certify the supplier's production and quality systems, or inadequate quality assurance and inspection.

Recently, the plant manager of a leading electronics manufacturer stated that if deficiencies in incoming material could be eliminated, he could increase throughput at his plant by 400% with no increase in equipment or labor.* The savings may far offset any incremental cost of materials, as shown in Exhibit 1-2.

Selecting the right material during design also will have a significant impact directly on productivity and manufacturing costs (and, in turn, on profits). Some materials are much more economical to work than others. For example, selecting bronze rather than lower-priced steel greatly reduces machining costs. As shown in Exhibit 1-3, the savings may offset any incremental cost of materials.

Productivity also is affected by procurement of the right supplies, capital equipment, services, and plant. Any additional cost for the right item of capital equipment may be offset many times through increased productivity and reduced maintenance, whether in a manufacturing, service, governmental, or construction setting. As shown in the case study at the beginning of this chapter, Ted saw that the procurement of a low-grade copy paper might have reduced purchase expenditures but it resulted in lower secretarial productivity and additional copier maintenance expense.

Service contracts have become a popular way of obtaining janitorial, security guard, transportation, and cafeteria services. Emergency rooms and pharmacies are operated under contracts at some hospitals. The quality and enforceability of the provisions and resulting contracts affect both the quality of services received and the number of personnel required to administer the contracts.

Procurement of the "right" type of construction also affects productivity. When an electronics manufacturer purchased two new manufacturing plants, it found that productivity in the two plants was significantly different! The first building consisted of two stories. The second plant consisted of one story and was cooled by 70-unit air conditioners located on the building's roof. In the first plant, the two-story construction posed material handling, management, and communication problems. Further, the central air conditioner became inoperable

---

*These defects resulted from the requirement for purchased components whose production processes had not stabilized. Defects in the purchased components could not be detected until the final assembly in which they were incorporated was tested. Specification of more proven components could have had relatively little effect on performance of the end product but would have avoided the vast majority of test and rework, thereby greatly increasing productivity!

Exhibit 1-2.   Effect of quality of purchased material on productivity and profits.

		Cost Totals With Standard Materials (costs in $1,000)		Cost Totals With High Quality Materials (costs in $1,000)
Sales (10,000 units)		$325		$325
Cost of goods sold:	*Man-Hours*		*Man-Hours*	
Purchased materials		100		110
Labor (production)	3,000	30	3,000	30
Labor (fault finding and rework)	12,000	120	6,000	60
Fixed		20		20
Totals	15,000	$270	9,000	$220
Operating income		$55		$105

Note 1: Productivity improvement (*productivity* is defined as the number of units produced per man-hour)
Standard materials: 15,000 hours to produce 10,000 units = .67 units per man-hour.
High quality materials: 9,000 hours to produce 10,000 units = 1.11 units per man-hour.
Productivity improvement = change to output per man-hour ÷ by original output = $|(.67-1.11)/.67| = 66\%$ improvement.
Note 2: Profit improvement: $|(55-105)/55| = 91\%$.
Note 3: This rather conservative analysis assumes that a higher level of quality of purchased material will result in greater material expenditures. In many instances, this may not be necessary.

on several occasions, which meant closing the entire plant. None of these problems existed at the second plant where productivity was considerably higher because of the selection of the right method of purchasing building construction. (Interestingly enough, the second plant cost only 37% as much as the first one on a square-foot basis.)

How Much Can Be Saved?

One of us recently met with purchasing executives from some 30 major manufacturing organizations. Annual sales at these organizations ranged from $200 million to in excess of $16 billion. The 30 organizations were well on the road to the integration of their procurement systems. The more significant components of proactive procurement and the IPS were described. Next, the traditional reactive approach to purchasing was discussed. Several executives indicated that they were familiar with firms that operate in this reactive mode. One stated that a recently acquired subsidiary had operated in this traditional reactive fashion "before I got my hands on it."

The executives were requested to estimate the savings incurred by transforming a reactive orientation to a proactive one. Estimates ranged from 6–30%

Exhibit 1-3. Effect of different materials on productivity and costs.

		Costs Totals (steel)		Costs Totals (bronze)
Sales		$100		$100
Costs of goods sold	*Man-Hours*	*Costs*	*Man-Hours*	*Costs*
Raw material cost		5		10
Direct labor (machining)	2	30	1	15
Variable overhead		6		3
Fixed overhead		50		50
Total cost		$91		$78
Operating income		$9		$22

Note 1: Productivity Improvement: $|(.5-1.0)/.5| = 100\%$ improvement
Note 2: Profit Improvement: $|(9-22)/9| = 144\%$ improvement

per year. Several executives offered the belief that although the savings potential was approximately the same for all sizes of firms, implementation of proactive procurement would be relatively easier in smaller firms. They felt that two areas of major savings potential were especially critical: adequate purchasing lead time and involvement during the design stage of one or two carefully prequalified potential suppliers.

How to Integrate Marketing, Production Planning, and Inventory Management Into the Procurement System

Purchasing managers must show missionary zeal in making Marketing, Production Planning, and Inventory managers aware of the cost and productivity implications of inadequate purchasing lead time. Managers should develop examples showing the results of adequate and inadequate lead time. These examples— some with happy endings and some of them virtual horror stories—should be used in support of this effort. Remember to praise publicly and discuss problems in private.

Through an understanding of production planning, forecasting, and inventory management provided in this book, the purchasing manager can better communicate with his or her colleagues in these areas. This communication, supported by the examples, is the key to obtaining the necessary cooperation. But once this cooperation is achieved, it must be maintained—*one of a proactive purchasing manager's most important responsibilities.*

Five Approaches to Doubling Profits

Virtually all managers want to improve their organizations' performance. For profit-making organizations, profits are a key indicator of performance. For government and other not-for-profit organizations, budgets reflecting successful cost control are common indicators of performance. The principle contained in the following example is easily transferable to any of these organizations. A hypothetical situation with our friends at Eagle Manufacturing emphasizes the profit-making potential of procurement.

Eagle has a product line with a sales volume of $2 million and expenses as shown:

Sales	$2,000,000
Purchased material	1,000,000
Labor	200,000
Overhead	700,000
Profit	$100,000

Eagle desires to double its profits to $200,000. This may be accomplished in any of the following five ways:

Increase sales	100%
Increase prices	5
Decrease labor costs	50
Decrease overhead	15
Decrease material costs	10

In most organizations, it is far easier to reduce purchasing expenditures for materials and services by 10% than it is to double sales, decrease labor costs by 50%, decrease overhead by 15%, or increase prices by 5% in a competitive market. Thus, we see that an investment in reducing purchasing expenditures will have a great impact on the organization's profitability. If we consider reduced quality, scrap, process yield losses, rework, field warranty, and inventory carrying costs resulting from implementation of the IPS, the savings and profit impact are even greater.

The return on investment (ROI) impact of a 10% reduction in the cost of goods purchased can be even more impressive, since such a savings affects both the pretax profit margin and the asset turnover rate.

Exhibit 1-4 shows the effect of such a savings on ROI at Eagle under the following conditions: inventory turnover rate is four times per year, accounts receivable is $50,000, cash on hand is $50,000, and fixed assets are $400,000. Exhibit 1-4 shows that ROI more than doubles (from 6.9% to 14.3%) as a result of a 10% reduction in purchasing expenditures.

The Integrated Procurement Systems in Different Settings

Proactive procurement (and the resulting integrated procurement system) is truly a broad, pervasive, cross-functional effort that involves nearly all major units of a business enterprise in harmony with the new concept of horizontal organization theory.[2] It is a system of great interaction and interdependency. Proactive procure-

Exhibit 1-4. Effect of purchasing savings on ROI.

Return on Investment	6.9%
	14.3%*

Pretax Profit Margin
5%
10%*

Asset Turnover
1.38
1.43*

Pretax Earnings
$50,000
$100,000*

Sales
$1,000,000

Sales
$1,000,000

Total Assets
$725,000
$700,000*

Sales
$1,000,000

Cost of Sales
$950,000
$900,000*

Current Assets
$325,000
$300,000*

Fixed Assets
$400,000

Labor
$100,000

Material
$500,000
$450,000*

Overhead
$350,000

Inventories
$250,000
$225,000*

Accounts Receivable
$50,000

Cash
$25,000

*These figures reflect the impact of a 10% reduction in the cost of purchased goods.

ment is not limited to any one industry: It works in virtually all organizations including manufacturing firms, hospitals, and government.

Manufacturing Firms

Proactive procurement begins in Design Engineering when concepts calling for alternative conceptual solutions are being considered in response to new product ideas developed by Marketing. Good procurement commences at this point. Exhibit 1-5 illustrates the functional organization of a typical manufacturer and its integrated procurement system. Since the publication of *Proactive Procurement* in 1984, several world-class manufacturers have elevated the reporting responsibility of Purchasing or Procurement so that it reports directly to the COO or the CEO.

Design Engineering chairs the team that sets objectives for the new product and then develops alternative solutions to product, subsystem, and component requirements. Quality Assurance should review proposed designs and manufacturing plans to ensure that the quality called for by Marketing is the quality that will result if the prescribed design is followed.

Source selection is also a team process. For example, Quality Assurance is involved in determining a prospective supplier's ability to develop robust designs (using DOE) for required assemblies to customer developed specifications.[3] Quality Assurance also is involved in ensuring that the quality of incoming materials is as specified on the purchase order or contract, when buying from noncertified suppliers.

The IPS determines the timing of and quantities on the resulting purchase order or contract. Although make-or-buy analyses should be made periodically throughout the manufacture or purchase process of an item or service, the most critical make-or-buy analysis for purchased materials should occur before the first item is manufactured or purchased.

After a decision to purchase an item or service has been made, the purchasing department becomes responsible for leading the cross-functional team, which selects the right source, establishes the price (including negotiation, if appropriate), and issues the purchase order. If negotiations are appropriate, Purchasing is the team leader of the negotiating team consisting of representatives of Engineering, Quality Assurance, Manufacturing and others, as required. Then Purchasing must act to ensure that the item or service is received on time and in the quality specified. To provide its maximum contribution to the well-being of the enterprise, Purchasing must actively develop and manage sources of supply to ensure that an optional number of qualified suppliers is available now and in the future.

Finance is responsible for timely payment to suppliers after delivery of the material. Finance monitors the firm's investment in inventory. In a well-run organization, Finance closely controls working capital and cash flows, based largely on sales forecasts and accurate purchasing delivery schedules.

In a sense, Marketing begins and ends the procurement activities. Marketing identifies the need for the item to be developed that leads to a requirement for purchased material or services. Marketing is responsible for the sale and delivery to the customer of the item that incorporates the purchased material. Purchasing

Exhibit 1-5.   The functional organization and procurement activities in the IPS: manufacturing.

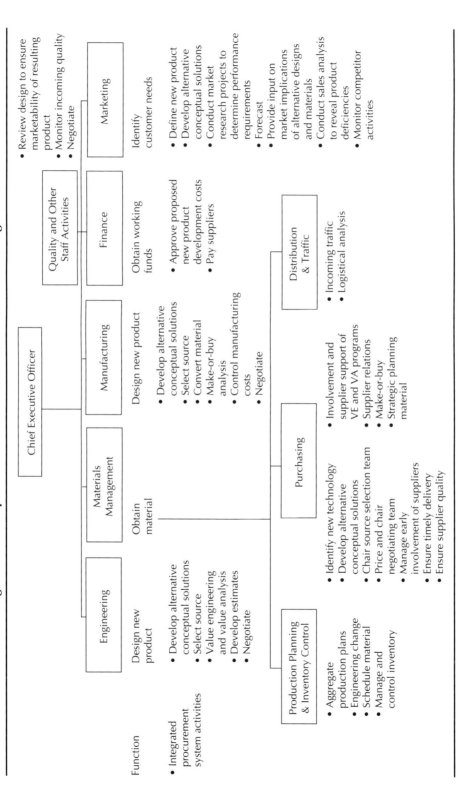

must maintain a good dialogue with Marketing on changes in material prices and availability and product acceptance relative to purchased components to allow Marketing to update sales quotations and current selling prices. Purchasing may have information that will influence Marketing's plans for future changes in its product lines.

Service Organizations

As with manufacturing firms, no one organizational chart can represent all service activities. However, the organization for a hospital in Exhibit 1-6 provides a vehicle for the discussion of proactive procurement and the IPS in a service setting.

Purchasing normally is responsible for 30–60% of the expenditures of a service organization. For hospitals, the expenditure for capital equipment, drugs, utilities, and supplies is approximately 33% of the annual budget. If food services, janitorial, pharmacy operation, and similar services are obtained through contracts, this figure may increase to 60% of the hospital's budget.

Most of a hospital's expenditures are of a repetitive nature. In the majority of instances, standards, descriptions, and stock levels for drugs, medical supplies, and administrative supplies already have been established. This repetition has led to the increased use of systems contracts involving the long-term contracting for entire groupings or families of related medical supplies. Saint Agnes Hospital in Fresno, California, is one of the large hospitals in the group of 14 operated by Holy Cross Health System. Saint Agnes has contracted with the Value Link Business Center of Baxter Healthcare Corporation, one of the nation's largest hospital supply distributors, to build a distribution center in Fresno. This center will service Saint Agnes Hospital on a JIT basis. The director of materials, Anthony P. Marino, C.P.M., estimates that $5 million dollars in savings will result over a five-year period through reduced warehousing costs, increased volume discounts, and labor savings under this creative "proactive" approach, which was achieved after two years of team study using the IPS approach shown in Exhibit 1-6.

Requirements for new equipment, drugs, or supplies must be controlled. More than ever, hospitals are confronted by funding limitations and must standardize as other organizations do. The Therapeutics Management Board (TMB) shown in Exhibit 1-6 is responsible for the review, approval, and ordering of priorities of all requests for capital equipment, drugs, and ordering of supplies not previously approved. The TMB consists of representatives of both Professional Services and Administrative Services (including Purchasing). Once an item has been approved by the TMB and funds are made available, Purchasing becomes responsible for the procurement.

Many hospitals frequently purchase some of their services such as food service, janitorial, security, radiology, pharmacy operation, and similar services. Decisions to purchase services are the result of one or both of two forces: the nonavailability of qualified personnel or the cost savings resulting in purchasing from an efficient specialist. When cost savings are used to justify a request to contract for services, a make-or-buy analysis, as described in Chapter 7, should be conducted.

Exhibit 1-6.   The functional organization and procurement activities in the IPS: hospitals.

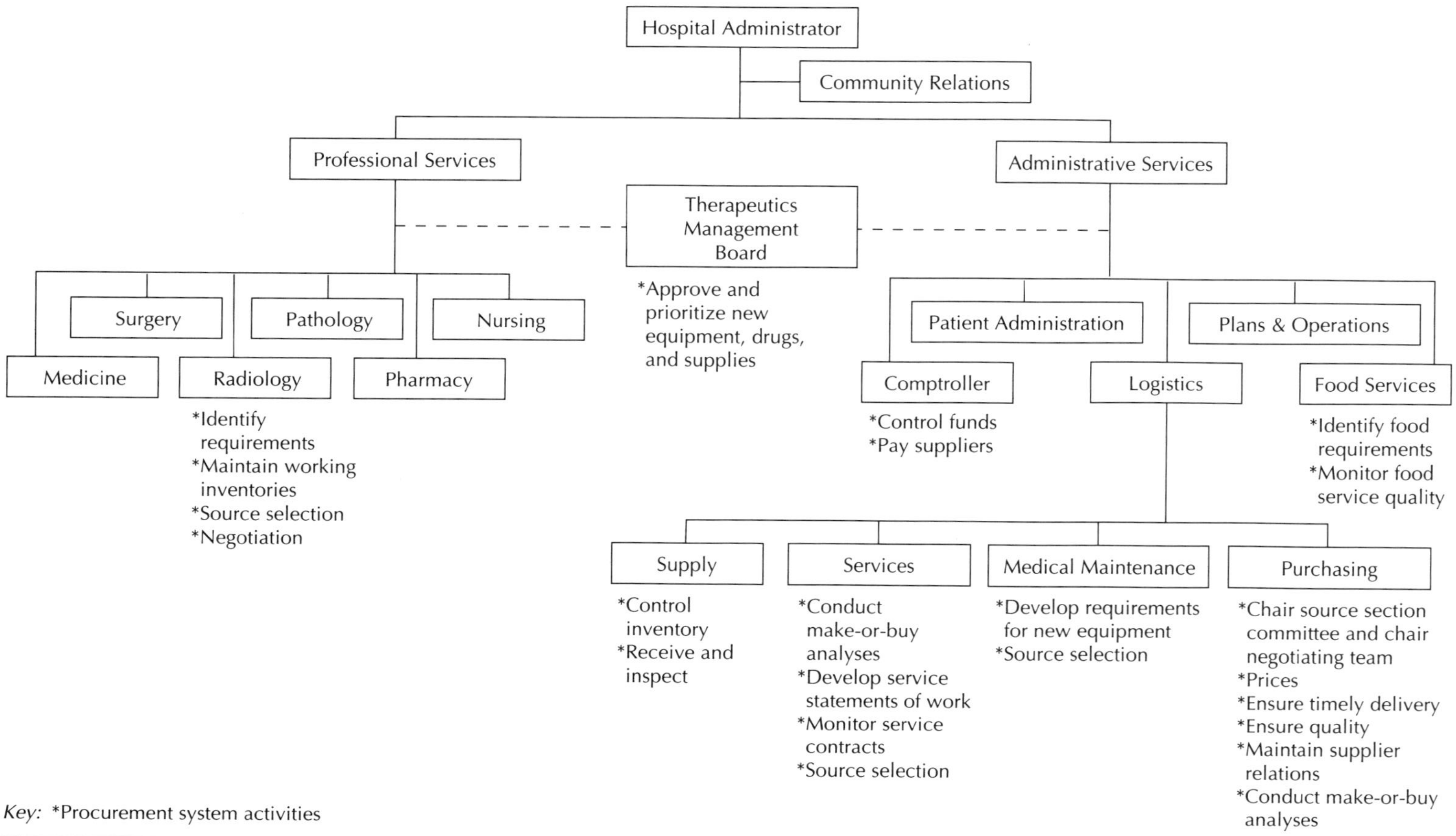

Hospital Administrator

Community Relations

Administrative Services

Professional Services

Therapeutics Management Board
*Approve and prioritize new equipment, drugs, and supplies

Medicine

Surgery

Radiology

Pathology

Pharmacy

Nursing
*Identify requirements
*Maintain working inventories
*Source selection
*Negotiation

Comptroller
*Control funds
*Pay suppliers

Patient Administration

Plans & Operations

Food Services
*Identify food requirements
*Monitor food service quality

Logistics

Supply
*Control inventory
*Receive and inspect

Services
*Conduct make-or-buy analyses
*Develop service statements of work
*Monitor service contracts
*Source selection

Medical Maintenance
*Develop requirements for new equipment
*Source selection

Purchasing
*Chair source section committee and chair negotiating team
*Prices
*Ensure timely delivery
*Ensure quality
*Maintain supplier relations
*Conduct make-or-buy analyses

Key: *Procurement system activities

Developing specifications and monitoring the resulting contract for such services are the extremely challenging responsibilities of the services branch of the logistics division as shown in Exhibit 1-6. These functions are discussed in Chapter 4.

Government

More than 80,000 government bodies in the United States have the power to spend public funds. For a number of historical and political reasons, no single approach to organizing the agencies and departments charged with providing government services has evolved. Exhibit 1-7 depicts an organizational approach that groups the many departments and agencies into six "systems," each accomplishing similar activities. Representative departments or agencies are listed under each system. In most governments, any of these departments or agencies may initiate requirements (within budgetary constraints) that will be acted on by Purchasing. Each department or agency develops specifications for services required to be performed under contract. Each department monitors the supplier's performance under the order or contract issued by Purchasing. Each department inspects, receives, and inventories supplies, materials, and equipment purchased for its particular needs. (The stores department of the Administrative Services System performs these functions for items common to two or more departments.)

Normally purchasing is responsible for chairing the cross-functional team that selects the source of supply, obtains a reasonable price for the supply or service, ensures timely delivery of the specified quality, and maintains good supplier relations.

The comptroller is responsible for controlling funds, paying suppliers, and monitoring the investment in inventory.

Construction

In many ways, the IPS for a construction firm is very similar to that described for a manufacturer.

As shown in Exhibit 1-8, Marketing or Sales initiates a procurement in a construction firm as it represents the firm in discussions with the client on the cost and quality implications of various approaches to satisfying the requirement. Each design approach has procurement implications. Purchasing must keep Sales informed of changes in material prices and availability to ensure accurate quotations and bids.

The engineering department in the construction firm, or an independent architect-engineering (A-E) firm, designs a project to meet a client's requirements. The design calls for work to be performed either by a construction firm's own employees or by subcontractors. The engineering department or A-E firm performs several procurement functions. Engineering specifies the equipment and materials. It is involved in any value analysis-value engineering activities. Engineering develops specifications for work to be performed under subcontracts. It develops its own estimates of equipment, material, and subcontract costs. These estimates will be used by Purchasing as a basis of comparison in negotiations. The

Exhibit 1-7. The functional organization and procurement activities in the IPS: government.

Administrative Officer				
Environmental Management System	Justice Services System	Fiscal Services System	Administrative Services System	Education and Recreation System
• Public Works	• Sheriff	• Auditor	• Personnel	• Recreation
• Planning	• Courts	• Comptroller	• Administration	• Libraries
• Parks	• Public Defender	• Accessor	• Counsel	• Department of
• Weights and Measures	• District Attorney	• Tax Collector	• Stores	Education

*Initiate requirements
*Member of sourcing and negotiating teams
*Develop specifications
*Monitor service, maintenance, and construction contracts
*Receive and inspect
*Maintain inventory

*Purchasing
*Chair source selection committee
*Price and chair negotiating team
*Ensure timely delivery
*Ensure quality
*Maintain supplier relations

Human Services System
• Health Care
• Hospitals
• Social Services
• Mental Health

*Initiate requirements
*Member of sourcing and negotiating teams
*Develop specifications
*Monitor service, maintenance, and construction contracts
*Receive and inspect
*Maintain inventory

Key: *Procurement system activities

Exhibit 1-8. The functional organization and procurement activities in the IPS: construction.

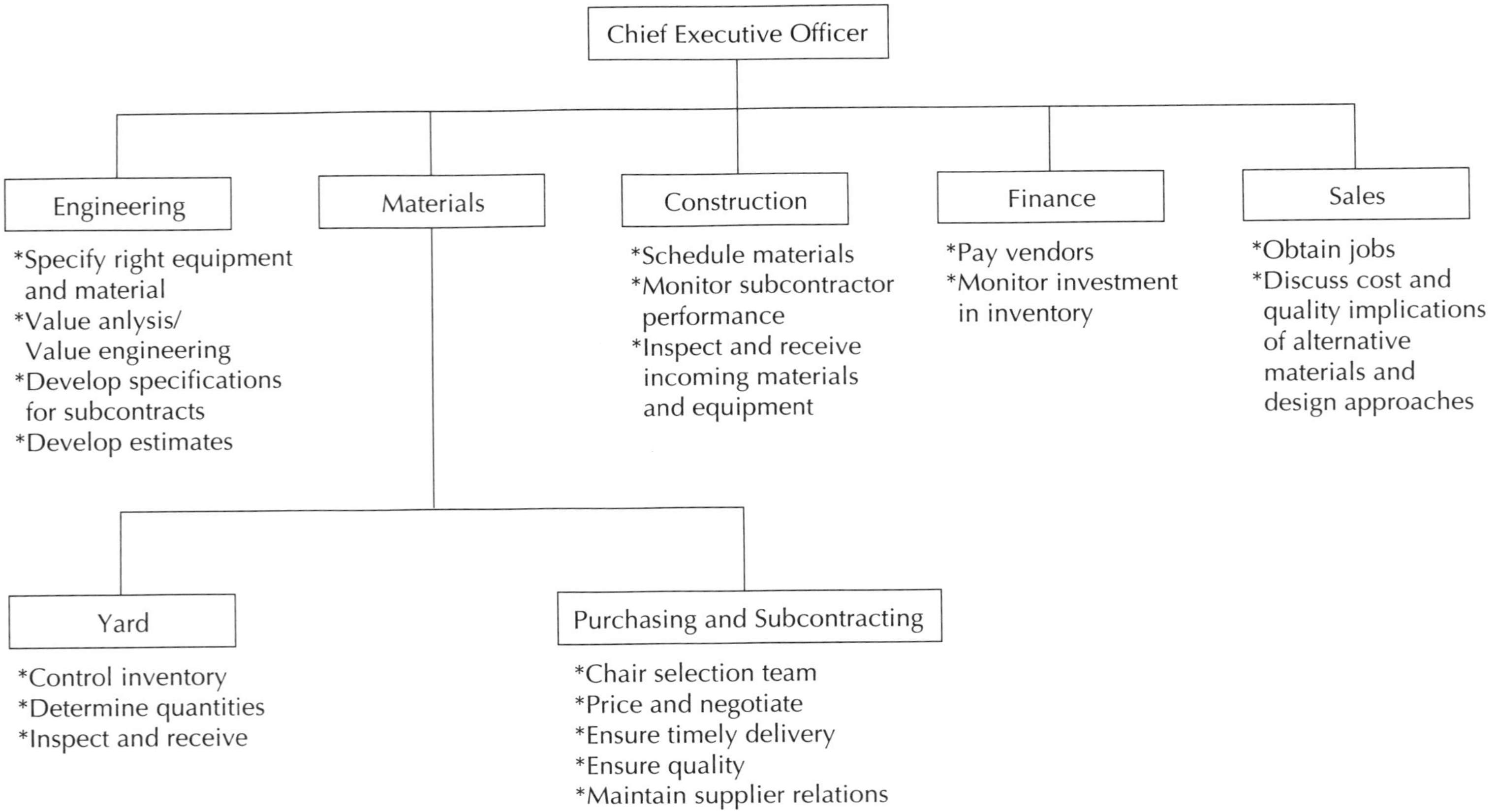

Chief Executive Officer

Engineering
*Specify right equipment and material
*Value anlysis/ Value engineering
*Develop specifications for subcontracts
*Develop estimates

Materials

Construction
*Schedule materials
*Monitor subcontractor performance
*Inspect and receive incoming materials and equipment

Finance
*Pay vendors
*Monitor investment in inventory

Sales
*Obtain jobs
*Discuss cost and quality implications of alternative materials and design approaches

Yard
*Control inventory
*Determine quantities
*Inspect and receive

Purchasing and Subcontracting
*Chair selection team
*Price and negotiate
*Ensure timely delivery
*Ensure quality
*Maintain supplier relations

Key: *Procurement system activities

importance of the availability of realistic estimates was illustrated in the Eagle Manufacturing case study earlier in the chapter. Engineering normally is involved in sourcing decisions for critical materials.

The material division consists of two branches: the yard (stores) and the purchasing and subcontracts branch. The yard is responsible for inventory control of capital equipment and expendable supplies common to several jobs. The purchasing and subcontracts branch is responsible for chairing the cross-functional team responsible for selecting sources, pricing, and negotiating purchase orders and subcontracts. Purchasing also is responsible for ensuring that the firm receives purchased material on time and of the quality specified. The yard and the construction division provide inspection and monitoring services to assist in these activities. To obtain the right supplies, services, and equipment at the right time and the right quality, purchasing must maintain viable sources of supplies, services, and equipment.

The construction division frequently is organized along project lines. Each actual or potential job is assigned to a project manager (superintendent) who becomes responsible for the project's successful completion. The project manager's responsibilities include the following IPS activities: participating in source selection and negotiations, scheduling materials and equipment, monitoring subcontractor performance, and inspecting and accepting material shipped directly to the job site. Finance makes timely payment to suppliers, monitors the firm's investment in inventory, and closely controls working capital and cash flows. This latter activity is based largely on information contained in the progress payment schedules and purchasing schedules. Purchasing must apprise Finance of any changes in delivery schedules that would affect working capital or cash flows.

Purchasing and Materials Management

In 1956 L. J. De Rose wrote the following timeless definition of materials management:[4]

> Materials management is the planning, directing, controlling, and co-ordinating of all those activities concerned with material and inventory requirements, from the point of their inception to their introduction into the manufacturing process. It begins with *the determination of material quality* [emphasis added] and quantity and ends with its issuance to production in time to meet customer demands on schedule and at lowest costs.

Materials management should and does result in improved communications and coordination among Production Planning, Inventory Control, Purchasing, and those other departments such as traffic, receiving, and warehousing that often are included. This improved communications and coordination means significant reductions in inventories, production disruptions and their resulting cost, administrative costs, and the cost of purchased materials.

Unfortunately, *materials management normally does not pay sufficient attention to determining the right item or material to be purchased.* The day-to-day problems confronting the materials manager are so challenging that no time or effort is available to interact with Design Engineering. As a result, the majority of organizations that have implemented materials management overlook the largest profit potential offered by the IPS. They buy the right quantities and buy them effectively. But they frequently are not buying to the right level of quality or the item that best satisfies the firm's true requirement.

When determining whether to implement an IPS or a materials management system (MMS) first, it is recommended that the IPS be the choice. Experience indicates that when an MMS is implemented, several years are required to gain control and develop a high degree of coordination among the formerly independent departments of the new organization. During this formative period, the day-to-day problems confronting the materials manager are so challenging that little time is available to pay proper attention to an effective requirements process.

The materials manager of one organization with sales in excess of $2 billion has addressed this issue by refusing the responsibility for production planning and inventory control. His materials management organization consists of four divisions: Material Engineering, Purchasing, Subcontract Administration, and Traffic. This executive has convinced top management that the assignment of additional responsibilities would reduce the savings his organization now makes. Much of the present savings results from the material engineering division's involvement in the appropriate stages of the design process and in value engineering. The IPS is not dependent on any one organizational structure. It can and does work in firms with a materials management organization. And it works in organizations with other approaches to procuring material, equipment, and services.

Richard Lamming, a key contributor to *The Machine That Changed the World*, suggests that teamwork between purchasing and the other departments we have identified in this chapter is necessary to achieve "lean supply."[5]

The rather recent term *value-supply chain management* is actually a combination of IPS and logistics early involvement (LEI). This approach looks up the supply chain toward suppliers and down the value-supply chain toward customers (including physical distribution).[6] The goal is to establish one master information linkage system among all carriers to minimize time and maximize integrated planning from raw material needs to final consumption of the finished product.

Several successful proactive purchasing managers have stated that top management is ready and waiting for the purchasing manager to take the initiative to reduce purchase expenditures systematically. As we have seen, such action also will result in improved product quality and greater productivity. If you share these objectives, you should:

1. Study and understand the wants and needs of the other activities (departments) involved in the procurement process. Begin from an informed position. Personal interviewing followed by a written summary of the findings is the best approach. (The next five chapters discuss the general principles.)

2. Make sure that your own house is in order. (Chapters 8 through 13 de-

scribe the major shortcomings found in purchasing activities and tell you how to do a better job.)

3. Portray the IPS for your organization adapting the figures in this chapter. Demonstrate the savings potential, using examples of previous "good" and "bad" procurements. Develop understanding and rapport with your fellow managers and offer to present the concepts and principles of a systematic approach to procurement and show the benefits to *their* activities. (Selected sections of this book may make useful reading for your colleagues.)

4. Translate dollar savings into earnings per share and the additional sales required to have the same impact on the bottom line. (These are big-time attention getters!)

5. Inform and sell top management on the plan to reduce procurement expenditures, as described in Chapter 16. Set up a task force to implement the integrated procurement system. Include the heads of all involved activities.

6. Publicize the resulting benefits to all levels of management, ensuring that all individuals involved in the program receive proper recognition for their cooperation and participation. (Again, translate dollar savings from cost reduction into earnings per share and additional sales required to have a similar impact on the bottom line.)

Summary

Procurement is the systematic process of deciding what, when, and how much to purchase; the art of purchasing it; and the process of ensuring that what is required is received in the quality specified on time. The procurement process cuts across traditional department lines to include activities that take place in Marketing, Design and Manufacturing Engineering, Purchasing, Operations, Quality Assurance, and Finance.

The quantity, quality, and price of purchased items affect the quality of the firm's product, the ability to produce it, productivity, and, most important, the firm's profitability. Determining what to buy does not begin when the purchase requisition is written but, rather, with the decision to produce the product.

An organization exercises the best control over the cost of purchased goods and services only when the various departments involved in the process operate as an interdependent, integrated system. Uncoordinated action by one department may optimize the success of that department but cause undesirable results in another, to the detriment of the organization as a whole.

Implementation of proactive procurement and the IPS differs greatly from reactive purchasing. With proactive procurement, all members of the procurement system recognize their role in the system. They cooperate in making the organization more profitable through more effective procurement. With this proactive approach, the purchasing department is involved in the requirements process by providing input on the commercial implications of alternative materials, equipment, and services. The purchasing department takes the initiative in making savings happen throughout the procurement system. In contrast to reactive purchasing, the purchasing department becomes involved in the procurement process at the very first stage of new or improved product-service development.

The introduction of proactive procurement and an IPS can create significant cost savings and increased productivity in many settings: manufacturing, service, and construction firms; not-for-profit organizations; and government.

In most organizations, it is easier to increase profits and ROI through a reduction in purchasing expenditures than through any other endeavor. If we consider the increased quality of finished goods (and the resulting market implications) and the savings in scrap, process yield losses, rework, field warranty, and inventory carrying costs resulting from implementation of an IPS, then the savings and profit impact are even greater.

In Chapter 2 we look at the most critical component of the procurement process—the determination of what material to purchase for operations.

Notes

1. Kathleen Kerwin, with James B. Treece and David Woodruff in Detroit, Kevin Kelly in Chicago, and Michael O'Neal in New York, "Can Jack Smith Fix GM?" *Business Week* (November 1, 1993), p. 131.
2. "The Horizontal Corporation," *Business Week* (December 20, 1993), pp. 76–81.
3. For a basic description of design of experiments, see Keki R. Bhote, *World Class Quality: Using Design of Experiments to Make It Happen* (New York: AMACOM, 1991).
4. L. J. DeRose, "The Role of Purchasing in Materials Management," *Purchasing Magazine*, March 1956, p. 115. Also see Gary J. Zenz with assistance from George H. Thompson, *Purchasing and the Management of Materials*, 7th ed. (New York: Wiley, 1994), pp. 99–105.
5. Richard Lamming, *Beyond Partnerships: Strategies for Innovation and Lean Supply* (Hertfordshire, U.K., Prentice Hall International (U.K.) 1993), p. 246.
6. See Jeanette Budding, "The Chains That Bind," *NAPM Insights* (August 1993), p. 49; M. C. Cooper and L. M. Ellram, "Characteristics of Supply Chain Management and Implications for Purchasing and Logistics Strategy," *International Journal of Logistics Management* (vol. 4, no. 2, 1993); David N. Burt and Michael F. Doyle, *The American Keiretsu: Strategic Weapon for Global Competitiveness* (Homewood, Ill.: Business One Irwin, 1993).

2

Determining What to Purchase: The Design Process

It is Friday, March 7. A design review is being conducted at the All American Test Equipment Company.

Robin Sagle, chief engineer, chairs the meeting. "Three months ago marketing indicated a likely market of 70 Digital Waveform Recorders a month at a selling price of $16,000, provided that we can begin deliveries by October 1. When I first looked at this requirement, I said, 'No way!' But two months ago a sales engineer from Duo Diodes described her firm's new analog-to-digital converter (ADC). Duo has been working on the development of this ADC for two years. It has developed a revolutionary new process that will produce 350 units a month at a selling price of $1,450. We have tested its ADC and have developed four prototype digital waveform recorders incorporating it. The prototypes meet our every desire."

Dick James, director of Purchasing, interrupts to ask, "Sagle, can anyone other than Duo produce this ADC?"

Sagle answers, "Obviously not. It's Duo's new process. We will be lucky to get in on its initial sales allocation. Don't get in a lather, Duo can be trusted."

Tom Ham, vice president of Operations, interrupts: "Sagle, the last time we incorporated some newly developed material, we had nothing but problems. We would go along fine for a while; then for no apparent reason, defects would jump so high that we'd be 200–300% over budget because of test and rework requirements. Those state-of-the-art materials you guys like so well are going to bankrupt us."

Steve Achtenhagen, vice president of Marketing, joins the fray: "Not only is this new digital wave recorder potentially very profitable, but it will help our sales representatives gain access to new customers. We expect this increased exposure to enhance our entire sales program. In fact, it's likely that our sales of test equipment could increase by 10% through the early availability of this digital wave recorder."

Perhaps the biggest failure of purchasing professionals is that of not becoming involved at the appropriate points in the requirements development process.

Probably this is a carryover from the days when purchasing was a reactive clerical function that issued orders based on the decisions and actions of others. But if Purchasing is to make its full profit contribution, it *must* be involved early in the requirements determination process.

A second major problem is the failure to integrate engineering constructively into the procurement system. In the late 1980s and early 1990s numerous trade books related to the new product design process and lean manufacturing were published.[1] Virtually all of these fine works stress the need to integrate suppliers into the design and operations planning phases of an organization. The concept of cross-functional teams and IPS are either explicitly or implicitly recommended in this recent trade literature. As Monczka and Trent observe, cross-functional teams substantially reduce new product development cycle time.[2]

The Development of Requirements

Determining what materials and services to purchase is the first and one of the most crucial steps in the procurement process. Responsibility for this determination varies with the requirement. In many cases, the using department is responsible. For example, Plant Engineering is responsible for developing equipment requirements. Plant Operations develops requirements for operating supplies such as drill bits, lubricating oils, and related items. Administrative Services initiates requirements for office supplies, equipment, and services.

The responsibility for determining which component materials to specify for newly designed products is a complex issue, complicated by the frequently conflicting interests, orientations, and biases of the many departments that have an interest in the end item or service. For example, Engineering may desire design excellence. Marketing may demand nonstandard and unique features. Operations prefers long production runs utilizing existing equipment, requiring few operators, and using high-quality, easy-to-work materials. Purchasing prefers to buy readily available materials from several dependable sources at reasonable prices.

Historically, Purchasing's contributions to the organization's success have been seen as being in two basic areas: ensuring the timely availability of required supplies and services and obtaining them at economic prices. However, these contributions are greatly expanded when purchasing is included at the beginning of the design process. For instance, as material requirements are developed, purchasing should ensure that only essential needs are incorporated in the requirement. The description of the requirement (usually a specification) should not contain features that unduly limit competition among qualified suppliers.[3] Further, purchasing can help the designer to be sensitive to the relative availability and cost of the alternative materials that may satisfy product requirements. Timely availability of required materials and services usually is enhanced by the availability of two or more qualified sources or carefully structured strategic alliances.

The implementation of proactive procurement and the other described and related concepts that lead to successful new product introductions require integrated product development. Lockheed Corporation's definition of this process is right on target:

Integrated product development is a concept of product development that integrates all the people, resources, control and communication systems, business methods, and program organizations around the product. It differs from most traditional approaches in that it focuses on and is organized around the product being developed rather than the disciplines required to produce the product. This integration concentrates resources and knowledge. It also provides employees with the sense of product ownership required for on-time delivery at the lowest cost.*

The Design Process and Procurement

Design is an interative process that results from the progression of an abstract notion to something concrete that has function and a fixed form. This form can be described so that it can be produced at a designated quality. (Describing requirements is discussed in Chapter 3.) The design stage is frequently the only point at which a major portion of the cost of producing an item can be reduced or controlled. If costs are not controlled at this time, they may be built into the item permanently, resulting in an expensive, noncompetitive product. General Motors states that 70% of the cost of manufacturing truck transmissions is determined at the design state.[4]

The design stage is the point at which the desired levels of quality and reliability must be engineered into the item. Quality is the basic nature or degree of excellence that an item possesses. Reliability is the degree of confidence or probability that an item will perform to requirements a specified number of times under prescribed conditions. J. M. Juran, a widely published authority in the field of quality, indicates that 20–40% of the field failures experienced by durable goods manufactured in America originate during development and design.[5] This chapter's opening case study showed how faulty purchased material drove manufacturing costs up on one of the company's previous production items. Had All American Test Equipment not had excellent test procedures in its manufacturing process, products containing faulty purchased components would have been sold to customers. Eventually, field failures would have occurred, resulting in postsales costs and customer dissatisfaction. Profitability and even a firm's survival require increased attention to the quality and reliability of its products from the earliest phase of the design stage.

The Investigation Phase

The design process, as illustrated in Exhibits 2-1, 2-2, and 2-3, begins with the investigation phase. The entire new product development process starts with a focus statement, usually called the product innovation charter or "blueprint," which gives the new product development team direction as to what to pursue.[6] First, the team develops a statement of needs, desires, and objectives. Needs and

---

*Reference Guide to Integrated Product Development, Lockheed Corporation, Calabasas, Calif., 1993, p. 1. Used with permission.

desires are based on Marketing's perception or knowledge of what customers want balanced against the organization's objectives and resources. Identified needs that are potentially compatible with the firm's objectives (profit, potential sales volume, payback period, etc.) and resources (people, machines, and management) are then considered for product or engineering development. Next, the product objectives, including performance, price, quality, and market availability, are developed. These needs, desires, and objectives then are transformed into criteria that guide the subsequent design, planning, and decision-making activities.

Alternative approaches to satisfying the needs and objectives are evaluated against these criteria. In Exhibit 2-1 these approaches are referred to as alternative conceptual solutions. Sound discipline by both design engineering and management is required to ensure the development of alternative approaches.

There is an unfortunate tendency to accept and proceed with the first approach that appears to meet the need. In many instances, less obvious alternatives may yield more profitable solutions. These alternative approaches should be evaluated on the basis of suitability, producibility, component availability and economy, and customer acceptability.[7]

The Laboratory Phase

In the next stage of the design process, the laboratory phase (see Exhibit 2-2), approaches are reviewed in detail for feasibility and likely risk. During this phase, efforts are taken to reduce risk to acceptable levels in all areas through the development and testing of prototypes for high-risk items. After tests demonstrate that risk has been reduced to an acceptable level, the most attractive alternative is selected.

When quality is a critical factor in designing a product for the marketplace, engineering should develop a quality map that describes the detailed design logic required to achieve the desired quality. This design logic starts with each desired end-product characteristic. It then identifies the characteristics of purchased materials and process steps that collectively contribute to building the desired attribute into the product. The quality map shows engineering, manufacturing, and purchasing specialists how the customer's expectations will be fulfilled. It details key relationships between (1) customer expectations; (2) specifications of raw materials, parts, and assemblies; and (3) relevant steps in the production process.

There is an understandable tendency on the part of many design engineers to develop truly advanced products that incorporate the latest developments or that push the state of the art forward. Although this tendency may advance the development and implementation of technology, it is frequently needlessly expensive. Not only does such an approach result in a proliferation of components to be purchased and stocked, but frequently items whose production processes have not stabilized are incorporated. Quality problems, production disruptions, and delays frequently result.[8]

Putting the product designer's logic into the form of a quality map serves several purposes. One is to invite purchasing specialists and suppliers to comment on the probability of obtaining the desired level of quality in purchased materials. Another is to allow Quality Assurance to review the design logic. This

Exhibit 2-1. The design process—investigative phase.

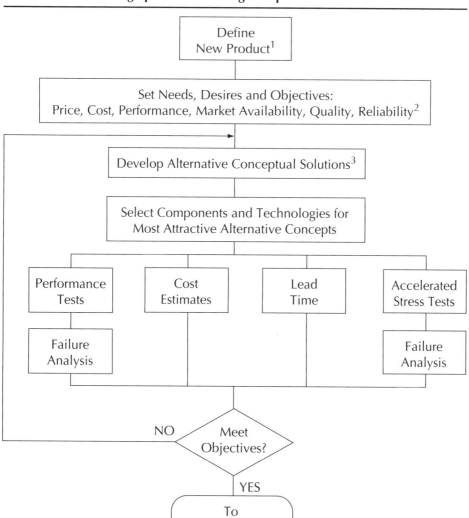

[1]Purchasing and suppliers should provide a window to new supplier-developed components, knowledge of which may allow marketing and engineering to identify new product possibilities.
[2]Purchasing and suppliers are the key source of information on the cost, performance, market availability, quality, and reliability of supplier furnished components that may be incorporated in the new product.
[3]Purchasing provides input on the economy and availability of the materials and subassemblies to be purchased under each approach.

review ensures that the quality specified by Marketing will result if Purchasing and Manufacturing each comply with the design criteria.

Consideration should be given to the desirability of using standard items or "shelf items" during the laboratory phase and carrying them over into the manufacturing phase. Many hidden costs are associated with an unnecessary variety of production items or purchased components: excess paperwork; short,

Exhibit 2-2.   The design process—laboratory phase.

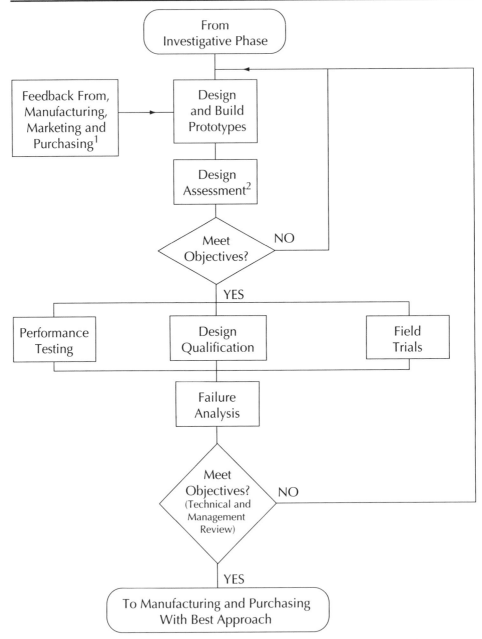

[1]Purchasing provides value analysis suggestions from suppliers. These suggestions may reduce cost, enhance performance, or both.
[2]Purchasing participates in the design reviews and provides information on the impact of specifications
and availability of items that are standard production for—and/or are inventoried by—suppliers.

needlessly expensive production runs; higher inventory costs; higher unit costs of small quantities of purchased materials; additional order processing costs; higher inspection and materials handling costs; additional quality problems; and an increased probability of stock outages. The use of standard materials, production processes, and methods resulting from standardization programs can greatly reduce the cost of designing and producing an item.

The Manufacturing Phase

In the manufacturing phase, detailed specifications, the manufacturing plan, and the procurement plan (frequently in the form of a bill of materials) are finalized. As shown in Exhibit 2-3, numerous tests take place throughout the manufacturing phase. Any time there is an unacceptable degree of risk or uncertainty about the performance of a component, subassembly, or the item itself, appropriate tests are conducted. These tests pinpoint failures in one or more of the following areas: the design, the supplier, the assembly and handling procedures, or the test equipment and test procedures.

Engineering Change Management

Any changes in components required to manufacture a product or in the product itself may have profound effects on its cost, performance, appearance, and acceptability in the marketplace. Changes, especially at the component or subassembly level, can have a major impact on the manufacturing process. Thus, unless changes to the configuration of an item or its components are controlled, manufacturers may find themselves in one of several undesirable states. They may possess inventories of unusable raw materials or subassemblies resulting in excessive material expenditures. They may possess materials that require needlessly expensive rework to be adapted to a new configuration. Or they may produce an end item that will not meet the customer's needs or that may otherwise be unacceptable in the marketplace.

Engineering change management (ECM), a discipline that controls engineering changes, has been developed to avoid such problems.* The need for and degree of application of ECM to an item will depend on many factors and will be a matter of managerial judgment. But, for most modern technical items, ECM is a necessity. In some cases, it will be imposed on the manufacturer by the customer.

Under ECM, the functional and physical characteristics of an item and its components are identified. Any changes to these characteristics must be controlled and recorded. Any proposed changes to the item's characteristics are relayed to Marketing and all departments or groups involved in the purchase, control, and use of purchased materials, who then comment on the impact of the proposed change. Such control and coordination is especially important when

*Engineering change management is the management of change to a product's design, specifically, its form, fit, and function. It is also a requirement of ISO 9000 certification as discussed in Chapter 12. The term "document control" is sometimes used as part of engineering-change management.

Exhibit 2-3.   The design process—manufacturing procurement phase.

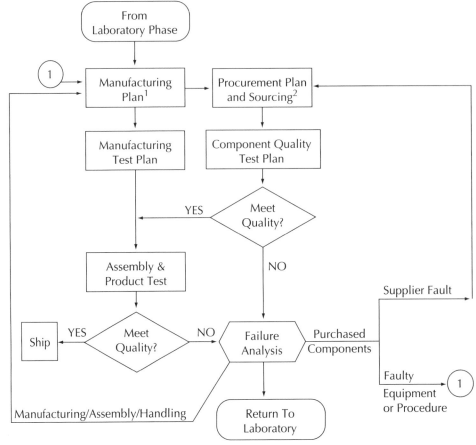

[1]Purchasing and suppliers provide input on the material cost and availability implications of a change in the item's configuration.
[2]As a result of its early involvement in the design process, Purchasing has developed contingency plans. These plans allow Purchasing to satisfy the firm's requirements for selected purchased components. Purchasing has worked with Design Engineering to select the appropriate type of purchase description. The appropriate plans are now formalized and implemented.

production scheduling and the release of purchase orders are controlled by a material requirements planning system.

Many organizational approaches to the responsibility for ECM exist. Ideally, an ECM board should be established with Engineering, Manufacturing, Marketing, Production Planning and Inventory Control, and Purchasing represented. When a materials management organization exists in the firm, it is recommended that Production Planning and Inventory Control chair the engineering change board.[9] The crucial issue is that Purchasing and the function responsible for material control must be involved in proposed engineering changes.

Adherence to this or a similar design process is key to the company's success. Product quality, cost, and availability all receive proper attention. And, as seen previously, Engineering, Manufacturing, Marketing, Quality Assurance, and Purchasing all have vital roles to play in the design process.

Key Points for Purchasing Input During the Design Process

At several points in the design process purchasing can or should provide input on the material to be purchased. In the investigation phase, Purchasing can make a major contribution during establishment of price, performance, timeliness, quality, and reliability objectives. Later in this phase, Purchasing is the source of information on the abilities of suppliers to meet the objectives being considered. Also, it can provide input on the likely costs (in rough terms) of purchased material and subassemblies. Such early involvement has the benefit of allowing Purchasing to initiate long-range plans to ensure an economic purchase.

After several alternative conceptual solutions to these objectives have been developed, purchasing should provide input on the economy and availability of the materials and subassemblies to be purchased under each approach. Often, direct supplier input is given at the design and development team meeting.

Design reviews are held at several points in the laboratory phase. This is the third point at which purchasing should be involved. At these reviews, particular emphasis should be placed on the use of standard items in the firm's inventory.

The design process results in a manufacturing plan that, in turn, leads to the procurement plan; see Exhibit 2–3. If Purchasing has *not* been involved in the earlier phases of the design process, this may be the first opportunity for Purchasing to provide input. At this point, Purchasing has the right and the responsibility to challenge requirements that do not appear to be economical or otherwise in the firm's best interest. (Obviously, Purchasing should not change the requirement. It can only challenge it!)

Finally, changes in an item's design configuration may appear to be desirable or essential during manufacturing. But such changes may have significant cost implications. Purchasing, together with Manufacturing, Marketing, and Inventory Control, should provide essential input when such changes are being considered. The transition from individual or unilateral configuration changes has given way to a team approach just as has design.[10]

How to Integrate Engineering Successfully Into the Procurement System

Requirements should be balanced between technical and functional considerations, manufacturing considerations, marketing implications of customer acceptance, and the procurement consideration of economy and availability. All too frequently, the design engineer attempts to address all these issues without obtaining the input and assistance of representatives of Marketing, Manufacturing, Quality Assurance, and Purchasing. Many engineers enjoy interacting with suppliers both on technical and *commercial* issues. These engineers believe that they are serving their employer's best interest, even while specifying materials that are in short supply or obtainable only from one source (unless that source is a preferred supplier).

Professional purchasing managers have their work cut out for them. Their objective should be developing and maintaining cooperative relations with engineering *that protect the profitability of the firm.* Once this objective has been embraced, the purchasing manager prepares the plan as described in Chapter 16.

When purchasing managers assume total responsibility for the integration of engineering into the procurement system, they must devise and implement a well-developed strategy. It is essential that the purchasing manager understand the orientation and dedication of the typical design engineer. Obviously, an ability to speak "engineering" is very helpful. A review of the principles of negotiation (see Chapter 14) is very desirable: After all, the purchasing manager is about to undertake a most crucial negotiation. In many situations, it will be possible to enlist the aid of an ally such as the director of marketing or finance. Under most circumstances, the purchasing manager's supervisor should be made aware of the objective and the planned strategy.

This chapter identifies several key points at which purchasing's involvement in the design process has the potential for making the organization more profitable. Several managers of proactive purchasing organizations indicate that they achieved success in the desired engineering–purchasing integration in the following manner. Whenever feasible, they provided advice on the commercial implications of designs under consideration in a positive and constructive manner. When the advice was accepted, the resulting savings were publicized in a manner to bring credit and recognition to engineering, even to the specific engineer involved. Eventually, these purchasing managers and their buyers were able to establish—through a history of accomplished savings—that the purchasing staff is a valuable resource to Engineering. Purchasing, then, is seen as a partner that takes care of business problems, thereby allowing engineers to concentrate on engineering challenges and problems.

Several successful approaches to obtaining the desired level of purchasing input during the design process are described next. One or a combination of these may be right for you.[11]

Material Engineers (Liaison Engineers)

One of the quickest and most successful ways of gaining the cooperation of engineers is to speak their language. Several successful material organizations consider only individuals with an engineering background as candidates for buying positions *when the responsibilities require involvement with design engineering.* Other purchasing organizations divide buying responsibilities into two specialties: material engineering and buying (sourcing, pricing, and negotiating). The material/liaison engineer is responsible for coordination with design engineering, for prequalifying potential sources (usually with the assistance of quality assurance), and for participating in value engineering and value analysis.

Engineers Temporarily Assigned to Purchasing

Several organizations have greatly improved working relations and the cooperation between Engineering and Purchasing by temporarily assigning engineering personnel to Purchasing. The assignment usually lasts for 6–36 months. While working in the purchasing department, the engineer provides invaluable assistance to Purchasing. On returning to Engineering, the engineer has a far better understanding of the role and responsibilities of Purchasing. Such individuals greatly facilitate the integration process.

No Dead End Streets, If You Please!

Purchasing is an ideal point of transition for an engineer who desires to advance into general management. Several forward-looking organizations do *not* look at Purchasing as an end assignment. Carefully selected employees are promoted from other functional areas into Purchasing. And carefully selected Purchasing employees are promoted to other departments.

Co-Location

Co-location calls for the placement of members of the purchasing staff in locations where design engineering is accomplished. Frequently, these individuals have technical backgrounds. They are available to assist design engineers by advising them on the procurement implications of different materials under consideration. They obtain required information from prospective suppliers. In some organizations, these members of the purchasing staff have the authority to purchase. In other organizations, they act in a liaison capacity only. This approach is especially effective when a company is bidding on a large project with a short bid time.

Design Review Committee

A design review committee consisting (as required) of representatives of Engineering, Marketing, Manufacturing, Quality, and Purchasing is established to review all designs prior to manufacture or purchase.

Project Teams

Project teams with members from the foregoing departments are established to develop and introduce the desired item into production. Membership on the project team may be either full time or on an as-required basis, preferably managed through the use of a matrix control system. Cross-functional teams are the most effective and efficient integrators provided they have empowerment and the leader has independent authority from department heads.[12]

Approved Components Catalog

The development and use of a catalog of approval components minimizes friction among engineering, purchasing, quality, and the standards engineer, while ensuring that the concerns of each of these functions is addressed. Parts in use are classified into three groups: recommended, acceptable, or not recommended. Engineers are free to select from the recommended group. The use of "acceptable" items or incorporation of new items not on the list requires approval by higher management. Purchasing, standards engineers, and quality engineers constantly monitor and update the lists to ensure currency.

The authors have had many discussions with proactive executives responsible for purchasing on the issue of integrating engineering into the procurement system. Several of the approaches just cited are based on suggestions offered by these pros. In addition, one or more of the following slightly paraphrased excerpts from these discussions may be of interest.

♦ **Major Primary Producer:** Hire engineers. Give them field experience. Put Purchasing and Engineering under the same boss. Rotate future top managers through Purchasing. Purchasing is not a dead-end street.

♦ **Electronics Manufacturer:** Co-locate buyers in Engineering. Motivate Engineering to accept commercial advice from Purchasing by making cost reduction a factor in determining their bonuses.

♦ **Appliance Manufacturer:** Have the good fortune to have a CEO with purchasing experience. Make sure that the purchasing manager has experience in Operations. As buyers, we have much to offer . . . this must be our self image.

♦ **Aerospace:** The purchasing manager must earn the respect and cooperation of other members of the procurement system. Hire engineers with floor experiences to be material engineers. Expect one to two years to orient them on commercial activities. Have material engineers work with design engineers to adapt textbook solutions to the realities of the supply marketplace.

♦ **Electronics Manufacturer:** Make engineers dependent on Purchasing. Provide an invaluable service. Make engineers use catalog items. If not in the catalog, require approval of engineering and purchasing managers.

♦ **Computer Manufacturer:** Raise field reliability objectives. This puts pressure on all members of the procurement system to increase coordination and cooperation. Make key managers' bonuses a function of profits and cost control. This makes other members of the procurement team receptive to cost-saving suggestions. Management has told engineering that 50% of its efforts should be allocated to design and 50% to cost control.

♦ **Conglomerate:** We are really hot on value analysis—not only does it save big bucks, but it really helps to break down organizational barriers!

♦ **Two Defense Contractors:** Co-locate!

♦ **Aerospace:** Hire engineers.

♦ **High-Tech Firm:** Co-locate. Use project teams when appropriate.

♦ **Public Utility:** Get a good procurement audit.

Summary

Determining what to purchase is one of the most critical steps in the procurement process. This determination is complicated by the frequently conflicting objectives of Engineering, Marketing, Manufacturing, and Purchasing.

The design stage is the only point at which many costs can most effectively be reduced or controlled. The design process begins with a statement of needs, desires, and objectives. It then proceeds through several iterations, starting with the development of alternative approaches and ending with the development of a set of requirements suitable for Manufacturing and Purchasing's use. Throughout this process, consideration must be given to technical, manufacturing, procurement, and marketing issues. The key output, from the point of view of the integrated procurement system, is the procurement plan. This plan frequently is in the form of a bill of materials, along with required delivery dates. Buying strategy then becomes the basis of subsequent tactical purchasing actions.

Standardization of materials and manufacturing processes and methods can greatly reduce the cost of designing and manufacturing an item. An effectively implemented standardization program avoids short, expensive production runs, higher inventory costs, higher costs of purchased materials, additional order processing costs, quality problems, higher inspection and materials handling costs, and the costs associated with stock outages.

Engineering change management (ECM), a discipline that controls engineering changes, is the final step in the design process. Under ECM the functional and physical characteristics of an item are identified. Changes to these characteristics are controlled and recorded. ECM helps a firm avoid material waste, excessive manufacturing effort and expense, and the possibility of producing an item that will not be compatible with customers' needs.

Efforts to increase profitability and productivity may be blocked if Engineering does not see and understand its role in the integrated procurement system. By understanding engineers' wants and needs and their reasonable requirements, purchasing can help to bring them on side, to the benefit of all departments in the firm and the firm itself.

Seven approaches to bringing engineering into the integrated procurement system are:

1. Material/liaison engineers
2. Engineers temporarily assigned to Purchasing
3. Promotional opportunities into and out of Purchasing
4. Co-location of Purchasing personnel in Engineering
5. Formal design reviews in which Purchasing participates
6. A project or cross-functional team approach to development
7. Use of an approved parts list.

No one approach is appropriate for all firms.

Once a decision has been made on what to purchase, it is necessary to select the most appropriate means of communicating this information to the buyer, potential suppliers, and inspectors. This process is discussed in Chapter 3.

Notes

1. For example, James P. Womack, Daniel T. Jones, and Daniel Ross, *The Machine That Changed the World*, based on the MIT 5-year study on the future of the automobile (New York: Rawson Associates, 1990); Michael L. Dertouzos, Richard K. Lester, and Robert M. Solow, *Made in America: Regaining the Productive Edge* (New York: Harper Perennial, 1989), the MIT Commission on industrial productivity; Kim B. Clark and Takahiro Fuji-

moto, *Product Development Performance: Strategy, Organization, and Management in the World Auto Industry* (Boston: Harvard Business School Press, 1991); Peter C. Reid, *Well Made in America: Lessons from Harley-Davidson on Being the Best* (New York: McGraw-Hill, 1990); Roy L. Harmon, *Reinventing the Factory II: Managing the World Class Factory* (New York: The Free Press, 1992); Steven R. Rayner, *Recreating the Workplace: The Pathway to High Performance Work Systems* (Essex Junction, Vt.: Oliver Wight Publications, 1993); and Richard Lamming, *Beyond Partnership: Strategies for Innovation and Lean Supply* (Hertfordshire, U.K.: Prentice Hall International, 1993).

2. Robert M. Monczka, and Robert J. Trent, "Cross Functional Teams Reduce New Product Development Cycle Times," *NAPM Insights* (Febuary 1994), pp. 64–66.

3. Two 1970s studies conducted by David N. Burt emphasize the importance of competition in achieving purchasing's economic objectives. The first study, entitled "Effect of the Number of Competitors on Costs," was published in the November 1971 issue of the *Journal of Purchasing*. The article indicated that over the range of one to five competitors, prices tended to decrease by 4% each time one additional qualified supplier submitted a price. Thus, an item costing $100 when only one bid had been obtained would tend to cost $92 if three bids were available. The second study, entitled "Reduction in Selling Price After Introduction of Competition," was coauthored with Dr. Joe Boyett and published in the May 1979 issue of the *Journal of Marketing Research*. This study found that an average savings of 12.5% resulted when material that previously had been purchased on a sole-source basis was purchased under competitive conditions.

4. See Daniel E. Whitney, "Manufacturing by Design," *Harvard Business Review* (July-August 1988), p. 83.

5. J. M. Juran, "Japanese and Western Quality: A Contrast in Methods and Results," *Management Review* (November 1978), p. 28. Also see Juran's book *Juran on Planning for Quality* (New York: The Free Press, 1988).

6. See C. Merle Crawford, *New Products Management*, 4th ed., (Homewood, Ill.: Irwin, 1994), pp. 23–45.

7. Suitability is concerned with technical considerations such as strength, size, power consumption, capability, maintainability, and adaptability. Engineering has primary responsibility for suitability.

   Producibility refers to the ease with which a firm manufactures an item. Frequently, an item's design must be constrained or revised to accommodate the firm's ability to produce it economically. Producibility is primarily a responsibility of Manufacturing at the designing firm or its suppliers.

   Component availability is a function of assured, dependable sources of supply. Component economy refers to the cost of the item or service. Component availability and economy are primarily Purchasing's responsibility.

   Customer acceptability considers likely acceptance of an item by potential customers. This is primarily a Marketing responsibility.

8. See Kaoru Ishikawa, *What is Total Quality Control?: The Japanese Way*, translated by David J. Lu (Englewood Cliffs, N.J.: Prentice-Hall, 1985); and David A. Garvin, *Managing Quality: The Strategic and Competitive Edge* (New York: The Free Press, 1988).

9. This recommendation is supported by Robert W. Holland and Thomas E. Vollman in "Planning Your Materials Requirement," in the September-October 1978 issue of the *Harvard Business Review*. The article reports on various forms of manufacturing organizations. One finding was that a significant loss of effectiveness occurs when engineering change control does not rest with those using the information (Purchasing and Production Planning and Inventory Control).

10. See Lisa M. Ellram and John N. Pearson, "The Role of the Purchasing Function: Toward Team Participation," *International Journal of Purchasing and Materials Management* (Summer 1993), pp. 3–9.

11. Also see David N. Burt and William R. Soukup, "Purchasing's Role in New Product Development," *Harvard Business Review* (September-October 1985).

12. See James W. Dean, Jr., and Gerald I. Susman, "Organizing For Manufacturing Design," *Harvard Business Review* (January-February 1989), pp. 28–36, and Daniel E. Whitney, "Manufacturing by Design," *Harvard Business Review* (July-August 1988), pp. 83–91.

3

Developing the Right Purchase Description to Save You Time and Money

Joyce Firstenberger, city manager of Great White Way, New York, faces a major decision. Great White Way's rapid growth has resulted in a shortage of classrooms. Revenue has not kept pace with the need for additional school physical plant. To accommodate the growth in student population, it has been necessary to adopt the use of shifts at the high school. Parents and students alike are unhappy with the situation. The school board is demanding a new high school.

This morning, Joyce met with the city comptroller, engineer, and purchasing agent. Hal Eyring, city engineer, indicated that preliminary engineering estimates for a new high school were $5 million. John Pasgrove, the comptroller, stated that the city could not afford a building costing in excess of $4 million. Hal responded that his estimates were for an austere structure and that $5 million seemed optimistic. Judy Hardy, the purchasing agent, then said that she had recently learned of an approach to purchasing construction through the use of a performance specification.

The performance specification describes the size and function of the building in explicit terms. Qualified builders are then invited to propose their design approaches and prices. When purchased in this manner, manufacturing plants tend to be 30% less expensive than when purchased through the use of detailed plans and specifications. Further, the use of performance specifications reduces the time required to complete such projects by one fourth.

After a spirited discussion, Hal Eyring summarized his position: "Every organization I've ever been with has purchased building construction through the use of detailed plans and specifications. I won't be party to Judy's new-fangled performance specification."

John Pasgrove commented, "If this performance specification approach is any good, the savings would allow Great White Way to get on with the needed school project. With building costs escalating at 10–15% a year, if the project does not go forward now, it will be many years—if ever."

Use of the right type of specification will significantly reduce procurement costs. And, as we saw in Great White Way, the right type of specification also can reduce the amount of time required to fill requirements. In an IPS, proactive purchasing can influence the development or selection of the right type of specification. This activity is critical! One of the most efficient manufacturers in America has assigned the development of specifications to the appropriate commodity buying team in its Purchasing department. Purchasing should be involved in this critical, but frequently overlooked, activity.

Two problems are common in the area of purchase descriptions:

1. Requiring activities frequently fail to consider the cost implications of alternative approaches to describing their requirements.
2. Purchasing departments often fail to conduct systematic procurement research and analysis on alternate materials when appropriate.

The word *requirement* means "need," not product or service type, which is a solution to a need. All purchasing starts with need determination, and this process eventually is translated into products or services, which then direct us to potential suppliers and the cost of the solution. Under appropriate circumstances, need determination may include carefully screened suppliers. Jumping to a product skips the essential first step of identifying alternatives and can result in automatic supplier selection, locked-in high costs, mistakes causing very expensive change orders, and users doing the buying—all potentially uneconomical actions. For example, if the need is to join two pieces of material together, we can weld, bolt, glue, screw, or use other methods to *fasten*, that is, the need is to "fasten together" and the requirement determination process is which method, then which product, then which supplier. This kind of thinking also forces the investigation of new methods and helps prevent the continued use of obsolete products/procedures.

Classifying an Inventory Catalog

An inventory catalog should be coded according to several classifications, easily done today with computer data systems. A few classic classifications are:

1. *Buying-Using Experience.* Is the product/service a new buy, modified rebuy (same product type, slightly different need), or straight rebuy? This will determine the amount of effort needed to determine the requirement. Most of the straight rebuys are via systems contracts, electronic data interchange (EDI), and such; they should be "automated" with requirements changed as the need dictates.

2. *Value-Volume Relationships.* This is the familiar ABC inventory analysis, which usually starts with a finding that A items account for 80% of the dollars spent but represent just 20% of the physical volume, B items represent 15% of the dollars spent for 30% of the physical volume, and C items represent 5% of the dollars for 50% of the physical volume. This traditional analysis targets candi-

dates for special study. Critical items that can shut the operation down also qualify as A items. Requirements for A items are obviously the top priority, for they are the real cost drivers.

3. *Type of Product or Service.* Capital goods, especially production machine tools, call for a vastly different requirement determination than most raw materials or maintenance, repair, and operating (MRO) supplies.

Coding your inventory catalog according to the above classifications can facilitate rapid computer printouts to give direction to purchasing research assignments. It helps the purchasing department focus activities to achieve the highest payoff. It also helps to explore the questions of simplification and standardization to avoid too many unnecessary requirements and/or slight variations adding little or nothing to value. The basic question is, "Why do we buy and stock 30 different grades, sizes, and types of many MRO items!"

Requirement Trade-Off Analysis

Using the well-known Consumer's Union "best buy" ratings for consumer products is a good way to resolve the often conflicting desires for high quality, reliability, suitability, and low cost. Remember that unit price is just one aspect of total cost. One must balance the total buy with the caveat that certain requirements for specific products are key requirements as set forth by safety or customer dictates. For example, aircraft bolts must have 100% reliability (extremely long mean times between failure, or MTBF ratings), they must be suitable, such as low in weight and capable of withstanding large temperature variations and be of the highest quality (conformance to specifications). The unit price per bolt is not critical, given the total cost of the aircraft and the potential cost of an accident. Most experts in industrial purchasing define quality as goods and services that fulfill a need or desired function at the lowest total cost of ownership.

The early Japanese automobiles provide another good example of highly *suitable* automobiles (low gas consumption), high *reliability* (low failure rates and correspondingly low maintenance costs) and relatively *low initial price*. Toyota was and still is considered by many experts as a "best buy" when considering customer demands. American automobiles (Saturn is a good example) and several European cars have improved greatly over the last five to six years, but they still suffer from some *reliability* problems when compared to Toyota and Honda's autos.

Purchasing plays the key role in resolving the trade-off between quality and cost during requirements communication with users, suppliers, and end customers (the really important actors in this play). The "how" used to describe the requirement must come only after a fairly exhaustive debate/analysis of the needs and the final agreement with all concerned parties. This is another reason why purchasing *planning* is so important today. Purchasing personnel must have adequate lead time for this investigation. Emergency buys must be reduced to real emergencies and not be the result of failure to plan ahead, which produces "purchasing by panic," a very costly luxury.

The Importance of the Purchase Description

Assuming the buyer has done his or her homework and knows the need, he or she can now write the purchase description that forms the heart of any procurement. Whether a purchase order or contract will be performed to the satisfaction of the buyer frequently is determined at the time the purchase description is selected or written. In no other form of communication is there a greater need for clarity and precision of expression. The extent of this precision has a major bearing on the successful completion of the procurement.

Purchase descriptions serve a number of purposes. Some of these are used to do the following:

- Communicate to the buyer in the purchasing department what to buy.
- Communicate to prospective suppliers what is required.
- Serve as the heart of the resulting purchase order.
- Establish the standard against which inspections, tests, and quality checks are made.

The purchase description can greatly influence the amount of competition. As seen in Chapter 2, the amount of competition has a major impact on the purchase price. The type of purchase description also may affect the "depth" of competition: This depth of competition may have an even more pronounced effect on the purchase price.

In the situation that opened this chapter, two very different approaches for describing requirements for a new high school were under consideration. The approach endorsed by the city engineer calls for the development by an architectural engineering company of a very explicit set of plans and specifications that meticulously detail how the successful builder is to construct the required building. Competition then is solicited on this one plan.

The alternative approach advanced by the purchasing agent calls for using an explicit performance specification to describe the intended use of the building. Under this approach, solicited prospective suppliers are free to bid on various methods to satisfy the building requirements. For example, one proposal may call for a built-up wood truss roof; another may call for the use of prestressed concrete for the roof. One method for meeting a requirement for comfort control might employ the use of one central air conditioner. An alternative proposal might call for the use of several unit air conditioners mounted on the walls or roof. The level of comfort obtained would be the same, but the cost of the two approaches differs substantially.

The use of performance specifications, then, can result in a "competition of concepts," with great savings enjoyed by the purchaser.

Five Approaches to Describe What to Purchase

Brand or Trade Name

The use of a brand name is the simplest way to describe what to purchase. A brand name is used by a manufacturer to distinguish a product and to aid in its promotion. Brand names ensure that the goodwill developed in satisfied customers is credited to the product. Such goodwill requires that the manufacturer provide consistent quality. Using a brand name description implies a reliance on the integrity and the reputation of the manufacturer. When purchasing by brand name, the purchaser has every right to expect that follow-on purchases of the brand name will possess the same quality as the original.

Normally, the expression "or equal" should be used immediately following a brand name to facilitate competition. When using an "or equal" after a brand name, it is desirable to set forth those salient physical, functional, or other characteristics of the referenced product that are essential to the purchaser's needs. The term *or equal* means that any proposed item should be able to perform the function to the same level of satisfaction as does the specified brand.

Although the use of brand names simplifies the procurement process, it tends to be expensive. Even when competition is introduced through the use of the "or equal" provision, higher prices tend to result than when several of the alternative descriptions of the item are employed. Brand-name products generally are sold at higher prices than unbranded products of similar quality. There are several advantages and disadvantages in specifying brand names.

Advantages

* Describing the desired item is simple for the requiring department.
* Purchasing by brand name is relatively simple.
* Brand-name products tend to be more readily available than unbranded items.
* The use of a brand-name purchase description may be the most efficient method of obtaining a desired level of quality or skill when this level of quality cannot be defined easily.
* The branded item may be advertised so widely and successfully as to aid in promotion of the product in which it will be incorporated.
* Inspection of brand-name items is relatively simple.
* Testing of an item may be impractical. The purchaser may avoid such testing by relying on the brand-name manufacturer's quality standards and test reports.
* The purchaser is assured that the manufacturer will stand behind his or her brand-name product.

Disadvantages

* Brand-name products usually cost more.
* Using brand-name products may mean that the purchaser is not taking advantage of improvements introduced by competitors of the brand-name manufacturer.
* The use of the "or equal" provision may mean that items are purchased from a variety of manufacturers. Since each manufacturer exercises its own quality control, the quality variation probably will be larger than if the item were purchased from one source only or purchased by detailed specification. When commonality of items from purchase to purchase is essential, the use of "or equal" is not desirable.

Samples

The need to develop a purchase description sometimes is avoided through the use of samples. Prospective suppliers are invited to match or duplicate the buyer's sample. Such an approach may be appropriate when special, nonrepetitive items are to be purchased and quality requirements are not a significant factor.

Advantage

- Use of samples is a very simple method of communicating what is required.
- It is almost mandatory when purchasing materials requiring a specific color, feel, finish, or look, such as painted printed surfaces, fabric, style, film, packaging, signs, letterhead stationary, and the like.

Disadvantages

- Detailed tests and inspections may be required to determine that the furnished item meets the sample.
- The inspection on a requirement such as color may be very subjective.
- No definite standards are established either for record-keeping purposes or as the basis of future purchases.
- If the sample is exactly reproduced, all performance warranty responsibilities shift to the buyer as the supplier has performed as per the instructions from the buyer.

Standard Specifications

Recurring needs for a consistent level of quality have led industry and government to develop standard specifications for many items. Standard specifications include commercial standards, federal specifications, and international specifications. Such standard specifications contain descriptions of the quality of materials and the quality of workmanship to be used in manufacturing the item. Testing procedures are included to ensure that those quality standards are met.

Advantages

- The use of standard specifications greatly facilitates communications. The requirer, purchaser, and supplier all know what is needed.
- The cost of developing a design specification is avoided.
- The use of standard specifications results in wider competition and lower prices.
- The use of standard specifications facilitates the firm's standardization program, resulting in savings in purchase price, inspection, materials handling, and inventory carrying costs.
- Standardized items tend to be more readily available.
- Designs developed by professional societies are often state of the art and thoroughly tested.

Disadvantages

- Standard specifications may be dated. Accordingly, the buyer may not be taking advantage of the latest technology.
- The specification may call for inputs or processes that are difficult or expensive to achieve.
- Testing costs might be higher than with brand-name products, as there is less performance history.
- As with samples, responsibility for the suitability of the purchased item rests with the purchaser. Normally, the supplier who produces under a specification cited in a purchase order is not responsible for ensuring that the item will satisfy the customer's need. (With a performance specification, this responsibility is shifted to the supplier.)
- The use of standard specifications results in the purchase of standardized items. The incorporation of such standardized items in the purchaser's end product may conflict with marketing's desire to sell a unique product.

Design Specifications

Design specifications* spell out in detail the materials to be used, their sizes, shapes, and tolerances, exact physical and chemical characteristics, and how the item is to be fabricated. They provide a completely defined item capable of manufacture by a competent manufacturer. They also describe test procedures to be used to verify that all stated requirements have been met. The specification must meet the requirements of many departments in the firm: Engineering's concern for technical adequacy, Marketing's concern with consumer acceptance, Manufacturing's concern for ease of production, and Purchasing's concern for availability and economy. As would be expected, design specifications often use commercial standards and other standard specifications.

Since design specifications frequently are the basis of competitive bidding, they must communicate what is needed without need for further clarification. Thus, critical dimensions must be spelled out in detail, and all necessary quality requirements must be fully described. Concomitantly, the specification must avoid imposing unnecessary conditions that would disqualify an otherwise acceptable product because it fails to meet a nonessential condition. The design specification must convey a complete and accurate understanding of what is required. The same word or expression is subject to different interpretations by different people. The supplier will interpret the specification to its own advantage.

A specification essentially is the means of transferring knowledge between minds. Each mind will test the words of a specification against its own experience. If the design specification is ambiguous, the ambiguity will be construed against

---

*For ease of discussion, blueprints and engineering drawings are included under the heading of design specifications. Blueprints and drawings should include a statement of function, i.e., what the part will be used for to facilitate insurance against an overlooked specification unique to function. For example, "This bearing will be used in a high-vibration environment on cargo ships of *x* tons."

the drafter (i.e., the firm using the specification to purchase the item). When design specifications control performance under a purchase order or a contract, there is a presumption that the specifications are adequate for the purposes intended and that, if followed, the desired outcome will be obtained. There is an implied warranty that the specifications are adequate. Thus, the supplier who produces under the customer's specification is not responsible for the suitability or acceptability of the resulting product. However, if the supplier knows (or perhaps from experience should know) that the desired product cannot be obtained, it cannot make a useless thing and expect to be paid for it. If the supplier knows (or should have known) that the specification is defective, it is obligated to notify the customer of the defect. The supplier discharges this obligation by making the defect known to the customer.

As might be expected, design specifications must be reviewed periodically and updated. Unfortunately, the use of design specifications tends to complicate purchase order administration (follow-up and expediting) and may increase costs, delay delivery, result in delivery of obsolete items, and sharply increase inventory carrying costs. The use of design specifications may create a costly storage and distribution system for items that are not generally commercially available.

There are several advantages and disadvantages in using design specifications.

Advantages

- The purchasing organization avoids having to purchase on a sole-source basis. As seen in Chapter 2, a savings of approximately 12% can be enjoyed by avoiding sole-source situations.
- The purchasing organization avoids paying premium prices on branded goods.
- Design specifications facilitate the corporate standardization program, and many savings are enjoyed through such a program.
- They can solve the problem of "no supplier can design it," if true.

Disadvantages

- Design specifications are expensive to develop. Both time and human resources are required.
- The purchaser is responsible for the adequacy of the specification and the buying firm may use obsolete technology.
- The use of design specifications may deny the purchaser the latest advances in both technical development and manufacturing processes.
- Using a design specification for material that is very similar to an item covered by a commercial standard may result in higher unit prices. Further, the item covered by the design specification will tend to be less readily available.
- The use of design specifications restricts competition to one approach or concept. As we have seen, competition of concepts resulting from use of a

performance specification may lead to significant financial and time savings.

♦ Purchase through the use of design specifications tends to complicate the purchase order administration function. Late delivery of unique items is much more common than it is for standard ones.

♦ The purchaser usually assumes the inventory responsibility for such unique items.

Performance Specifications

Performance specifications generally describe a product by its capacity, function, or operation instead of by its physical, chemical, or quality characteristics. The supplier need only demonstrate acceptable performance to achieve acceptance of the product.

A performance specification provides a description of the intended use of an item (whether component, plant, or equipment). A performance specification may include a statement of the qualitative nature of the item required. When necessary, it may set forth those minimum essential characteristics and standards to which such item must conform to satisfy its intended use. Performance specifications describe in words what the item is to do instead of describing the item in terms of its physical and chemical properties.

Although a performance specification is much shorter and easier to develop than a design specification, caution must be exercised in its development. Once again, engineering, marketing, manufacturing, and purchasing requirements must be considered.

The following general principles apply to the development of performance specifications:

♦ The performance specification must not be so narrow that it stifles creativity.

♦ While unnecessarily restrictive performance specifications are undesirable, the performance specification must be sufficiently specific to obtain desired objectives. If it is written too broadly, potential suppliers may choose not to respond because of the uncertainty and risk involved, their inability to relate work requirements to their talents and capabilities, or difficulties in estimating costs.

♦ The performance specification serves as the nucleus of the purchase order or contract. The resulting performance is a direct function of the quality, clarity, and completeness of the specification.

♦ The element of risk to the supplier inherent in producing under the performance specification should affect the type of pricing on the resulting purchase order (e.g., firm fixed price, fixed-price incentive). Appendix D examines the relationship between the degree of risk and uncertainty and selection of the right type of pricing.

As with other approaches to defining and communicating the requirement, the use of performance specifications has inherent advantages and disadvantages.

Advantages

- Performance specifications are relatively easy to prepare.
- Their use tends to avail the purchaser of the latest technology.
- Using performance specifications ensures that the purchaser obtains the specified (desired) level of quality.
- When several already designed, developed, and produced items can meet the performance specification, the depth of competition is enhanced and purchase costs are reduced.
- Performance specifications allow a greater degree of innovation by suppliers. Under performance specifications, the supplier assumes the responsibility of providing a product suitable to the purchaser's need.

Disadvantages

- Marginal suppliers look for loopholes in specifications. Care and effort must be taken to screen potential suppliers to ensure that only reputable ones are asked to submit proposals. The use of performance specifications is restricted by purchasing's ability to select capable and ethical suppliers—the kind who do not look for loopholes.
- Competition tends to be reduced when the performance specification requires potential suppliers to perform considerable engineering in preparation for submitting a bid or proposal. Reduced competition may result in higher prices.

The advantages and disadvantages of these five approaches are summarized in Exhibit 3-1.

How to Select the Right Approach to Describing Requirements

Although the decision on what type of purchase description to use may appear to be simple, many factors complicate the issue. For small, noncritical procurements, brand names or samples frequently best describe requirements. The use of a brand name as a purchase description is appropriate to:

1. Obtain the desired level of quality or skill when these are not described easily,
2. Gain the benefits of wide advertising of the brand-name item that would aid in promotion of the purchaser's end product,
3. Accommodate users who have a bias or prejudice (whether founded or unfounded) in favor of the brand. Such prejudices can be virtually impossible to overcome.

When brand names or samples are inappropriate for describing requirements, some type of specification is employed. When selecting or developing the

Exhibit 3-1.   Advantages and disadvantages of five approaches to describing what to purchase.

Approach	Advantages	Disadvantages
Brand or trade name	Easily described Easily purchased Readily available Facilitate obtaining special workmanship Promotional pull of incorporated brand name Easy inspection Avoid testing Assurance of quality	Limited competition Higher prices Miss competitors' improvements
Samples	Easy communication of requirements	May require detailed test/ inspection No definite standards
Standard specification	Facilitate communication Avoid cost of developing design specification Wide competition Facilitates standardization program Readily available materials State of the art—in some cases Available test data	Specifications may be dated May require expensive manufacturing processes High test costs Purchaser has responsibility for suitability of purchased item Standardized material may conflict with marketing's desires for unique products
Design specification	Avoid sole source Avoid premium prices Facilitate standardization program	Expensive to prepare Purchaser responsible for adequacy of specification Miss latest technology Higher cost than standard item Less readily available More expediting problems Late deliveries Larger inventories
Performance specification	Easily prepared Gain latest technology Obtain specified level of performance Increased depth of competition	Possible loopholes in specifications Decrease breadth of competition

specification, consideration must be given to the importance of competition and the desirability of avoiding unnecessarily restrictive criteria.

Once a need has been identified and functionally described, and when the size of the contemplated purchase warrants, procurement research and analysis should be conducted to investigate the availability of commercial products able to meet the company's need. Normally, these commercial products are described by one of the standard specifications. This research and analysis also should provide information to aid in selecting a procurement strategy appropriate to the situation. Procurement research and analysis involves obtaining the following information as appropriate:

- The availability of products suitable to meet the need (with or without modification)
- The terms, conditions, and prices under which such products are sold
- Any applicable trade provisions or restrictions or controlling laws
- The performance characteristics and quality of available products, including quality control and test procedures followed by the manufacturers
- Information on the satisfaction of other users having similar needs
- Any costs or problems associated with integrating the item with those currently used
- Industry production practices, such as continuous, periodic, or batch production
- The distribution and support capabilities of potential suppliers

If a suitable commercial product is unavailable at a reasonable price, a determination should be made on whether to use a design or a performance specification.

Summary

Once the need or required function is determined, the purchase description forms the heart of the procurement. The organization's satisfaction with the purchased item frequently is determined at the time the purchase description is selected or developed. Purchase descriptions communicate to the buyer what to purchase, communicate to prospective suppliers what is required, serve as the principal element of the resulting purchase order or contract, and establish standards for inspection.

Five types of purchase descriptions have been described: brand or trade names, samples, standard specifications, design specifications, and performance specifications. Each has inherent advantages and disadvantages; no one approach is right or best in all circumstances.

The procurement of services is a little understood, yet increasingly important, activity. This frequently overlooked issue is discussed in Chapter 4.

4
Procuring Services

Gerald Brown, purchasing manager at Brandywine Products, has just had an uncomfortable discussion with Silas Eaton, owner-manager of Brandywine. Not even during his days as a pledge in a well-known national fraternity some 20 years earlier had Gerald experienced such humiliation. Silas Eaton was livid. Accounts receivable show that $500,000 is being held up by Brandywine customers. It seems that these customers will not pay for their new vibration sensing equipment until they receive the technical manual that Marketing promised to provide with the instruments. Marketing indicates that it is losing sure sales because of the forecasted nonavailability of the manual. (The manual is to contain technical data, installation and operating instructions as well as troubleshooting and maintenance information. It also is to be used as a sales aid.) Eaton holds Gerald Brown personally responsible for the snafu. Eaton claims that every day of delay in the availability of the manual is costing Brandywine thousands of dollars in lost sales.

The vibration sensing equipment has been under development for three years. The equipment was designed to detect potential malfunctions on expensive heavy equipment. In this way, corrective action can be taken before a catastrophic failure destroys the equipment monitored by the vibration sensing device.

Eight months ago, the program manager for the vibration sensing equipment forwarded a memo to technical publications at Brandywine requesting the development of a technical manual. A month after receiving this request, the head of Technical Publications told the program manager that it would be more cost effective to purchase the completed manual than to do the work in-house. The technical publications manager said that if her section were to do the work, she would have to hire two artists and several technical writers.

The program manager then contacted Gerald. After a few minutes' discussion, the program manager agreed to develop a statement of work describing his requirements. A one-page statement together with four glossy prints of the new equipment arrived in Purchasing three days later. The statement of work stated that Brandywine's engineering department would provide requested technical advice to the supplier of the technical manual on request. The estimated cost of 500 finished manuals was $300,000. The manual was to consist of not less than 400 pages. The specified completion date was six and one-half months.

Recognizing the sensitivity of this procurement, Gerald assumed personal responsibility for its satisfactory completion. He contacted three technical writing consulting companies, described Brandywine's requirements, and requested a price from each firm. Only two of the companies were willing to meet the tight delivery schedule.

One of these firms, the C. Y. Hadley Company, employed 23 individuals. Of these, 20 were artists, draftspersons, or technical writers. The firm had been in business for 17 years. Samples of recent Hadley work showed it to be satisfactory. Gerald's efforts to lower its price of $290,000 were unsuccessful. Carole Hadley, owner of the firm, stated that she was operating near capacity and would have to use considerable overtime to meet Brandywine's schedule. But she guaranteed to meet the required date if her firm received the purchase order within two days.

Brown had better luck with the A-B Commercial Art Company. Discussions with Messrs. Angst and Biddle, co-owners of A-B, indicated that they fully understood the requirement. They stated that they would have no difficulty in meeting the schedule. An examination of A-B's work showed excellent artistic and technical competence. The quality of A-B's work appeared to be superior to C. Y. Hadley's. The partners explained that it was their practice to do the artwork themselves and subcontract the technical writing to any of six local technical writers. Angst and Biddle both had been employed by C. Y. Hadley prior to establishing their own firm 10 months ago. A-B's initial price was $260,000. Through an examination of the firm's estimated costs and subsequent discussions, Brown was able to negotiate a price of $240,000 with a guaranteed delivery of six months.

Gerald Brown awarded a purchase order to A-B Commercial Art Company, incorporating the statement of work he had received from the program manager. The purchase order stipulated that the finished technical manual would contain not less than 400 pages. Progress payments at the rate of $500 per page would be made on a monthly basis. All work was to be done to the satisfaction of the program manager.

At the end of the second month, the first 10 pages arrived with a request for a progress payment of $5,000. Gerald Brown visited A-B and was assured that the project was under control and the stated completion date would be met if Brandywine engineers would be more responsive to A-B's requirements. Gerald contacted the program manager and received a commitment for improved Engineering support.

Two weeks later, only 20 more pages had arrived. Gerald visited the firm's loft office to find things in a state of total disarray. Messrs. Angst and Biddle were involved in a bitter argument. It soon became obvious that they would never meet the required delivery date.

Gerald then contacted Carole Hadley to see if she would be willing to "pick up the pieces." Carole stated that her firm simply did not have the capacity. Gerald tried, without success, to locate another supplier willing to meet the required delivery date. He then reported his findings to the program manager who immediately went to see Silas Eaton. Silas, in turn, had a very heated discussion with Gerald.

Six Problems to Avoid

We often hear that the United States is becoming a service-oriented society. Expenditures on services by commercial firms, not-for-profit organizations, and government increase each year. Traditionally, such procurements were for services which "obviously should be bought"—such as the maintenance of the reproduction equipment or landscaping services. Today, many traditional in-house services such as payroll processing, management information processing, and even some or all of the purchasing function are being outsourced. The criticality of services to the successful operation of these organizations frequently is more important than the amount of money spent. *The well-run procurement system must be as efficient at obtaining services as it is at obtaining materials, equipment, and supplies.*

Six of the major problems encountered in the procurement of services are:

1. *As was true at Brandywine, many companies treat service requirements with indifference.* The procurement of services frequently represents a sizable expenditure. Of greater importance, such procurements influence the efficiency, productivity, profitability, and morale of the organization. In Chapter 1, we saw another example of how critical the procurement of services can be. Ted Jones, purchasing manager at Eagle Manufacturing, had been called twice in one month by the president's secretary who had complained that the janitorial service had not washed the president's windows properly. This may not be Ted's most critical contract from the point of view of Eagle's profitability and success. But it may be a most important one from the point of view of Ted's success—and even his employment!

2. *Many organizations fail to identify their primary objective when purchasing services.* In Brandywine's case, the primary objective was to obtain an adequate technical manual *on time.* Timeliness was far more critical than was the artistic excellence of the manual or its price.

3. *Another common problem is failure to develop an adequate statement of work (SOW) with appropriate inspection procedures.* In no other area of procurement is there a more complex interdependency between the SOW, the method of compensation, source selection, inspection procedures, and a satisfied customer. Standard specifications are unavailable for many service requirements. Thus unique, *enforceable* SOWs must be developed. Purchasing's early and detailed involvement frequently is the key to a successful service procurement.

4. *Pricing frequently is not tailored to motivate the supplier to satisfy the organization's principal objective.* Once we know what the primary requirement is (whether timely completion, artistic or design excellence, low cost, etc.), we must structure the purchase order to motivate the supplier to meet our needs. We also should reward good service and penalize poor service.

5. *Make-or-buy analyses (also referred to as outsourcing analyses) do not underlie most decisions to accomplish services either in house or by contract.* The services area is a dynamic one. Changes occur in the availability of suppliers and the cost of obtaining services under contract. The cost of performing work with the firm's own employees also may fluctuate. Periodic reviews of these costs can lead to a make-or-buy decision and significant savings. As is true in other make-or-buy analyses, consideration of control, availability, and technical excellence also must be weighed.

6. *Selecting service contractors is done in an unsystematic manner.* Source selection is much more of an art when purchasing service requirements than when

purchasing material. Because of the many problems involved in services procurement, it is essential that established, reputable suppliers be selected. Normally, competitive procedures should be employed. In addition, because we are buying intangible talents and skills that cannot be measured objectively, much more thorough background checks must be employed to assess the personal characteristics of the providers. This process must involve personal interviewing and cannot be restricted to telephone and mail contacts. We often forget that service contracts are almost always "single source," causing the kinds of potential problems experienced by Gerald Brown in the case study opening this chapter. The A-B Commercial Art Company was a new firm with no real track record on delivery; given the critical nature of the purchase, price should not have been the major selection factor.

Three Classes of Service

Professional Services

Lawyers, consultants, and A-E firms are examples of the individuals and organizations whose services are obtained through professional service purchase orders and contracts. To obtain a satisfactory procurement when purchasing professional services, it is essential that the individuals involved in the development of the SOW know what is *really* required. For example, the vast majority of industrial, not-for-profit organizations, and government agencies lose sight of their true objective when purchasing professional services. Many of these organizations enter into what can best be described as a contract designed to reward inefficiency.

The purchase of A-E services is typical of inept procurement of professional services. Frequently, the purchasing organization and the A-E agree that the fee will be a stated percentage of the cost of the building to be designed. (In many cases, a fee ceiling is established.) Under the logic of basing the fee on the cost of the building, the A-E's income increases as the building cost increases. *This is truly a reward for inefficiency.* Fortunately, most A-E firms are ethical and do serve their clients' best interests, even though their financial rewards would be greater if they complied with the incentive provision in the contract. Of equal madness is the approach of compensating A-Es with a firm fixed-price contract. As discussed in Appendix D the firm fixed-price type of pricing rewards suppliers for their cost control. Every dollar that costs are reduced results in a dollar of additional profit to the supplier. A fixed-price contract places the A-E in a most awkward position. If design cost is tightly controlled, the A-E's profits increase. But such frugality may result in the design of a building that costs the client considerably more than if the building had been designed for economic construction and low maintenance. Again, the vast majority of A-Es will not slight their professional responsibility and loyalty to their clients. But why take chances? It would make far greater sense to reward the A-E with a reasonable fee by using a cost plus fixed fee or cost plus incentive fee contract. To this fee should be added an incentive for designing the building whose cost is less than the previously established target cost.[1]

Once management in the procuring organizations has established exactly what professional service is required (e.g., the design of a low-cost functional building), it is relatively simple to develop a SOW and proceed with the procurement. Unless the professional or professional firm possesses some truly unique skills or reputation, competition *should be* solicited. Provisions for review and approval of work in progress should be established. Since the resultant supplier (contractor) is a professional and since his or her reputation is of critical importance, inspection ordinarily is not a major problem.

A variety of compensation schemes is appropriate for professional services: hourly, daily, or weekly rates; firm fixed-price when the supplier's reputation has been established; cost plus incentive or fixed fee; and cost plus award fee. The most effective compensation scheme when purchasing A-E services calls for the use of a cost plus fixed fee contract with a cost ceiling *and* an incentive fee that is based on how well the A-E controls construction cost. Such a compensation scheme is similar to a cost plus award fee contract. The various types of contract pricing are discussed in Appendix D. Some organizations are negotiating flat fees with law firms as opposed to time charges.

Technical Services

Technical services include research and development (R&D) work; the development and installation of management information systems (MIS) and materials requirement planning (MRP) systems; and the development of technical manuals, printing services, and repair services. In virtually all cases, competition should be based on the quality of the services offered, delivery time, and the prices. As with professional services, it is essential that those responsible for the procurement focus on what *really* is required.

The completeness of the SOW and required inspection procedure is a function of the size and urgency of the requirement and the availability of reputable suppliers. For example, if an item of production equipment requires immediate repairs, time does not permit the development of an extensive SOW. If, on the other hand, a requirement exists for the development and subsequent fabrication of a new robot for manufacturing, then a carefully worded performance specification or SOW can be developed to describe what the machine is to do. Again, the key to a satisfactory and successful procurement is the identification of the firm's real requirement. Once this has been established, the development of a SOW, with appropriate inspection provisions, is relatively straightforward.

R&D services frequently are purchased on a fixed-price basis. When large expenses are likely to be incurred by the supplier, a cost plus fixed fee or cost plus award fee contract generally is more appropriate. Another approach to purchasing R&D services is to allow the supplier to amortize the R&D expenses over a stated production run. This approach is acceptable when no proprietary or patentable processes or equipment would result. If it appears likely that additional orders for the item being designed will occur, then title to and possession of the development data should be obtained. These data will allow the purchasing firm to solicit competition on all reprocurements, which will result in significant savings during follow-on procurements.

The procurement of the development and/or adaptation of standard computer software systems such as MIS and MRP systems is most challenging. There are far more examples of faulty procurements of software than of efficient ones. The first prerequisite to a successful procurement of computer software is the realization that a team effort must take place both within the procuring organization and between the customer and supplier. Appropriate levels of management within the procuring organization must participate in the development of the SOW. Care must be taken in the development of the SOW to ensure that the resulting purchase order or contract does not become a bottomless pit. Identifiable milestones should be established to serve as the basis of progress payments. Termination provisions must be established to allow the purchaser to disengage from a hopeless situation. A small working project team with representation from all interested activities should be appointed. This project team will assist Purchasing in selecting the best qualified supplier.

Such software development services are costly. Pricing approaches range from firm fixed price to labor hour to cost plus award fee. *If* the scope of work is very specific and relatively little uncertainty is present, the firm fixed-price approach usually is appropriate. When these conditions are not present, other approaches must be adopted. The labor-hour purchase order is simple to negotiate and administer but has the disadvantage of rewarding inefficiency. Under a labor-hour purchase order, overhead and profit are built into the hourly rate. The supplier's contributions to overhead and profit increase as the number of hours worked increase. The cost plus award fee contract rewards excellent performance, punishes poor performance, yet ensures that the supplier's costs are reimbursed. Unfortunately, the cost plus award fee contract requires considerable administrative effort on the part of the procuring organization. Obviously, judgment and skill are required to tailor a contract to the specific situation. The responsible purchasing manager, as part of the preparation for the purchase, should talk with colleagues from other organizations who have had experience with such procurements. By openly discussing lessons learned, many errors can be avoided.

The purchase of services such as the development of technical manuals and printing is relatively straightforward, once a determination has been made as to what is *really* required. Competition usually is available. The keys to a successful procurement are a sound statement of work; selection of an established, reputable supplier; and good purchase order administration. Fixed-price contracts usually are appropriate. Because of the nature of these service industries, progress payments may be required. When progress payments are necessary, the purchaser needs to develop a list of identifiable progress milestones against which payments can be made.

The purchase of repair services varies from emergency situations to periodic maintenance. The best way to cope with emergencies is to anticipate them. Equipment does break down. Sewer lines do get clogged. In many cases, the source (and even price) of such repairs can be established before the emergency occurs. Purchasing personnel recognize that when an emergency occurs, getting the repair done is usually more important than its cost. The vast majority of tradespeople are ethical and will not take advantage of an emergency situation. Thus, if the procuring organization has not anticipated such emergencies, time and materials contracts serve the best interests of both parties. "Requirement contracts" are common in the procurement of repair and maintenance services with payment schedules and procedures for unexpected maintenance.

Requirements for periodic plant and equipment maintenance should allow reasonable time to develop a realistic SOW that includes inspection provisions. When the cost of such services warrants and when competition exists, Purchasing then can solicit competitive bids. Warranty provisions on equipment items may require that maintenance service be purchased through the manufacturer's service organization. But as soon as this warranty period expires, the feasibility of obtaining competition should be explored. As we discuss in Chapter 5, the time to establish maintenance prices for new equipment is *during* the competitive stage of selection of the equipment source. This is the time when the most attractive price, service arrangements, and warranty can be obtained.

Operating Services

Operating services are those services that could be performed by the organization itself but that, for any of several reasons, are performed under contract. Examples include janitorial and guard service, grounds maintenance, food service, and the staffing and operation of hospital pharmacies. Private industry, not-for-profit organizations, and government have found that it frequently is more cost effective to purchase such services than it is to hire and supervise the required personnel.

The operating services area is fast-changing. The availability and cost of suppliers can vary dramatically in the course of a year or two. The cost pattern of performing the services in-house also can fluctuate over a short period of time. Labor laws, practices, and costs may change. Based on the dynamic nature of this area, it is recommended that a make-or-buy analysis be conducted on any significant service requirement on a semiannual basis.

Again, the key to the successful procurement of such services is a well-developed SOW that includes detailed inspection procedures. In most instances, the SOW describes what is to be done rather than how it is to be done. Identifiable, measurable tasks must be established for both pricing and subcontract administration purposes. A second requirement for success is the selection of a supplier who has the experience and resources to provide the specified level of services. The third key to success is the development of a compensation scheme that rewards the supplier for good service with appropriate penalties for poor service. Of equal importance is the establishment and continued operation of a monitoring (inspection) system that protects the procuring organization's interests.

Selection of suppliers for such services is usually straightforward. Once a good SOW is available, purchasing can solicit competition on a regional or national basis. Widespread competition is desirable and appropriate. Nationwide competition may be possible. For example, janitorial services for a hospital in New York State can be provided efficiently and cost effectively by a supplier whose home office is located in a small town in California.

Selecting the method of compensation normally is routine. In most cases, a firm fixed-price purchase order should be used. Such a purchase order must contain detailed provisions for price reductions, should any portion of the work not meet established criteria during any period of the contract. When considerable uncertainty exists on the expenses likely to be involved and when the size of the procurement warrants, a cost plus award fee contract is generally more appropriate.

Statement of Work (SOW)

Although we have already addressed many aspects of the SOW in the foregoing pages, it is now appropriate to give more detail on the subject. Do the security guards carry loaded weapons? Are all guards subject to police background investigations? (Not all states require this, so it is possible to have a guard force with a number of former convicts.) Do the janitors replace burned-out light bulbs—if so, who supplies the light bulbs? Are all appropriate personnel licensed? Does "cleaning the floor" mean sweeping only or does it include washing and waxing and how often? These and other questions must be addressed.

Calvin Brusman, a widely published authority on procurement, offers an excellent list of "language ground rules."

- Use mandatory language such as "shall."
- Avoid ambiguous statements and words with multiple meanings such as "including," "adequate," etc.
- Include only necessary, essential requirements, i.e., don't tell the service provider *how* to wash the floor.
- Do not repeat requirements described in other documents: Reference them when necessary.
- For government funded contracts, use Sub-Contractor Data Requirements List (SDRL), DD Form 1423, and DD Form 1664, as applicable.
- Do not expect a supplier to infer a requirement. Be specific if you need something.
- Write the SOW in a manner that encourages competition (i.e., don't have unnecessary restrictions that favor a particular contractor).
- Do not tell the supplier how to do the work unless the work is being performed under a design specification. Remember, design specifications relieve the supplier of the risks and responsibilities of performance.
- Use simple language and short sentences to describe the work requirements.
- To avoid confusion when a part is referenced, use the same descriptive part terminology throughout the SOW.
- Do not include an "Agreement to Agree" type provision as it seldom works as intended.
- Include or reference applicable specifications, illustrations, diagrams, tables, charts, and so on in the SOW if they assist in describing the work or related requirements.[2]

Brusman then gives a typical SOW descriptive outline that includes scope, background, applicable documents, deliverables, delivery/performance schedule, packaging, packing, marking and shipping instructions, technical specifications, inspection, test and acceptance, quality assurance, configuration control, data and documentation, repair parts, management, approvals of work, conferences and meetings, government/contractor furnished equipment and data, special requirements, and exhibits attachments.[3,4]

If the above recommendations seem to be overkill, remember how vague the term "services" is. We must be very specific as to what kind of service we are buying. Management consulting contracts can be even more subjective and the client must know exactly the role of the consultant regarding areas of investigation, reports, distribution of reports, training vs. implementation, authority, compensation including limits, completion dates, degree of involvement with client personnel, schedules, required references, and so on.[5] The only way to retain a consultant is to conduct a personal interview with reference checks with former clients.

Summary

Many organizations treat service requirements with indifference. Yet such procurements frequently affect the efficiency, productivity, profitability, and morale of the organization. In addition to indifference, five other major problems frequently are encountered in the procurement of professional, technical, and operating services.

The most critical problem encountered in the procurement of services is the failure to identify the *primary* objective. Design, artistic, or technical excellence; timeliness; and low cost are three common objectives. Frequently, these objectives conflict. Therefore, the primary objective must be identified and must be the focus of the procurement.

Many organizations fail to develop an adequate SOW that contains appropriate inspection procedures. Enforceable SOWs are an essential prerequisite for successful service procurements.

The method of compensation frequently is *not* tailored to motivate the supplier to satisfy the customer's primary objective. Once this objective is known, purchasing should structure the compensation scheme so that the supplier will maximize his or her income by fulfilling the customer's needs.

The services area is dynamic. Changes occur in the availability and cost of services furnished under contracts and in the cost of performing the work with the firm's own employees. Periodic make-or-buy analysis on the cost, control, availability, and technical implications of making vs. buying will lead to significant savings.

The last problem discussed deals with the source selection process. Source selection is much more of an art when purchasing services than when purchasing materials. Because of the many problems involved in services procurement, it is essential that established, reputable suppliers be selected. Prospective suppliers should be screened with extreme caution. In most cases, it is possible and desirable to use competitive procedures as a tool in source selection, including extensive checking with past clients.

Notes

1. For a more extensive discussion of this issue, see David N. Burt, "Selecting and Compensating Your Next Architect-Engineer," *Michigan Business Review* (January 1972).
2. Calvin Brusman, "A Statement of Work Primer," *NAPM Insights* (April 1994), p. 50.
3. Ibid. p. 51. Reproduced with permission.
4. Also see Leroy H. Graw and Deidre M. Maples, *Service Purchasing: What Every Buyer Should Know* (New York: Van Nostrand Reinhold, 1994), pp. 151–163.
5. See "The Craze For Consultants: Companies Are Hiring More Soothsayers—And Giving Them Bigger Roles," *Business Week* (July 25, 1994), pp. 60–66.

5

How to Stretch Your Equipment and Building Dollar

Wilbur Segerson, purchasing manager for Fairburn Manufacturing Company, is involved in a spirited discussion with Harry Worell, the plant manager at Fairburn.

Harry: Wil, as you know, I have authorization and $100,000 to purchase two new lathes. Yesterday, I had a visit from Paul Jacobs, sales manager for Wellbuilt & Sleezy. We have four other Wellbuilt & Sleezy machines and they're tops. Jacobs said that demand is really heavy for the lathes we want but that, as a personal favor to me, he will guarantee delivery within six months if he gets an order this week—and at an installed price $1,000 below my budget. What sort of paperwork do you need to wrap this up?

Wil: Wait a minute, Harry. How do we know that Wellbuilt & Sleezy has the best-suited equipment? How do we know that they will give us the best service, cooperation, and price?

Harry: Wil, you simply don't understand industry conditions. These are good prices. And Wellbuilt & Sleezy is the only make that Tom Jones in Production and I would let on our floor. If we don't grab this offer of six months' delivery, we will have to wait 12 to 18 months. Production needs those machines and as soon as humanly possible!

The procurement of new plant and equipment has a profound impact on the capacity, profitability, and productivity of the organization. Such procurements are complex. They require considerable planning, coordination, and cooperation on the part of all personnel. Substantial dollar amounts are involved. These expenditures have a significant effect on fixed overhead costs and break-even levels because they become employed assets vs. expensed materials.

The productivity of individual workers and the organization is a function of the capacity, precision, and labor requirements of the equipment purchased. Downtime and maintenance expense can contribute significantly to costs.

The availability of new plant facilities has a major impact on the firm's ability to introduce new products or to enter new markets in a timely manner. The productivity of the entire organization is affected by the physical layout and flexibility of the plant.

In most organizations, procurement decisions on plant construction and equipment are made infrequently. But once such a decision is made, the organization normally lives with it for many years.

Seven problems commonly exist in the procurement of capital equipment.

1. Purchase descriptions tend to be either too precise or too broad.
2. The requisite purchasing skills frequently are absent because plant engineers and other technical personnel frequently handle all the buying activities.
3. Emphasis is placed on the cost of acquiring an item rather than on the total cost of owning (TCO) and operating it.
4. Because they are one-shot purchases, most buyers (and engineers for that matter) are not as knowledgeable about new equipment as opposed to expensed material ordered frequently.
5. In many instances, only one or two sources are available and single sourcing is common. Thus, purchasing does not have the leverage of competition.
6. When replacing equipment, buyers and users may fail to check for the *compatibility* of the new model with existing tools, software, power requirements, floor weight maximums, worker knowledge, and so on.
7. Installation often runs 25–35% of the equipment cost and, for major production machines, installation is often the most difficult and risky step. This area must be a major negotiation topic.

When obtaining new plant construction, selecting the wrong method of purchasing construction results in the needless waste of millions of dollars. Purchasing can play a vital role in the procurement of the right equipment and facilities at the right price. We will look first at the procurement of capital equipment and then at the procurement of new plant facilities.

Purchasing Capital Equipment

The Buying Team

As depicted in Exhibit 5-1, the purchase of an item of capital equipment involves personnel from many areas of the firm. Production and Manufacturing Engineering are vitally concerned with the operating characteristics of the equipment. Plant Engineering is concerned with the equipment's physical size and mounting dimensions, power and maintenance requirements, safety features, and pollution characteristics. Design Engineering is concerned with the equipment's ability to produce items meeting standards. Engineering also may be concerned with the equipment's ability to meet likely future requirements. Finance is concerned with the initial cost and prospects for payback. On large expenditures, Finance is con-

Exhibit 5-1. The procurement of capital equipment.

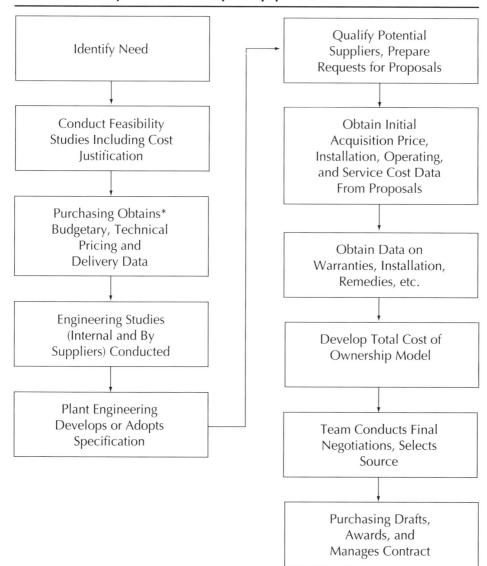

*If at this point a potential supplier deals directly with the engineer, it can result in a single source procurement incompatible with the lowest all-in-cost.

Adapted from: David N. Burt, Warren E. Norquist, and Jimmy Anklesaria, *Zero Base Pricing™: Achieving World Class Competitiveness Through Reduced All-In-Costs* (Chicago, Ill.: Probus Publishing Company, 1990), p. 72.

cerned with credit arrangements and other sources of funds. Because of the importance of the procurement, top management frequently is involved throughout the process and generally makes the final decision on timing, sourcing, and the method of financing, based on recommendations from Purchasing and the departments just noted. Normally a special project or commodity team is assigned the task of buying major equipment with Purchasing serving as the key coordinator and "gatekeeper" regarding the use of suppliers.

Reputable equipment manufacturers understand their particular machine technology and application much better than any member of the buying team. Thus, early supplier involvement (ESI) is critical to prevent unrealistic or uneconomical specifications. For this reason the supplier(s) should help by conducting application surveys at the feasibility stage of the procurement cycle (see Exhibit 5-1).

Purchasing has the responsibility for obtaining necessary information as the procurement process moves from preliminary analysis, through technical and economic analysis, to a commitment to purchase. Purchasing should ensure that the specification is adequate to meet the organization's performance, quality, and cost needs without being unduly restrictive. Purchasing also is responsible for negotiations, consummating an adequate legal document, and managing the resulting purchase order.

The Process Flow of Procuring Equipment

The typical procurement of capital equipment begins with the identification of a need. Next, initial feasibility studies are made. Production or plant engineering initiates and forwards to Purchasing a request for general information about equipment that might satisfy the need. Many organizations call this Request for Information (RFI) and develop a form to send suppliers when asking for preliminary data and interest. Purchasing *must* be responsive to such requests from its internal customers and obtain the requested preliminary technical, delivery, and pricing data. The least lack of cooperation at this point will cause the customer (user) to start dealing directly with potential suppliers.

Next, engineering studies are undertaken. In many instances, the users will want to meet with one or more equipment manufacturers' technical representatives. These individuals can provide invaluable information. A question may arise as to how much presale engineering work the purchasing firm can receive without incurring a legal or moral obligation to the technical representative's organization. This issue must be addressed before any possible problem arises. Caution is the key word. The responsible buyer needs to determine the amount of "free" sales engineering work common to that particular industry. (This so-called free work is a selling expense that must be absorbed by purchasers of the supplier's products if the supplier is to remain in business.) If the cost of an engineering study that appears to be especially desirable exceeds normal industry practice, the purchasing firm should pay for the study, with this fee refundable if an order is placed with the particular supplier. If a "free" study is offered, the wise buyer ensures that neither he or she nor the firm will be under any obligation to purchase the proposed equipment.

Engineering now should be in a position to develop or adopt a specification. The key in developing the specification is to create an explicit statement of what the item is to do without unduly restricting competition. The specification should indicate whether the equipment is to be used for a particular specified purpose or to be adaptable to a variety of purposes. The machine's ability to meet and hold tolerances (precision); the size of the parts that are to be machined; the capacity per unit of operating time; the derived power requirements and consumption; the desired operator requirements; a description of desired motions; the desired range of feeds and speeds; the desired or required safety objectives, maximum size, and special features; software interface; maintenance and operating manuals; maintenance schedule and cost; training costs-who pays-where; installation; union approvals; OSHA conformance; building permits; the equipment's ability to be moved without difficulty; its pollution characteristics; and similar requirements should be specified. To encourage a desirable level of competition, minimum standards or requirements should be established. Normally, a performance guarantee should be included in the specification. This provision guarantees that the equipment supplied under the purchase order or contract will be capable of the performance set forth in the specification. If any adjustments, changes, or requirements are required, they will be accomplished at no additional cost to the purchaser.

Classification of Capital Equipment

Equipment falls into one of the three following classifications:

1. Equipment standard to an industry
2. Standard equipment that is customized to meet special requirements
3. Unique equipment

Equipment can also be classified as to production, test, and accessory, such as a computer. The term *capital* means the item becomes an asset and goes on the books of the organization for a period of time.

Normally, an adequate level of competition can be obtained by specifying an item that is standard to an industry and that is produced by three or more suppliers. This competition results in the right quality of equipment and service at attractive delivery and price terms with the lowest cost of ownership.

When standard equipment must be customized to meet the purchaser's unique needs, the required unique feature must be clearly defined so that it can be completely understood by all potential suppliers. The potential suppliers should be required to indicate in their bids exactly what the additional feature will consist of, how it will affect the machine's operation, and what it will cost.

Two approaches commonly are employed to meet unique equipment requirements. When the procuring organization is concerned with what the machine will do and some freedom exists in how the machine will accomplish the task, the use of a performance specification is appropriate. The previously developed statements of what the item is to do and the identified technical characteristics will serve as the basis of such a specification. Competition can and should be solicited.

In some process industries, it may be desirable to purchase unique equipment by using detailed technical specifications. The firm may develop these specifications with its own engineering staff or through a professional services contract. Either approach allows the firm to solicit competition for the fabrication of the required unique equipment. A less preferred approach is to invite two or three carefully prequalified engineering firms to submit proposals for the development of the required specifications under a cost plus fixed-fee basis. The firms invited to submit proposals should indicate their planned technical approach, rates, overhead, fee structure, and ceiling costs for design and development. Separate overhead rates, fee structure, and ceiling costs also should be obtained for the fabrication of the required equipment. The procuring organization should specify that it retains the right to award the follow-on fabrication work to the selected engineering firm or such other supplier as it may choose.

Installation

The installation issue requires special attention. For major equipment, a great deal of construction and excavation may be required. It is critical to check union rules of both the buyer and seller since some union contracts call for hiring a specified percentage or number of the trade people employed in the buying company. In addition, many permits such as building code approval, helicopter authorization if the moving of generators or other large machinery is to be done by air (a common occurrence in high-density city areas), and other approvals may be required. We know of a case where after completion of a custom test machine at the supplier's plant, the machine had to be dismantled when it was discovered that the machine would not fit on a standard flatbed delivery truck. The use of a turn-key supplier is recommended to ensure proper installation with single responsibility and coordination.

Request for Proposals

On receipt of an adequate specification and when competition is present, the purchasing department prepares a request for proposals (RFP). This request should set forth the terms and conditions that will be incorporated into the resulting contract. Many equipment suppliers will attempt to have the purchase contract drawn up on their standard sales agreement form. The purchasing firm should establish that its terms and conditions will govern and that any deviations or exceptions will result in the bid being rejected as nonresponsive. Negotiation may have to be employed to resolve conflicts over terms.

Several benefits are gained by adopting this approach:

1. It is easier to analyze and compare proposals since they are all submitted under the same terms and conditions.
2. The buyer gains a better negotiating position.
3. The time and effort required for negotiations are reduced.

In most instances, the request for proposals should require suppliers to bid on the equipment specified (including installation as a separate line item) and, in addition, allow the suppliers to propose alternate equipment that they recommend.

Many standard and several nonstandard issues must be addressed in the terms and conditions. These include payment terms, performance standards, inspection procedures, warranties against defects, unique shipping requirements such as size, weight, a performance warranty, supplier responsibility for postsale services, indemnity for patent infringement, operator training responsibility, installation responsibility, insurance including the extent of liability for employee accident, compliance with state and OSHA safety requirements, special packaging for protection during shipping, and the supplier's responsibility for maintaining an inventory of spare parts. The RFP should request prices for periodic and emergency maintenance and repairs. *The time to get such prices is when competition exists.*

On receipt of proposals, Purchasing should discuss the proposed procurement with Finance, allowing Finance to update its economic analysis with current ceiling price information. If the analysis indicates that the procurement will be financially attractive and feasible, Finance will give Purchasing instructions to proceed. The buyer then should properly prepare for and conduct negotiations on price and any other issues that are unsatisfactory. This is often called the two-step approach under which the buying firm first calls for proposals from three or four suppliers and then selects one or two for negotiation. The term *RFQ* is not used because a request for quotation implies a final offer only; RFQ also has a "low bidder gets the business" tradition, which is inappropriate for major capital equipment procurement.

Supplier Selection

The buying team must weigh many factors during the source selection process. The seller's reliability, past experience making such equipment, evaluations from other users, willingness and ability to provide required technical assistance, ability to provide spare parts quickly, service history, and an acceptable price including total life cycle cost all must be considered. Frequently, two or more items of equipment will satisfy the firm's needs. These items will have different prices and other characteristics such as operator requirements, fuel consumption, life cycle costs, expected life, and likely salvage values.

Total Cost of Ownership (TCO)

The TCO approach to pricing allows the purchaser to determine the most likely cost of owning and operating an item over its anticipated productive life. This approach is the only rational way to determine a true basis for comparing the costs of owning and operating equipment. Further, by considering all the significant costs over the life of the item instead of merely the initial acquisition cost, the firm gains increased competition. Firms whose products have higher initial prices but lower subsequent ownership costs may be able to compete.

The cost of ownership includes the initial cost of the item together with installation and start-up costs, the likely cost of operating it (e.g., fuel or power consumption or salaries for operators required), finance, training, maintenance (a function of the reliability and the maintainability of the equipment), and insurance costs, as well as tax considerations and the likely salvage value of the item. The present value of the expected stream of expenditures less expected salvage value should be employed to accommodate for the time utility of money—the fact that most people would rather have a dollar today than one, in say, five years.

This concept is expressed as follows for a simplified example where initial (acquisition), training, operating, and maintenance costs and salvage value are the only variables under consideration:

$$TCO = A + P.V. \sum_{i=1}^{n} (T_i + O_i + M_i - S_n)$$

where:

TCO $=$ total cost of ownership;
A = acquisition cost;
$P.V.$ = present value;
T_i = training costs in year i;
O_i = operating cost in year i;
M_i = maintenance cost in year i;
S_n = salvage value in year n.

When the buyer is conducting price analysis on items of capital equipment, the price to use is the item's TCO as determined by the appropriate model. The accounting-finance department will also conduct various return studies such as payback period and discounted cash flow methods such as net present value (NPV), ROI, and return on assets (ROA). It is very important to inform all suppliers what financial tests the buying firm is using so they can submit appropriate data for financial evaluation.

Financing vs. Leasing, Used vs. New

Once a decision has been made about which item to purchase, two other issues should be addressed. Many equipment suppliers now provide excellent financing packages. The cost of such financing should be compared with the cost of alternative sources of funds. If supplier financing appears to be of interest, the buyer should recognize that the rates and duration may be as negotiable as are price and delivery terms. One last point: The buyer should hold back 25–30% of the final payment until the equipment has passed all operating tests.

Leasing frequently is a viable alternative to purchasing the desired item and is a popular method of acquiring industrial equipment. There are many arguments in favor of and also against leasing. In the final analysis, the acquiring firm must look at the actual effect of leasing on its profit and loss statement. The legal department should be requested to determine if the lease is an actual operating lease (which is a true lease) with payments deducted as expenses vs. a capital lease, which is actually a deferred payment plan (if you own it) with depreciation rights.[1]

Buyers should not overlook the good buys in used equipment but such equipment must be evaluated by senior equipment operators, set-up personnel, maintenance specialists, and other very experienced individuals.[2] In other words, if your organization is thinking about buying a used executive jet, the company pilots and mechanics must have veto-approval power.

Having looked at some of the major issues involved in the procurement of capital equipment, we now turn our attention to the purchase of new facilities.[3]

Purchasing Plant Facilities

Not long ago expanding demand and a low cost of capital (by today's standards) allowed many firms to acquire new facilities with little regard to minimizing costs. The president of one large manufacturing company summarized this attitude by saying, "When you need more physical plant, what's $500,000 extra?" But conditions have changed. Building costs have continued to escalate and the cost of capital is significant. Changing market conditions, global competition, new product developments, and obsolete plants continue to make new plant facilities attractive to many organizations. But now, increased attention is, or should be, focused on minimizing expenditures for such facilities.

The purchase of new facilities is a commitment for the future. Quality, productivity of the new plant, the time required to effect the purchase, and cost all must be considered. Aesthetic and time requirements and the availability of highly qualified designers and builders all will influence the selection of a purchase method. However, even before the purchase method can be selected, long-range planning is required.

Top Management Functions

Top management must be involved in the planning phase of the acquisition of new plant facilities.

- Top management should review facility requirements when corporate plans and long-range goals are reviewed.
- If at all possible, additional facility requirements should be identified at least two years before their actual need. Within reason, the more lead time available to those responsible for purchasing the new facilities, the better will be the procurement.
- Top management should agree on the general location for the new facilities.
- Space requirements at the time of building completion should be established. Requirements for five years in the future should be estimated. A preliminary budget should be established. Present and future space re-

quirements and the size of the budget are vital items of information that must be discussed with the designer-builder or architect-engineer.

♦ Top management must determine whether to lease or buy the proposed facilities.

♦ The use and amount of performance bonding must be addressed. Under such a bond, a bonding company guarantees timely completion of the construction. The cost of such a bond is usually passed on to the purchaser.

♦ Payment terms, including withholding amounts pending acceptance must be established.

A task group should be formed to accomplish the facility procurement. This group should establish detailed requirements for the facility and should recommend the appropriate purchasing method. Purchasing, Plant Engineering, and Plant Maintenance should be represented in the group to ensure that cost, plant layout, and maintenance considerations are all addressed.

Alternative Methods of Purchasing Construction

There are five methods for implementing the purchase of construction; however, it is unlikely that any one of the five methods will consistently be the proper choice for all building requirements. Exhibit 5-2 provides a graphic presentation of the various steps involved in each method from start to completion of a construction project.

The *conventional method* is the most frequently used approach to buying building construction in the United States. With this approach, the required facility is designed by architects and/or engineers without the involvement of a builder. Design of the facility is completed before potential contractors are requested to submit bids. Two separate organizations are responsible for the design and then the construction phases of the work.

The *design and build firm-agreed-price method* could be described as construction with gratuitous design. The owner determines the basic facility requirements such as size, temperature, electrical, mechanical, and so on. These requirements become the basis of a performance specification. This specification is furnished to carefully prequalified builders who, with their prospective subcontractors, prepare a bid package consisting of a design and price proposal. The purchasing firm awards a firm-agreed-price contract for construction to the builder whose bid, consisting of a design and price proposal, is most attractive.

With the *design and build cost-reimbursable method* only one contract is awarded for both design and construction. Design is accomplished by architects and engineers employed by the general contractor. Thus, the builder has ample opportunity to influence the design of the required facility. With this approach, construction of a work element (excavation, structural work, and so on) proceeds when the design of the *element* has been complete. It is not necessary to await design of the total project since one firm is responsible for both the design and the construction phases. This approach is particularly useful when a structure is required within a very short time period.

With the *building team* approach, the owner retains both a designer and a

Exhibit 5-2. Sequence of steps involved with alternative methods.

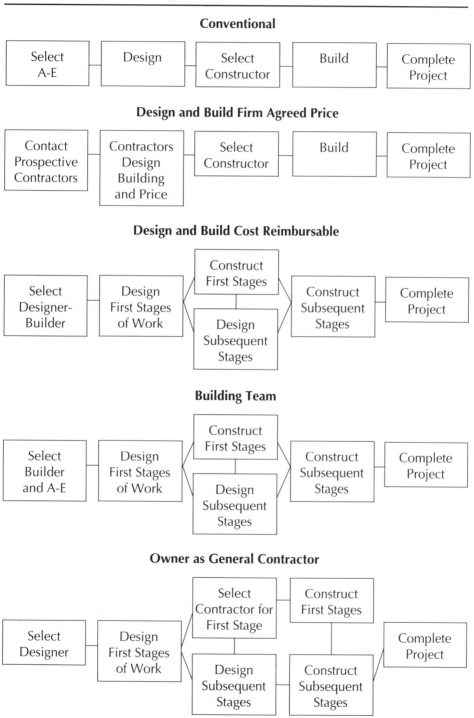

builder concurrently. In contrast to the conventional method, the builder is re-tained during the design phase and is expected to contribute information on costs, procedures, and time requirements to the designer. As the A-E completes the plans and specifications for a work element, the builder either accomplishes the work with its own forces or obtains prices from several qualified specialists in the work (subcontractors) and awards the work to the qualified subcontractor making the best offer (price, time, and quality considered). As with the other methods, the general contractor oversees and integrates the efforts of the subcon-tractors.

With *the owner as general contractor* method, the owner contracts directly for the various work elements and performs the functions of integrating and control-ling that would otherwise be accomplished by a general contractor. Since pur-chase orders and contracts are awarded on a work element basis, it is possible for construction to proceed prior to completion of the total design phase.

Research on these five methods and the resulting cost of purchasing building construction shows that the conventional method is, by far, the most costly ap-proach to obtaining construction.[4] Savings of approximately 30% are likely to result when the design and build firm-agreed-price method is used in lieu of the conventional method. Savings of 9% are likely when either the design and build cost-reimbursement or the building team method is used in lieu of the conventional method. A savings of 5% is likely when the owner acts as general contractor.

The amount of time from first contacting the designer or builder until com-pletion of the facility varies significantly with the methods used. On a typical 130,000-square-foot manufacturing plant, 16 months are required with the con-ventional method, 11.5 months with the design and build firm-agreed-price method, 12 months with both the design and build cost-reimbursable method and the building team methods, and 15.5 months when the owner acts as contractor.

We see that selection of the most appropriate method of purchasing plant facilities can significantly reduce the cost and time required to purchase new facil-ities.[5]

Summary

The procurement of new plant and equipment profoundly affects the capacity, profitability, and productivity of the firm. These procurements require planning, coordination, and the cooperation of all involved. An organization normally lives with plant and equipment procurement decisions for many years.

When purchasing new equipment, competition often is not possible. Since users are inclined to insist that only one make of equipment is acceptable, Pur-chasing must act to ensure that the equipment specification provides an explicit statement describing what the item is to do without unduly restricting compe-tition.

When two or more items of equipment satisfy a firm's needs, the total cost of ownership should be determined. This cost, also known as the life cycle cost, is computed by aggregating the initial cost of the item together with installation and start-up costs and the present value of likely operating costs and deducting the present value of the item's estimated salvage value. This is the only rational approach to determining a true basis for comparing the cost of owning and operating different equipment. This approach also allows the firm to increase competition, because products that have higher initial prices but lower subsequent ownership costs may be considered.

The most common problem encountered when purchasing new plant construction is selection of the wrong method of contracting. Research conducted on the subject shows that the most commonly employed method of purchasing construction is not only the most costly but requires the most time for completion of a building. Selection of the most appropriate method of purchasing new plant facilities can save both time and money.

In a production environment, purchasing often lacks sufficient lead time to develop procurement plans and to purchase in a cost-efficient manner. In the area of production materials, such lead time is a function of Production Planning and of Inventory Control. Chapter 6 discusses these challenging areas.

Notes

1. See B. J. Holmes, "Lease-Buy Decision Analysis" *International Journal of Purchasing and Materials Management* (Fall 1991), pp. 35–40; and James L. Schallheim, *Lease or Buy? Principles for Sound Corporate Decision Making* (Boston: Harvard Business School Press, 1994).
2. See the *MDNA Buyer's Guide* (a yearly publication), published by the Machinery Dealers National Association, 1110 Spring St., Silver Spring, Md. 20910.
3. For additional information on equipment procurement, see the dated but classic *Major Equipment Procurement* by Joseph Auer and Charles Edison Harris (New York: Van Nostrand Reinhold, 1983). Although out of print, try business libraries as this work has excellent contract examples.
4. David N. Burt, "Stretching Your Building Dollar," *California Management Review* (vol. 15, no. 4, Summer 1973), pp. 54–60.
5. Also see Anthony Stephen, *Contract Management Handbook for Commercial Construction: How to Plan, Form, and Administer Commercial Construction Contracts* (Santa Barbara, Calif.: Naris, 1984).

6

Two Key Interfaces: Production Planning and Inventory Control

Bob Meckline, president and general manager of the Lone Star Manufacturing Company, is addressing his first- and second-line managers: "Ladies and gentlemen, we are confronted with a most fascinating and frightening situation. Don Mann tells me that sales are better than ever. But according to Everet Smith, we are in a situation of near cash starvation. According to some projections Ev discussed with me yesterday, we are in a situation of profitless prosperity. Ev and I are convinced that the most important thing we can do to get back on track is to reduce our inventory of purchased materials. Moneybags, how about sharing your thoughts."

Everet replies, "Thanks, Bob. Well, as Mr. Meckline was saying, and as most of you know, sales are looking pretty good so far this year. But our investment in inventories is eating up most of our profits. Purchased material inventory turnover has fallen from 4 to 1 just 18 months ago to 2 to 1! We now have $9 million tied up in inventories. Our inventory carrying costs are about 33% of the value of the inventory, on an annual basis. My latest pro forma shows our net income before taxes is only $1 million. Now, I figure that if we cut our inventory in half to $4.5 million, we will save about one half of our current inventory carrying costs. This, in turn, would increase profits by $1.5 million to a respectable $2.5 million. Ladies and gentlemen, there is no quicker way to increase profits!"

Don Mann, vice president of Marketing, is the first to respond. "Ev, as you know, we in Marketing have done an unbelievable job. Not only have sales doubled in the last 18 months, but our market share has risen from 8% to 14%. And we've done this in spite of having virtually no increase in finished goods inventory. When Charlie and Al talked with me about a way to support an increase in sales without an increase in finished goods inventory, I thought that they were nuts. But they claimed that with a decent inventory of purchased materials, fast purchasing action, and a highly responsive production system, we would be able to support our tremendously successful marketing program. They also pointed out that an increase in purchased materials

72

inventory would be less costly than would an increase in finished goods. No labor investment. As I said, I was skeptical, but now I'm a believer."

Charline Teplitz, vice president of Operations, joins in: "Large inventories of purchased materials have three major advantages, from my point of view. They allow greater flexibility in planning and scheduling, they minimize production disruptions, and they facilitate longer production runs. I'm certain that you are all aware that both labor and management learn more efficient ways of doing things during long runs, resulting in increased productivity and lower unit costs."

Next, Al Englehart, director of Purchasing, offers his thoughts, "Frequently, large inventories are necessary to allow us to buy economically. Just yesterday, I signed a P.O. for 500 steel castings. The unit price was 13% lower than if we'd bought only 199 castings.

"As most of you know, the price of most purchased materials is based on changing supply and demand patterns. Temporary favorable buying situations and the likelihood of future adverse supply situations are good grounds for hedging or laying in inventory in advance of requirements. In effect, an expected higher cost of goods is avoided.

"Administrative costs in Purchasing, Inspection, Receiving, Warehousing, and Finance tend to be lower on a unit price basis when high inventory levels allow us to process fewer relatively large orders for materials and supplies. Additionally, larger, less frequent orders allow for more efficient utilization of my staff. My buyers are free to concentrate on the development of new sources and on more extensive and better negotiations. Lower unit prices result. Fewer orders reduce the purchase order-contract management work load, resulting in better monitoring of the remaining work load, better control, and the probability of improved timeliness of delivery and quality of material received.

"Further, maintenance and repair supplies are required to operate and maintain our plant and equipment. Paper, pencils, and similar items are required throughout the organization. We need fuel, lubricants, and replacement parts for our vehicles. The availability of such operating supplies is essential for our successful operation. When supplies are not available, efficiency and productivity are greatly reduced, and we can't perform effectively."

Sue Anderson, traffic manager, then chimes in: "Carload and truckload freight rates are a fraction of smaller, less-than-truckload rates. Large purchase orders result in considerable savings for my traffic budget."

Meckline was becoming severely agitated. "Boy, Ev, we really opened a can of worms on this one. How do we know what the optimal level of inventory is?"

Determining the right time at which to make purchases and the right quantity to buy have major impacts on an organization's success. These decisions affect the firm's responsiveness to its customers, its productivity, the cost of its purchased materials, and its administrative, handling, and storage expenses. Many purchasing managers view inadequate lead time as their number one problem. A second major problem in this area is that of inappropriate or suboptimal purchase quantities resulting from faulty inventory policies. In the foregoing case study, we see that Lone Star Manufacturing is far in advance of many other manufacturers: At least Lone Star management is aware of some of the many issues underlying sound inventory policies.

In proactive procurement, purchasing must interact with those responsible for forecasting, production planning, and inventory management. For this interaction to result in cost-effective decisions, purchasing managers must have a basic understanding of production planning, forecasting, and inventory management.

Production Planning

Time is a valuable resource in the procurement process. The more time available, the better or more optimized is the design process (assuming that the additional time is employed to develop the most cost-effective design and *not* to "gold plate" a design, as happens all too frequently). More time provides the opportunity for better specifications and better cost estimates.

Adequate time is essential for economic purchasing. The amount of time available will affect the quality of the solicitation request, the number of sources solicited, the quality of the negotiations, and the resulting price. For example, if sufficient time is not available to seek competition, we may be forced to purchase on a sole-source basis.* As mentioned in Chapter 2, sole-source procurements tend to cost about 12% more than competitively solicited procurements.

The amount of lead time allowed for purchasing is usually insufficient, resulting in excessively high prices, lower quality of material received, and late delivery. To avoid such situations, personnel in Marketing, Design Engineering, Production Planning, and Inventory Management must become familiar with purchasing's need for realistic lead times and then must endeavor to provide such lead times.

Production planning—also referred to as aggregate planning, operations planning, and aggregate scheduling—is concerned with the overall operation of an organization over a specified time. Based on customer orders and forecasts for a period 6 to 18 months into the future, Production Planning determines the size and training of the workforce, inventories, aggregate material purchases, overtime, and subcontracting** required. These decisions then can be converted into a production budget, which becomes the source of personnel plans (hiring, training, firing), warehousing needs, purchasing plans, and cash requirements.

The production plan is the basis of the short-range (one- to six-month) master schedule. Development of the master schedule involves checking on capacity and allocating the resources acquired as a result of the production plan to specific products in specific time periods. The master schedule is the basis of a third activity, dispatching, which involves taking corrective actions required as a result of late receipt of materials, absent workers, inoperable machines, changes in pri-

---

*Sole source means only one supplier exists because of patent, capacity, or some other advantage. *Single source* means the buyer has elected to use just one supplier (i.e., by choice, not default).
**Throughout this chapter, the word *subcontracting* refers to purchase of an end item that normally is manufactured by the firm.

Exhibit 6-1. Production planning and scheduling.

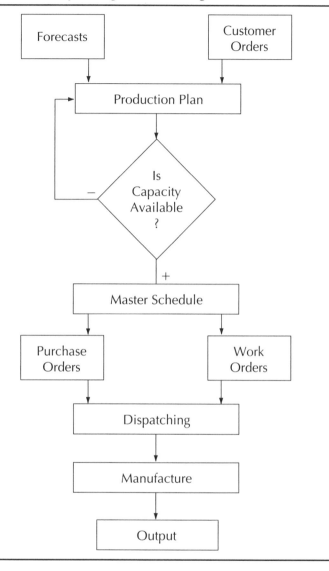

orities, new or canceled orders, and a host of other events that make the master schedule appear to be a wish or an idle dream. Dispatching ranges from coercing suppliers to expedite deliveries of needed materials, to expediting the production of component parts, to appeasing customers while telling them that their order will be late.

Exhibit 6-1 shows the relationship between these activities. Customer orders and sales forecasts are the basic input to the production plan. Ideally, the production plan will cover a period of one to five years. If adequate capacity is available, the production plan becomes the basis of the nearer-term master schedule. The master schedule commonly is for a period of six months. The master schedule is the basis for releasing purchase orders for materials and work orders. Dispatching then is required to juggle available and additional resources, customers, and production activities.

Production planning involves the development of a series of interrelated shorter-term plans, including the master schedule, an input or resources plan, and an output plan. The master schedule specifies the amount of production (or subcontracting) to be accomplished over a series of future periods. The input plan specifies the inputs to the master schedule by indicating the size of the workforce, the length of the workday, and the materials that will be required. The output identifies the destination of the manufactured goods to inventory or distribution.

Production planning begins with a forecast of future demand. Normally there are a number of ways that the resources, rates of production, and output rates can be balanced to meet the forecasted demand. Each alternative is likely to have different cost and operating implications. For example, the manufacturer may be able to:

- Vary the size of the workforce
- Utilize overtime
- Subcontract or "outscore," as many now call it
- Vary the product mix
- Accept back orders
- Stabilize demand by adding countercyclical products to the product line
- Vary price and promotional efforts to influence demand

Let us now consider a simplified manufacturing process. If forecasted demand is 1,000 units in month 1 and 2,000 units in month 2, how can input, production, and output rates be varied to meet anticipated demand (forecasts)? One approach would be to vary the input, production, and output rates simultaneously as we move from month 1 to month 2. In month 1, sufficient labor and materials would be input to produce exactly 1,000 units. In month 2, these inputs and the rate of production could be doubled to produce exactly 2,000 units of output. A second alternative would be to produce 1,000 units in each of the two months and *subcontract* for 1,000 units for delivery in the second month. A third alternative would be to keep all inputs and production at a constant rate, one equal to the average demand. Under this alternative, 1,500 units would be produced in month 1 with 1,000 going to distribution and 500 to inventory. In month 2, all 1,500 units produced together with 500 units from inventory would go to distribution. Obviously, there are many additional alternatives.

The attractiveness of each alternative depends on the relative costs associated with changing input and production rates and the costs associated with the various ways of routing the outputs (i.e., distribution or storage).

As we have seen, the key inputs to the production planning process are customer orders and forecasts. The receipt of customer orders requires no elaboration. Forecasting, on the other hand, frequently appears to be something of a black art.

Forecasting

A major manufacturing firm recently learned the importance of accurate sales forecasts. Its sales forecasts for two years were based, in large measure, on bleak economic predictions for the period. These forecasts proved to be approximately 25% below actual demand. This firm operated in an industry where long lead times and allocation of materials by suppliers were common. The firm purchased supplier capacity for its annual materials requirements based on its sales forecasts. Accordingly, it purchased approximately 75% of its actual material requirements from its traditional suppliers. The balance of the material required to meet actual demand was purchased on the open markets from middlemen at premium prices. Not only did the firm pay more, but quality became a major problem.

No single forecasting method gives uniformly accurate results. Accordingly, when forecasting accuracy is of critical importance, it is desirable to use several methods, with each method acting as a check on the others. The two basic approaches to long-term (in excess of one year) forecasting are top-down and buildup. With top-down forecasting, we

- Obtain or develop a forecast of general economic conditions
- Determine the industry's total market potential for the product
- Determine the firm's share of the total industry market
- Identify likely changes in historic activity due to competitive action, pricing, promotional efforts, and so on
- Develop the product's sales forecast

Under the buildup method, we accumulate estimates of future demand from various organizational units in the company. This method may draw on one or more of the following four classes of forecasting techniques: consensus of executive opinion, a sales force composite, users' expectations, and quantitative methods.

Consensus of Executive Opinion

Consensus of executive opinion is the oldest and simplest technique for developing sales forecasts. The opinions of top managers from various departments are obtained and averaged in an effort to develop a sounder forecast than could be developed by a single individual. This technique is quick and relatively simple. But it is based entirely on opinion rather than on facts and analyses. Furthermore, averaging opinions disperses the responsibility for their accuracy.

Sales Force Composite

Using sales force composite, members of the sales department are solicited for their opinions concerning expectations of future sales in their territories. The estimates are reviewed by regional sales managers and then by the general sales manager. This technique also is simple and has the advantage of being based on the specialized knowledge of those closest to the market. But the technique suffers from several disadvantages. Many salespersons tend to be overly optimistic. Others are risk averse and will play it safe by underforecasting. Such action ensures that the salesperson's forecast will be met without the individual having to exert himself or herself. Other problems with this technique include giving customers and prospects unrealistic lead times to get the business.

One of the authors worked with XYZ Company, which regularly promised three to six weeks lead time to develop rather sophisticated prototypes with the hope of taking business away from competition. Marketing ignored normal supplier and manufacturing lead times, which caused frantic rush work, expediting with suppliers, rework because of hasty transition from prototype to production runs, and poor documentation. The results of increasing sales and lower profits were and are predictable. In addition, such *unplanned* operations caused XYZ to issue at least twice as many purchase orders as normal to find suppliers who could meet short lead times. To quote one of XYZ's engineers, "We can always find another supplier to meet our delivery requirements." This kind of thinking produces an ever increasing number of suppliers who charge high prices for schedule changes and other typical related problems such as poor prints. Superior suppliers will not tolerate customers who cannot plan a reasonable schedule. Indeed, one of the best machine shops supplying XYZ Company dropped it as a customer because of the disruptions and problems caused by the lack of realistic forecasting and planning.

User's Expectations

Manufacturers in industries with relatively few customers may ask their customers how much they expect to purchase in the forthcoming period. The sales forecasts are based directly on this information. This method of forecasting is relatively inexpensive; however, the basis of the forecast is expectations, which are subject to change. Further, the firm's customers may be too optimistic or too pessimistic.

Quantitative Techniques

Many organizations rely on one or more quantitative techniques to supplement personal judgment and to increase the accuracy of sales forecasts. These quantitative techniques allow the forecaster to predict the future from past internal data. These techniques, which are beyond the scope of this book, may be obtained from a number of texts on the subject.[1]

The experienced forecaster will develop a forecast and then modify it, if appropriate, by the expected influence of factors that cause deviation from historic trends. Such factors include competition, market demand, economic conditions, proposed legal changes, and the availability of materials. We see that forecasting is both an art and a science! It is wise to use several techniques to give a range of estimates.

Aggregate Planning

With the revised forecast in hand, the production planner is now able to plan on an aggregate basis. This plan will be the basis of material input requirements, total workforce, total production, the size of inventories, the amount of subcontracting, and the master schedule. Although considerable effort is being devoted to operations research approaches to aid the production planner, charting techniques are still the most commonly used approach to carrying out this difficult task.

With charting, once an approved forecast has been developed for the planning period, a table is constructed for the cumulative product requirements. The production planner then investigates alternative strategies calling for different production rates, different workforce sizes, different levels of subcontracting, and/or different inventory levels with the objective of maximizing profits. The costs that are investigated include:

1. Costs due to production rate variation (overtime or excess idle time)
2. Costs due to variation in the size of the workforce (hiring and training costs, severance, and unemployment pay)
3. Incremental costs for materials (quantity discounts, price breaks, etc.)
4. Costs resulting from subcontracting for requirements that cannot be produced by the firm under a particular production plan
5. Carrying costs of different levels of inventory

The most attractive strategy becomes the production plan.

Assuming adequate capacity is available, the adopted production plan becomes the basis for the master schedule. The master schedule provides information both on the total quantity to be produced and on variations in quantities by time period. In extremely simple operations, this information can be applied to the bill of materials for the item under study and used to forecast material requirements. These requirements can be checked against available inventory, ultimately becoming the basis of purchase activity. But, in most manufacturing operations, the number of items produced, the variety and quantities of required purchased materials, and the frequent changes in the master schedule require considerable intermediate-level planning. More and more, we find that this intermediate-level planning is being accomplished through the assistance of a computer-controlled materials requirement planning (MRP) system. Even when a computer-controlled MRP system is not employed, the following logic is useful in understanding the process of converting the production plan to work orders and purchase orders.

Manufacturing Resource Planning (MRPII) expands the basic MRP to include interrelated modules such as accounts payable, purchasing, payroll, and financial analysis in a closed-loop system. This closed-loop system gives financial figures and enables the users to simulate the manufacturing system. It also facilitates almost instant comparison of planned to actual performance on a wide variety of factors such as inventory turns, production control, costs, profits, and so on. At some buyer firms, the MRPII system is compatible with the supplier's MRPII system, which means the buying firm can actually activate scheduling at the supplier firm. Finally MRPII software is often used to link operations in computer integrated manufacturing (CIM) systems.

Material Requirements Planning

MRP is a new name applied to an old established procedure.[2] It is simply a computer program for production scheduling, inventory control, and the scheduling of purchase orders. MRP allows management to time efficiently the ordering and manufacturing of the components and subassemblies that make up completed products of dependent demand—that is, one automobile requires four tires and a spare. MRP includes a precise scheduling system, an efficient material control system, and a rescheduling system for revising plans as changes occur. The major objectives of the MRP system are simultaneously to:

- Ensure the availability of components and subassemblies for planned production of end items for delivery to customers or inventory.
- Maintain the lowest possible investment in inventory.
- Plan purchasing and manufacturing activities.
- Reschedule purchasing and manufacturing activities, as required.

The four principal elements in an MRP system are:

1. The production schedule, which comes from the master schedule.
2. The product structure (bill of materials) file
3. The inventory status files: in stock, on order, encumbered (allocated)
4. The MRP logic

Exhibit 6-2 depicts a traditional MRP system. We see that the production plan is the basic input and drives the MRP system. But the production plan is constrained by projected production capacity. If projected capacity in the form of facilities, equipment, personnel, and purchased materials (especially long lead components) is not adequate to meet the production plan, resources will have to be increased, excess requirements will have to be obtained from subcontractors, the plan will have to be revised, or marketing will have to be advised that projected demand cannot be met.

Inventory status records indicate the actual inventory level of each item, quantities on order, quantities previously allocated (encumbered), lead times, and lot sizes. Lead times should be long enough to be feasible without resorting to special efforts by suppliers such as expediting, premium time, and the use of premium transportation. MRP systems that update lead times based on the time the supplier required on the last order can result in production disruptions, premium prices, premium transportation, and extraordinary expediting efforts. There is no guarantee that 10 weeks lead time will be adequate today, even though

Exhibit 6-2. A materials requirement planning system.

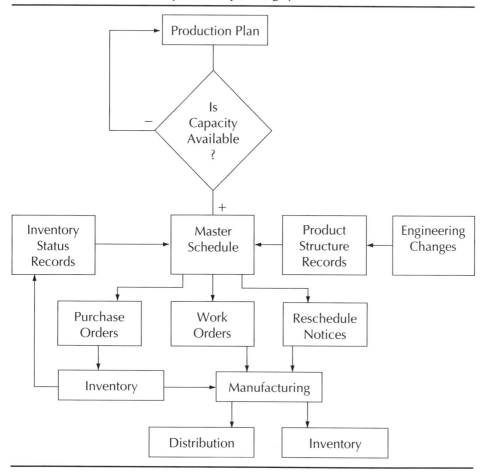

10 weeks were required for delivery on the last order. There are at least three ways of coping with the need for current *and* adequate lead times.

1. One of the approaches to purchasing recurring requirements with guaranteed lead times specified is the use of planner-schedulers, as discussed in The Changing Role of Purchasing section later in this chapter.
2. The lead times contained in the inventory records can indicate maximum likely time required. Then when the MRP system issues a requisition for material, the requisition should indicate the required availability date.
3. The timing of purchases can be at the discretion of the buyer based on the production schedule. If this approach is employed, the buyer must be informed when manufacturing activities are rescheduled and then must take appropriate action.

The MRP logic takes into consideration lot-sizing techniques based on balancing the costs of ordering and holding inventory. These techniques are discussed later in the Trade-Offs section of this chapter.

Product structure files are based on the bill of materials. They show every component or assembly required to produce end items together with the sequencing of manufacturing and assembly operations required to manufacture an item. When an item is designed, an engineering drawing and a bill of materials are created. A process planner then develops route and operation sheets on the actual manufacture of the item including operational times. This logic is captured in the item's product structure record.

To understand the logic of an MRP system, suppose that the production plan calls for delivery of a child's wagon in 14 weeks. We know from the wagon's product structure record that the wagon consists of six parts:

1. A steel body
2. Four wheels
3. Two axles
4. Four axle brackets
5. Four axle nuts
6. A handle

Additionally, a set of assembly instructions and a printed corrugated shipping box are required. A check of the inventory status records for these items shows that we have only the axle nuts, axle brackets, and the printed instructions in inventory. These records also indicate that the procurement lead times are as follows:

Body: 10 weeks   Handles: 4 weeks
Wheels: 2 weeks   Printed corrugated boxes: 8 weeks
Axles: 2 weeks

We also know that it will take a week to assemble the wagon. To ship during the fourteenth week requires that all components be available for assembly in week 13.

We could place orders for all of these items right now, but what would happen if we did? We would have the body in inventory for 3 weeks, wheels in inventory for 11 weeks, and so on. For one wagon, this would not cause much worry. But what if we are talking of 100,000 wagons?

Instead of ordering all items now, let's work back from our shipping date of week 14. We will need all the wagon's components in week 13, so we can simply calculate when to place our orders by subtracting lead times. We would order the body in 3 weeks, the printed box in 5 weeks, the wheels and axles in 11 weeks, and the handle in 9 weeks.

Now consider the substitution of a body manufactured in our own facilities for the purchased one. We will simplify by assuming that the body is pressed from purchased sheet steel that requires 6 weeks lead time. It then is painted with red paint requiring 2 weeks lead time. Each of the two internal operations (pressing and painting), together with materials handling times, requires one week. Recognizing that the body must be available at the beginning of week 13, our action times would be:

order steel week 5	press body week 11
order paint week 10	paint body week 12

Next, consider a disruption in the production schedule. Suppose that a machine breaks down, throwing a component two weeks off schedule, ultimately affecting end-product delivery by two weeks. As a result of the delayed completion date, there is no reason to hurry the other components along as planned. To do so would merely result in their sitting needlessly in inventory. Instead, the due dates for these items could be delayed by two weeks. Such a revision (slippage) has three important benefits:

1. If the item is produced internally, it frees up production capacity for other jobs.
2. It avoids the "hurry up and wait" syndrome that is so common in manufacturing operations and that is responsible for excessive in-process inventories.
3. It allows us to reschedule supplier deliveries for purchased components, reducing our inventories of purchased materials.

Now, visualize a manufacturing plant with hundreds of operations and purchased components. Although the planning and controlling of the actions required for one wagon can be done by hand, it is not difficult to imagine the complexity of planning for and controlling many products and parts that interact with one another. Such complexity defies manual control procedures. MRP considers not only the time dimension in planning but also the current and planned quantities of parts and products in inventories. MRP takes into account the dynamics of both time and quantity for interrelated parts and products. With the significant reductions in the cost of high-speed computation we have gained in the recent past, MRP can now rapidly and inexpensively update order priorities weekly or daily if changes in plans and expectations require. Rapid computation is required to explode component requirements from the schedule while simultaneously referencing inventory records to check stock status and lead times and to keep the entire plan sufficiently current to be useful in spite of revised schedules and late material arrivals.

The following benefits result from successful MRP applications:

• *Reduced inventory investment.* Inventories of purchased material and work in process decrease by 10–30%.
• *Reduced administrative effort.* Scheduling, inventory control, and purchasing should become more efficient, making the assignment of personnel to more productive tasks possible.
• *Reduced manufacture of obsolete components.* Through the use of product structure records that reflect planned engineering changes, manufacturers

are able to coordinate changes with the consumption of dated parts. Such coordination decreases scrap costs substantially.

* *Improved customer relations.* MRP can be used to determine the likelihood of meeting proposed delivery dates before marketing makes delivery quotations. In addition, if an item with a promised delivery goes off schedule and cannot be brought back on schedule, customers can be notified in a timely manner so that they can revise their plans with minimum inconvenience.

Although MRP appears to be highly desirable, there have been many unsuccessful applications. To be implemented successfully, six prerequisites are essential:

1. A commitment by *all* levels of management
2. Stable employment for those who implement and use the system during its initial stages of operation
3. The availability of timely and accurate data including scheduling, accurate bill of materials, precise inventory records and stores counts
4. The active involvement of those who will use the system in its design and implementation
5. Schedule stabilization for designated production periods, perhaps one month, a minimum of one week
6. Computer data input discipline: If you use it, report it.

Just-in-Time Systems

MRP systems are *push* production-inventory control systems since they are internally generated from a master schedule, that is, the forecast at the front end *drives* all the shop floor scheduling, ordering from suppliers, and operations. JIT systems copied from the Japanese concept of *kanban* are *pull* systems and work in reverse of MRP by literally waiting for an actual order (for delivery to a customer or inventory). At a certain reorder point at each workstation, a production release device (card, light, signal), directs the products of, for example, workstation one to move to workstation two in a continuous flow. This system includes materials requisition devices for suppliers. In theory, we have "just enough" at "just the right time" at any particular workstation. Multiple daily deliveries in small lots is the requirement. With the trend to "Build to Order" production, such as that of Gateway computers. Suppliers must be on the same JIT system.

Like MRP, but more critical, JIT systems require:

* 100% Defect-free material
* Cycle time reduction
* Workers trained to be their own quality control inspectors
* Quality detection systems such as statistical process control (SPC)
* Fewer but better partnership suppliers working on long-term contracts featuring a release scheduling system

+ Fast transportation systems direct to workstations
+ Schedule stabilization[3]

One major disadvantage to JIT is its very advantage—little or no buffer inventory. It requires stable demand. Several users have experienced stock outs. Accurate forecasting and schedule stabilization are prime prerequisites.

Xerox; Honda of America Manufacturing; General Motors; Ford; Hewlett-Packard; Sony in San Diego; IBM; John Deere; Motorola; and many other U.S. firms have increased sales, lowered manufacturing costs, and drastically reduced inventory—all with much better quality through the implementation of JIT. For example, after certification and qualification, all incoming inspection is avoided. Except for the occasional spot check, there simply isn't the time or the storage space for such non-value added activities. In addition, returnable containers and bar coding have facilitated the successful use of JIT. Quite obviously, this concept favors using suppliers located as close as possible to the operating facility.

The Changing Role of Purchasing Under MRP and JIT

The early use of MRP and JIT made it mandatory to rethink the entire procurement process. Now we really had to negotiate the entire supply chain rather than merely place orders for each required delivery. We had to reduce the paperwork and buyer time. The only way to do that was to contract with fewer suppliers who would match our production control to their production and shipment capability.

The key first step was to consolidate suppliers to one prime and perhaps one backup supplier to provide larger value orders to induce suppliers into better pricing, faster delivery, much better quality, and more services. In other words, we had to ask much more from fewer suppliers who would be rewarded with larger and more profitable long-term contracts. No more "three quotes and a cloud of dust" as Bob Stone, a former director of purchasing at General Motors often said to both authors. Consolidation also facilitates simplification and standardization; rarely would any buying company need to stock 50 different gaskets from 10 different suppliers. Buying teams soon discovered that a partnership based on trust and commitment would be a necessary development during negotiation.

Although we explore the partnership concept in more detail in later chapters, a word about scheduling is appropriate here. It became apparent under MRP and JIT that the buyer should negotiate the contract and that direct release authority should be given to "someone" in production control called a *planner/supplier scheduler*. It is a waste of buyer time and a non-value-added extra step to have a planner go through purchasing simply to schedule releases under a contract that has been negotiated by a buyer. The old system also often produced a purchase order for each release, adding to paperwork delays and expense. It is best if the planner can also be the supplier scheduler. Under a concept called JITII, a registered service mark of Bose Corporation in Framingham, Massachusetts, the supplier replaces the planner-scheduler and salesperson with a full-time individual called *in-plants*.[4] These in-plants execute the releases back to their own plant and in their spare time, work as advisers to the customer's design engineering staff. A company need not establish partnerships to achieve the advantages noted, but it is mandatory to do so under MRP and JIT systems.

The Trade-Offs Involved in Determining the Right Levels of Inventory and Quantities to Purchase

A high degree of interdependence exists between the inventory level for an item and the optimal quantity to purchase at any point in time. Inventory policy involves a determination of desired turns, average level, and buffer or safety stock. Determining the right inventory level and the right quantity to purchase has very significant impacts on the successful operation and profitability of the organization. As we saw at Lone Star Manufacturing, this determination requires an analysis involving many trade-offs. But the savings potential makes the required effort well worthwhile.

Theoretically, demand and supply of production materials and supplies required for the operation of the organization could be coordinated to such an extent that inventories would be unnecessary. Such a situation is approximated when an organization employs an MRP system. But for many items and many situations, it may be impossible to know future demand with total certainty. Further, it may be impossible to guarantee availability of all items at a particular moment. Thus, inventories serve as buffers between the demand for and the supply of required materials and supplies. In addition, MRP is *not* appropriate for all organizations. Inventories allow greater flexibility in production. This flexibility has two benefits: (1) The firm can better respond to customer demands for its products, and (2) economies result in the production operation. Inventories also allow a reduction in the overall cost of purchased material and supplies through purchasing, transportation, and administrative economies. And inventories serve as hedges against future price increases and other contingencies such as transportation difficulties, strikes, natural catastrophes, and so on. History shows that large purchase order quantities tend to be associated with large inventories.

Inventory carrying costs currently run between 15% and 45% of the value of the inventory on an annual basis. No published studies have ever documented the popular use of 30–35%. Further, inventories tie up needed working capital and may preclude a firm from being able to take advantage of otherwise attractive investment opportunities.

If we can significantly reduce the amount of inventory required to support a given level of operation without adversely affecting the various costs and impacts in the areas of production, purchasing, and transportation, then we could improve the organization's efficiency and profitability. Such a reduction in inventory requires effective inventory and purchasing management and a close coordination between the two. The following example illustrates the impact of such improved inventory and purchasing management.

The Clearwater Company produces farm equipment to order. It relies on a large inventory of purchased material and a responsive production department to meet its customers' needs. Clearwater has an average of $12 million in purchased materials in inventory. Its sales are $24 million, for an inventory turnover ratio of 2.

$$\frac{\text{Sales}}{\text{Inventory}} = \frac{24}{12} = 2$$

Increased emphasis is placed on inventory and purchasing management resulting in a reduction in inventory from $12 million to $8 million. Note that the inventory turnover ratio improves from 2 to $24/8 = 3$. Inventory carrying costs are 35% per year of the value of the average inventory. The $4 million reduction in inventory will lead to a reduction in inventory carrying expenses of $4 million $\times$ .35 = $1.4 million (assuming that the unused capacity in space, equipment, and workforce can be released or that this capacity would be absorbed by allowing increased sales with no corresponding increase in inventory.)

If pretax profits for Clearwater were $8 million, this savings of $1.4 million in inventory carrying costs would increase pretax profits by $17.5%! Further, by improving the inventory turnover ratio, Clearwater has freed $4 million that it can invest or use to reduce its current or long-term liabilities.

Several quantitative approaches exist for determining the optimal inventory level and reorder point. These are beyond the scope of this book. But the underlying logic of inventory management can be examined by looking at the tabular approach. We can determine the optimum inventory level for an item by summing the appropriate costs discussed earlier and selecting the inventory level associated with the minimum total cost. An example provides further insight into this concept.

The Apex Manufacturing Company purchases blank castings from outside suppliers and machines them to customer orders. Apex uses an average of 2,000 castings per year. Purchase prices and transportation rates for differing quantities are as follows:

Units per Order	Purchase Price FOB* Origin	Transportation per Unit	Total Delivered Price
0 to 199	$190	$20	$210
200 to 499	175	10	185
500 and over	160	10	170

The administrative costs associated with purchasing, receiving, inspecting, warehousing, and paying the supplier are estimated to be $200 per purchase order. Apex maintains no safety stock of purchased material. Average inventory, then, is one-half the size of each purchase order quantity. Marketing believes that lost sales

*FOB stands for free on board, and FOB Origin usually means the buyer selects the carrier, pays for transportation, and assumes liability.

costs will be a function of the number of orders placed per year, since an out-of-stock condition for the castings will occur between use of the last casting and receipt of a new shipment. Marketing estimates the lost sales cost (based on expected value analysis) to be $50 each time an order is due in. Production does not begin work on a order until all required blank castings are on hand. Thus, production believes that inventory and ordering policies will have no impact on the productivity of its operation. Hedging is not considered to be feasible by top management. Inventory carrying costs are estimated to be 35% per year.

We now develop a table to determine the total costs associated with several different order sizes (and inventory levels). Most of the quantities selected are at points of a price break since experience has shown that the optimal order quantity usually is at such a point.

Apex Manufacturing Company

Data

Order quantity (Q)	50	100	200	500	1000
Average inventory ($Q/2$)	25	50	100	250	500
Number of orders					
($2,000/Q$)	40	20	10	4	2
Delivered price per unit	$210	$210	$185	$170	$170

Annual Costs

Purchasing and transportation ($2,000$ units)	$420,000	$420,000	$370,000	$340,000	$340,000
Administration costs (no. orders × $200)	8,000	4,000	2,000	800	400
Cost of lost sales ($50 × no. orders)	2,000	1,000	500	200	100
Inventory carrying costs (.35 × $Q/2$ × delivered price per unit)	1,838	3,675	6,475	14,875	29,750
Total costs	$431,838	$428,675	$378,975	$355,875	$370,250

Another way of looking at the optimal level of inventory is to study the relation between the incremental savings and the incremental costs associated with different levels of inventory as shown in Exhibit 6–3. The incremental savings include:

- Avoided lost sales
- Improved manufacturing productivity
- Lower per unit costs of purchased material because of price breaks, better sourcing, improved negotiations, and hedging
- Reduced per unit administrative costs due to economies of scale
- Lower unit transportation costs

Exhibit 6-3.   Costs associated with various levels of inventory.

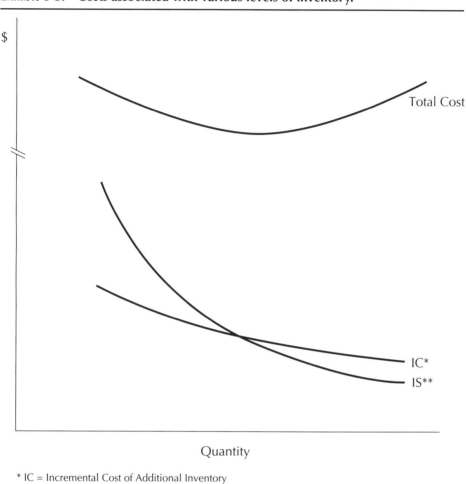

Quantity

* IC = Incremental Cost of Additional Inventory
**IS = Incremental Savings Associated with Additional Inventory Resulting from:
       Avoided Lost Sales
       Improved Manufacturing Productivity
       Lower Unit Costs of Purchased Goods
       Lower Unit Transportation Costs
       Lower Unit Administrative Costs

The incremental costs are largely from carrying additional inventory. Because inventory carrying costs are a function of the value of the material in inventory, the incremental cost of additional inventory declines (slopes downward). This phenomenon is based on the fact that larger inventories allow us to purchase and ship in larger quantities. Consequently, we enjoy lower delivered unit prices. This, in turn, leads to lower interest and tax liabilities, resulting in lower inventory carrying costs.

As previously indicated, quantitative techniques exist for determining the optimal level of inventory. When demand for an item has a random pattern, a fixed order quantity model normally is employed.

Frequently, we will want to coordinate inventory review and ordering for several items of the same class. Such action reduces inventory management and administrative expenses. Also, it allows the organization to enjoy discounts in purchase prices and transportation because of consolidation. In such cases, fixed period order models are appropriate. A useful variation of the fixed period ordering system is appropriate for continuous flow types of manufacturing operations. This procedure calls for the establishment of period contracts (e.g., six months) with delivery scheduled on a daily or similar basis throughout the period of the contract. Daily visual review is made of the inventory of such items with any imbalance reported to purchasing and production control. Any changes in production schedules must be furnished to the responsible buyer in purchasing so that delivery schedules may be revised.

The Fallacy of the Economic Order Quantity

For years, management believed that economic order quantity (EOQ) analysis could be used for inventory control. The concept itself is simple, using the following formula

$$Q_{opt} = \sqrt{\frac{2RS}{KC}}$$

where:
    R = annual demand
    S = setup or order preparation cost
    K = carrying cost to hold inventory
    C = delivered purchase cost.

Q_{opt} is the minimum number of units at the point where order cost and carrying cost are equal, which, in theory, is the point where total carrying costs and order costs are the lowest. But this formula is almost useless because of the following major limitations:

- It is not compatible with MRP and JIT.
- All the demand inputs are yearly estimates so the output is just an estimate.
- Only incremental costs are appropriate, that is, the cost of the next setup, the next purchase order preparation, the cost of the next stored unit (warehouse cost). Most users of this technique erroneously use "average costs," which destroys the logic. Until you need to build a new warehouse, there is no increase in "sunk" warehouse cost as inventory increases.
- For inventory that moves from location to location, one set of costs does not apply.
- The carrying costs are usually badly overstated.
- Purchase ordering costs for long-term contracts are one-shot expenses. Release costs would be or are fractions of a cent or, for a fax, $1.00. Few firms

have accurate studies of K (carrying cost to hold inventory) beyond the cost of capital of the material. This cost could never be much beyond the going commercial loan rates and average rate of return of the firm.

♦ The opportunity cost aspect of EOQ is gigantic assumptions such as storage cost. Most warehouses are on the books at sunk costs with zero alternative use in the short term.

♦ EOQ assumes constant demand for the next year.

We agree with Gardner, a leading author and consultant in materials management, when he says:

> In the same vein, suppose there is excess storage capacity from time to time. The accounting department will tell you to include all available space into carrying costs because if you were not using the space, it could be rented out. They are dealing in pure fantasy. Whom are you going to rent it to? How would you go about finding someone who would inconvenience himself by renting out a few feet of your floor space on a temporary basis at your stated rate when he could get all the space he needs at a public warehouse and probably save money in the bargain?[5]

Catalogs: A Profitable Investment

In most organizations, an inventory catalog will pay for itself many times over. For example, the typical industrial firm stocks between 10,000 and 50,000 items. To control such a large number of items effectively, it is essential to know what the items are; their cost, use, and lead time; and any special considerations. All inventory items should be identified, described, and cross-referenced to the manufacturer's part number and the user's part number. Proper cross-indexing allows users to be aware of the interchangeability of items and opportunities for consolidation.

The catalog serves as an important medium of communication. It allows engineers and production personnel to communicate more effectively with purchasing personnel and Purchasing with the firm's suppliers. The catalog facilitates the standardization program discussed in Chapter 2. If a designer knows that one of two or three suitable alternatives is a stock item, he or she knows that procurement costs and lead times will tend to be better than for the nonstocked alternatives.

The development and use of an inventory catalog reduce the likelihood of duplicate records and redundant inventories for identical items. Lower inventory levels and a reduced probability of a stock outage result.

Once an inventory catalog has been developed, it then is desirable to analyze the inventory preparatory to controlling it effectively. Each item should be studied in terms of its cost, use, lead time, and other relevant information. The items should be arrayed by size of inventory investment, the classical ABC analysis. Typically, 20 percent of the *inventory* items (A) account for approximately 80 percent of the inventory investment, and 30 percent of the items (B) represent approximately another 15 percent of inventory investment, with the remaining 50 percent of the items (C) representing only 5 percent of total inventory investment. This same principle is present in virtually all organizations, be they manufacturing firms, hospitals, banks, or government agencies. Such an analysis allows management to focus on those areas of greatest savings potential.

Distribution Resource Planning

The inventory and production control systems discussed thus far are basically for traditional industrial manufacturing concerns. What about the Wal-Marts of the world? What about the Proctor and Gamble type firms who, although manufacturers, must interact with a vast network of distribution centers at both the wholesale and retail level? One answer is distribution resource planning (DRP), which has played a major role in channel integration. Using many of the same tools applied in JIT and TQM (such as bar-coding and electronic data interchange), DRP uses a system called quick response continuous replenishment or QR/CR.[6] Although the details are beyond this book, QR/CR is a paperless resupply system with the buying company directly ordering from the supplier, often bypassing wholesalers for shipment to major distribution centers who, in turn, ship to retail outlets. This is accomplished electronically by computer and usually includes one month of firm shipments with forecasts out many weeks into the future. There are no purchase orders, no confirmations, and no individual invoices, only monthly statements. It is a variation of MRPII but integrates MRPII with DRP to plan and schedule inventories in the entire channel of distribution. Transportation and warehouse logistics are key elements of DRP along with accurate master production schedules (MPS). The huge retailers, such as Wal-Mart, Kmart and Target, are now dictating this new ordering and shipping system, even to giant manufacturers such as Proctor and Gamble.[7]

Electronic Data Interchange (EDI)

We list this as a special section because EDI is a total corporate electronic information transfer system that can only be justified on that basis. You do not need EDI just to send releases to your suppliers, a task that can be done for nominal amounts of money by phone, fax, or speed letter. When using third party mailboxes, this is especially true as the fees are significant. Although many manufacturers such as Ford link EDI with their JIT systems and others link it to MRP systems as a tool, it is not a substitute for negotiation, personal communications with suppliers, and simple releases by fax (a much, much cheaper and "fast enough" system for most firms). There are many advantages to EDI when accomplished on a companywide basis, but we have not read, seen, or heard of an EDI system justified purely on the basis of communication with industrial suppliers.[8] Significant cost savings in paperwork, lead time, data input errors, and inventory are reported, but it does not produce much labor savings.[9]

We feel the essential step is to eliminate the paperwork rather than automate it by EDI. For the key, large volume materials, negotiate one- or two-year long contracts and then have planner/supplier schedulers release orders by a simple one-page fax message with copies (or via computer input) to Accounting, Receiving, and Inspection. After negotiating the contract, Purchasing should not be involved unless there are problems and or until the evaluation of the supplier prior to the next negotiation or sourcing period. Bar coding automates the documentation at the receiving end and instantly adjusts inventory records, routing to testing, stores, and Accounts Payable. Again, we are not against EDI, we simply feel in many instances there are faster and cheaper methods for accomplishing much the same thing. Very few operations need the incremental speed of computer time over fax time. In addition, it is not necessary to keep sending an entire purchase order just to give a release quantity.

Purchasing Credit Cards

Most major banks and credit card companies now offer a special procurement credit card. This concept is another attempt to reduce paperwork involved with "odds and ends" maintenance, repair, and operating (MRO) buying for single or very small quantity items. Selected managers have credit cards to buy limited items up to a certain dollar limit from approved suppliers who have agreed to accept the cards. There are no purchase requisitions or purchase orders. This method can substantially reduce the purchasing cycle time and administrative costs. However, the purchasing department must solicit proposals from several sources as fees and terms vary considerably. The credit card procedures must prevent abuse such as excessive buying of a wide variety of special tools and other items when one type is sufficient.[10]

Summary

Determining the right time at which to make purchases and the right quantity to buy has a major impact on an organization's productivity and profits. Many purchasing managers view inadequate lead time as their number one problem. A second major problem is that of inappropriate or suboptimal purchase quantities, resulting from faulty inventory policies.

Because it is concerned with the overall operation of an organization over a specified time horizon, production planning is one of the keys to adequate procurement lead time. Production planning begins with orders and a forecast of future demand. It then determines the size of the workforce, overtime, the size of inventories, the size and timing of material purchases, and the amount of subcontracting. Normally, there are several alternative ways of balancing the rate of production and projected demand.

Once the production plan has been developed, it is possible to derive the master schedule which, in conjunction with inventory information and the product structure record, is the control mechanism for releasing work orders and purchase orders.

An increasing number of manufacturers are employing an MRP system for intermediate-level planning. MRP, a computer program for production scheduling, inventory control, and the scheduling of purchase orders, facilitates production planning and scheduling, ensures that required materials are available when required, reduces the firm's investment in inventory, and assists in rescheduling purchasing and manufacturing operations.

In addition to easier and more efficient scheduling of the firm's production capacity, MRP potentially can reduce investment in incoming materials and work-in-process inventory, reduce scrap previously associated with the implementation of engineering changes, help to improve customer relations, and aid in long-range planning. MRPII is a closed-loop system with feedback measuring output to objective, including the financial consequences.

The JIT system is a pull system versus the push system of MRP. It involves multiple deliveries of very small lots of 100% defect-free material moved ahead one workstation at a time with each movable storage container having the exact number of parts needed for the next operation. The movement starts from the end of the production line and signals with a card as it "pulls" each remaining tub to the next station as it is needed. Both JIT and MRP have forced organizations into a much smaller supply base with long-term contracts for 100% defect-free materials. Supplier schedulers issue direct releases against contracts issued by Purchasing. Paperwork is greatly reduced and time is now spent on professional buying activities. When appropriate, EDI can augment both MRP and JIT systems.

Determining the right inventory and the right quantity to purchase on a particular purchase order has a significant impact on the operation of any organization. The cost of lost sales, lost productivity due to nonavailability of needed material or supplies, administrative costs associated with purchasing and receiving the items, and inventory carrying costs are all affected by the size of inventory and the size and frequency of purchase orders. As we have argued, old concepts such as EOQ do not work.

Marketing, Operations, Purchasing, and Materials Handling all have arguments favoring large inventories and relatively large quantities on each purchase order. Finance is concerned both with inventory carrying costs and the amount of money invested in inventory. Management's objective is to find the right balance between these conflicting positions.

The field of DRP has exploded with the advent of mass distribution centers built by Wal-Mart and others. Direct electronic communication with the supplier is critical in DRP.

We now will look at another area where several departments do or should interact: the make-or-buy decision. Although this is a relatively straightforward area, it is one that continues to be misunderstood and one in which numerous costly mistakes are made. Accordingly, the potential for improving productivity and profits is tremendous.

Notes

1. See James A. Gardner, *Common Sense Manufacturing: Becoming a Top Value Competitor* (Burr Ridge, Ill.: Business One Irwin, 1992), pp. 39–67; J. Holton Wilson and Barry Keating, *Business Forecasting* (Homewood, Ill.: Richard D. Irwin, 1993).
2. See the classic work, Oliver W. Wight, *MRP II: Unlocking America's Productivity Potential* (Boston, Mass.: CBI Publishing, and Williston, Vt.: Oliver Wight Limited, 1981).
3. See A. Ansari and B. Modarress, *Just-in-Time Purchasing* (New York: The Free Press, 1990).
4. Lance Dixon, "JITII: When You're Doing It," *Purchasing*, May 6, 1993, p. 17; and Fred R. Bleakley, "Strange Bedfellows: Some Companies Let Suppliers Work on Site and Even Place Orders," *The Wall Street Journal* (January 13, 1995), pp. 1 and A6.
5. Gardner, *Common Sense*, p. 24.
6. See Andre J. Martin, *Distribution Resource Planning: The Gateway to Quick Response and Continuous Replenishment*, 2nd ed. (Essex Junction, Vt.: Oliver Wight Companies, 1992; distributed by Dearborn Trade, Chicago, Ill).
7. See Roy L. Harmon, *Reinventing the Warehouse: World Class Distribution Logistics* (New York: The Free Press, 1993).
8. See Margaret A. Emmelhainz, Ph.D., *EDI: A Total Management Guide*, 2nd ed. (New York: Van Nostrand Reinhold, 1993).
9. Joseph R. Carter, *Purchasing: Continuing Improvement Through Integration* (Homewood, Ill: Business One Irwin, 1993), pp. 40–43.
10. See Fred R. Bleakley, "When Corporate Purchasing Goes Plastic," *The Wall Street Journal* (June 14, 1995), p. B1.

7

To Make or To Buy: That Is the Question

The Tarheel Tool Company, located in Raleigh, North Carolina, manufactures hydraulic and electric handtools. The company was founded by two veterans of the Vietnam conflict. Originally, Tarheel purchased all its components. It then began making its gears and, later, its housings and most of its fields and armatures. Sales at Tarheel have grown to $40 million per year.

Three years ago, Jack Thomas, the surviving cofounder and the president of Tarheel, established a make-or-buy committee. The committee consists of Tim Whitney, the chief engineer; Jim McAdams, the vice president of operations; Tom Cervantes, the purchasing manager; John Brooks, the plant engineer; and Judy Jones, the controller. The committee meets at the call of Thomas, who normally participates in the discussions. A month ago, Thomas requested that the make-or-buy committee members gather information on the merits of making or buying a new gear fabrication machine. We now observe the make-or-buy committee in action.

Jack Thomas begins: "I know that you are all very busy, but we have an important item to discuss today. We have the funds to upgrade our gear production operation. Basically, we must decide whether to make the machine ourselves or to purchase the new gear fabrication machine."

Jim McAdams comments, "As you may be aware, our gear cutting equipment is 20 years old. It is labor intensive and it is so shopworn that even our senior machinists have trouble holding tolerances. Tom and I have located two machines that will satisfy our projected gear requirements for the next five years. I'd be happy with either machine. Tom, how about a few words on the cost implications."

Tom Cervantes contributes his thoughts. "As Jim indicated, we have identified two suppliers. One is the Hamilton Machine Works with a delivered price of $120,000. The other is the Lexington Tool Company with a price of $147,000. I've performed a total cost of ownership analysis on the cost of acquiring and operating both machines for the next five years. The Lexington machine's life cycle cost is a good $100,000 less than Hamilton's."

Jack Thomas then says, "Well, we have a good handle on the cost of purchasing and operating the machine. But based on some reading I've been doing recently, I thought it might be a good idea to look at the implications of making our own gear fabrication machine. Tim, what have you been able to learn?"

Tim Whitney: "As is so often the case, things aren't quite as simple as they initially appear. When Jack asked me to look into this, it seemed pretty far-fetched. But I've gathered data on the cost of designing and assembling our own equipment. Based on costs that Tom's people obtained, the material required to build this machine would cost about $105,000. Jim, John, and I figure that we could pool talent from Production, Plant Engineering, and Design Engineering to assemble and install the machine. Most of the work would be done on an overtime basis since the people we want are already busy. Our best guesstimate is that our out-of-pocket labor costs would be $60,000 to $70,000. Thus, we feel that the machine would cost us about $165,000 or so to make.

"But there is a major, yet subtle, offset. In both Europe and Japan, we find that manufacturing firms make much more of their own equipment than we do here in America. Everything I've read on the subject indicates that the active involvement of the firm's engineering and production personnel in the design and fabrication of required capital equipment results in a more productive piece of equipment. Based on my research, I'm convinced that we should make the new gear fabrication machine."

John Brooks adds his concurrence to this comment.

Judy Jones interjects, "I hear what Tim is saying, but I have two questions: Can we be sure that the resulting equipment will be more productive? Are our costs any more realistic than on our last fiasco? As we all recall, costs grew by some 240% when we built our own chuck assembler!"

"Judy, I'm glad you asked me that," replies Tim. "I've used Tom's life cycle cost model with two assumptions: first, the initial out-of-pocket cost of making will not exceed $300,000, under a worst-case scenario, and, second, our own gear fabrication machine will be 10% more effective than any we purchase. With these assumptions, we still would save well over $500,000 during the next 5 years."

Mr. Thomas interrupts, "I think we've heard enough. I think we should build our own machine. Anyone disagree?" Silence and nods of agreement from all.

The make-or-buy issue confronts most organizations continually. Every job release and every purchase request implies a decision to make or to buy. Most organizations have two basic sources of supply: their own operation and that of outside suppliers. This is as true of requirements for janitorial services as it is for fuel injection pumps. The U.S. auto manufacturers are a good example with the trend for all of them to purchase more parts than they make themselves. Along with the trend to more purchasing of parts, the auto manufacturers are encouraging the part suppliers to engage in more design work. As Alex Taylor III writes:

> Don't confuse this fragmentation with the industry's former infatuation with outsourcing. That meant sending detailed specifications for a particular part around the world in search of the lowest-cost producer. Today's automakers are seeking suppliers capable of not just making a part but also designing it.[1]

Many chief executives consider the make-or-buy decision to be among the most critical and most difficult confronting their organizations. Not only are billions of dollars needlessly wasted if the wrong decision is made, but scarce management resources frequently are stretched past the breaking point. *Outsourcing* is a term being used in the trade press primarily relating to services such as accounting, maintenance, security, promotion, stocking, and the like. The basic issues are the same concerning the question of doing it yourself or contracting with an independent outside the buying firm. We prefer the term *make or buy.* The strategic issue requires the firm to identify its core competencies—the things that differentiate it and make it viable. If an item or service at or near the heart of the firm's core competencies is to be outsourced, it should only be supplied by a carefully selected supplier under a tightly woven strategic alliance.

Top management has the ultimate responsibility for make-or-buy decisions. In most cases, this responsibility can be satisfied through operating procedures that develop and pool all relevant information surrounding a make-or-buy issue. Purchasing is a source of much of this information. Also, Purchasing frequently should identify candidates for a make-or-buy analysis.

Five major problems are common in the make-or-buy area:

1. Make-or-buy decisions are made at too low a level in the organization.
2. Not all factors are considered when conducting a make-or-buy analysis.
3. Decisions are not reviewed on a periodic basis. Circumstances change!
4. The *estimates* underlying the cost of making are less objective and accurate than the purchase *facts.*
5. Members of the buying company assume they know more than the supplier about the material or service.

Make-or-Buy Issues

The Strategic Issue

"What kind of an organization do we want to be?" This issue is the first, and perhaps most critical, to be addressed. Pride or purely emotional reasoning plays a major part in many decisions. Pride in self-sufficiency can become a dominant factor that can lead to many problems. While self-sufficiency in some areas is desirable or even necessary, it is impossible for even a large firm to become entirely self-sufficient as Henry Ford found out in the 1920s. Mr. Ford wanted to make everything in what became the world's most vertically integrated manufacturing firm, a far cry from the Ford today, which buys 50% of its parts.[2] The more a firm strives for self-sufficiency, the larger it becomes, with the management task increasing in complexity and diversity. In such a situation, it is entirely possible that management will be spread too thinly to effectively manage the business. If at all possible, purely emotional reasoning should be omitted from the make-or-buy decision.

Many years ago, a major truck manufacturer had marginal success at a time when one of its objectives required a high degree of self-sufficiency. Today, this

Exhibit 7-1   Make-or-buy cost data: An example.

	Make	Buy
Material (incl. freight) (variable)	$ 79.25	$213.00
Direct labor (variable)	80.00	—
Material burden (variable)	2.25	7.00
Labor burden		
Fixed	20.00	
Variable	48.00	
Tooling (fixed)	20.50	
Total cost	$250.00	$220.00
Variable costs	209.50	220.00
Fixed (sunk) (20.00+20.50)	40.50	

firm purchases most of its components and assemblies. The firm is far more successful now that it focuses on design, assembly, and marketing.

Cost

Two keys prerequisites are essential to a thorough and sound analysis of the cost considerations of a make-or-buy decision.

1. Cost must be segregated between fixed costs and variable or incremental ones. Such cost figures must include all relevant costs, both direct and indirect, near term and anticipated changes. Realistic estimates of in-house production costs must include expected rejection rates and spoilage. These estimates also should consider the likely effects of learning resulting from long production runs. It is interesting to compare the Big Three auto manufacturers per labor hour cost (wages and fringes) of an average of $42.00 per hour per assembly worker to the $14.00 per hour labor cost of ITT automotive, the world's largest supplier of antilock brakes.[3]

2. Accurate and realistic data must be available on the investment required to make or to buy an item. Frequently, the working capital required in the manufacture of an item can equal and even exceed the investment required for facilities and equipment. It is essential to consider both the facilities and the working capital components of an investment.

Exhibit 7–1 provides an example of the cost considerations involved in a typical make-or-buy analysis. Assume that we have an annual requirement for 5,000 units that we may purchase at $213 plus a charge of $7 for materials burden per unit. The total unit cost of making these items is $250. There is idle plant capacity adequate to produce the item.

At first glance, it would appear less expensive to buy ($220) than to make ($250). But when we look at variable or out-of-pocket costs, we see that the variable cost of making is $10.50 less per unit ($209.50) than is the cost of buying ($220). The total savings are $52,500 (5,000 × $10.50) per year.

Before concluding that we should make the item, we must consider the net investment required to manufacture it. Let us assume that the net investment required for equipment and working capital is $430,000 if the item is made. The return on investment becomes 12.2% ($52,500 savings/year ÷ $430,000). While such a return may sound attractive to many executives whose firms struggle to make 10% on investment before taxes, it is only an average return for many operations. Thus, what appeared to be a most attractive candidate for in-house manufacture based on marginal dollar savings ($52,500) may prove to be less attractive as an investment (ROI = 12.2%) than other alternatives!

Quality

When there is a significant difference in quality between items produced internally and items purchased or when a specified quality cannot be purchased, then management must consider these quality considerations in the make-or-buy decision. One argument for making over buying is the so-called impossibility of finding a supplier capable or willing to manufacture the item to the desired specifications. But further investigation should be conducted before this argument can be accepted. Why are these specifications so much more rigid than those of the rest of the industry? The manufacturer should reexamine the specifications and make every effort to secure the cooperation of potential suppliers to ensure that the quality specifications are realistic and that no satisfactory product is available. Frequently, suppliers can suggest alternatives that are just as dependable if they know the intended purpose of the item.

On the other hand, the firm may desire a level of quality below that commercially available. Suppliers may be selling only a quality far above that which would fully satisfy the need in question and may, at the same time, have so satisfactory a volume at the higher level as to have no interest in a lower quality product. If this is the case, the user may be justified in manufacturing the item.

Frequently, it is claimed that in-house production may better satisfy manufacturing's quality requirements. The user of an item usually better understands the operational intricacies involved in the item's use. With a make decision, a better degree of coordination will probably exist between those responsible for producing the item and those responsible for assembling it. Communications between the two groups are facilitated compared with the situation in which the item is furnished by an outside supplier. If the firm has a weak purchasing department, such assumptions may be true. But with a professional purchasing operation, the flow of information and coordination between purchaser and supplier should result in no more problems than between two production activities of the same firm.

Since quality must be controlled in either the purchased or manufactured items, a competent quality assurance staff and a TQM (total quality management) program must be employed. The purchase order may state that the purchaser's quality assurance inspectors have access to the supplier's manufacturing, inspection, and shipping departments. Thus, the purchaser can maintain significant control and still not incur the additional cost resulting from manufacturing the item.

Quantity

One of the most frequent reasons for making over buying is that a requirement may be too small to interest suppliers. Small volume requirements of unique, nonstandard items may be difficult to purchase. The firm may feel that it is forced to make such items; however, it may be economically imprudent to do so. The costs of planning, tooling, setup, and purchase of required raw materials may be exorbitant. It may be far more cost effective to purchase the required item in larger quantities or to identify a suitable substitute.

If a large quantity of an item is required on a repetitive basis, then the analysis described in the Cost section should be made. The company should have a high degree of confidence that its requirements for the item will continue to the point that it receives a satisfactory ROI before deciding to make such an item.

Frequently, a firm will follow a conscious policy of making an item at a level of production sufficient to meet its minimum requirements and purchase additional items as required. This policy builds a degree of stability into the firm's production activities and provides accurate comparative cost data. Such a policy should be adopted only after investigating the willingness and ability of suppliers to fill such fluctuating demand.

Service

Service often is defined simply as reliable delivery. In a broader sense, it includes a wide variety of intangible factors that lead to greater satisfaction on the part of the purchasing firm. This consideration must be judged fairly and the purchasing firm must not be given undue credit with respect to service simply for emotional reasons. Merely because the item is produced in-house is not proof that service will be superior to that of a supplier.

Assurance of supply is a primary service consideration. When the lack of an item causes serious problems, such as total production stoppage, and totally reliable suppliers are not available, the decision to make rather than buy may be justified.

When a purchaser is faced with a monopolistic environment, the service accompanying the product is generally somewhat poorer than in a highly competitive market. Such a situation may induce the would-be purchaser to make the product. If an item is used as a subcomponent on a product the purchaser is selling and is causing the entire product to be unreliable, the resulting loss of goodwill and sales may be significant enough to justify a make decision, even though the cost analysis does not support such a decision.

Specialized Knowledge

Frequently, a supplier possesses specialized knowledge, abilities, and production know-how that would be very expensive to duplicate. Suppliers may have a large R&D budget leading to improved and/or less expensive products. As the U.S. auto industry has discovered, developing such experience and expertise tends to be cost prohibitive and time consuming. The protection of innovation achieved by the supplier is a critical aspect of trust, that is, the buyer *must not under any condition* give this innovation to a supplier's competitor or use the technology were it to make the item.

Design or Production Process Secrecy

Occasionally, a firm decides to manufacture a certain part because additional industrial security can be provided, especially when the item is a key part for which a patent would not provide adequate protection. This justification must be used with caution, however, as the firm can provide very little protection against design infringement after sale. In short, if a patent will not protect a certain part, then in-house manufacturing may not either. Frequently, a firm may have developed a unique or proprietary production process. Such circumstances may support a decision to make over buying.

Urgent Requirements

The firm usually can purchase a small quantity much more readily than were it to produce the item. If the requirement is urgent, such as to preclude stopping an assembly line, the payment of a higher price to buy the item is justified.

Labor Problems

The production of any new item may require labor skills that the company does not possess. The hiring, cross-training, and upgrading of personnel may be a troublesome and complex process, especially if a union is involved. The company may be entering a field in which it has no experience and no adequately trained personnel. Labor problems are easily shifted to someone else, namely, the supplier, through a decision to buy.

The presence of unions within the company also may be a significant factor. Unions often have clauses in their contract prohibiting the purchasing of items that can be manufactured within the plant. The history of labor problems in the supplier's company also may influence the make-or-buy decision.

Plant Capacity

Obviously, the more significant the item in question is relative to the company's size, the greater the probability that the item will be purchased rather than produced in house. When the item would require a significant investment, the smaller company has no rational decision other than to buy.

Generally, the more mature company will try to integrate items currently purchased into its production more often than will a new company. The new company understandably concentrates on increasing output and has very little excess capital or plant capacity to divert to production of components. Quite the opposite is true for the more mature company. Such a firm tends to have extra facilities, capital, and personnel and, therefore, is in a better position to increase profit by producing what was formerly purchased. Excess plant capacity and the likely duration of the excess capacity should always be considered in the make-or-buy decision as should additional expenses such as tooling, setup, and training.

Capital Equipment

Manufacturers sometimes find it necessary to make a needed item, simply because a suitable supplier does not exist. This is most frequently the case with highly specialized manufacturing equipment.

As we saw at Tarheel Tool, another potential advantage results from a manufacturer's developing and fabricating its own equipment: Integrating the firm's production and engineering experience into the design and fabrication of the equipment may greatly increase productivity. Many Europeans and Japanese have found this to be the case.

Use of Idle Resources

A make decision can prove profitable to a firm even when suitable supplies are available. In periods of recession or business slumps, a firm is faced with the problem of idle plant equipment, labor, and management. By making a product that it may have been buying, a firm can put its idle machinery to work, retain skilled employees, and spread its overhead costs over a larger volume of production.

Perhaps the biggest benefits obtained from a make decision during a slump are in the area of labor relations. Employee morale can be maintained and layoff penalty costs can be avoided by timely use of the make decision. Even in times of recession, most firms find it desirable to retain highly skilled production personnel. These personnel can be kept at work and a stable workforce maintained by a decision to make. The long-run benefits from good labor relations are obvious.

Great caution must be taken when basing a make decision primarily on temporary idle resources. Make decisions tend to be permanent. A decision to make temporarily an item under such circumstances should be reviewed when demand increases.

Make and Buy

Some firms make and buy critical nonstandard items to ensure that a reliable second source is available in case of difficulty with the supplier. Such a policy also provides data that are useful in reviewing internal production and management efficiency.

Making the Decision

Make-or-buy decisions can have a critical effect on the economic health of a firm, even on its survival. Frequently, these decisions are made at too low a level in the organization. On many occasions, no conscious decision appears to have been made. Things just happen! The decision to make is often weaker than the decision to buy because buy costs are known whereas make costs are estimates. Obviously, the amount of time and effort and the level of managerial attention appropriate are functions of the amount of money involved and the criticality of the item to the firm's well-being. Normally several departments should be interested and involved in make-or-buy decisions: Production, Purchasing, Engineering, Finance, and Marketing. See the Appendix A for an example of a make/buy policy and procedure.

Any of the following situations should precipitate a make-or-buy analysis:

- *New product development and modification.* Every major component should be reviewed.
- *Unsatisfactory supplier performance.* If purchasing is unable to develop reliable sources for an item, the item should be reviewed and analyzed to ensure that the specified quantity level is essential and to ensure that suitable substitutes are not available. If the item, as specified, passes these reviews, it becomes a candidate for in-house sourcing.
- *Changes in sales.* Sales demand that exceeds capacity calls for a make-or-buy review of those items produced in house that contribute the lowest ROI. Declines in sales and production should prompt a review of candidates for in-house production.
- *Periodic review of previous decisions.* Changing costs and other considerations can convert a good make-or-buy decision into a bad one very quickly. Major make-or-buy decisions should be reviewed as a component of the firm's annual planning process.

Summary

The firm's objective is, or should be, that of optimizing the utilization of its production, managerial, and financial resources. The make-or-buy analysis and resulting decision is a key ingredient in this optimizing process.

Many considerations influence a make-or-buy decision, or outsourcing as it is often called in the service sector. It is far easier to reverse a make-or-buy decision *before* its implementation. Therefore, the make-or-buy analysis should take place during the planning of new product items. Because of rapidly changing costs, sales, and conditions of supply, the make-or-buy decision should be re-examined on a periodic basis.

The make-or-buy decision is among the most critical and most challenging confronting an organization. The cost implications of a faulty decision will reduce the firm's profitability. A decision to make items that differ from those currently being produced can so dilute management that no area receives the right level of managerial attention. Profits, productivity, and quality all suffer.

The lasting nature of a make decision causes it to be far more critical than for a buy decision. Once a firm begins making an item or service, all sorts of justifications can be found to support a continuation of the activity, even in the face of evidence supporting a buy decision.

Each make-or-buy analysis is unique. Each requires the consideration of many factors. Rarely will all relevant factors favor a make or a buy decision. The decision must be based on the composite effect of many factors on the firm's operation.[4] The fact that the make decision is usually weaker than the buy decision seems to be reinforced by the recent long-range trend to buying vs. making.[5]

This chapter completes the most critical and least understood part of the procurement process: the determination of requirements. We now turn our attention to what happens to a requirement that has been soundly developed and determined to be appropriate for purchase from outside sources.

Notes

1. Alex Taylor, III, "The Auto Industry Meets the New Economy: Everything From Designing Cars to Building Factories Will Get Cheaper as Auto Companies Quit Making Their Own Parts and Rely More on Suppliers," *Fortune* (September 5, 1994), p. 53.
2. Susan Helper, "Supplier Relations Hold the Key to Competitiveness in the Auto Industry," *Strategy* (July 1994), the Weatherhead School of Management, Case Western Reserve University, Cleveland, Ohio.
3. Taylor, *Fortune*, p. 53.
4. See M. R. Leenders and J. Nollet, "The Gray Zone in Make or Buy," *Journal of Purchasing and Materials Management* (Fall 1984), pp. 10–15.
5. "Outsourcing Solving More Supply Problems," *Purchasing* (May 18, 1989), p. 21.

8

How to Select the Right Supplier

The California Gas & Electric Company (CG&E) is being confronted with many problems: increasing costs of diesel oil for its diesel-fired electric generators, delays in planned nuclear plants, a decrease in rainfall leading to reduced hydroelectric generation, reduced net income, and a decrease in bond rating. Many of these issues led to a significant increase in electric rates, which, in turn, caused a storm of consumer protests.

A recently completed study by CG&E engineers and a leading geothermal engineer recommended construction of a geothermal plant in the Mohave Desert. One of the key components of the new generating station is a revolutionary heat exchanger capable of operating in a very hostile environment.

CG&E engineers developed a performance specification for the required heat exchanger. Purchasing identified three companies that were technically and managerially capable of developing and manufacturing the heat exchanger. Each company submitted a preliminary or conceptual solution to the requirement, a fixed-price proposal for development, and a target price for manufacture of the machine. Purchasing, with the concurrence of CG&E top management, decided to enter into a two-phase contract. Phase I was to be a firm fixed-price contract for detailed development of the heat exchanger. Phase II, to be covered by an option in the basic contract, would call for a fixed-price incentive type of contract for manufacture of the heat exchanger. Appropriate preaward surveys and negotiations were conducted.

Charlie Holt, purchasing manager for CG&E, was confronted with a predicament. No one supplier was clearly superior. For example, the Akron Manufacturing Company demonstrated the best understanding of the technical requirement and the best delivery schedule, but the worst price. The Bakersfield Scientific Company had the best price, but only second best delivery and technical understanding.

Charlie knew that technical considerations, price, and delivery were all important. He wanted to recommend to top management either who the supplier should be or, at least, how to select the supplier. But Charlie saw no clear-cut solution to his predicament.

Perhaps the most critical activity for which the purchasing department has primary responsibility is selecting the right source—one that can provide the right quality of materials or services, on time, at a reasonable price and with the services required to create a satisfied customer. Although internal users have veto power, Purchasing must provide qualified candidates.

Nine problems are common in the source selection process:

1. Short lead time to investigate potential sources and negotiate
2. Requirements that dictate a particular supplier
3. Insufficient attention to the screening of prospective suppliers
4. The habit of buying from current but marginal suppliers
5. Failure to take full advantage of global sources of supply
6. The tendency to buy from those who call on the buyer
7. The underuse of competitive bidding as a source selection process in the private sector and its overuse in the public sector. In addition, only formal negotiation can be used for complicated buys requiring extensive information exchange between buyer and seller
8. Actual "back door" buying by users
9. The tendency to place orders without any investigation

Exhibit 8-1 provides an outline for the sourcing procedure. The details of each step are given in this chapter. If the procedure appears too involved, remember the old adage "an ounce of prevention is worth a pound of cure." Most serious procurement mistakes can be traced to vague requirements in the hands of marginal suppliers. Both authors have found numerous buying firms who merely look up suppliers in trade directories, call on the telephone to place an order, and follow up with a purchase order (P.O.). While some routine, standard MRO items can be purchased this way, the large dollar and critical buys can not. Even with simple requirements, telephone ordering tends to inflate the number of suppliers and neglects negotiation for blanket orders, systems contracts, and other options.

Prescreening Potential Suppliers: The First Step in Supplier Certification

It is imperative to eliminate potential suppliers who are not qualified to perform in accordance with the buyer's requirements. This may seem obvious, but even large firms often spend enormous amounts of time negotiating with sellers who should never have been in the bid-proposal pool. An obvious waste of time and resources for both sides, such ill-advised interaction burns lead time, may preclude discussions with the proper suppliers, and usually results in ill feelings and potential lawsuits. Poor buyer company planning often results in rushing into negotiations with the first available potential supplier versus capable suppliers as buyers work with insufficient lead time. This may be the fault of the requisitioners, but it is Purchasing's responsibility to inform users of lead time requirements and

Exhibit 8-1.   Sourcing outline for major purchases.

1. *Requirements.* Think performance but have all you know regarding specifications, quantity, quality, and delivery in clear terms with room for supplier input. Know the standard industrial classification (SIC) code for the material.

2. *Prescreening.*
   A. Partnership vs. transaction. Which mode do you need?
   B. Who makes it? Directories, past records, trade associations, trade shows, trade magazines, foreign consulates, data sources such as Information Handling Services in Englewood, Colorado, fellow buyers, NAPM, editors of trade magazines, etc.
   C. Which channel? Direct to original equipment manufacturer (OEM), distributor?
   D. Pre-experience supplier evaluation forms. Send survey to prospective supplier, get D&B, get literature, *call* references (given and not given). This is the request for information (RFI) phase.
   E. Form commodity evaluation team.
   F. Visit supplier plant operation.
   G. Complete pre-experience forms.
   H. Select final 2 or 3 potential suppliers for request for quote (RFQ), request for proposal (RFP).
   I. Determine ground rules for cover letter and cost breakdown data, if appropriate.

3. *Study Bids, Proposals.* Obtain missing information.

4. *Rate in a Matrix Form by Supplier According to Criteria.* Use 1, 2, 3, 4 or A, B, C, or +, −, 0.

5. *Final Negotiations* with leading one or two candidates.

6. *Preaward Final Meeting.* "One more time," are we talking the same language?

7. *Postaward Meeting.* Are we ready? Who does what? Do we have all permits, etc.?

8. *Managing the Contract.* Progress reports, clarification, handling problems and conflicts.

9. *Supplier Evaluation After Completion (in writing).*

10. *Post Mortem.* How can we improve?

qualifying criteria. Further, under proactive procurement, Purchasing should be informed and aware of unusual requirements, which will require longer lead time. With this knowledge, Purchasing can work in parallel to compress total process cycle time.

For significant buys including large quantities of raw material, custom components, subassemblies, construction, capital equipment, and special supply systems such as in JIT delivery, the prescreening activities must start well in advance of the release date. Some high-tech firms take as long as three years. Remember, we are talking about prescreening and negotiation lead time, not the delivery lead time after the supplier receives the purchase order. Even if you are just starting a formal sourcing program, the current suppliers must also be "screened" in the same manner as potential suppliers—for comparison purposes, to complete the sourcing records, and to ensure that you are getting the best available supplier.

The Pre-experience Supplier Evaluation Form shown in Exhibit 8-2 highlights the essential data that must be obtained prior to negotiations or formal requests for action of any kind. This form must be expanded in appropriate sections with individual questions for the supplier to complete and with requests for supporting documents such as annual reports, facility descriptions, equipment lists (including model, serial number, and age), samples, customer lists, backgrounds of key individuals, and financial statements. Some buying firms issue an RFI at this stage and include various questionnaires and/or checklists for the supplier to complete by a specified date.

At this point (or before, depending on the circumstances), a personal visit must be made to the supplier's location. Using the data collected as per the foregoing, the sourcing or commodity team is prepared to ask the proper questions. There is no substitute for personal interaction and visual inspection. In some cases involving machinery, construction, and other systems; visits to customer plants of the potential supplier will be necessary.

Aside from the direct inquiry to the potential supplier for information, the buying team will be compiling its own information, including Dun & Bradstreet reports, brochures, videotapes, trade publication articles, recommendations from internal users, reports from other customers of the potential supplier company and knowledgeable individuals in the industry of the selling company (association officials, technical editors of trade magazines), and even financial statements from auditors of privately held firms. While Dun & Bradstreet reports have been subjected to criticism over the last few years, they are a good benchmark and provide the basis for questions relative to financial stability.

After the completed questionnaires are received from the potential supplier, the visits to the supplier and its selected customers are completed, and the internal buyers' files contain all relevant data, the initial assessment begins with particular attention to the following areas.

Management and Ownership

The experience, education, philosophy, and depth of the top and operating management levels are critical, as the buyer and seller managers must have a "fit" or mutually agreeable style—call it "chemistry" if you will. There must be confi-

(text continues on page 112)

Exhibit 8-2. Pre-experience supplier evaluation form.

[*Note:* Elaborate when appropriate with attached commments and other supporting documents, and surveys.]

Date of evaluation _____

1. Supplier name   _____

    Supplier mail address _____ Telephone _____

    _____ Fax # _____

    Supplier contact (name and title) _____

    Source of supplier contact (catalog, sales call, etc.) _____

2. ☐ Distributor   ☐ Manufacturer

3. Location of branches, warehouses _____

    _____

4. Dun & Bradstreet Report: Secure historical summary and most recent credit report.
    Sales _____ Year _____ Total # of employees _____

5. Overall D&B financial rating _____ (Financial strength _____
    (Excellent, very good, good, fair, poor)

6. Ownership _____

7. Union?   ☐ Yes   ☐ No   If yes, contract expiration date(s) _____
    If yes, relationship? _____

8. Years in business _____

9. Principal products _____
    _____

10. Facilities list (plant and equipment list with age of machines, etc.). See attached and *rate housekeeping.* (Rate A, B, C, D) _____

11. Present capacity, rate, expansion ability _____

12. Patent activity? _____

13. Samples?   ☐ Yes   ☐ No   If yes, attach sample report.

14. Top management depth and skill. (Rate A, B, C, D) _____

15. Engineering management depth and skill. (Rate A, B, C, D) _____

16. Production management depth and skill. (Rate A, B, C, D) _____

17. Production control procedures. (Rate A, B, C, D and state the system used such as MRP, etc.) _____

18. Purchasing management depth and skill. (Rate A, B, C, D) _____

19. Bar coding ability? ☐ Yes ☐ No   _____

20. EDI availability? ☐ Yes ☐ No   _____

21. Quality control procedures, training, equipment and personnel. ISO 9000? SPC, PCI*, DOE**. Rate and elaborate.

   _____

   _____

22. Service organization: Number, location, experience _____

23. Warranty policy. (See attached)

24. Inventory policy: (Make & hold, warehouses, etc.)

25. Delivery-freight policy such as JIT abiliy _____

26. Contracting flexibility (Blanket orders, systems contracts, etc.) _____

   _____

27. Reports from other users. (See attached)

28. Plant tour reports. (See attached)

29. Past purchasing evaluation reports (if any).

30. Affirmative action–EEO compliance _____

31. Government regulation compliance _____

32. Other _____

33. Comments _____

   _____

   _____

   _____

   _____

   _____

   _____

   _____

   _____

   _____

*Product capability index.
**Design of experiments.

dence in one another regarding ability, honesty, and ethics. With remote owner-ship so popular today, this issue is very important. For example, if the supplier reports it is backed up by a parent company in Europe, the question is "to what extent?" If there is a crucial issue, say one of financial backing for the project, then the buyer must obtain a guarantee letter from the parent company as the relationship of the parent to the selling company may be "a tub on its own feet" or the association may be very remote. The issues of backup management and skill are also very important, especially for small, family-owned firms.

Financial Strength

For large projects of any kind, the financial resources of the seller must be ana-lyzed in detail. Inadequate capital can cause quality, delivery, and completion problems. Progress payments are normal for long lead time and large dollar proj-ects, but down payment requests are not. Any hint of a need for financing must be known. Although a buyer company may elect to help finance a seller, this decision must be made prior to negotiation and the risk must be carefully ana-lyzed. Aside from the credit record and rating of a particular seller, the two most important ratios are:

$$\text{The Current Ratio} = \frac{\text{Current Assets}}{\text{Current Liabilities}}$$

Two to one is the usual adequate current ratio for large manufacturing firms.

$$\text{Quick or Acid Test} = \frac{\text{Current Assets} - \text{Inventory}}{\text{Current Liabilities}}$$

One to one is the usual adequate acid test for most manufacturing firms. This is the real test of a liquidity or the ability to pay the bills.

Exhibit 8-3 gives the standard ratios for several key items. Buyers must com-pare the seller's ratios to those ratios in a particular industry. This comparison can be accomplished with the help of your credit and finance departments and by using ratio reports furnished by Dun & Bradstreet, Robert Morris & Associates, *The Almanac of Business and Industrial Financial Ratios* by Prentice Hall, Moody's, Standard & Poor's, and others.[1] The financial status of a prospective supplier, like the other critical information, must be verified by an auditor, CPA, bankers, or SEC-type report, in particular, the 10K SEC reports. The financial analysis must be reviewed at least once a year and preferably quarterly for key suppliers. In addition, the supplier should have a good cost accounting system to accurately track costs. Ideally, the potential supplier will have adopted activity-based cost-ing (ABC).

Production Capacity

Can the supplier really produce the material or complete the equipment on time? Can it expand if needed? Will overtime be required with potential cost overruns

Exhibit 8-3.   Standard financial ratios.

Ratio	Formula for Calculation
I. Liquidity	
1. Current	$\dfrac{\text{current assets}}{\text{current liabilities}}$
2. Quick or acid test	$\dfrac{(\text{current assets} - \text{inventory})}{\text{current liabilities}}$
II. Leverage	
3. Debt to total assets	$\dfrac{\text{total debt}}{\text{total assets}}$
4. Times interest earned	$\dfrac{\text{earnings before interest and taxes}}{\text{interest charges}}$
5. Fixed charge coverage	$\dfrac{\text{income available for meeting fixed charges}}{\text{fixed charges}}$
III. Efficiency	
6. Inventory turnover	$\dfrac{\text{sales}}{\text{inventory}}$
7. Average collection period	$\dfrac{\text{receivables}}{\text{sales per day}}$
8. Fixed assets turnover	$\dfrac{\text{sales}}{\text{fixed assets}}$
9. Total assets turnover	$\dfrac{\text{sales}}{\text{total assets}}$
IV. Profitability	
10. Profit margin on sales	$\dfrac{\text{net profit after taxes}}{\text{sales}}$
11. Return on total assets	$\dfrac{\text{net profit after taxes}}{\text{total assets}}$
12. Return on net worth	$\dfrac{\text{net profit after taxes}}{\text{net worth}}$

Source: Standard Accounting Ratios; for more details, see J. Fred Weston and Thomas Copeland, *Managerial Finance,* 9th edition (Fort Worth, Tex.: The Dryden Press, 1992). For guidelines as to actual desirable ratio numbers for particular industries, see Dun & Bradstreet, Robert Morris Associates in Philadelphia, and other such sources.

and quality problems? To answer these questions, we must know the capacity potential and current capacity position. Does the potential supplier have adequate equipment, tooling, space and line workers along with efficient procedures and plant layout? Aside from current facility/equipment lists, only a tour of the supplier plant by the proper commodity or sourcing team of experts will answer production ability questions.

Experience With the Product, Material, Service

Has the potential supplier ever made this particular product, including size, performance, complexity, and features, before? Can it do turnkey installations, a very important aspect of capital equipment procurement? It is extremely risky to have one supplier manufacture the equipment or system and another install it. Has the potential supplier offered this service (such as JIT) before?

Quality Control and Assurance

Although quality control and assurance is part of the production capability analysis, it is so important today that it must be addressed in a separate section.

A company may have the very latest plant and equipment and yet produce poor quality. We must know and verify the seller's process capability index (PCI), its statistical process control (SPC) philosophy, charting techniques, and employee quality training.[2] The supplier survey on quality issues must be very detailed and again, verified. Any firm can tell you it uses X and R bar charts, but the buyer or quality member of the sourcing team must see the evidence. A sound total quality control (TQC) program is the key to controlling costs for any organization and has a direct effect on cost and prices for both buyer and seller. Is the supplier ISO 9000 qualified? Detailed quality control techniques and procedures will be covered in Chapter 12.

Research and Development Ability

If the buying company needs heavy design input and value engineering analysis assistance, then it must check the track record of the supplier regarding patents, design suggestions, and value engineering activities. More and more, buying companies are engaging in Early Supplier Involvement to obtain more efficient interface with their suppliers to reduce engineering changes, lower costs, and increase product performance.[3] In addition, the supplier should have an organized value engineering program to control its own costs while improving the performance of its products. Remember, unit price is just one part of total cost, and poorly or isolated purchase part designs can dramatically increase a buyer's manufacturing and assembly costs.

On-Time Delivery

Delivery problems have always been a trouble area for buyers, even before the JIT concept and system. Assuming the buyer has not conducted business with the supplier in the recent past, the only way to verify its delivery reliability is to telephone and visit costumers of the supplier. The supplier will give you a list but try to find other customers in the event the supplier-furnished contacts are "the only satisfied customers." Ask the customers on the list for others to contact as a check. It is also prudent to try to obtain a representative sample and remember, all organizations experience some delivery problems, so look for the realistic batting average. If your requirements are extremely high for a JIT operation, then delivery, transportation, packaging, and materials handling capability must be thoroughly evaluated.[4]

Purchasing Expertise

Does the prospective supplier have an adequate source of required raw materials and purchased components? Is adequate and effective competition obtained? Are there special relations with certain companies and affiliates? Does the prospective supplier determine financial, quality assurance, and other capabilities of his or her prospective key suppliers and subcontractors? Does the potential supplier follow modern purchasing practices and employ qualified purchasing personnel? Is there good documentation of materials inventory and work-in-process (WIP)?

Price/Cost Controls and Documentation

With the trend to single sourcing, the qualification process should be even more demanding and in particular, the analysis of the supplier's cost structure must be more rigorous.[5] Using industry averages, buyers must review detailed and documented cost breakdowns furnished by the supplier. Such ratios as material to labor and sales and general and administrative costs should be compared to industry averages and target figures.[6] Confident suppliers will give these data to buyers provided nondisclosure statements are signed.

Total quality control, learning curve analysis, value analysis, equipment modernization and cost control programs are essential to improving productivity. The buyer or sourcing team must see the evidence of such efforts through plant tours, submission of questionnaires, and review of records. Extra effort in pre-screening suppliers will reduce the actual negotiation time, while minimizing the risks associated with selecting a new source.

All prospective suppliers should be graded against the selection criteria in a matrix form, that is, suppliers listed by rows and criteria in columns. A simple yes-or-no scale can be used or a more elaborate numerical score. Just remember to conduct all screening in a dignified, positive, and professional manner. Avoid the hint of an "investigation" and focus on the word "survey" or "qualification."

Direct or Indirect, Local or National Sources?

Direct vs. Indirect

One of the first considerations is a prospective supplier's place in the channel of distribution. Is the supplier the manufacturer (sometimes called the original equipment manufacturer [OEM]), a distributor, or a manufacturer's representative? The focus should be on the services required and the prospective supplier's ability to satisfy these requirements. A manufacturer normally provides the right combination of price and service for large quantities. Custom parts made to the purchaser's design specification (and perhaps performance specification) are usually purchased directly from the manufacturer, regardless of quantity. Small lots, requirements for immediate delivery, and credit considerations usually result in purchases from distributors. Normally, distributors carry a wide range of products from several manufacturers. Distributors buy in large quantities, warehouse the items, and resell in smaller quantities to purchasers in their area. If these services are performed both by the manufacturer and its distributors, then the purchaser must decide which prospective source provides the more attractive package of price and service.

Many firms object to dealing with manufacturers' agents on the grounds that the agents' commissions are excessive. Also, it frequently appears that many manufacturers' representatives are only errand boys between the buyer and supplier, thereby complicating the information flow. Although these objections frequently are valid, for many manufacturing firms, this method of marketing distribution is the most practical and economical available. Again, we must look at the service being provided. In the case of manufacturers' representatives, this service frequently is access to additional sources of supply. Furthermore, many agents are extremely competent.

Desired Number of Proposals

A second concern is the number of suppliers from whom proposals should be solicited. The ideal situation is to have sufficient qualified potential suppliers to ensure free and adequate competition. Usually three to five firms will satisfy this criterion. If a significant investment for bid preparation is required, it may be desirable to solicit quotations from only two qualified sources. Two interested and highly motivated firms are likely to provide better competition on such a procurement than are five firms that are only half interested. Obviously, this issue is judgmental and one reason that a competent buyer is a prized resource.

Local or Distant Suppliers

A third issue concerns whether to favor local suppliers over those not in the surrounding area. For small quantities, a local supplier frequently will be able to provide the best price and service. Communications generally are simpler. If the material is to come from the local supplier's inventory, delivery will be more certain, since there is less opportunity for delays during transportation. If a local supplier is highly reliable, it may be possible to transfer much of the buyer's inventory carrying function to the supplier. In addition, community relations are strengthened by purchasing locally. This consideration is especially critical for nonprofit organizations that depend on the local community for part of their operating funds.

Buying in regional or national markets tends to be more attractive than local buying in certain circumstances. Large national firms usually can better provide technical assistance. Economies of scale allow the national firm to sell at lower prices. National companies usually have more production capacity and are more able to cope with fluctuating demand. However, companies using JIT systems obviously favor local sources and even develop them under long-term contracts and occasionally, offer financial assistance. Part of Japan's success with JIT is the fact that most suppliers of Japanese plants are located in the immediate area, a condition caused by the highly geographically concentrated Japanese industry. There is a good rule, "the further away your supplier, the greater the need for a more thorough contract and partnership."

How Many Suppliers Do You Need?

Purchasing managers frequently are confronted with the question, how many suppliers should there be for a particular item? Several issues are involved. Generally, caution must be exercised when purchases by one customer exceed 20% or so of a supplier's sales, unless a strategic supply alliance exists. (If this is the case, 60 to 70% of the supplier's capacity should be the limit.) If purchases appreciably exceed 20 percent or so, the purchaser begins to assume a moral responsibility for the economic well-being of the supplier. The purchaser loses needed flexibility in such a situation and may find itself morally committed to a supplier who is no longer competitive or capable of performing the desired services. An explosion at Sumitomo Chemical plant in Nihama, Japan, on July 4, 1993, pushed spot prices of computer memory chips up 50% because this plant produced 65% of the world's supply of an expoxy resin used to seal computer chips into their plastic packages.[7] Thus, it may be desirable to employ two or more suppliers to retain freedom of action.

If a significant dollar amount is involved (say, $100,000), then allocating the amount between two suppliers frequently proves to be advantageous. Allocating 75% to one supplier and 25% to a second has many benefits. The supplier with the majority of the allotment can enjoy economies of scale that can be passed back to the purchaser in the form of lower prices. Further, this supplier has the incentive and the profit to perform additional services such as maintaining a local warehouse to provide nearly instantaneous delivery. Ideally, the supplier receiving the 25% allocation should be able to provide backup support if the other source encounters difficulty. Further, the supplier with 25% of the allotment will tend to "yap at the heels of the big guy and keep him in line on price, quality, delivery, and service."

It is important to distinguish between single source, which is one supplier by choice, and sole source, which means only one supplier is available, such as a monopolist.

If the purchaser is buying a critical item from a new source, dual sourcing should be the rule. Many major manufacturers have made this an ironclad rule as a result of previously unsatisfactory sole-source experiences with new suppliers.

The argument for single sourcing comes from the Japanese use of one supplier (although they frequently have two suppliers for an item) to gain maximum clout or power to ensure top quality, design input, low prices, and 100% on-time delivery plus other services. In fact many U.S. automobile manufacturers use just one source per part to facilitate quality tracking, commitment and total production control interface. The obvious trade-offs include vulnerability to interrupted supply for a wide variety of reasons, possible complacency due to lack of competition, and restricted future options if the total supply base produces just a few remaining giants. In some instances, abnormal R&D investment, high tooling cost, and unique customization actually require just one source in order to attract the desired supplier. In any case, the use of single sources requires a much more thorough management of the supplier with constant and organized reporting systems, contingency backup plans, and excellent communication. In addition, the buyer should continually search for and screen potential substitute suppliers—have a plan ready "just in case." Newman's fine article contains more detail on the advantages and disadvantages of single sourcing.[8]

Global Sources

Approximately half of all manufacturers purchase some of their materials overseas. Contrary to popular belief, quality, technology, and delivery considerations are often the primary reasons for purchasing from nondomestic sources; however, price normally is the major consideration.[9] Nondomestic manufacturers can be and are excellent sources of supply, but the realistic buyer must be aware of the many additional problems involved when dealing with overseas sources.

The Great Global Trading Areas

The current best global sources for many technical components and raw materials are in Asia with Japan; the four tigers of Hong Kong, Singapore, South Korea, and Taiwan; and, with emerging China, Malaysia, Thailand, Indonesia, and Vietnam. Next comes the European Union, the largest trading partner for the United States, and by far the most organized and complicated.[10] The North American Free Trade Agreement (NAFTA) is providing great potential trade sources as are the former Soviet Union and Eastern European countries.[11]

China is predicted to become the Asian leader through Chinese connections within Singapore, Hong Kong, Taiwan, and the rest of the Chinese in the Far East. The sun has set (or is setting) on the current giant Japan, which will remain very powerful but not the Asian leader as the Chinese affiliation grows, especially after 1997 when Hong Kong returns to China.[12]

Culture

Cultural differences pose the largest obstacles to developing mutually profitable business relations with overseas sources. The nature, customs, and ethics of individuals and business organizations from two different cultures can raise a surprising number of obstacles to successful business relations. What is considered ethical in one culture may not be ethical in another. The intention of filling commitments, the implications of gift giving, and even the legal systems differ widely.

Communications

Language differences and nuances pose significant barriers to successful international business relations. Both parties may think that they know what they have said and what the other party has said, but true agreement and understanding may be missing. Think, for instance, of the confusion the simple word "ton" can create. Is it a short ton (2,000 lb), a long ton (2,240 lb), or a metric ton (2,204.62 lb)? Most American businessmen doing business in Japan have discovered that when the Japanese say *hai* ("yes"), it doesn't always mean they agree. Frequently, it means that they understand.

Financial Constraints

Currency exchange rates cause great problems. Some leading firms that buy internationally do business only in their own currency. Others normally conduct their business in the currency of the supplier's country. And other firms adopt a flexible policy. This variability of approaches demonstrates that no one best way has been discovered. Carter and Vickery define several methods for coping with the exchange rate issue.[13]

Many international transactions now contain offset provisions. In effect, we have advanced international commerce to a revolutionary concept known to seventeenth- and eighteenth-century traders as *barter*. Offset provisions complicate such transactions, yet they can be mutually advantageous.[14]

It is the custom in many countries for payments to be made prior to commencing work. Such payments may be necessary to agree on otherwise highly attractive conditions. But this provision ties up the purchaser's capital. Letters of credit also are common in international commerce. Again, the purchaser's funds may be committed for a longer period of time than if a domestic source were involved.

Documentation

Many unique documents are required for international commerce: export-import licenses, customs documentation, international bills of lading, and certificates of origin. The proper product and use description should be included on all customs documents to eliminate custom duty overcharges.

Ancillary Services

Transportation and insurance procedures and provisions are significantly different from and, generally, more complex than those for domestic material purchases.

Quality

Overseas suppliers frequently are used because they can and do provide the desired level of quality or in the case of some equipment and components, they are the only source. *But* problems do exist. The United States is the only major nonmetric country in a metric world. This frequently leads to manufacturing tolerance problems. Also, nondomestic suppliers tend to be less responsive to necessary design changes than their domestic counterparts.

Total Landed Costs

Sourcing from overseas suppliers introduces many issues: higher transportation and insurance costs, broker and other fees, additional travel and administrative costs, capital tied up under advanced payments or letters of credit, additional buffer stocks, and political and economic uncertainties. When considering travel costs, for example, the purchaser must take into account the additional cost for overseas travel for the preaward survey team (if required) and for likely expediting or subcontract management trips. If buying is based on price, many experts say the difference must be at least 50% to achieve significant price advantage because the *extra* transaction costs are much higher than usually expected.

Larger buffer stocks generally are required to accommodate larger variances in delivery time. Such variances arise from variable shipping schedules, documentation and customs problems, and strikes in the suppliers' plants and by stevedores and maritime workers.

In addition, the purchaser must investigate the likely stability of the government and the prospect of nationwide strikes and civil disorder. Obviously, a high degree of certainty of supply is a key consideration for all critical purchased material.

When overseas suppliers are under consideration, the source selection process is little different than when only domestic sources are involved. Initially, a purchaser may find it both simpler and more cost effective to deal with sales agents, brokers, import merchants, or trading companies. Many buyers have found that the problems associated with overseas sources are best avoided by using domestic or overseas trading companies. In most cases, the trading companies offer shorter lead times, easier communications, and more enforceable quality guarantees.

If the dollar value, frequency of purchases, and probability of continuing relations justify the administrative effort, the purchaser should deal directly with potential foreign suppliers.[15] Again, a necessary prerequisite to such transactions is an understanding of the other party's culture and business customs. Also, additional time must be available to develop the business relationship. (These and other nuances of doing business overseas are discussed at greater length in Chapter 14, titled The Winning Ways of Negotiation). Once a purchaser becomes a significant customer of an overseas supplier, he or she usually is treated as an honorable and valuable member of the supplier's family.[16]

Request to Bid, Quote, Propose, or Give Information

When the buyer sends out invitations to submit offers, great care must be taken in the instructions to the prospective supplier. The terms we use such as Request for Bid (RFB), Request for Quotation (RFQ), or Request for Proposal (RFP), have no inherent legal meaning. No one really knows what the difference is between the words "bid," "quote," or "propose," if indeed there is a difference. However, they all can be used to ask for an offer. For this reason some buyers prefer to use Request for Information (RFI) when asking only for product data or general qualifying information regarding the supplier company as RFI inquiries avoid a request for an offer.

What Is an Offer?

The words *quote* and *quotation* are dangerous, as pure price quotes are not offers. As one leading business law textbook advises, statements that are not in themselves proposals of conduct (promises) but are preliminary thereto are called negotiatory statements.[17] If there is no offer, there can be no acceptance. The prerequisites for an offer include: the language of commitment, serious intent, definite and complete terms, plus communication to the offeree (the buyer in this example).[18] If the buyer wants to receive an offer, the RFP term seems to be a stronger request, but the reply may be nothing more than statements of fact (our product costs $5.00 each) and/or preliminary statements to start the negotiations, which may lead to an offer. In addition, the buyer must remember that a purchase order response to an *unsolicited* price quote will probably constitute an original offer, which may be ignored or accepted by the supplier. The good news is that "invitations" are not offers to buy unless such an offer is specifically stated.

Lower Bid Implications

There is some legal implication, and trade practice assumes that the buyer is willing to do business with the firms receiving invitations to bid, quote, or propose. This is why it is critical to prescreen and prevent later charges of unfair treatment, fraud, or unfair trade practices. There have been recent court cases in which the losing bidder charged the buyer with concealment, discrimination, and unfair trade practices. The buyer will usually win such cases, but the costs are enormous.

   Under the trade custom rules of competitive bidding, the implication is that the lowest bidder will receive the order. This is required in many government buys.[19] While such bid requests usually state "assuming compliance to required specifications," there is an assumption that the buyer has checked the supplier's ability to perform and meet all other requirements and thus the low bidder will receive the order. Every government buyer knows that a low bid is not always the best price and the entire concept of competitive bidding ignores the total cost or life cycle cost concept.

When to Use Competitive Bidding for Source Selection

Should competitive bidding procedures or negotiation be used to select the source and to arrive at the price to be paid? Notice that competitive bidding does both in one step! Under competitive bidding (also referred to as "advertised procurement" in the public sector), the firm prepares a request for bids with the intention of awarding a purchase order or subcontract to the supplier offering the most attractive price *without* further discussions. To employ this procedure successfully, the firm preparing the request for bids must ensure that certain prerequisites or situations have been met:

- The specifications must be clear and adequate so that prospective suppliers can estimate their costs with a high degree of precision. If this accuracy is not present, suppliers will still submit bids, but they will include contingencies to protect themselves from any uncertainties.
- The amount of money involved is sufficient to warrant use of competitive bidding. For low-dollar-value requirements, less formal procedures are faster and require less administrative time and effort.
- Adequate competition must be present. Not only must a sufficient number of potential suppliers be available, but a reasonable proportion of these potential suppliers must be willing to price competitively.
- Sufficient time is available to use source selection. The amount of time and effort involved with this technique is considerable. A formal request for bids, mailing, opening the resulting bids, and evaluating the bids requires more time than might be expected. Additionally, adequate bid preparation time must be afforded to the prospective suppliers.
- Face-to-face communication is not necessary, such as the case of buying generic raw materials, for example, Kellogg buying salt, etc.
- Postsale service (other than delivery) is not a factor.

In addition to satisfying these six prerequisites, competitive bidding as the means of source selection should *not* be used if:

- Price is not the only variable. For example, quality, technical specifications, schedule, design input, and service may be the critical variables subject to negotiation.
- The purchaser anticipates changes in the specification or some other aspect of the purchase order or contract. When unscrupulous suppliers anticipate changes, they may buy in with the expectation of getting wealthy on the resulting changes.
- Special tooling and/or setup costs are major factors. The allocation of such costs and title to the special tooling are issues best resolved through negotiation.
- The requirement is unique and supplier input is desirable.

If these prerequisites and conditions are satisfied, then competitive bidding *usually* will result in the lowest price and is the recommended method of source selection *provided all the suppliers who have received the bid package are qualified and have been prescreened*. To ensure that the lowest prices are obtained, the competing potential suppliers must be assured that the firm submitting the low bid will receive the award. If the purchaser gains a reputation for conducting negotiations subsequent to or after the opening of bids, then future bidders will tend *not* to offer their best prices initially, believing that they may do better in any subsequent negotiations. They will adopt a strategy of submitting a bid low enough to allow them to be included in any negotiations, but their initial bid will not be as low as when they are confident that award would be made to the low bidder without further negotiation.

When these prerequisites and conditions to the use of competitive bidding are not satisfied, negotiated procedures should be employed to select sources and to arrive at a price. The term *negotiated procedures* is applied to both low-dollar procurements (frequently using telephone solicitation of proposals) and to larger requirements that involve extensive preparation and skill in face-to-face negotiations with prospective suppliers. Another procedure is to inform all those requested to bid or quote that the two-step bidding procedure will be used. This means the best one or two bidders will be invited to negotiate the final contract.

One of the obvious disadvantages of straight competitive bidding is its focus on price vs. total life cycle costs. To overcome this inherent flaw, bidders *must* be asked to submit total cost of ownership data in addition to price. Finally, if you need a *partnership* or strategic supply alliance, only negotiation will achieve this objective.

Selecting the Source

In most instances, one prospective supplier will be so obviously superior to the competitors that selection will be a very simple matter. Unfortunately, the choice is not always so clear. A mathematical rating system can greatly facilitate source selection in such cases. We will look at two examples to see how such a selection process can work.

The mathematical rating system (easily accomplished on a spreadsheet program) calls for two activities: the identification of the key factors in the source selection decision and the assignment of weights to each factor.

These factors and weights usually are assigned by a committee of interested members of management called a *sourcing* or *commodity team*. Let us consider the situation described at the beginning of the chapter. CG&E has the necessary information on which to base a source selection decision. Yet, no one supplier is obviously superior.

The ideal way in which to cope with such a situation is *before* it arises! A sourcing or commodity team consisting, perhaps, of members of Engineering, Quality, Operations, the controller's department, and the buyer should have gathered together and identified the key factors in the purchase. Then the group should have assigned weights to the factors. We see the results of such an effort under the headings "Factors" and "Maximum Rating" in Exhibit 8-4. The data shown for suppliers A, B, and C are based on field investigations of each supplier's technical understanding, capability in each of several areas, and the outcomes of negotiations. Assuming that Purchasing has a firm fixed price offer and estimated life cycle costs from each of the three suppliers, the rating for this aspect of the factor "price" is objective. It is based on the relationship between each supplier's proposed price for development of the heat exchanger and CG&E's target price. But when a contract calls for some degree of cost reimbursement

Exhibit 8-4. Source selection rating matrix (development and production).

Factors	Maximum Rating	Supplier A	B	C
Technical				
Understanding the problem	10	10	8	7
Technical approach	20	18	16	15
Production facilities	5	4	5	4
Operator requirements	3	2	3	2
Maintenance requirements	2	1	2	2
Totals	40	35	34	30
Ability to meet schedule	20	18	15	12
Price and life cycle cost	20	16	20	2
Managerial financial & technical capability	10	10	8	8
Quality control standards	10	9	8	7
		88	85	59

(fixed-price incentive or a cost-plus type of contract as described in Appendix D), the price rating is subjective. The buyer and other members of the sourcing team rate how well they believe the prospective supplier will do in the area of cost control. Thus, that part of the "price" rating for the production portion of the prospective contract with CG&E is subjective. All the other ratings (understanding of the problem, etc.) are subjective and are arrived at in a similar manner. In effect, the mathematical rating system takes a complex problem and breaks it down into several components leading to a fair result.

A somewhat more mundane, but important, area of source selection concerns selection of a supplier who will furnish Reilly Manufacturing with MRO supplies under an annual requirements contract. Estimated annual expenditures are $5 million. The Reilly purchasing department has solicited quotations and has conducted inspection of the facilities of the four distributors under consideration (a simplified pre-award survey). The findings, together with ratings, are shown in Exhibit 8-5.

In this example, it appears that supplier X is the most attractive source.

Source Development

What happens when the sourcing or commodity team comes up empty handed, that is, no qualified source emerges or submits a proposal? The team now has to approach a potential supplier who could produce the equipment, material, or service. This involves visiting or calling in suppliers who have the equipment, facilities, labor, and experience in producing something similar to what the buy-

Exhibit 8-5. Source selection rating matrix (MRO distributor).

Considered Factor	Maximum Rating	Supplier W	Supplier X	Supplier Y	Supplier Z
Price and life cycle cost	25	20	20	22	18
Product lines available	20	17	18	15	15
Meantime for delivery	20	15	18	17	17
Technical service capacity	15	13	15	10	10
Management rating	5	4	5	5	3
Inventory positions	5	4	5	5	3
Credit terms	5	5	3	3	3
Housekeeping	5	3	5	4	3
	100	81	89	81	72

ing team wants. This form of sourcing is the most challenging and expensive (initially). The buyer may have to provide technical, managerial, purchasing, and financial help.

The Triax Company of Cleveland, Ohio (now called the Webb-Triax Company of Chardon, Ohio), the pioneer and leader in automated storage and retrieval systems (AS/RS) was nourished to adulthood by such giants as Dupont, Western Electric, GE, GM, and Ford. In the late 1950s, this tiny firm had the basic patents for AS/RS application but needed the engineering assistance and patience of the giants to grow and eventually become part of the great material handling engineering firm, the Jervis B. Webb Company of Farmington Hills, Michigan. The Webb-Triax AR/AS system for painting operations at the Saturn plant in Spring Hill, Tennessee, is a splendid application of this type of system.[20]

Supplier Certification

The term *certification* means *vouched for* or *guaranteed* for something. In the context of *sourcing*, it means the buying company actually issues, through a formal program, some kind of status to prospective and current suppliers after trials, tests, surveys, and documentation as to the supplier's design, process, and quality systems. Normally, such certification eliminates the necessity of incoming inspection. The terms *preferred, acceptable, marginal, unacceptable* or *qualified* are common and are given to suppliers after prescreening, trial such as post first article inspection, or annual surveys. The old term *qualified bidders list* or *QBL* essentially means the same thing, but is less involved: that is, the supplier has made the approved list, and this list is distributed to appropriate individuals in the buying firm. Certification also means that the buying firm has formally notified the supplier of his or her exact status with suggestions for improvement as needed. The surveys and personal visits we mentioned in the prescreening and pre-award survey sections of this chapter are the typical tools of certification.[21] Thus, *certification* is a rather recent term for what have always been the requirement for good sourcing versus order-placing without a thorough investigation. In Chapter 12, Quality Assurance Overview, the supplier certification process will be reviewed. Appendix J contains a supplier quality survey instrument.

Supplier Contract Management

Once a contract has been awarded, the real work begins as people execute the agreement, not pieces of paper. A reporting system must be developed, personal contact points established, progress monitored, and inevitable problems solved. Excessive change orders on the part of the buyer will dramatically increase costs, delay shipments, contribute to rework, decrease quality, and harm the partnership basis of supply management. Planning for adequate lead time is key: Without *some* degree of schedule stabilization, haste will make waste.

During source selection, always make a sincere effort to help the prospective supplier through the process. The supplier welcome booklet, *A Navigational Guide to Sea Ray Purchasing,* in Appendix B, is the finest we have seen.

Finally, it is critical to evaluate performance in writing with a form such as the example in Exhibit 8-6. Keep this form simple as buyers do not have the time (nor is there any need) to complete elaborate and involved forms. These ratings should be completed for every contract period, usually once a year and obviously prior to the next negotiation session.

Suggestions to Help Reduce Mistakes

If you are slightly overwhelmed at this point, it means you understand the complexity of the issue. But there is hope. The following guidelines should help a great deal.

1. One more time, request offers only from suppliers you have prescreened and with whom you are prepared to do business.

2. For routine, shelf items or generic material, use the competitive bidding method and the term RFB or better yet, request for offer (RFO).

3. For custom material, capital equipment, facilities, long-term contracts, and other large dollar buys, use negotiation to reach a final agreement acceptable to both sides.[22] Use the term *RFP*, but state that the best proposals (two or three) will be selected for final negotiation. Complicated purchasing cannot be completed by mail or telephone communication as there are too many options to discuss and evaluate.

Exhibit 8-6. Supplier rating form.

Supplier Name _____   Material _____
_____   Supplier Code # _____
                                                     Supplier Part # _____
                                                     Buyer Part # _____
P.O Numbers and Dates _____ _____ _____ _____ _____ _____
Period Covered _____   Prepared by _____   Date _____

  I. Quality
      A. No. of orders rejected _____ Percent of Total _____
      B. No. of units rejected _____ Percent of Total _____
      C. % Rejection × weight, say 40% = _____ points
      Dollar cost of rejection: Paperwork _____ Telephone _____
      Travel _____ Repair _____ Scrap _____ Reorder Costs _____
      Comments _____
      _____

 II. Price
      A. Price in relation to lowest price received during period as a %.
      B. Price changes from start to finish as a %.
        Price % × weight, say 25%
      Comments _____
      _____

III. Life Cycle Cost to Date
      Amount. Describe _____

IV. Delivery
      % of late shipments _____ % of early shipments _____
      % × weight, say 25%
      Comments _____
      _____

 V. Service
      A Postsale technical service response time to requests _____
        Your cost to obtain service $ _____
      B. No. of service calls _____
        Rate A, B, C, D, E on "some" standard.
      Comments _____
      _____

VI. Total Weights and Final Score _____

VII. Extend Contract?
      ☐ Yes   ☐ No   ☐ Yes, but
      Comments _____
      _____

VIII. Comments _____
_____

4. For all invitations, have complete instructions and rules regarding required data, samples, documents, terms, selection criteria, and conditions. In writing, reserve the right to reject any or all bids or proposals at any time. Be consistent with selection criteria. For example, if you state the bidders/proposers will be subjected to various economic tests such as discounted cash flow techniques and a certain number of years will be used to calculate financial returns, apply the same criteria to all bidders/proposers. Document and retain all evaluation data because the losers may challenge the award.

5. A representative from Purchasing must be present during all negotiation and/or prescreening meetings with suppliers. This will help prevent premature commitment to terms, specifications, conditions, or even selection of the supplier. The actual selection of a supplier must be a team effort with representatives from Purchasing, Design Engineering, Quality, Manufacturing, Product Planning, Finance and related functions.[23] Using the screening criteria developed in the first section of this chapter, the sourcing or commodity team negotiates to final selection through a process of elimination.

6. When in doubt, use trial order when appropriate.

The previous guidelines will help prevent misunderstandings and even lawsuits. Although this chapter is not about specification determination, custom purchases and sophisticated buys require early supplier involvement, which can only happen if we negotiate (prior to contracting) with responsible suppliers with both sides communicating all the necessary information. We now address the question of what happens after the contract is awarded.

Notification to the Losers and the Postaward Meeting for the Winner

What we say or write to the losers is critical both to avoid poor public relations and/or possible lawsuits and to protect our base of potential suppliers. Form letters can and should be used for the routine competitive bidding method. While we do not reveal the final contract price, it is normal to state who won the contract and the general indications as to why the sale was lost such as high price, poor warranty, excessive life cycle costs, unacceptable delivery, inexperience, or poor quality and service.

Remember, the implication/intention of competitive bidding is that "other things being equal," the low bidder gets the order. We should have screened out suppliers who fail the "other things being equal" criteria prior to issuing the invitation to bid. Thus, the form letter may simply be a thank-you with a statement that the addressee was not the low bidder. A word of caution: Never reopen bids unless you reopen to all the last bidders. We write the losers as a form of industrial courtesy, to maintain good supplier relations, and to provide useful feedback that may help the supplier improve.

A formal meeting is recommended for losers of negotiations for significant contracts. They undoubtedly have invested considerable time, energy, and resources in their attempt to secure the order. Presumably they are an excellent potential supplier and should be kept in the pool for future solicitation. The sourcing team should go into some detail regarding the buying decision while honoring all nondisclosure types of agreement and trade custom. Some firms believe it is good business practice to pay for proposals that go beyond normal marketing efforts as this avoids the charge of "free engineering." Whether to pay some fee depends on the extent of the requested information and if supplier surveys provide valuable information even without the purchase.

The postaward meeting with the winner is essential for an effective start or contract execution. It often is combined with a formal contract signing. All individuals who will be working together meet and review the contract for clarification, timetable details, and reporting procedures. It is usually concluded at a formal dinner with top executives from both sides in attendance. The postaward meeting offers an excellent opportunity to answer questions, begin the formation of close working relationships, and to launch the project on a high, positive note. Contract signing is like school commencement: It is the beginning, not the end.

Summary

Selecting the right source of supply probably is the most critical activity for which Purchasing has primary responsibility. The right supplier is one who can provide the right quality of materials or services, on time, at a reasonable price, and with the services required to maintain customer satisfaction.

The purchasing firm should know enough about its prospective suppliers to provide a satisfactory level of confidence as to their ability to perform. On small, routine purchases, awareness of the supplier's place in the channel of distribution, the services he or she performs, and his or her other financial capability will provide adequate insight.

The degree of competition to solicit is a judgmental matter. Usually three to five interested, qualified firms will provide adequate competition. If the requirement necessitates significant investment for bid preparation, two highly interested, highly motivated firms are apt to be more aggressive and provide better prices with the lowest life cycle costs than are five firms who are only half interested.

There are several occasions when purchasing in the local market may be attractive: Communications are simpler; delivery times are shorter and more certain. A local supplier may perform many of the purchasing firm's inventory requirements. On the other hand, regional or national buying tends to result in lower prices and better technical assistance. National firms usually have greater production capacity and are more able to cope with fluctuating demand.

The question of how many suppliers to have per type of material is a tough one and the answer is situation specific. We generally feel one prime and one backup is sufficient. Single sourcing is becoming more popular but requires a formal supplier management system.

Purchasing from global sources has become a way of life for the majority of manufacturing firms. While international purchasing poses certain problems not present with domestic purchasing, an overseas supplier can be a valuable and dependable source of supply, provided the buyer engages in extensive study of the particular country and accounts for the additional administrative-transaction costs.

A pre-award survey is an in-depth analysis of a prospective supplier. Such an investigation should be conducted before solicitation of proposals for an item that is critical to the well-being of the purchasing firm. The pre-award survey normally looks at the prospective supplier's facilities; production and quality systems; engineering; purchasing, financial, and managerial capabilities; industrial relations; and past performance. The pre-award investigation is a major feature of certification programs.

Competitive bidding is the recommended method of source selection and pricing when several conditions are satisfied. If any of these conditions is not met, negotiation procedures or the two-step approach, which selects the best proposals for final negotiation, should be employed.

Usually one prospective supplier is obviously superior to his or her competitors. But when several factors play a role in source selection (e.g., price, technical considerations, service, and/or schedule), a mathematical rating system should be utilized to aid in source selection. Finally, the contract must be managed.

In some instances, we must actually develop the source. This may require substantial financial, technical, and managerial assistance on the part of the buying firm.

Determining a fair and reasonable price to pay for goods or services requires the analysis of many factors and variables. Obtaining such a price affects the firm's financial health and even survival. Price analysis is the subject of the next chapter.

Notes

1. See "Duns Industry Norms and Key Business Ratios" from Dun & Bradstreet Analytical Services, Murray Hill, N.J.; Robert Morris Associates, Philadelphia, Pa. and database services such as Dialog in Palo Alto, Calif.
2. Richard G. Newman, "Insuring Quality: Purchasing Role," *Journal of Purchasing and Materials Management* (Fall 1988), pp. 14–21.
3. Somerby Dowst, "Early Supplier Development gives Design Team the Winning Edge," *Purchasing* (March 12, 1987), pp. 52–60.
4. Richard J. Schonberger and Abdolhossein Ansari, "Just-in-Time Purchasing Can Improve Quality," *Journal of Purchasing and Materials Management* (Spring 1984), pp. 2–7. Also see Albert F. Celley, William H. Clegg, Arthur W. Smith, and Mark A. Vonderembse, "Implementation of JIT in the United States," *Journal of Purchasing and Materials Management* (January 1987), pp. 9–15; G. H. Manoochehri, "Suppliers and the Just-in-Time Concept," *Journal of Purchasing and Materials Management* (Winter 1984), pp. 16–21.
5. Richard G. Newman, "Single Source Qualification," *Journal of Purchasing and Materials Management* (Summer 1988), pp. 10–17.
6. Ibid., p. 12.
7. David D. Hamilton, "*Chokepointe*, Computer Makers Run at Risk of Disruption From Supply Cut Off," *The Wall Street Journal* (August 27, 1993), p. 1.
8. Richard G. Newman, "Single Sourcing: Short-Term Savings Versus Long-Term Problems," *International Journal of Purchasing and Materials Management* (Summer, 1989).

9. "The Why, How, and What of Overseas Purchasing," *Purchasing* (June 25, 1987), p. 54. Price as the major reason for offshore sourcing was noted by 74% of the managers. Quality was second at 46%.

10. Richard L. Pinkerton, "The European Community—'EC 92': Implications for Purchasing Managers," *The International Journal of Purchasing and Materials* (Spring 1993), pp. 19–26.

11. *NAFTA: The North American Free Trade Agreement: A Guide to Customs Procedures* (January 1994). U.S. Customs Service Publication No. 571, Washington, D.C.: Dept. of the Treasury.

12. See *The World Factbook*, 1993, by the Central Intelligence Agency; *International Business Practices*, January 1993, by the U.S. Dept. of Commerce with Federal Express Corp.; *Destination Japan: A Business Guide for the 90's*, December 1991, by the U.S. Dept. of Commerce and the International Trade Administration; and *The China Business Guide*, January 1994, by the U.S. Dept. of Commerce and the International Trade Association. All sources in this note are available from the U.S. Government Printing Office, Washington, D.C. 20402–9328.

13. Joseph R. Carter and Shawnee K. Vickery, "Managing Volatile Exchange Rates in *International Purchasing*," *Journal of Purchasing and Materials Management* (Winter 1988), pp. 13–20.

14. See Kenton W. Elderkin and Warren E. Norquist, *Creative Countertrade: A Guide to Doing Business Worldwide* (Cambridge, Mass.: Ballinger Publishing, 1987).

15. The National Association of Purchasing Management (NAPM) in Tempe, Ariz., maintains a list of correspondents in 20 foreign nations who have agreed to provide data on suppliers in their countries. The NAPM, in turn, has compiled a guide on purchasing in the United States for members of the International Federation of Purchasing and Materials Management.

16. For more detail, see Thomas K. Hickman and William M. Hickman, Jr., *Global Purchasing: How to Buy Goods and Services in Foreign Markets* (Homewood, Ill.: Business One Irwin, 1992), and Victor H. Pooler, *Global Purchasing: Reaching for the World* (New York: Van Nostrand Reinhold, 1992).

17. J. David Reitzel, Gordon B. Severance, Michael J. Garrison, and Ralph D. Davis, *Contemporary Business Law and the Legal Environment: Principles and Cases*, 5th ed. (New York: McGraw-Hill, 1994), pp. 220–232.

18. Ibid.

19. Michiel R. Leenders, and Harold E. Fearon, *Purchasing and Materials Management*, 10th ed. (Homewood, Ill.: Irwin, 1993), pp. 308–310. A great many terms are used, or misused, in this area. Commonly employed terms include request for quotation, request for bids, invitation to bid, invitation for bids, request for proposal, and inquiries. We attempt to use the most accurate and most descriptive terms. Accordingly, request for bids will be reserved for situations in which competitive bidding is employed to select the source. The term *requests for quotation* will be reserved for situations in which formal competitive bidding procedures are not employed. But the instruction cover letter dictates the rules regardless of the terms used.

20. See Charles A. Watts and Chan K. Hahn, "Supplier Development Programs: An Empirical Analysis," *The International Journal of Purchasing and Materials Management* (Spring 1993), pp. 11–17.

21. See *Supplier Certification* by Peter L. Grieco and Jerry Claunch, Plantsville, CT, PT Publications, 1988.

22. Donald W. Dobler, David N. Burt, and Lamar Lee, Jr., *Purchasing and Materials Management: Text and Cases*, 5th ed. (New York: McGraw-Hill, 1990), pp. 205–208.

23. David N. Burt, "Managing Suppliers Up to Speed," *Harvard Business Review* (July-August 1989), p. 129.

9
Price Analysis

Morley Amsterdam, senior buyer at QRS Products, is wrapping up another purchase order. The order is for an estimated 100,000 molded plastic bases. This is a very tricky seven-cavity mold. The delivered cost is $4.07 per unit. For the third year in a row, Precision Plastics is the low bidder. After preparing an abstract of bids, Morley turns his attention to an informal analysis of the price for which he was about to contract.

Three years ago, QRS had estimated its requirements for the plastic base at 40,000 units. The purchase request cited an estimated unit price of $5.00. Having good specifications and adequate time and knowing that the molded plastics business was highly competitive, Morley had chosen to use competitive bidding to aid in source selection and pricing. He had requested bids from six suppliers, four of whom submitted bids. The prices received three years ago (including an allowance for transportation costs) were as follows:

Memphis Molding	$3.75
Precision Plastics	3.65
Injection Processes	3.90
Meadville Plastics	4.00

An estimated requirements order was issued to Precision Plastics. The supplier performed very satisfactorily. The following year QRS's estimated requirements for the base unit increased to 75,000. Again, Morley solicited competitive bids. Again, Precision Plastics was low bidder, with a price of $3.90. Morley knew that the price of plastics was up over 10% on similar items, so he was very pleased with only a 7% increase in Precision's price.

This year, estimated requirements increased to 100,000 units. Once again, Precision submitted the low bid after considering transportation costs:

Memphis Molding	$4.15
Precision Plastics	4.07
Injection Processes	4.22
Meadville Plastics	4.27

Having completed his price analysis, Morley begins drafting the estimated require-ments contract. He is on the verge of turning the order in for typing when Josh Keough, the sales representative from Injection Processes, stops by to see how his firm has done. On learning that he'd lost once again, Josh says, "Morley, no one is ever going to beat Precision's price. The way you're doing business on a one-year basis, we have no choice but to amortize our special tooling and setup costs over your annual requirements. We figure these costs at $50,000. Not only can we not compete with Precision, but I'd bet you're paying too much to those rascals."

After Josh departs, Morley thinks, "Were those sour grapes, or does Josh have something?"

Basic Supplier Pricing Strategies

Before we discuss the details of pricing, we must first look at the various pricing strategies used by our suppliers—how do they price their proposals, products, materials, and services? In addition, we must always remember that price is just one part, the starting point, for the total cost of purchasing and processing (or incorporating) the item into the end product. We also must consider storage, handling, conversion, process yield loss, scrap, rework, and the costs associated with defective purchased material resulting in field failures.

Our suppliers, like our buyers, analyze supply and demand and then, using total actual costs as a floor, estimate "what the market will bear" or what the buyer is willing and able to pay. So far, so good. If this sounds like the start of a basic economics class lecture, it is. For example, as business improved in March–April of 1994, steel firms experienced higher utilization of capacity and started raising prices even though the cost per pound went down as the fixed costs were amortized over more pounds; the increase in price had nothing to do with costs. It had everything to do with increased demand and a more restricted supply. The marketing managers at the steel companies are probably using a price strategy called *maximum current profit* or *maximum current revenue*.

Other pricing strategies include

- *Survival* during periods of overcapacity, intense competition, or changing customer needs
- *Market penetration pricing* to maximize sales growth and market share by setting the lowest possible price
- *Market-skimming,* which sets a very high price, the highest possible price to skim the top of each market segment before competition copies an inno-vation or some other competitive advantage
- *Product-quality leadership pricing* based on superior product performance and service.

Thus, pricing strategy is a function of demand, costs, competitor pricing, and product-service attribute differentiation.[1]

With a strategy as a guide, the marketing manager now selects a pricing *method* such as *markup or cost plus, target return pricing* for a particular desired ROI, or *perceived-value pricing*. Perceived-value pricing is the method used by Caterpillar to justify a higher price over competition by assigning dollar value numbers for superior service, durability, reliability, and other attributes. *Going-rate pricing* is common in industries dominated by a few companies that sell generic products such as steel and paper, with the few smaller firms simply following the price leader. *Sealed-bid pricing* involves forecasting competitor bids using the probability of getting the bid, which gives expected profit at different probabilities (the probability percentage × the profit at that bid price equals the expected profit). Of course, discounts, transportation, installation, training, rebates, financing, service contracts, and other such "add on" or "takeoff" factors all affect the actual price.

Most industrial buyers face the *markup* or *cost plus* methods, sometimes referred to as the *full cost absorption method*, which adds labor, material, and overhead to arrive at total cost, then applies a profit figure to arrive at a proposal price. This price can be adjusted according to the other factors we will call options, such as freight and service contracts. Thus industrial buyers must either request and get the individual cost components and percentages from the supplier or estimate the total price breakdown. With today's typical ratio of material cost to labor cost 3:1, buyers need to question and probe the accuracy and reasonableness of material costs more than they did in the past. As some costs go down (such as labor due to increased automation), many suppliers are increasing the overhead percentage rates beyond reasonable levels to inflate costs in an effort to maintain a desired dollar profit margin.

Pricing Elements Under the Control of Purchasing

Several prerequisites to good pricing are controlled by Purchasing, including:

- The right amount of competition when competition is available or can be developed
- Adequate price analysis
- Thorough cost analysis when price analysis is inadequate or inappropriate
- Selection of the right method of contract pricing (firm fixed-price, fixed-price incentive, etc.)
- Use of the right type of contract (requirements contract, indefinite quantity contract, etc.)
- Partnerships and long-term contracts
- Use of negotiation rather than competitive bidding
- Application of the principles of Zero Base Pricing™

Chapters 2 and 8 addressed the importance of obtaining the right degree of competition. Chapter 8 described how to select the right source, being aware that the right source is one that provides, among other things, the right price.

This chapter examines the critical but frequently misunderstood and misused purchasing activity, price analysis. Chapter 10 addresses cost analysis.

The vast majority of procurement requirements can be satisfied through the use of a firm fixed-price purchase order or subcontract. But many high-value requirements can be priced much more successfully through the use of other than the firm fixed-price method of contract pricing. A whole family of alternatives exists. Selection of the proper approach can and does save the purchaser significant sums. Since few buyers properly understand and use these alternate methods of contract pricing, they are examined in the Appendix D.

Defining Fair and Reasonable Pricing

In one way or another, our jobs are all concerned with answering the question "What's it worth?" The determination of what something is worth is, among other things, a reflection of its availability, quality, and utility. The impact of such factors is translated into money or price, usually through the interaction of supply and demand. The asking price attached to an item or service is generally a summation of labor, material, overhead, and profit.

The worth of the item may be the result of many considerations, including the need, the competitive situation, supply and demand factors, cost comparisons, historical trends, engineering evaluations, actual cost data, and judgment. Our ability as purchasers to assess the proper worth of an item presents as many facets as the criteria used by the supplier to establish his or her concept of price. Arriving at a conclusion of worth in purchasing is called *pricing*. The process involved in making a sensible decision about the price proposed by the offeror or supplier is known as *price analysis*.

From a procurement point of view, the objective of pricing is to ensure that the purchaser pays a fair and reasonable price for the timely delivery of the desired quality of a required supply or service at the lowest life cycle cost. A fair and reasonable price is one that is fair to both parties of the transaction, considering quality, delivery, competition, and the probability of the supplier's producing as required by the purchase order or contract. There are several ideas as to what a fair and reasonable price is:

- *Market Price.* One view is that the market price is the fair and reasonable price. Assuming competition among potential buyers for the available material and competition among potential sellers for the available demand, competition determines what quantities will be bought and sold and at what price.
- *Seller's Point of View.* A fair and reasonable price is one that covers the seller's cost of production plus a reasonable profit. This price may change to meet market conditions (e.g., the degree and effect of competition).
- *Buyer's Point of View.* A fair and reasonable price is one that must be paid to obtain a needed item. How much the buyer is willing to pay may be influenced by the intensity of the need, the item's quality, its utility, its cycle total cost, and the availability of alternatives.

No one price is fair and reasonable from all viewpoints. All three viewpoints cited must be considered in concluding that a price is fair and reasonable. In summary, fair and reasonable describes a conclusion concerning price.

To understand pricing, it is necessary to apply a consistent meaning to the following terms:

Cost. All elements of expense with the exception of profit
Price. All elements of expense plus profit
Profit. The net proceeds obtained by deducting all elements of cost from the price

In deciding on the fairness and reasonableness of the price for a product or service, the buyer must determine the kind of information to use as a basis for the decision. If competition has established the price, the marketplace has in essence satisfied the need for a price analysis. Therefore, the buyer can accept that price as a sound basis for the pricing decision. In the absence of effective price competition or where it is lacking altogether and when the purchase is of a significant size and unique requirements, cost analysis along with price analysis may become necessary for arriving at a decision on the reasonableness of the price.

The Price Analysis Process

The techniques of price analysis and cost analysis are clearly and distinctly different. Price analysis is a broad term that means those actions taken by the buyer to reach a price decision without recourse to cost analysis. Price analysis may be done by comparing prices with prices of previous contracts, purchases of similar services or products, independent cost estimates, or by engineering estimates. Price analysis does not include evaluation of the offeror's detailed cost estimate; that is cost analysis.

In competitive bidding, price analysis is used to determine if the price is reasonable. Price analysis may include a look at what suppliers have done on previous contracts, a comparison with prices paid for the same or similar product or service, or a comparison with an independent cost estimate as described in Chapter 10 and Appendixes E and F.

Much of modern procurement is founded on the principle that free and open competition is the one sure way to get a fair and reasonable price. The buyer must decide in every case, however, if there is competition for the requirement and if the competition is adequate. As we saw at QRS Products, this decision frequently cannot be made until after an evaluation of the proposals received in response to a request for bid. Adequate competition cannot be guaranteed even though many suppliers are asked to submit bids. It is possible that each supplier does not have an equal chance of winning the competition. The fact that several suppliers do submit bids does not mean that the price of the low bidder is fair and reasonable. For example, the low bidder already may have amortized significant setup costs that are included in a competitor's costs. The low bidder may be far down the learning curve, resulting in lower labor and material costs. Or the low bidder may be the only source of manufacture for the item, with his or her apparent "competitors" being distributors of the product. Good pricing should identify such situations for purchases of a significant value. In such circumstances, cost analysis and negotiations may be necessary to arrive at a fair and reasonable price.

If a comparison of bids does not provide decisive information on the adequacy of competition, the buyer should make a more detailed analysis using past prices, quantities, production and delivery rates, and similar information. When competition is not adequate to support a determination that a price is fair and reasonable, it may be possible to use information from past purchases or cost estimates (prepared in engineering or purchasing) without recourse to cost analysis.

Price analysis is basically a comparative process. Therefore, it is meaningful only if the data being compared are truly comparable. This may not be the case, for example, when prices have been based on different assumptions about technical or performance requirements. The danger of comparing apples and oranges becomes particularly great when quotations from earlier purchases are used for comparative purposes, because differences in such factors as specifications, quantities, delivery schedules, buyer-furnished material, improvements in efficiency, and general economic conditions may have an important bearing on price.

Competition

Competition has been described as rivalry in selling goods. One of the basic principles of goods procurement is that open competition among sellers is the one sure way to get a fair and reasonable price. It must be decided in every case, however, that there is competition for the requirement and that the competition is adequate. A buyer cannot decide this until evaluating the prices offered and until it has been determined that at least two responsible suppliers who can satisfy the requirement have competed independently.

If this condition has been met, the buyer can assume price competition unless it is learned that:

- The low bidder has an unusual advantage over the competition. For example, the low bidder may have written off all costs of special tooling and plant rearrangement to previous sales. Another example might be that the low bidder is the manufacturer of a vital component that competitors must buy from it.
- The conditions of the solicitation unreasonably denied one or more known and qualified sources the opportunity to compete.
- It was not possible for suppliers to estimate costs with a high degree of certainty. (In such situations it is likely that contingency allowances have been included in the bids.)

A price can be based on adequate price competition, even when there is no active rivalry between would-be sellers. Such a conclusion is based on a comparison of current prices for the same or similar items bought in comparable quantities under purchase orders previously awarded *after adequate price competition*.

To see if competition really exists, a buyer must test past prices, examine the range of prices and experience offered by competing companies, note the exceptions taken to the specifications by a supplier, and compare delivery schedules or other terms of the invitation for bids or request for proposals.

Catalog or Market Price

The prospective supplier may claim that the quoted price is fair and reasonable since the price has been shaped by the "harsh realities" of the marketplace. To test this contention, the supplier's sales record for the recent period should be reviewed on the basis of such information as pricing policies, current prices quoted to others, current catalog price lists, and discount sheets.

Price Comparisons

Comparative price analysis involves comparing a proposed price with another or other prices. The base price may be another supplier's offer on the same purchase, or it may be a price paid on earlier purchases of the same or similar items. One must be sure that the base price is fair and reasonable and represents a valid standard against which an offered price can be measured. If an original price is being used, it is not enough for the present offer to be lower than the last price paid or even lower than all prices previously paid. Consider the example of an item bought repeatedly from the same supplier:

Buy	Quantity	Unit Price
1st	180	$86
2d	200	79
3d	172	70
Present	212	58

A steady downward trend in price is often pleasing to the buyer, but it is not proof of reasonableness. Unless one of the previous prices has been established by competition, detailed cost analysis, a cost estimate, or testing of the market for the same or a similar item, there can be no assurance that the present bid is reasonable.

If there is little variation in the quantities in the example for comparability, there should be little difference in price. As a general rule, one expects to pay less per unit as the quantities purchased increase. It is for this reason that consolidation of requirements is urged continually. It does not necessarily follow, however, that a proposed price lower than the last purchase price is reasonable just because the present quantity is greater than on the last buy. Neither does the coupling of a higher price with a smaller quantity prove a price reasonable. Although the relative price change is logical and should be expected, other factors requiring attention are the nature of the item, the number to be purchased in relation to the number sold in a comparable period, and the existence of a price list with quantity breaks that may be used in selling the item to all classes of customers.

Usually price comparison is a starting point that reveals differences to be explained before a price decision can be made. The supplier may be the only source for needed answers, however, and a discussion with the buyer may be necessary before a decision can be made. In any event, the buyer must proceed with great caution in analyzing differences, because plausible answers may not be the actual ones.

In a particular situation, the supplier may contend that material and labor costs have gone up in the interval since the last purchase; therefore, a higher price is justified for the item. A general increase in material and labor costs, however, may not influence the unit cost of a particular item unless the price of the actual material used has gone up, unless the rates actually paid workers have gone up, and unless there have not been compensating economies in the amounts or costs of material and labor used in manufacturing or in other direct expenses.

This is the fallacy of escalation–de-escalation provisions in a contract. As a rule, these clauses in a contract or proposal only use the language *escalation*, which means the price can only go up, and they usually use the general producer's price index (PPI) and/or Bureau of Labor Statistics (BLS) indexes. These government or other such industry producers indexes are very general "basket" averages by SIC code and may have (they usually do not) nothing to do with one particular company's experience. In particular, for repeat sales of the same item from the same supplier, learning curve experience and amortization of original setup costs should lower costs on future orders. The only value of using such indexes is to compare the industry average with the performance of a particular supplier. Even if the term *formula pricing* is used to allow both increases and decreases, such clauses should *not* be used in POs or contracts. If the contract extends for a long time, reopener clauses can provide a safety valve for both sides in the event of real and unexpected changes in cost elements.

A supplier may contend that the last buy of the item was made while the end item of which it was a component was still in production. Now, as an out-of-production part, the item must take full setup costs spread over a smaller quantity. Therefore, the supplier contends, a price increase is justified. In this instance, the last buy may have been made while the end item was being manufactured, but even at that time, the particular part may have been produced in a special, small-quantity run and have carried a full setup charge. Thus, on closer investigation, we find that the cost of manufacture today should not differ appreciably from the previous cost. In addition, with modern numerically controlled processes and flexible computer machine systems, setup charges may be minuscule.

Price comparison requires easy access to price history on an item-by-item basis. Item history cards or machine printouts showing price, quantity, purchase order number, date, supplier, and delivery schedule should be available in any well-run purchasing organization. But care must be taken in using these prices. The mere fact that past prices exist does not make them valid bases for comparison. The buyer also must establish production or delivery rates, learning curve experience, the kinds of purchase (competitive, sole source, or similar characterization), and the presence or absence of special considerations before deciding to use a price as a standard.

Exhibit 9-1.   Pricing analysis—a decision chart.

Estimated $ Amount Basis for Decision	$0–1,000	$1,001– 50,000	$50,001– 250,000	≥$251,000
Competition	If prices considered reasonable, may bypass competition	Generally limited to 3 sources	Maximize to extent consistent with requirement	Maximize to extent consistent with requirement
Catalog or Market Price	Good source	Acceptable	Acceptable	Acceptable
Price Comparisons	Acceptable	Acceptable	Acceptable	Acceptable
Engineering Estimate	Acceptable	Acceptable	Acceptable	No
Cost or Pricing Data	No	No	When appropriate	Yes
Negotiate	Last resort	Permissible	Permissible	Yes

Source: David N. Burt, *Proactive Procurement* (Englewood Cliffs, N.J.: Prentice-Hall, 1984), p. 129.

Engineering Estimates

An offered price may be compared with an engineered cost estimate to establish reasonableness when price comparisons are not possible. To be useful, however, the basis for the estimate and its reliability must be established. It is important to determine how the estimate was established, what information and estimating techniques were used, the source of the information, and how earlier estimates compared with resulting contract or purchase order prices.

Exhibit 9-1 sets out pricing actions in a go/no-go sequence.[2] The purchaser starts with competition as a basis for a decision and goes only as far as necessary to assure himself or herself that the price is right. The buyer starts with an evaluation of the proposals. If effective price competition exists, the price is right. If competition is not effective, the buyer may look to catalogs and market prices. If these do not do the job, the buyer moves to price comparisons and then to engineering estimates. If no price analysis method works, it may be necessary to use cost analysis.

Analysis and decisions probably will not follow this sequence to the letter. Experience frequently will allow one to take shortcuts to reach the decision that an offer should be accepted or negotiated to an acceptable level. *Remember the objective: an acceptable price achieved with minimum effort.*

Keeping Total Cost Low

Altogether too frequently, great emphasis is placed on the initial cost of acquiring a material while ignoring or neglecting the total cost of owning and processing the material. In Chapter 5 we discussed the need for placing attention on the cost of ownership or life cycle cost of equipment. By considering costs over the life of the item instead of merely the initial acquisition cost, we gain an increase in competition because firms whose products have higher initial prices but lower subsequent ownership costs on a total life cycle cost basis may be able to compete.

When the purchaser considers cost of ownership, it may be best to purchase a higher unit price production drill bit if the bit will last longer. A more elaborate example concerns the actual case of a large university negotiating with three major manufacturers of office copiers. The buying team established a target of 25% less than the previous contract price. Negotiations for this large order continued for many weeks until a new foreign competitor submitted the winning proposal at a machine rental price of 25% less than the competing and past supplier's prices. One year after the contract award, not only had the total operating cost failed to meet the 25% target cost reduction, the actual costs had exceeded the previous supplier's cost by 10%. What happened? If you are wondering if they asked about service and maintenance cost, the answer is "yes but." There were distinct limits in the rental and service agreements. The buying team failed to probe the maintenance issue in depth and consequently did not negotiate a proper service agreement. If you ask a supplier selling team the simple question, "Do you have good service?" in all probability, unless the supplier team has a death wish, the answer will be "yes."

Service Costs

In the copier example, an entire line of questions should have been asked in order to determine the real service costs. For example:

- How many service people do you have?
- Where are they located?
- What is your response time to a call?
- Do the maintenance people speak English (remember, this was a new foreign competitor)?
- Are your maintenance manuals in English?
- Who is using your copier? Try to learn the experience and recommendations of present users recommended by the seller.
- What exactly does the service contract cover and for how long?
- How long does it take to get supplies and repair parts and at what cost?
- Will the seller negotiate a redetermination clause to resolve cost overruns?
- What happens after the warranty period regarding cost of service calls?
- What is the supplier's policy on parts inventory?

This list is by no means exhaustive and yet seemingly minute oversights can lead to trouble. For instance, one U.S. capital equipment buyer purchased a complicated and expensive machine tool from a German manufacturer only to discover that the electrical diagrams and schematics were all in German electrical symbology: The German firm refused to have the installation wiring diagram translated, forcing the buyer into the unusual and embarrassing situation of trying to find a German-reading electrical engineer in central Ohio!

Transportation Costs

Transportation and freight charges are another easily hidden cost. The customer usually pays the freight cost one way or another unless it is a specific form of price concession achieved through negotiation. Some buyers think they can escape all freight cost by negotiating FOB buyer's plant, when in fact, most sellers will hide the freight cost somewhere in the price of the product. This does not mean the seller is evil, it simply reflects a very real cost that must be recovered.

The Negotiated Rates Act (NRA) passed in December 1993 and the Trucking Industry Regulatory Reform Act (TIRRA) passed in August of 1994 dramatically changed the transportation industry. The details of these amendments to the Motor Carrier Act of 1980 are well beyond this book, but buyers must now use their own contracts because carrier contracts will shift the risk to the other parties. Although common carriers no longer have to file their tariffs with the ICC, undercharge claims and other restrictions can still be written into the carrier contracts. These rates, rules, liabilities, penalties, and other such tariffs of the National Motor Freight Classification (NMFC) for trucking, the Uniform Freight Classification for rail, and the Association of American Railroad's (AAR) loading pamphlets still apply. The NRA also restricts the use of "off-bill discounting," which allowed suppliers offering goods on a "freight prepaid and add" basis to receive hefty refunds from carriers if they negotiated "off-the-freight bill" discounts. Under the NRA, both buyers and sellers can negotiate discounts from carriers but the terms of sale must contain precise wording as to who is entitled to the discount. The buyer must seek the professional advice of the in-house traffic department or a freight auditor-consultant to obtain legitimate discounts and to avoid paying "unknown" and "surprise" charges.[3]

Two-Step Procurement

When a performance specification (see Chapter 3) serves as the basis of a solicitation, a procedure known as two-step procurement may be employed to select the source and determine the price. During the first step of this procedure, interested potential competitors are requested to submit unpriced technical proposals on how they will meet the requirement. Personnel in the requiring organization then review these technical proposals and accept those technical approaches deemed to be satisfactory. In step 2, companies having submitted acceptable technical proposals are requested to submit a price with cost element breakdowns to perform under a purchase order or contract using the technical approach they previously submitted. On receipt of the price proposals, the purchaser can select a supplier in either of two ways:

1. *Price competition.* With this approach, award will be made to the qualified bidder submitting the lowest price. With adequate competition, this approach allows price analysis to serve as the basis of a determination that the price is fair and reasonable.

2. *Combination of technical and price considerations.* In this case, a combination of price and technical considerations is the basis of selecting the supplier. A decision must be made as to the adequacy of price analysis alone or the need to include formal cost analysis as part of the process leading to a decision that the price is fair and reasonable. Many suppliers will not submit a cost breakdown. However, nothing is lost by asking for a cost breakdown. At a minimum, such a request alerts the supplier as to your objectives and needs and to your intent to analyze potential suppliers' costs (as discussed in the next chapter).

The Special Case of "Price in Effect at the Time of Delivery"

During the high inflation period in the United States, 1974–1984, industries with reputations for heavy-handed dealing started to quote "price-in-effect at time of delivery." No other pricing tactic quite so angered the purchasing community as this obnoxious practice. This tactic may again appear if inflation and high demand occur.

Luckily, the practice is actually an unenforceable contract clause under the Uniform Commercial Code (UCC) (§ 1-102 comment 2), and UCC § 2-302 according to the principle of the prevention of oppression and unfair surprise.[4] Few courts would ever enforce such a contract even if the buyer signed a contract containing such a clause. Second, once the product has been "made," the manufacturer knows exactly what the product costs. Thus, the price-in-effect at time of delivery is a blatant attempt to induce by commercial pressure a signed "blank check" where the seller fills in the amount with no possible chance for the buyer to question the price. If the supplier states he or she does not know the exact price of raw material (in particular, for precious metals), negotiate a surcharge clause, which calls for documentation.

How do you handle such a practice? First, refuse to sign any type of contract with a one-way and arbitrary price determination. Second, analyze prices and costs as appropriate. Third, negotiate a price change warning clause of, say, 60 days notice with the right to renegotiate and require documentation. Finally, if the seller persists, notify your legal department and have it send a formal complaint to the president of the selling firm. Appendix G goes into detail on managing or "fighting" price increases.

Target Pricing and Cost Drivers

In many firms, the marketing department establishes a target price for the firm's products and services. This is the optimum price the market will tolerate in view of competition and product differentiation and one that will provide a desired ROI at the seller's predicted production level. Another definition of target price is the price that will optimize the firm's net revenues. This "price" obviously dictates the target production cost and gives direction to the firm's engineering, production, and purchasing departments. The need for IPS, concurrent R&D work with early supplier involvement, and the need to first determine cost goals are the essence of proactive target-costing management. We establish cost limits for internal and external operations (suppliers) to satisfy the target price rather than wait and set the price after the costs are merely summarized.

Target pricing, when conducted professionally and ethically, begins with Marketing's "optimized" price. This price then is adjusted for target profits and target cost. The target cost, then, is allocated to the various components or subassemblies that compose the end product. Target costs for components and subassemblies obtained from outside suppliers become the basis of discussions and negotiation. Personnel from the firm's buying and engineering staffs work with the potential supplier's design and production staffs in order to develop processes that allow the supplier to produce the required item at the target cost, while having the ability to earn a fair profit.[5]

Part of this process involves identifying cost drivers within the buyer's plant and the supplier's operation. For example, one of the key cost drivers in motors is horsepower and the more you want, the higher the cost. Another example is computer memory. These key cost elements become candidates for value analysis (the subject of Chapter 11) within the buying organization and its suppliers. The philosophy is to control costs as opposed to merely accepting them. To accept them means that they are passed along within the value chain and, ultimately, to the end customer, the source of funds feeding the value chain. As previously noted, the subject of managing or "fighting" price increases is covered in Appendix G. These techniques are important tools for containing costs.

These cost goals are actually another application of benchmarks based on the best competitive standards for the most efficient and effective producers. These benchmark standards usually trigger the need for cost estimating and the need for cost reduction techniques such as value analysis, cycle time reduction, and cost breakdown analysis of purchased materials. What are the big cost factors and how can we reduce them? When comparative price analysis fails to resolve these issues, we use cost analysis, the subject of Chapter 10.

Summary

The worth of an item may be the result of many considerations: one's need for the item, the competitive situation, cost comparisons, historic trends, and judgment. In purchasing, the process of arriving at a conclusion about the worth of an item is called pricing. The purchaser's objective is to pay a price that is fair and reasonable for the timely delivery and desired quality of a required item or service. A fair and reasonable price is one that is fair to both buyer and seller, considering quality, delivery competition, and the probability of the supplier's producing as specified.

Price analysis is a broad term that includes those actions taken by the buyer to reach a decision on the reasonableness of a price without recourse to cost analysis. A basic principle underlying modern procurement is that free and open competition is the one sure way to obtain a fair and reasonable price.

When a comparison of bids does not provide decisive information on the adequacy of competition, the buyer should make a more detailed analysis using past prices, quantities, production and delivery rates, and similar information. It may be possible to make adjustments in pricing data based on past experience by looking at cost behavior patterns.

A hierarchy of preferred pricing methods has been developed. Competition is the preferred method, with catalog or market price analysis second, price comparisons third, the use of the firm's engineering estimates fourth, the analysis of supplier-supplied cost or pricing data fifth, and negotiations being the final (and most costly) basis of reaching a decision on the fairness and reasonableness of a price.

Notes

1. Thomas T. Nagle, *Strategy and Tactics of Pricing: A Guide to Profitable Decision Making*, 2nd ed. (Englewood Cliffs, N.J.: Prentice-Hall, 1994).
2. Adapted from Richard P. White, "How to Price Contracts Using Price Analysis," *NCMA Journal* (January 1979), p. 25. Quoted in David N. Burt, *Proactive Procurement* (Englewood Cliffs, N.J.: Prentice-Hall, 1984), p. 129.
3. David L. Jordan, "The Wheels of Change Keep Turning," *NAPM Insights* (November 1994), pp. 8–9, 12; and William J. Augello, "Transportation's Correct Compliance on Off-Bill Discounting," *NAPM Insights* (November 1994), pp. 8–9, 12.
4. Donald B. King and James J. Ritterskamp, Jr., *The Purchasing Manager's Desk Book of Purchasing Law*, 2nd ed. (Englewood Cliffs, N.J.: Prentice-Hall, 1993) (with periodic updates), pp. 168–173.
5. For more detail on both target pricing and target costs, see Richard G. Newman and John M. McKeller, "Target Pricing—A Challange for Purchasing," *International Journal of Purchasing and Materials Management* (Summer 1995), pp. 12–20.

10
Cost Analysis

David Richards, a 37-year-old graduate of the University of San Diego's graduate Supply Management Program, was recently appointed VP Supply for the Tough Tractor Company of Fresno, California. Prior to working on his MBA, David had gained 16 years of experience at General Dynamics and Lorel, where he had positions as a materials manager. Tough Tractor is number three in its industry with sales of $1 billion a year. Cost of goods sold (CGS) is 75% of sales, with purchased material representing 72% of CGS.

David is sitting in his new office preparing for his first staff meeting later in the day. A memo from Mr. Columbine, the CEO, indicates that the meeting will focus on Tough Tractor's above-industry CGS. During the interviewing process, David learned that Tough Tractor has implemented JIT, MRPII, quality circles, MBO, and TQM, all with success.

Since joining the firm, David has learned that 10 contracts represent 80% of all production procurement dollars. Tough Tractor's normal practice is to award two or three contracts for most production items. Sourcing is done by Engineering, with Purchasing playing a support role. The key criteria against which sources are selected include performance, reliability, and availability. Very close relationships exist between Tough Tractor and its suppliers' engineers. Costs are agreed to by the engineers from Tough Tractor and its key suppliers in very open discussions.

David realizes that purchased material costs offer a major source of cost reduction for the firm. He wonders how much resistance he will encounter from both suppliers and his engineers while implementing the principles of basic cost management.

Today, billions of dollars are being squeezed out of supply chains as purchasing professionals work with their suppliers to understand the suppliers' costs and the forces that drive these costs and then to reduce them. Most buying firms have an array of relationships with their suppliers, ranging from traditional arms-length ones to strategic supply alliances. When price analysis does *not* allow the buyer to determine that a price is fair and reasonable, a cost analysis must be tailored and applied based on the supply relationship. With arms-length relationships, the procurement professional will invest energy understanding the supplier's likely costs. With strategic supply alliances, members of both firms will jointly investigate the likely costs and *their drivers* in an effort to reduce costs incurred in producing the required materials, subassemblies, or services.

Traditional Relationships

When conducting cost analysis within a prospective traditional supply relationship, the buyer has several sources of data to use in determining or negotiating an acceptable cost: the supplier's cost breakdown submitted with its proposal, estimates prepared by the buyer's estimating department, or estimates prepared within its purchasing department.

The Supplier's Cost Breakdown

When it is anticipated that a cost analysis will be required, the professional buyer requests prospective suppliers to submit a bill of materials and/or blueprints with their proposals. When warranted, an engineering or work sequence list revealing the step-by-step cycle progression of the part through all of the various workstations and the various operations to be performed is requested. This engineering-production sequence list is the key to understanding labor costs. *If* a supplier ignores the request for such data, then we frequently recommend that the proposal be treated as nonresponsive—unless it is otherwise so attractive that the buying firm is willing to invest the time and energy required to develop its own estimate of the supplier's likely costs, as described below. The following discussion applies to the situation wherein the prospective supplier has submitted the requested cost data. From the buyer's point of view, costs may be divided into four groups: material, labor, overhead, and profit.

Materials and Components

Direct materials and components are consumed or converted during the production process. Materials and components are normally purchased by the prospective suppliers and from their subcontractors. If the items are produced or partially processed in other plants or divisions of the suppliers' operation, the proposed costs must be carefully analyzed for internal transfer charges and mark-ups. These are all variable costs, directly traceable to a specific operation.

If the buyer knows a material cost should be $2.50 per unit and the supplier proposes $3.00, the buyer may be able to suggest different purchasing procedures or sources of supply. The same observation holds for components. In some instances, the buying firm may make the item available to the supplier at its lower cost.

Two other issues require attention: scrap rates and learning applied to the procurement of materials and components. Assuming that the supplier employs the design of experiments and statistical process control, as discussed in Chapter 12, its scrap rate normally should approach zero. *If* the supplier must purchase materials and components for the project which it has not purchased in the recent past, a well-run purchasing organization should drive material costs down with experience. (The learning curve is discussed in Appendix C.) We have observed learning curves of 95% for such material procurements.

Direct Labor

The proactive buyer must analyze a prospective supplier's cost proposal for design and development efforts, tooling and setup expenses, and then production and, possibly, test labor. Experience and the assistance of design and manufacturing engineers are required. Again, the learning curve (see Appendix C) should be applied to items to be produced specifically for the buying firm. Direct labor is also a variable cost, 100% traceable to a specific operation.

Production costs include machining, assembly, inspection, handling, and other direct work force input. Many suppliers attempt to use standard costs in their proposals. The buyer must determine if the *actual* labor costs for the products *being purchased* are (or should be) below the "standard." The buyer may discover that either the wrong labor rate is being used or that the time is incorrect. Some suppliers also charge for overtime, begging the question, "Why on my order?" Unless the delivery is a rush caused or required by the buying firm, these charges are inappropriate. The industrial engineering department and cost accounting group of the buying firm can be very helpful in this area.

If there is great uncertainty on the amounts of prices of labor and/or materials, and if the size of the expenditure warrants, then the professional buyer will use one of the alternative methods of contract pricing, as described in Appendix D.

Overhead

The analysis of materials and labor as variable costs is relatively straightforward compared with the analysis of overhead costs, which are indirect and often fixed costs, although some are semivariable. Normally, the potential supplier's proposal will reflect its accounting department's effort to allocate overhead costs to the suppliers' products.

Three basic issues are involved when dealing with overheads:

1. The acceptability of the individual overhead cost (or its driver): Should this cost properly be allocated to "our" job?
2. The reasonableness of the individual overhead costs and, thereby, the reasonableness of the overhead pool: Is the "size" or amount of cost reasonable?
3. The allocation of the "reasonable pool" to our job. This is (or should be) based on the supplier's forecast of total work to be done while our share of the supplier's resources are being applied to our order. Quite obviously, the supplier is motivated to estimate or forecast its total volume of work very conservatively. Such a practice will ensure that our work carry its full share of overhead and, frequently, then some! Thus the buyer must study both the size of the overhead pool and the reasonableness of its allocation!

The three major overhead pools of particular interest to the buyer are manufacturing; engineering; and sales, general, and administrative costs.

1. *Manufacturing overhead.* Manufacturing overhead includes direct tool setup charges, direct assignment of machine tool depreciation costs based on running time, supplies, maintenance, utilities, supervision, insurance, taxes, safety costs, and the like. Most suppliers will use a standard percentage rate based on direct variable labor. The buyer must inquire as to the particular allocation method used and determine if it is appropriate.

2. *Engineering overhead.* When the supplier has a separate engineering department, probably it will charge this rate as a separate overhead item or as part of some other overhead rate. In other instances, the engineering costs are included in a plantwide rate often called *manufacturing and engineering overhead.* In either case, as we have previously advised, the buyer should ask what is included in these rates, are they reasonable, and is the buying firm using engineering resources of the seller. Never pay for a function you are not using. If there is supplier engineering effort, what is it? How many hours are involved? What is the hourly rate? Many buyers blindly accept engineering charges they have not incurred because the charges are buried in other cost components.

3. *Sales, general, and administrative overhead costs (SG&A).* Typical SG&A costs are exceptionally common costs for the entire firm. They include personal selling expenses such as travel, salaries, commissions; sales office rental; service; advertising, sales promotion, and other marketing expenses. On top of these "field expenses" are added just about everything else in the way of home office and staff support expenses such as executive compensation, legal staff, office space, insurance, purchasing, taxes, pure R&D costs, accounting, clerical, taxes, principle and interest on nonproductive facilities, association and club dues, and charity donations.

It is in the SG&A area where the buyer must question what is included to avoid duplication of items in manufacturing overhead and charges for services not used. Such services include R&D (if the buyer firm has the patent), tooling, prints, and so forth. Some suppliers subcontract large amounts of an order and although the subcontract administrative expenses are appropriate charges, other staff costs, such as engineering, may not be involved to any great extent and should not be charged at a normal rate. In the area of selling expenses, long-term contracts such as blanket orders and systems contracts should substantially reduce personal selling and related distribution expenses. The buyer team has every right to ask for a reduction in this element of SG&A and avoid accepting routine sales calls if they are not necessary.

Many of the same allocation methods used in direct or factory overhead costing are also used in SG&A allocation. A supplier is entitled to a fair recovery of SG&A, but the big question is "what is fair?" Buyers must avoid actually paying excessive profits based on inflated overhead. The direct costing method would eliminate allocation of SG&A to unit cost. This is another reason to urge suppliers to use several costing methods. Unfortunately, such action is a very difficult concept for suppliers to accept. By training and custom, accountants are very prone to allocate all costs to each unit sold even though this practice can badly distort an individual product's profitability.

Activity-based costing. The foregoing or traditional approach to allocating overhead pools has a large element of arbitrariness. Further, as direct labor costs have shrunk to an average 10% of total costs, they have become a less logical and realistic basis on which to allocate indirect costs.

During the 1980s, Professors Robert Kaplan and Robin Cooper developed what has become known as activity-based costing (ABC)—a tool that more accurately identifies and allocates indirect costs to the products they support. Recently, ABC has evolved into activity-based management (ABM).[1]

ABC or ABM can be used to identify opportunities to reduce the supplier's indirect costs. ABC goes beyond identifying and allocating these indirect costs to products: It identifies the drivers of these costs. Some examples of cost drivers are the number of orders, length of setups, specifications, engineering changes, and liaison trips required. This identification allows management to identify and implement cost savings opportunities. Quite obviously, if the supplier's management does not implement the required changes, an alert buyer can "encourage" such action.

If a supplier uses some form of ABC accounting, the price quoted includes an overhead allocation. The buyer still must judge whether the size of the overhead pool and its allocation are reasonable.

Perhaps the most helpful comment concerning overhead allocation is: There are many different methods, and the selection of the appropriate one will vary by product type, past history, and the ease of tracing costs. Certainly the supplier is entitled to recover overhead costs and the buyer should avoid unreasonable positions during negotiation. But the buyer should know what method is being used and what costs are included, so that inappropriate ones can be eliminated or reduced. If the supplier uses the direct costing approach and uses profit as a contribution to overhead, the question of allocation is eliminated. However, the buyer then needs a much more thorough analysis of the profit rate.

Profit

Enlightened buyers realize that their suppliers must earn a reasonable profit to ensure a healthy long-term relationship and to preserve the supplier as a source of supply by establishing a realistic and viable target profit. Although some buyers take a cavalier attitude that it is up to the supplier to make sure it remains solvent, it is dangerous to allow a supplier to sell on a marginal basis. Sooner or later the supplier will cut corners on quality, safety, service, and delivery. In the short run during slack periods, many suppliers will cut profits and seek only to recover variable costs in order to retain skilled workers, but this cannot continue for indefinite periods. Sufficient profits are essential to:

• *Encourage entrepreneuring.* Investors must obtain a sufficient ROI and assets in order to reinvest in the business and to stimulate risk taking. Profitable suppliers modernize their plant and equipment while the marginal operators engage in "milking" and eventually cause buyers excessive costs in terms of inefficiency, rejects, follow-up, and other corrective action. Thus, the buyer must understand how the supplier has and will use profits from this job.

♦ *Stimulate high quality production standards.* A financially healthy supplier is able to take the time and make the financial investment necessary to produce to the required specifications without excessive scrap or cost. Sufficient labor rates attract skilled workers with high morale and foster good postsale service assistance. There is a direct, but subtle, relationship between profit and quality: Suppliers with small or no profit margins frequently reduce quality costs to a bare minimum, thereby reducing quality.

♦ *Ensure delivery.* There is no question that financially weak companies have trouble buying their materials in sufficient quantities, thereby affecting the unit price and possibly the quality, and also delaying production. The inability to purchase sufficient support equipment, such as modern material-handling storage systems or adequate test equipment, may, and often does, interrupt the process and delay delivery. Underskilled and insufficient labor, including weak engineering and shop management, can also cause delays, higher costs, and poor quality. Obsolete production equipment is an obvious handicap.

♦ *Support R&D.* New product development, patent activity, good value engineering, and technical assistance all add to overhead and, as a result, the supplier must earn enough profit on unit sales to recover these costs. High technology industries such as electronic components, computers, aerospace, telecommunications, pharmaceuticals, and special machinery are good examples of how rather high profits stimulate innovation.

♦ *Benchmark profits.* There are several sources of general industry profit and margin ratios and other economic indicators: the *Prentice Hall Annual Almanac of Business and Industrial Financial Ratios,* individual Dun & Bradstreet reports, *Dun's Key Business Ratios, The Wall Street Journal, Barron's, Forbes, Fortune, Business Week,* Robert Morris Associates in Philadelphia, the NAPM Report on Business® included in *NAPM Insights,* and many other industry magazines. Again, negotiation experience and literature review will eventually provide the buyer or buying team with the background records to reveal normal profits and industry practice.

Many sellers simply use an industry standard markup, which may or may not be appropriate for the particular order in question. Practically speaking, normal or fair profit and at times, high profits, are required to induce the seller to:

Accept the order
Meet high quality standards
Produce efficiently
Deliver on time
Provide adequate postsale service
Offer technical assistance
Remain healthy and interested in repeat business.

Good suppliers will always be scarce. If has often been said that prudent purchasing managers are those successful at getting suppliers to do special tasks for the buying firm. Profit, good communications, and fair treatment are the major inducements.

At the same time, the buyer must remember that profits must be earned through value-added performance based on risk assumption, quality, cost, delivery, and service. *Profits are the reward for satisfying requirements, not an inalienable right based on the industry average.*

Estimates Prepared by the Estimating Department

Appendix E describes a variety of techniques commonly employed by cost estimating departments. Prior to employing such estimates as the basis of analyzing and negotiating a prospective supplier's proposal, the buyer *must* know the likely confidence limits (e.g., ± 1%, ± 10%) around these estimates.

Purchasing Department Estimates

Assuming the supplier will not reveal the cost component breakdowns and if the buyer has little or no internal cost accounting help or cost element knowledge, secondary sources can be of great assistance. Appendix F describes several techniques.

Price Increases

With some 70 years of experience in purchasing/procurement/supply management between us, we remain amazed at how otherwise effective purchasing departments deal with the issue of requests for price increases. The proactive procurement professional fights price increases aggressively, in some cases even turning such a request into a price decrease. Appendix G summarizes actions that can be taken when dealing with requests for price increases.

Just remember that the incumbent supplier has an inherent advantage over competition. It probably has amortized most of the startup production costs, possibly all tooling costs, and obviously has learning curve experience. This means that this supplier has the burden of proof to justify a price increase. In addition, never grant a price increase on the total invoice price: Only grant the increase if legitimately based on the cost element (material, labor, or overhead). Failure to do so will magnify the price increase. For example, assume the last total invoice price was $10 per unit and the supplier's materials costs were $7. If he justified a 10% material cost increase, the revised total price should be $10.70, not $11.

Strategic Supply Alliances/Partnerships

Although strategic supply partnerships are relatively few in number, they frequently account for 50–80% of the firm's purchasing expenditures. Establishing such partnerships is described in *The American Keiretsu* by Burt and Doyle.[2] The key issue of concern to us here is that such alliances require open books. That is, the supplier's cost data are available to the buying firm and its orders and sales projections are available to its supply partners.

Once this information is available, interfirm teams composed (as appropriate) of designers, process engineers, quality and manufacturing managers, and purchasing professionals from the buying and supplying firms systematically examine the largest cost items in the areas of materials, labor, and overheads, in an effort to identify costs that can be reduced or eliminated. In some cases, value analysis and value engineering techniques, as described in Chapter 11, are applied. In other cases, application of industrial engineering techniques (currently referred to as reengineering) can drive labor costs down. In some instances, it is necessary to identify the cost driver (how many horsepower, number of trips, etc.) in order to drive costs down. In some cases, these techniques are applied to the supplier's supplier—all the way through the supply chain back to Mother Earth.

Target Costing

Target costing is our favorite approach to cost and pricing. In Chapter 9, we introduced the concept of target pricing to the reader. It is so important that we want to review its application in a price-cost relationship. Management guru Peter Drucker shares our advocacy of this approach to the establishment of an optimal price. He maintains that one of U.S. business's major sins is the use of cost-based pricing. Drucker argues that businesses must embrace cost-based or cost-lead pricing as do Marks and Spencer of the United Kingdom, Toyota of Japan, and Chrysler of the United States.[3]

In several world-class firms, the marketing department establishes a target price for the firm's products and services. This is the optimum price the market will tolerate in view of competition and product differentiation, and one that will provide a desired rate of ROI at the seller's predicted production and sales level. According to another definition, it is the price that will optimize the firm's net revenues. This "price" obviously dictates the target production cost and gives direction to both the firm and its suppliers' engineering, production, and purchasing departments. This is the essence of proactive management as we establish cost limits for internal and external operations to satisfy the target price rather than wait and set the price after merely summarizing the costs.

Target costing, when conducted professionally and ethically, begins with marketing's "optimized" price. This price then is adjusted for target profit and target cost. The target cost, then, is allocated to the various components or subassemblies that compose the end product. Target costs for components and subassemblies that are obtained from outside suppliers (normally strategic supply partners as discussed in Chapter 15) become the basis of discussions and negotiations on how to meet the cost objectives. Personnel from the firm's buying and engineering staffs work with the potential supplier's design and production staffs in order to develop designs and processes that allow the supplier to produce the required item at the target cost, while having the ability to earn a fair profit.

Part of this process involves identifying "cost drivers" within the buyer's plant and the supplier's operation. These drivers become candidates for value analysis within our own organization and that of our suppliers. The philosophy is to control costs as opposed to merely accepting them. To accept them means that they are passed along within the value chain and, ultimately, to the end customer, the source of funds feeding our value chain—or a competitor's value chain!

Summary

Billions of dollars are being squeezed out of supply chains as purchasing professionals work with their suppliers to understand the suppliers' costs and the forces that drive these costs and then work to reduce the costs. Most buying firms have a variety of relationships with their suppliers, ranging from traditional arms-length ones to strategic alliances. Accordingly, when cost analysis is required, it must be tailored to the relationship.

With a prospective traditional supply relationship, the buyer has several sources of data for use in determining or negotiating an acceptable cost including the suppliers' cost breakdown, estimates prepared by the buyer's estimating department, or estimates prepared within the purchasing department.

When conducting a cost analysis, the buyer studies four areas of costs: material, labor, overhead, and profit. Direct materials and labor costs are relatively easy to analyze; overhead and profit objectives are far more challenging. Normally, the potential supplier's proposal will reflect its accounting department's effort to allocate overhead costs to the supplier's products. The buyer must analyze and (when appropriate) challenge both the costs in the overhead pools and their allocation to the supplier's products.

Many purchasing professionals mistakenly assume that the relatively new activity-based costing (ABC) or activity-based management (ABM) will solve their need to understand and accept the prospective supplier's allocations of overhead. While ABC and ABM will help identify potential overhead cost savings, the buyer still must determine whether the size of the overhead pool and its allocation are reasonable.

A supplier should be allowed to recover reasonable overhead costs. But the buyer must be able to understand the drivers of overhead costs, their reasonableness, and the allocation of the resulting costs.

Proactive procurement professionals realize that their suppliers must have the opportunity to earn a reasonable profit to ensure a healthy long-term relationship and to preserve the supplier as a viable source of supply. Many factors must be considered in tailoring this profit objective. These buyers also recognize that profits should be the reward for satisfying requirements, not an inalienable right based on industry averages.

Target costing is our favorite approach to cost and pricing. With this approach, the marketing department establishes a target price for the company's products and services. This price is designed to provide a desired ROI at the seller's predicted production and sales level. The target price, less its profit objective, provides the target cost. This cost is allocated to the various components and subassemblies that compose the end product. The resulting target costs for items to be purchased become the basis of discussions and negotiations with prospective suppliers on how to meet the cost objective. We believe that success in the global marketplace soon will require this approach to establishing both market prices and purchased materials price objectives.

Value Analysis/Value Engineering, one of the most powerful and, ironically, least utilized approaches to controlling costs, is the subject of our next chapter.

Notes

1. Robin Cooper and Robert S. Kaplan, "Profit Priorities from Activity-Based Costing," *Harvard Business Review* (May-June 1991), p. 30. Also see James A. Brimson, *Activity Accounting: An Activity-Based Costing Approach* (New York: Wiley, 1991), and Mary Lu Harding, "The ABCs of Activities and Drivers," *NAPM Insights* (November 1994), p. 6.
2. David N. Burt and Michael F. Doyle, *The American Keiretsu* (Homewood, Ill.: Business One Irwin, 1993).
3. For further insight into Drucker's thoughts on this issue, the interested reader is encouraged to obtain Peter F. Drucker, "The Five Deadly Business Sins," *The Wall Street Journal* (October 21, 1993), p. A-18. See also "The Information Executives Truly Need," *Harvard Business Review* (January-February 1995), p. 58; Richard G. Newman and John M. McKeller, "Target Pricing—A Challange to Purchasing," *International Journal of Purchasing and Cost/Price Analysis Tools to Improve Profit Margins* (New York: Van Nostrand Reinhold, 1993.)

11

Value Analysis and Value Engineering

Two days ago, Irv Applebaum, president of the Marysville Manufacturing Company, held a special meeting of line and staff managers. The meeting was brief. Applebaum said, in effect, that if costs were not reduced by 15%, there would be no Marysville Manufacturing Company this time next year. Applebaum stated that in 10 days he would devote a full day to suggestions from all present on how to reduce costs by 15%.

On returning to his office, Alan McDowell, the purchasing manager, called his four buyers together. Alan described the severity of the situation and asked for ideas on how to reduce purchasing expenditures by 15–20%. Several ideas were discussed and Alan planned to introduce the better ones at the general meeting in 10 days. Sue Shaffer, the new MRO buyer, suggested that Marysville implement a value analysis (VA) program.

Alan and his buyers were so enthusiastic about the VA program that they agreed to act immediately. (Alan felt that such aggressive action would not go unnoticed. He planned to present an implemented action, not a plan, at the forthcoming meeting.) The first action called for each buyer to contact his or her major suppliers to seek suggestions for reducing material expenditures. The suppliers would be requested to make suggestions in any of the following areas: substitutions, changes in materials, order quantities, tests, tolerances, finishes, and simplifications. The second action was for Purchasing to develop a checklist covering these areas of possible savings. The checklist became available the next day and was included as a part of all requests for quotations and purchase orders with values in excess of $10,000.

The following Monday, four days before Applebaum's meeting, Jon Hobbs, director of R&D, stormed into Alan's office. "Who gave you the right to second-guess my staff?" he bellowed. "It's my job to design products and your job to buy the materials we specify!"

Before Alan could respond, Hobbs left. Alan's blood pressure was up. He felt anger and resentment. He also realized that his "surprise" was backfiring. Maybe a good idea would not get a fair chance.

Development of Value Analysis and Value Engineering

During World War II, many essential materials used in production became scarce. The war effort drained many resources to the point that material substitutions were the order of the day. H. L. Erlicher, then Vice President of Purchasing and Transportation at General Electric (GE), noticed that creative people in the design and planning functions at GE were able to suggest or accept alternative materials that performed satisfactorily. Indeed, many of these substitutions turned out to be improvements. Either they were more reliable at the same price, or they were of adequate quality at a lower price. In 1947, L. D. Miles, who was then working as a purchasing agent for GE, was assigned the task of developing a systematic approach to the investigation of the function-cost aspect of existing materials specifications. Miles and his associates not only accomplished this task successfully but subsequently pioneered the scientific procurement concept GE called *value analysis.*

According to Miles, VA is "an organized creative approach which has for its purpose the efficient identification of unnecessary cost."[1] The term *value engineering* is sometimes used to describe the application of value studies before designs reach the hardware stage. Typically, however, the two terms *value analysis* and *value engineering* are used synonymously. Here, the term *value analysis* is all inclusive.

Other pioneers include C. W. "Smokey" Doyle of General Dynamics Corporation, J. K. "Dusty" Fowlkes of GE, Carlos Fallon of RCA, and Thomas J. Snodgrass. Snodgrass deserves special attention as he is the former value engineer at GE who played a key role in "saving" the GE appliance line by using VA techniques. In addition, Snodgrass became a professor (now emeritus) at the University of Wisconsin engineering Extension Division in Madison where he developed the excellent VA training program for practitioners. Professor Snodgrass is one of the very few individuals to receive the coveted Larry D. Miles Award for distinguished contributions to the field of VA and engineering.

What Is Value Analysis?

Perhaps the most attractive feature of VA is that it works. The VA technique involves a rigorous analysis of cost vs. function. The function of the item is defined in its simplest terms, and determinations are made as to which design characteristics are really required. Alternative materials, designs, and procedures then are considered along with their respective costs. The alternative finally selected must meet the item's performance criteria at a lower cost, without compromising quality. When applied properly with proper emphasis, the benefits can be substantial.

Purchasing is one of the departments most concerned with the costs of purchased material. When properly motivated, the firm's suppliers can be a major source of cost-saving suggestions. It is, therefore, very desirable that purchasing personnel understand and employ VA.

The Purchasing Handbook defines VA as

The organized and systematic study of every element of cost in a part, material, or service to make certain it fulfills its function at the lowest possible cost; it employs techniques which identify the functions the user wants from a product or service; it establishes by comparison the appropriate cost for each function; then it causes the required knowledge, creativity, and initiative to be used to provide each function for that cost.[2]

VA is concerned with the elimination or modification of anything that contributes to the cost of an item or task but is not necessary for required performance, quality, maintainability, reliability, or interchangeability. VA is not intended to reduce the quality or performance characteristics of an item or task, and it is not pure cost reduction as performance is always considered. In fact, VA often leads to an increase in productivity.

Five major problems are commonly found in the area of VA:

1. Personnel in top management, Purchasing, Engineering, Operations, Marketing, and Finance do not understand what VA is and what it can do for the organization's profitability and productivity.
2. The two aspects of VA—in-house programs and supplier programs—do not receive equal attention.
3. The development and implementation of VA programs frequently is haphazard and, therefore, unsuccessful.
4. VA programs often turn out to be cost-reduction exercises at the expense of performance or at a high risk of function degradation.
5. VA programs are sometimes viewed as a one-shot project rather than an ongoing program.

Principles and Techniques

The fundamental approach of VA is that it takes nothing for granted and attacks everything about a product including the necessity for the item itself. The techniques employed are usually described in terms of a checklist. Although there are as many different checklists as there are writers, VA checklists usually can be simplified into five basic questions that require valid and complete answers:

1. *What is the item or service?* The answer to this question is usually quite readily determined from objective information on the item and from functional analysis.

2. *What does it cost?* Costs are often obtainable from recent in-house and procurement data. However, accurate costs are sometimes difficult to obtain, especially for a system or item in development. It may be necessary to estimate the cost, using the best available cost data and cost estimating techniques.

3. *What does it do?* This question can best be answered by identifying the function in its simplest terms. By defining the function, the value analyst learns

precisely which design characteristics are really required. In VA, an attempt is made to express the function in two words—a verb and a noun object. The use of two words avoids the possibility of combining functions or attempting to define more than one simple function at a time, for example, the item "conducts current," "supports weight," "saws wood," or "makes toast." When looking at what the item does, several questions should be asked:

Can it be eliminated?
Does the item contribute value?
To what uses is it put?
How reliable is the item?
How does it perform?
What features does the customer want?
How strong should the part be?
How should the part look?

It is also helpful to break function into three components. For example, a light bulb produces light, the basic function, but it also produces heat, a secondary function, and it creates a mood, the aesthetic function. We can now cost each of these functions and decide which ones to adjust and at what cost.

4. *What else would do the job?* This phase of the analysis perhaps is the most difficult. To a large degree, the comprehensiveness of the answer determines the success of the entire VA effort. No matter how thorough the search, other alternatives will always remain, some of which may be effective. Alternatives can be obtained by various means including "brainstorming" sessions. In any event, the search for alternatives must be exhaustive. A checklist similar to the following list of questions should be used:

Can a standard item be substituted?
Are all of the features required?
Does the item have excess capacity?
Can the item's weight be reduced?
Are specified tolerances and/or finishes necessary?
Is unnecessary machining performed on the item?
Is the item made on the proper equipment?
Can less expensive materials be used?
Is a commercial quality specified?
Can the item be made (bought) more cheaply?

Other creative problem solving techniques such as the fresh eye technique, Heuristic Ideation Technique (HIT), and Forced (FIT) relationships technique are very useful.[3] However, there is no substitute for the requirement to have creative people on the VA project team.

5. *What would the alternative cost?* Costs of alternatives are derived by cost analysis and study. At this stage, perfection in cost data for each alternative is not

necessary. Cost estimates within a range of ±5% are considered sufficient, and costs within a range of ±10% will help to determine whether particular alternatives are worthy of additional consideration.

One of the finest VA examples was the decision by Kodak to remove the tissue paper instructions wrapped around the film (which few people read) and then print very simple yet adequate instructions on the inside of the outer cardboard box container. Just imagine the total yearly savings of such an innovation. Further, the new instructions are easier to read.

Answers to many of these questions often lead to simplified and less costly production methods and to increased productivity. The three following examples demonstrate how GE's VA program increased productivity.[4]

- Stainless steel disks used in a dispensing machine were chamfered on one side. VA revealed that the chamfer did not add to the value of the machine. Its elimination significantly increased productivity.
- A hub had been made as a two-part riveted assembly. VA showed that a one-piece casting would be equally suitable. The assembly operation was eliminated, resulting in increased productivity.
- A stainless fitting had been purchased and then machined to provide the desired weld embossing. VA led to a different production procedure utilizing an automatic screw machine. Again, productivity increased significantly.

Recent VA savings in other industries include:

- A user of 60-pound weld wire saved 4 hours of downtime per 1,000 pounds of wire through the substitution of copperless welding wire for the previously used weld wire.
- A manufacturer of forgings was able to substitute cold forgings for the previous process that called for the machining of parts from bar stock. Productivity more than doubled.

The VA-VE Procedure

Over the years, VA specialists have developed the following sequence of steps for VA projects.[5]

- *The Preparation Phase.* The preparation phase includes selection of the appropriate team members, team organization, charter, meeting schedules, procedures, and the like.
- *Information Phase.* The information phase is the fact-finding phase and includes in-house and purchased material cost breakdown analysis. Most VA teams disassemble the product and lay out all the parts and pieces on a "study board" with detailed descriptions and cost of each part, a form of reverse engineering. Supplier input and involvement may be required during this phase.

Exhibit 11-1. Function analysis systems technique.

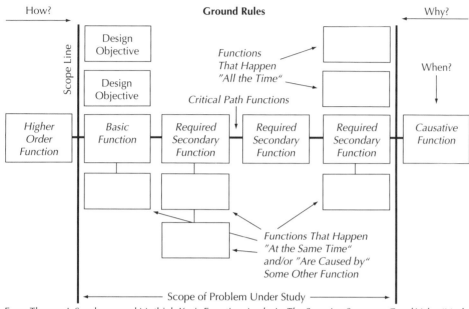

From Thomas J. Snodgrass and Muthiah Kasi, *Function Analysis: The Stepping Stones to Good Value* (Madison, Wisc.: Board of Regents, University of Wisconsin-Madison, 1986), p. 44. Used with permission.

• *Evaluation Phase.* What are the basic, secondary, and aesthetic functions? There may be just one basic function but we always try to describe a function with a verb and a noun, such as drills make holes, fasteners hold, and so on.

• *Creative Phase.* The next step is to match costs with functions and analyze where we can improve or at least get the same function at less cost. Brainstorming and other creative problem-solving techniques are used to find alternative manufacturing methods, substitute materials, change from custom to standardized parts, standarde sizes to reduce the number of variations, look for opportunities to use common parts, modularize, use better and less costly packaging, improve transportation, use fewer forms, lower unnecessarily high specifications, replace hand labor with automation, stamp vs. machine, and so on. When appropriate, involve suppliers and customers during this phase. Do not forget the final customer has the final say.

Snodgrass and Kasi developed technical FAST diagramming as depicted in Exhibit 11-1 to help organize all the facets of this function-cost relationship.[6] This procedure is extremely useful as it gives structure and direction for the investigative steps.

• *Selection and Presentation Phase.* In this phase, we list all the alternatives with their effects in costs and functions. Recommendations are listed in order of choice and presented to the management group that has authority to change manufacturing methods, materials, and specifications. This is the selling part of the VA activity and includes written reports and oral summaries with charts, transparencies, mockups, models, samples, and so on. Remember, most of us resist change so the burden of proof is on those advocating anything new.

    ♦ *Implementation Phase.* The implementation phase involves preparation of a time line action chart of who does what, where, when, and how. It is imperative to have precise change dates to force action.

    ♦ *Follow-up and Audit Phase.* Progress checking is mandatory with corrective action as necessary. Finally, we must audit or document the savings to prevent exaggerations and to calculate the economic worth of the project.

The Two Faces of Value Analysis

VA may be conducted either as an in-house activity, as a supplier program, or as both. As might be expected, the greatest benefits result when the two activities are pursued simultaneously by a buyer and seller who communicate with each other on joint projects.

In-House Activity

Many savings result through the identification of items that are promising candidates for VA. The selection of candidate items should be based on maximizing returns on VA investment (returns of 20 to 1 are common). Generally, potential savings are greatest on those components representing the largest annual outlay. Complexity also provides a clue. Usually the more complex an item, the greater the potential for improved value. An item that was developed in an accelerated time frame frequently will be overdesigned and may be a good candidate for VA study. Nonstandard industrial items have more potential for savings than do standard ones. Items with high scrap or rework costs and those requiring many operations also are good candidates for the VA program. Once a candidate has been identified, the VA procedures should be applied with the objective of improving marketability, reducing cost, or both.

    Three approaches to in-house VA programs are common:

1. Dedicated value analysts assigned to the purchasing office
2. The committee approach
3. The integrated approach

The employment of dedicated value analysts is common in large manufacturing firms. The ideal value analyst has a background in design engineering, industrial engineering, and purchasing. He or she possesses knowledge of basic physics, strength of materials, and manufacturing processes and is familiar with the firm's product lines, suppliers, and principal customers. Of even greater importance, a good value analyst possesses an open, inquisitive mind and develops close relations with top management. Thus, a good value analyst has considerable informal authority and is able to overcome resistance to his or her proposals. The most obvious disadvantage of this approach is its cost. Such experienced personnel are not inexpensive, but savings of 5 to 20 times their salary expenses are common.

The American Society of Value Engineers (SAVE) located in Northbrook, Illinois, was founded in 1959 under the leadership of Larry Miles. SAVE has a certification program called Certified Value Specialist (CVS) and we recommend key individuals involved with VA join SAVE and earn their CVS designation.

The committee approach calls for the assignment of experienced personnel from Engineering, Production, Purchasing, Quality Assurance, Industrial Engineering, and Marketing. Each operating participant develops a better awareness of the techniques and potential contribution of VA. Ideally, this carries over to the individual's day-to-day activities. The VA committee reviews proposals submitted by employees under a VA or cost reduction program. Promising proposals are reviewed by a working subcommittee that asks the questions listed under Principles and Techniques. The committee coordinates implementation of recommendations based on its studies. The committee approach uses teamwork to overcome resistance to change. However, it has the two inherent weaknesses of most committees: an inability to gain support and cooperation and conflicting demands on committee members' time.

The integrated approach requires the exposure of Operation Engineering, Purchasing, and other selected personnel to VA training *on a repetitive basis.* The objective of this training program is to develop an awareness of the importance of value analysis, an understanding of how to conduct a VA study, and a dedication to the use of VA. This approach reduces the resistance to changes in product design and specifications that frequently is encountered. The training program does, however, require time and money.[7]

Supplier Program

Suppliers are a gold mine of ideas for the VA program. Usually a supplier knows more about products and their capabilities than does the customer. Once an item is being produced, it is possible that suppliers of the required components will be able to suggest significant savings. Frequently, they are aware of suitable lower-cost substitute items than those being purchased. A supplier's assistance may be obtained in two ways: informally and contractually.

With the informal approach, the purchasing firm may include a supplier checklist with requests for quotations and/or with purchase orders. Exhibit 11-2 contains such a checklist. The firm may conduct value engineering clinics or post VA project candidates in an effort to obtain VA suggestions. If a supplier submits a suggestion that is implemented, he or she usually is rewarded with additional business.

A formal supplier VA program calls for the inclusion of a VA provision in the purchase order or subcontract. In this VA provision, the purchasing firm agrees to share in the savings resulting from an implemented proposal. One major purchaser includes such a clause in all purchase orders of over $100,000. This purchaser agrees to share net savings resulting from implemented proposals on a 50/50 basis. It also agrees to share savings on future buys for a period not to extend beyond three years, but at a reduced rate. Many firms have had good

Exhibit 11-2.   Supplier checklist for value analysis study.

Part name and number _____

Estimated annual usage _____

Buyer _____

Questions	Yes	No	Recommendations

Do you understand the part function?

Could costs be reduced by relaxing
    requirements:

☐ Tolerances?

☐ Finishes?

☐ Testing?

☐ By how much?

Could costs be reduced through
    changes in?

☐ Material?

☐ Ordering quantities?

☐ The use of castings,
    stampings, etc?

☐ By how much?

Could you suggest other changes
    that would:

☐ Reduce weight?

☐ Simplify the part?

☐ Reduce overall cost?

Do you feel that any of the
    specifications are too stringent? Why?

How can we help alleviate your
    greatest element of cost in
    supplying this part?

Do you have a standard item that
    could be substituted for this part?

Other suggestions? _____
_____

Supplier _____ Date _____

Address _____

Signature _____ Title _____

Please add additional comments

success with informal programs. But more positive motivation in the form of a sharing of the savings results in wider and more active participation by suppliers and even greater savings. Many buyers require their suppliers to have a VA program. This sourcing criteria promotes high-payoff joint buyer-seller VA efforts.

The Keys to Successful Implementation

If the principles of an IPS have already been implemented, the establishment of a VA program will meet little resistance. The cooperative attitude will carry over to this very logical approach to improving profits and productivity. If, on the other hand, purchasing is moving from a reactive to a proactive profit-making status, care and effort must go into the development and implementation of a VA program.

The key prerequisite to a successful VA program is a cooperative attitude on the part of all involved departments and their personnel, especially those in Design Engineering. Those responsible for developing, implementing, and managing the VA program must recognize people's inherent tendency to identify with that which they create or initiate. Care must be taken to ensure that designers realize that they are not being second-guessed. Those participating in the VA program should have the benefit of different points of view, experience, and knowledge. The initial design serves as an essential first step. Its subsequent review and possible revision must be seen as a necessary and normal process of product development.

Purchasing is the logical department to initiate, promote, and sponsor the VA program for these reasons:

- Every requirement and specification for material passes through purchasing. Accordingly, Purchasing is the logical organization to review and identify candidates for VA.
- Purchasing personnel have the responsibility of obtaining maximum value of all materials to be purchased. They also have the responsibility of challenging any questionable requirement.
- Purchasing personnel have many of the skills and perform many of the tasks required in a formal VA program.
- Through daily exposure to sales representatives and their product offerings and literature for new products, purchasing personnel are in an excellent position to identify suitable substitutes.
- Purchasing personnel can be more objective than the designer who may take great pride in the design.
- Under a VA program, purchasing serves as a solicitor and a conduit for the flow of suggestions from suppliers.

A VA program will be easier to develop and implement and will be more successful if it is seen by Purchasing and Design Engineering as a collaborative effort. (Remember what happened to the purchasing manager in the case history at the beginning of the chapter?) The managers of these two activities have the same objectives: the survival and profitability of the organization.

Assuming that a cooperative atmosphere exists, several approaches to initiating the program are possible.

- The purchasing manager and the chief engineer together attend a VA seminar.
- The purchasing manager provides the chief engineer relevant and succinct literature on the subject.
- A buyer who has especially good relations with a design engineer plants the seed so that the idea for a VA program emerges in engineering.
- The purchasing manager discusses several recent *friendly* examples of informal VA (involving purchasing and engineering) and suggests that the program be formalized.

When relations with engineering are somewhat more formal, purchasing has two logical allies in its efforts to develop and implement a VA program: Finance and Marketing. The CFO is acutely concerned with anything that will make the firm more profitable. The marketing manager is equally concerned with anything that will result in goods of a higher quality at the same cost or goods of the same quality at lower cost. If resistance from Design Engineering is experienced, Purchasing should obtain the cooperation and support of these two departments in an effort to enlist Engineering's cooperation.

A VA program can be implemented as a result of a directive from top management, but such an approach frequently encounters informal resistance from some of those involved. This resistance severely limits the success and profit contribution of the program.

Frequently, spectacular success will be experienced during the first year or two of the VA program's life. But after these initial successes, enthusiasm may begin to wane. Since significant savings still are possible and likely, it is important that action be taken to foster a positive attitude toward VA. Possible actions include:

- If dedicated value analysts are employed, management should avoid the temptation to assign non-VA work to VA personnel.
- If the VA committee approach is employed, the committee should meet on a periodic basis and ensure that a sufficient number of projects are undertaken. (Value analysts, by their nature, will take similar action.)
- The company newspaper, bulletin boards, purchasing newsletter, and other media should report on successful projects.
- Lobby displays and contractual VA clauses should be used to encourage supplier participation.
- VA workshops should be conducted to bring engineering designers, purchasing personnel, and suppliers together.

Summary

VA and value engineering concepts have found widespread application and have resulted in great savings since their inception in the 1940s. VA does not sacrifice quality or performance. Rather, it is a systematic approach to ensuring that every part fulfills its function at the lowest possible cost. VA requires answers to the five following questions:

 * What is the item or service?
 * What does it cost?
 * What does it do?
 * What else would do the job?
 * What would be the alternative cost?

The VA procedure includes the following phases: preparation, information, evaluation, creative, selection and presentation, implementation and follow-up, and audit. Technical FAST diagrams help reveal possible areas to improve function while lowering cost.

VA should be conducted under both in-house and supplier programs. Three in-house approaches are the employment of dedicated value analysts, the committee approach, and the integration approach, which calls for frequent VA training.

Purchasing is the logical department to initiate, promote, and sponsor the VA program. The VA program is easier to develop and implement and is more successful when it is a collaborative effort. Ideally, a cooperative attitude should exist on the part of all those involved in the VA effort.

Under the supplier program, suppliers are requested to submit VA proposals with their bids and under the resulting POs. Suppliers also are invited to participate in VA clinics. VA provisions calling for a sharing of net savings resulting from adoption of VA proposals should be included in major POs and contracts.

We now turn our attention to the issue of quality, the purchasing criterion that has replaced price in our efforts to obtain the lowest cost of ownership.

Notes

1. Lawrence D. Miles, *Techniques of Value Analysis and Value Engineering*, 2nd ed. (New York: McGraw-Hill, 1972). Still the best book on the subject.
2. Harold E. Fearon, Donald W. Dobler, and Kenneth H. Killen, eds., *The Purchasing Handbook*, 5th ed. (New York: McGraw-Hill, 1993), p. 438–439. Reproduced with permission.
3. Alvin J. Williams, Steve Lacy, and William C. Smith, "Purchasing's Role in Value Analysis: Lessons From Creative Problem Solving," *The International Journal of Purchasing and Materials Management* (Spring, 1992), pp. 40–41.
4. Stewart F. Heinritz, Paul V. Farrell, Larry C. Giunipero, and Michael G. Kolchin, *Purchasing: Principles and Applications*, 8th ed. (Englewood Cliffs, N.J.: Prentice-Hall, 1991), p. 357.
5. Richard L. Pinkerton, "Value Analysis Revisited," *Midwest Purchasing* (February 1983).
6. Thomas J. Snodgrass and Muthiah Kasi, *Function Analysis: The Stepping Stones to Good Value* (Madison, Wisconsin: The Board of Regents, University of Wisconsin System, 1986). This fine manual is available from the University of Wisconsin extension book-

store, 432 North Lake St., Madison, Wisc. 53706. This same source also sells *Excerpts from Techniques of Value Analysis and Engineering,* 2nd. ed., by Lawrence D. Miles (New York: McGraw-Hill, 1972). The best text ever written on the subject.

7. The best VA training is available at the College of Engineering, University of Wisconsin-Madison, Department of Engineering Professional Development, 432 N. Lake St., Madison, Wisc. 53706. This program includes short courses, videotapes, and seminars for the working professional, and one need not be an engineer. Contact Prof. William W. Wuerger for details at (608) 265-2001.

12

Quality Assurance Overview

Jack Jones, the director of Materials at Ajax Manufacturing Company, is worried and frustrated. He has just returned from an ISO 9000 team meeting and is alarmed over the arguments he heard regarding the quality of incoming materials. No one seems to have the same definition of quality, and they seem unclear as to how ISO 9000 procedures would interface with the recent supplier certification program his purchasing manager developed. The representatives from Engineering, Manufacturing, Purchasing, Quality Planning, and Marketing all have different versions of the quality problem and a variety of definitions for the many quality terms including SPC, DOE, QFD, TQM, CI, and so on.

In addition, the ISO 9000 team seems to be taking over the company and the selection of suppliers, or at least the survey part of source selection. A few suppliers reported to the purchasing manager they were receiving mixed signals from various managers, were not sure in what direction Ajax was moving, and communication was becoming difficult. Jack decides to call his old professor of logistics at California State University, Fresno, prior to meeting with the materials group, which includes Purchasing, Production and Inventory Control, Traffic, and Stores. Jack hopes his former mentor can give him an overview of modern quality terms, methods, and how they fit with the ISO 9000 movement.

Defining Quality

The first agenda item for the old professor would be to arrive at a good definition of quality. Most experts agree that "quality" from the producer's point of view simply means conformance to required specifications that define specific properties of material, parts, assemblies, and, finally, the stated performance of the final item. The problem is we often insert the adjectives "high" or "low" before the noun "quality" without regard to what level of quality is required. We do not always need the "best" part or machine. In fact, we can overspecify and pay too much for unnecessarily high quality.

The desired level of quality starts with the final customer and works backward through the producer or provider of the good or service who defines the requirements for all internal and external operations necessary to deliver this economic value. The term *economic value* is critical because it means what the customer is willing to pay for a particular level of quality.

One of the authors of this book drives a Saturn SL1, which, for him, is the "best buy." That is, it is the highest level of overall quality he can get at a price he is willing to pay. The other author drives a luxury auto as he is willing to pay twice the price of the Saturn for *what he believes* is twice the quality. In other words, both authors have different benchmarks. High quality should mean the right quality for the intended use, criteria, and price.

One of the rather subtle problems with the entire concept of benchmarking is it can lead people into overbuying and overorganizing. Although consumers often use the term *excellence* and quote the relative rankings of products on some kind of scale, the term is meaningless to the producer. Juran, like Deming, a pioneer in quality and consultant to the Japanese, said it all when he wrote that quality is "fitness for use."[1]

David Garvin of the Harvard Business School describes the eight dimensions of quality as:

1. Performance: such as speed, accuracy, and other functions.
2. Features: the extras beyond the basic function or options that help performance.
3. Reliability: mean time between failure (MTBF).
4. Conformance: are desired quality standards satisfied?
5. Durability: how long will it last?
6. Serviceability: the cost, frequency, and ease of maintenance.
7. Aesthetics: styling, appearance.
8. Perceived quality: what the individual thinks the quality level is[2]

This list is an excellent basis for a checklist for supplier survey teams, negotiation, and contract language. It helps to clarify the discussions of quality and provides a common meaning to terms often used loosely and without serious understanding. One can immediately see the value of determining what is needed vs. what is the best. If you plan to turn in your automobile every year, then you do not need a durable car or an extended warranty. The same analogy can be used when we purchase materials: Buy what you and your customers need; that's what is best in your environment.

Total Quality Management

The father of TQM is the late Dr. W. Edwards Deming. His theories were rejected by most of the major U.S. corporations. In 1950 Dr. Deming went to Japan on the invitation of the Union of Japanese Scientists and Engineers (JUSE) to help the Japanese overcome their reputation for inferior quality goods.[3] The rest is history. His 14 points are the foundation of TQM. The now famous 14 points are:

1. Create consistency of purpose toward improvement of product and service with a plan to become competitive, stay in business, and provide jobs.
2. Adopt the new philosophy. We are in a new economic age. We can no longer live with commonly accepted levels of delays, mistakes, defective materials, and defective workmanship.
3. Cease dependence on mass inspection. Require, instead, statistical evidence (statistical process control) that quality is built in to eliminate the need for inspection on a mass basis.
4. End the practice of awarding business on the basis of price tag. Instead, depend on meaningful measures of quality, along with price. Move toward a single supplier for any one item, on a long-term relationship of loyalty and trust.
5. Improve constantly and forever the system of production and service to improve quality and productivity, and thus constantly decrease costs.
6. Institute modern training methods and aids at the job level.
7. Supervise never-ending improvement.
8. Drive out fear, so that everyone can voice their opinions and report problems and thereby work effectively for the company.
9. Break down organizational barriers. Everyone must work as a team to foresee and solve problems (what is good for the company vs. the department).
10. Replace numerical goals, posters, and slogans with never-ending improvement.
11. Replace management by numbers with never-ending improvement. Concentrate on quality measures, not piece work and other such quotas.
12. Remove barriers that rob employees of their pride of workmanship. Involve workers at all levels on how to achieve high quality.
13. Educate and retrain everyone in quality techniques including statistical training.
14. Create a structure that will push the prior 13 points every day.[4]

These 14 points are based on a philosophy that places quality assurance in the hands of all workers with the quality department being used as a resource and training unit. Historically, U.S. quality control departments stressed sampling plans and inspection techniques to achieve certain average outgoing quality levels (AOQLs). The objective was to discover what is the statistical probability of x percentage of defects either entering the production system in the form of purchased materials and parts or going out the door to customers. The Deming philosophy is to prevent any defects by training workers in simple statistical control techniques to detect a process going out of control and by empowering them to stop the process *before* defects are made. If buyer production and the supplier production workers could stop the lines *prior to* providing defects, there wouldn't be any in the entire supply chain.

Anyone who worked in factories following World War II to almost 1985 knew the American management philosophy of volume at all costs. Most factory production managers were paid a bonus for high production and were never penalized for defects. In fact, defects were acceptable until American consumers discovered they could buy defect-free Japanese products. It seems so logical to eliminate defects instead of finding them after the fact. It is hard to believe it took American senior management so long to measure the costs of rework and lost market share. Arrogance, terrible worker relations, a focus on price vs. cost, bonus systems based on volume, and other similar factors eventually produced such a loss in market share that major stockholders demanded action from top management who were out of touch with both the workers and the marketplace. Why was top management out of touch with reality? One reason is a reward system based on numbers themselves rather than where the numbers came from or how they were achieved.

Mapping TQM

Organizations soon discovered they had to take final customer requirements, or quality dimensions as Garvin describes the components of quality, and track the various operations in the producing organization that produced these components of quality. The mapping starts with the customer needs as articulated by the marketing department using such well-known techniques as marketing research, sales analysis, service records, and customer satisfaction surveys and then matches these needs to the design and production functions necessary to achieve them. One such popular technique is the House of Quality (HOQ), which uses a matrix to rate a firm's product/service on desired attributes and perceptions to those of competition.[5] This matrix mapping process relates these needs to the various processes and design factors necessary to achieve them. It also identifies gaps between desired requirements and current status, which reveals a need for corrective action. Obviously, Purchasing must monitor the performance of suppliers in this mapping process.

Quality Function Deployment

Quality function deployment (QFD) links all the operations together starting with customer input from surveys, focus groups, or any other source and traces the flow of quality input throughout the organization. QFD identifies who is responsible for what and in what sequence. For example, QFD may reveal that poor internal document control is a major reason why suppliers are occasionally using the wrong blueprint, which in turn produces defects and rework. QFD started in Mitsubishi's Kobe shipyard in 1972, followed by Toyota and Ford Motor Company as a leader in the United States.[6] HOQ and quality circles/teams all help the QFD process. When the entire organization is practicing TQM, the environment is sometimes called *companywide total quality control* or CWTQC.

Continuous Improvement

It is unfortunate that we need a separate section to discuss continuous improvement (CI), but we do because some firms, consultants, and instructors think it is something new or different from TQM. If we reread Deming's 14 points and other such works, we note that TQM means that working on quality improvement is never ending and it must be organized as an ongoing system. The only value of using this redundant term is to remind U.S. management that TQM must be a permanent way of life and not just this year's project. TQM is a new way of doing business, and management must develop the habit of always improving quality, a habit purchasing must instill in its suppliers. TQM was *not* last year's project, it's forever.

The Major Technical Quality Tools

Procurement and materials executives must learn the basic quality tools that are available and the fundamental mechanics of how they work in order to identify which suppliers are using them . It is not necessary to become a statistical quality engineer but it is necessary to know when to send for one and to be able to carry on a reasonable conversation when discussing these techniques.

Statistical Process Control

Statistical process control (SPC) is the granddaddy of quality control. It measures process variation. Its basis is sampling statistics based on normal curve assumptions. Its use goes back to the period 1924–1929 when it was developed by Walter A. Shewhart and his colleagues at Bell Labs. One of the authors worked as an automatic screw machine operator at Hy-Level Screw Machine Company in Cleveland, Ohio (a leading firm in its field and getting bigger and better). The author had to sample the pieces, use a micrometer to measure dimensions, and then plot them on a metal plate above the machine, a type of $\bar{x}$ chart or average of the sample. The years were 1948–1950 and the author was working his way through high school. But he had the authority to stop the machine before the pieces went beyond control limits. SPC is not new; it has just been rediscovered. Appendix H contains a thorough description of SPC mechanics.

If the process is going out of control, we must stop the machine or operation and isolate the assignable causes such as tool wear, improper setup, defective material, power surges, excessive temperature, incorrect pressure, worker error, or other causes. Once we eliminate assignable or "abnormal" causes of variation, we are left with the natural or normal variation we expect from any continuous running operation. Deming always maintained that the systems created by management caused 85% of the quality problems with just 15% caused by worker error. One of the main reasons we *now* use workers at the line level to diagnose quality problems is that they know the causes, whether poor design, defective incoming materials, or incorrect assembly systems.

Deming and his assistants, along with other experts such as Juran, taught managers and trainers how to teach SPC techniques to line workers. The quality control department (or quality assurance department as it is often called) sets up the initial SPC system, which includes decisions as to how many observations per sample (usually three to five), how many samples to take, time between samples, and the number of standard deviations to use. The common goal today is to reduce defects to either zero or parts-per-million (ppm) levels.

The Process Capability Index

It is important to remember that the upper and lower *control limits* in SPC charts are what the machine is capable of producing, not the upper and lower tolerance limits of parts or material. The ratio of design tolerance to the natural capability range of the machine or process is called capability index, which should be at least 1. In our Appendix H illustration, the process capability index or PCI is:

$$PCI = \frac{\text{Absolute design tolerance range}}{\text{Natural capability range of the machine or process}}$$

$$\text{Golf Ball PCI} = \frac{1.562'' - 1.437''}{1.535'' - 1.465''} = \frac{.125''}{.07''} = 1.79$$

Our PCI of 1.79 exceeds the minimum goal of 1.00, which means the capability range of the machine just matches the design tolerance. At a PCI of 1.79 we are almost double the minimum goal and much less likely to produce rejects. Fernandez and others use more sophisticated PCI formulas using six sigma (six standard deviations) and a stronger test incorporating range data to test the assumption that our $\bar{x}$ and $\bar{R}$ charts are a normal distribution.[7] Six sigma deviations allow for a possible shift in the normal curve $\bar{x}$ (or mean) of $\pm$ 1.5 sigmas, which will reduce the number of defects to just about zero.

Precontrol Charting

To overcome the problem of sample error and the possibility of the failure of SPC to identify a process out of control, the concept of precontrol was developed by Frank Satterthwaite and the consulting company of Rath and Strong.[8] Precontrol establishes two precontrol lines in the middle half of the specification width by dividing the specification width by four, that is, the boundaries of the middle half become the precontrol lines. This area is called the green zone and if all five consecutive units from a process are in the green zone, assume the process is in control. Once production starts, check two consecutive units from the process periodically.[9] It is beyond the scope of this chapter to go into any more detail but this process substantially reduces the risk of accepting bad product and rejecting good product. Eventually precontrol will probably replace SPC.

As Phil Crosby, another quality pioneer, wrote in *Quality Is Free*, zero defects should be the goal of every manufacturer and supplier as the long-term savings of reduced returns, rework, and field failure more than offset the additional cost of quality assurance programs.[10] The problem has always been that management has not installed accurate accounting systems to track the costs of poor quality since nobody is rewarded for such statistics. In fact, some managers hide returns and rework for fear of low performance ratings.

Attribute Process Control

The illustration in Appendix H is based on actual dimensional measurements of golf balls being produced. What about attribute process control that uses $\bar{p}$-charts

Exhibit 12-1. $\bar{p}$ Chart for attribute process control.

Upper Control Limit	$\bar{p}+3\sqrt{\dfrac{\bar{p}\,(1-\bar{p})}{n}}$
99.73% $\bar{p}$	
	$\bar{p}-3\sqrt{\dfrac{\bar{p}\,(1-\bar{p})}{n}}$
Lower Control Limit	

Source: Joseph R. Biggs, "3.26 Statistical Process Control (SPC)," *Guide to Purchasing* (Tempe, Ariz., The National Association of Purchasing Management, 1989), p. 10. Reproduced with permission.

or just the percent of good vs. bad parts? The familiar go/no-go gauge is a typical example and is a device that simply tells the observer that the part or piece conforms or does not conform to tolerances. But it does not measure dimensions.

Exhibit 12–1 gives a simple explanation of attribute process control that uses the statistics of binomial distribution in relation to normal distribution.

Remember, as in $\bar{x}$ and $\bar{R}$ charts, the control limits must be based on actual experience with the particular operation producing the parts.

Some machine tools and engineered systems have SPC and PCI built into the apparatus. These tools and systems monitor themselves and shut down when going out of control. Many also have built-in $\bar{x}$ and $\bar{R}$ charts that can be observed on monitors, tapes, or computer disks.

The Investigative Tools of Quality Assurance

SPC and CPI analysis only identifies when we have or are going to have a quality problem, that is, the process is either going out of control or is out of control.

What happens when normal failure analysis such as checking for broken tools, leaking pumps, reduced speed, or defective incoming material does not correct the problem? We can use a number of investigative techniques or tools, including design of experiments (DOE); Pareto analysis; cause-and-effect diagrams (often called *fishbone diagrams*, and CEDAC: cause-and-effect diagrams, with the addition of cards); plan, do, check, act (PDCA); histograms; check sheets or tally sheets; and even brainstorming.

Design of Experiments

Design of experiments (DOE) is by far the most sophisticated analysis method to uncover the cause of quality problems or perhaps we should say "failure." However, DOE is also one of the least understood concepts in the United States and, except for Japan, perhaps around the world. It is not uncommon for statistical quality control engineers to have no or very little knowledge of the technique. Keki R. Bhote, former senior corporate consultant on quality and productivity improvement at Motorola, is the exception. For this reason, Appendix I is a review of Bhote's classic and unique book, *World Class Quality: Using Design Experiments to Make It Happen.*

Pareto Analysis

Pareto analysis is derived from the work of Italian economist Vilfredo Federico Pareto who gave us the 80/20 rule, which states that in most distributions, 80% of a number result (sales, profits, errors, and so forth) is caused by 20% of the customers or other causes. In other words, look for the few major causes of quality problems such as poor prints, too many engineering changes, bad tooling, poor adjustments, and so on. J. M. Juran is usually credited with the original application of the Pareto rule to the field of industrial quality control.[11]

Juran's application of Pareto includes using flow diagrams that include all the activities or tasks of an operation or process under study. Each activity is written on an index card and each member of the analysis team ranks each activity in order of importance. These rankings are then entered on a spreadsheet and by consensus; the team selects the "vital few" to investigate. The team may come back to the other activities but they start with the most likely causes to save valuable time. This technique is much like medical diagnostic work or how a good automobile mechanic starts the search process; both use a test for the most likely problem and then keep going until a solution is found.

We often associate the term *root cause* with Pareto analysis but all investigative techniques have this same objective, which is to keep searching for the primary or few interrelated causes. Symptoms give us clues as to what might be the real problem. Too many companies treat symptoms rather than correcting the problem.

Cause-and-Effect (or Fishbone) Diagrams

Although many quality experts doubt the real value of fishbone charts, they are so popular we must include them in our tool bag. They were developed by Dr.

Exhibit 12-2. Example of fishbone diagram.

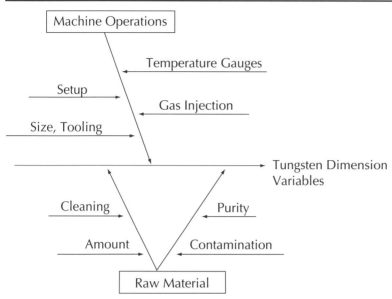

Note: Not a technically correct example. But it illustrates that temperature changes, etc. can change a dimension of tungsten variables.

Kaoru Ishikawa, a distinguished Japanese statistical engineer.[12] These diagrams are often called Ishikawa diagrams and are extremely popular with plant workers in Japan who are members of problem-solving teams. Exhibit 12–2 illustrates the basic principle of determining the step-by-step process of making something and identifying what could cause variation in that part or material. Brainstorming is often used, but engineering sequence directions, shop orders, and bills of materials are necessary to draw the diagram to guide the individuals through the analysis of what could cause variation. It is a much simpler yet much weaker technique than DOE. The DOE exponents say their techniques are faster and more accurate because fishbone diagrams require too much subjective judgment and cannot examine interaction effects among multiple causes of variation.

Fishbone charts do facilitate some experimentation as single cause factors can be varied and the result measured. The addition of data cards for worker input improves the technique into what is known as CEDAC, or cause and effect diagram with the addition of cards.[13] The cards allow the workers to instantly capture raw data and/or phenomena. CEDAC also allows workers to change the branches of the diagram.

Plan, Do, Check, Act

Plan, do, check, act (PDCA) was first introduced in Japan by Deming in 1950 during an eight-day seminar sponsored by the JUSE.[14] It involves the following six sequential steps in what the Japanese call a *control circle:*

1. Determine goals and targets—planning
2. Determine methods of reaching goals (standardizing)—planning
3. Engage in education and training—doing
4. Implement work—doing
5. Check the effects of implementation—checking
6. Take appropriate action—action

These steps are repeated over and over to achieve continuous improvement. The technique, which involves the entire company and all functions, was and still is the heart of TQM. It includes using all the methods and techniques discussed in this chapter. PDCA was probably the initial effort by Deming in formulating his famous 14 points.

The Poka-Yoke *System*

These Japanese words mean "mistake proofing" is a problem-prevention system devised by Shigeo Shingo, the brilliant Japanese industrial engineer at Toyota.[15] The goal of *poka-yoke* is zero defects. It accomplishes this by instantaneous feedback of human, mechanical, and electronic systems using 100% early warning inspection with sensors, motion detectors, and other such devices. As we have warned, it is possible for a process or machine to suddenly go out of control. SPC would not catch this situation until the next sample, thereby producing a number of defects. SPC is also subject to sampling error and other statistical limitations including the human judgment error of misreading the trend plots, that is, letting the process get too close to control limits. Unless one takes more and more observations in more and more samples, the sample error can be fairly significant, say 5% and individual piece measurements can be outside the control limits. *Poka-yoke* is a system to eliminate all these risks and is an ultimate method for CI.

Histograms, Frequency Distributions, and Other Static Charting Techniques

Histograms are bar charts depicting the frequency of occurrence of certain events. Scatter diagrams, tally sheets, and other such graphic devices are useful to communicate past statistics of data such as the number of defects in a production run, but none of these "pictures" identify what causes changes over time nor do they give us any clues as to assignable or unassigned causes of variation.

SPC charts are an important improvement over these static measures. They relate time and variance and they warn us when a process is going beyond the normal or unassigned variation. Unassigned variations are those normal fluctuations in a process well within our control limits and design tolerances, and they do not require corrective action. The static charts help the analyst identify a problem. But aside from stimulating the thought process, they are not useful for root cause explanation.

It should now be apparent that DOE and *poka-yoke* are the most powerful of the investigative tools. We will now discuss ISO 9000, what it is and what it is *not*, and how Purchasing interacts with this worldwide quality assurance program.

The International Standards Organization and the 9000 Certification Program

The International Standards Organization (ISO), located in Geneva, Switzerland, includes the national standards organizations of 91 countries including the American National Standards Institute (ANSI) in New York City.[16] Do not confuse ANSI with the National Institute of Standards and Technology (NIST) in the U.S. Department of Commerce, which compiles commercial standards and is located in Gaithersburg, Maryland (formerly called the National Bureau of Standards). ANSI is a federation of over 100 organizations, trade associations, and technical societies. ANSI reviews proposed standards, which, if approved, become a U.S. standard. The United States supports European efforts at adopting the 9000 certification program, ISO 9000. More than 30,000 European companies were ISO certified by mid 1992 compared to about 300 U.S. companies. There is a frantic movement to ISO certification now occurring in the United States.[17] The European Union organization has been the big promoter of ISO 9000 in its member states where it is designated EN 29000.[18]

In 1987, ISO published the 9000 series and, although the standards are the same the world over and accepted by all members, member countries often assign a different designator such as BS 5750 in the United Kingdom and ANSI/ASQC Q90–1987 series in the United States. The standards are revised periodically so an organization must have the latest version. The American Society for Quality Control (ASQC) in Milwaukee, Wisconsin, is the administrator for ANSI on quality and has formed an affiliate, the Registrar Accreditation Board (RAB), to screen and authorize individuals and organizations called registrars who conduct ISO 9000 "audits" and grant certification to those who pass. Write ANSI for the complete set of ISO 9000 materials.

The five major ISO 9000 standards are:

1. ISO 9000: The overview and directions; ISO 8402 has definitions, vocabulary.
2. ISO 9001: A quality assurance model for research and design, production, installation, and servicing of products and services. It consists of 20 major areas including purchasing, document control, design control, process control, statistical techniques, and so on. The purchasing section deals with assessment of subcontractors, purchasing data, and verification of purchased product.
3. ISO 9002: A quality assurance model for conformance in production and installation. It does *not* cover R&D or servicing.
4. ISO 9003: A quality system model for conformance in final test, inspection standards, and training.

5. ISO 9004 *Part One:* Provides guidance in the establishment of a quality system.

Part Two: Provides guidance for services organization including policy, objectives, systems management, human resources, and documentation. This part includes reference to recommend input from customers via marketing research.

Section 4.6 in ISO 9001 defines the responsibilities of purchasing and Section 9.0 of ISO 9004 has additional guidance for procurement. The standard promotes most of the concepts we have developed in this book such as defined sourcing surveys and criteria, cross-functional teams with supplier involvement, partnerships, and other indicators of a close buyer-seller relationship.

ISO 9000 is not a set of product standards for any industry nor does it define quality. It is a set of defined procedures to document what an organization states as its quality standard and product-service specifications. It also provides methods and procedures to monitor an organization's system, how mistakes are corrected, and how changes can be made. It facilitates implementation of TQM by providing guidelines on how to organize and document the policies necessary to consistently deliver the quality promised to customers.

ISO 9000 uses almost all the techniques and philosophies covered in this chapter and tells you how to write a TQM manual. Although the standards do not require a manual, most firms have discovered that one is necessary to achieve compliance. It accomplishes this mission by using appointed "assessors" who are companies or organizations (not individuals) employed by the registrars. The assessors serve as representatives of the registrars and conduct an independent audit of the firm's quality system, after the firm has prepared and implemented the required procedures prescribed by a particular standard—one or all of them. If the firm passes, it is certified and registered by a registrar certified to issue ISO 9000 certification. The registration period is from two to three years with subsequent audits required for recertification. The assessor, who conducts the audit, should be from another firm than the registrar to avoid a conflict of interest.[19]

If a firm has a loose quality control system, the preparation for certification will take about two years after the first step, which establishes an ISO 9000 steering committee or council to study ISO 9000 materials. The next major step is selection of the registrar (certification) agent who conducts an initial assessment and provides an assessor. The cost of the project will vary from $20,000 to as high as $250,000 depending on complexity of the company, size, status at the start, amount of required training, amount of help needed from the assessor-registrar and the like. Most organizations discovered they have had to hire an ISO 9000 consultant to help them through this process.

Is ISO 9000 certification and registration worth the effort? We think it is mandatory as more and more customers require their suppliers to be certified. The European Union countries are requiring certification and the movement is growing in the United States. The preparation also stimulates the installation of TQM. The savings from better quality should more than offset the costs. Firms must be careful not to allow their ISO 9000 steering groups, committees, and leaders to overapplying ISO standards or to engage in power trips. Not all company operating procedures must go through an ISO 9000 steering committee. Avoid becoming "ISO 9000 paranoid," use common sense, and do not create a huge paper or human bureaucracy that can delay necessary management action while waiting for the ISO 9000 committee to act.

One criticism of ISO 9000 is that it may promote a status quo in quality as it does not require significant customer input and it ignores competition. A firm could be ISO 9000 certified and wind up with zero customers as competition develops better products. ISO 9000 certification merely means you have a documented quality control system complete with procedures and this system is periodically audited. But, what if you have the wrong system for the current marketplace? This is the area that the Baldrige Award addresses.

The Malcolm Baldrige Annual National Quality Award

Public law 100–107 established the Malcolm Baldrige National Quality Award in 1987. It is named after the late Malcolm Baldrige, former Secretary of the U.S. Department of Commerce.[20] It was established partly to provide a similar award to the Deming prize awarded since 1951 by JUSE for outstanding use of both SPC and QFD. Florida Power & Light won the Deming Award in 1989. It was and still is embarrassing to U.S. officials that the world's most prestigious quality award is awarded by the Japanese in honor of an American. It was only natural for our country to sponsor an award to stimulate improved quality in U.S. products and services. The National Institute of Science and Technology manages the award and is assisted by ASQC. Awards have been made since 1988 and are based on the following criteria:

Customer focus and satisfaction	300 pts.
Quality and operational results, including 35 pts for supplier quality results	180 pts.
Human resources development and management	150 pts.
Management of process quality, including 20 pts. for supplier quality	140 pts.
Leadership	95 pts.
Information and analysis	75 pts.
Strategic quality planning	60 pts.
Total points	1,000

Supplier related criteria are worth 55 total points. The real difference and advantage of the Baldrige criteria over other standards is 30% of the score is customer driven, as opposed to less attention in ISO 9000 and to some extent, the Deming prize. A five-member board of examiners reviews applications but an army (like ISO 9000) of Baldrige expert consultants has evolved to assist the preparation process, which can be very expensive.

The Baldrige Award is rather controversial in that the cost of application is usually at least six figures. Some firms have found the requirement to help other noncompeting companies via the lecture circuit. A fascination with winning has hindered growth and continuous improvement. However, it does stimulate the move to TQM. Like the J. D. Powers Awards, it provides wonderful copy for major advertising campaigns. Marketing departments and company presidents love these prizes.

Supplier Certification

We are now ready to explore this rather broad subject in some detail. In Chapter 8, we explored sourcing and briefly mentioned certification, but cautioned readers that it is not a substitute for initial screening and sourcing efforts. We must first select the proper candidates for certification and gain some experience with them or carefully examine past records if they have supplied the buying organization for some time. Quality is the key criterion today along with on-time delivery, so it is appropriate that we address supplier certification. Certification is a procedure whereby selected suppliers move through a series of developments with audits to verify that they have achieved specific target performance goals. It concentrates on quality procedures to achieve zero defect production. It avoids incurring inspection, allowing material to be delivered directly to workstations. The procedure is a progression of the following steps:

♦ Select the candidates from your present supplier base (or new ones if none of the present suppliers has the potential). Not all suppliers need to be certified so select those delivering A items that can shut down the buying organization.

♦ Prepare a supplier audit survey concentrating on quality control procedures much like ISO 9000 and the other topics covered in this chapter (see Appendix J for an example). Do suppliers use SPC? What is their PCI? Do they utilize DOE? What is their defect rate? What is their AOQL? Do they have document control, are they going for ISO 9000 certification? Do they have a quality manual and so on.[21] List the criteria to achieve various ratings from "preferred" to "not qualified" and what must be accomplished and documented within each rating. Mail this survey to the candidate and allow at least one month for completion and return to the buying organization.

♦ Plan an initial meeting to discuss the survey results. This meeting should be held at the supplier's location with a team from the buying organization including representatives from Purchasing (team leader), Quality, Engineering, Manufacturing, and others as needed. Discuss the audit results, tour the facility, and develop quality assurance plans with the supplier to correct deficiencies and establish a time line for accomplishment. This includes a program to sample selected runs to check on PCI and defect rate reduction. Offer assistance to the supplier.

♦ Inspect and test sample runs. Discuss results and again, offer assistance, such as sending a quality engineer to the supplier.

♦ After a designated number of inspections and tests, designate the appropriate rating for the supplier with suggestions for correction, if appropriate.

♦ The supplier now ships directly to the buyer workstations with no buyer inspection or testing.

♦ Conduct periodic random inspection as a check for consistency.

♦ Continue regular meetings with the supplier to ensure open communication and suggestions for continuous improvement.

This procedure is not the only way to certify a supplier but it is pragmatic.[22] Avoid having such an elaborate procedure that both sides become buried in a mountain of paperwork. Do not require suppliers to work toward applying for the Baldrige Award as the cost of doing so outweighs the benefits for most companies. Requiring ISO 9000 certification is appropriate: Just give them time and support to do it.

Benchmarking

Michael J. Spendolini is a pioneer in benchmarking, as the word is now used in quality assurance. Following his original work at Xerox, he became a leading consultant and trainer in the field. He defines *benchmarking* as "a continuous, systematic process for evaluating the products, services, and work processes of organizations that are recognized as representing best practices for the purpose of organizational improvement."[23]

While "best practices" could mean any area of an organization, modern benchmarking was developed as part of the TQM movement in the 1980s. The process usually involves literature searches and personal visits by teams of managers of one organization visiting managers at another organization judged to be best in certain quality aspects of manufacturing, service, marketing, ROI, purchasing practices, and any other performance index or factor. One excellent source for Purchasing benchmarks is the Center for Advanced Purchasing Studies (CAPS) in Tempe, Arizona.

World automobile manufacturers have long compared each other on the number of hours required to produce comparable models in terms of type and quality. Teams of purchasing managers visit organizations thought to be proactive and very effective. The teams measure the gap between the best organization's practices and their own and then study "the best" process used to achieve the desired results. Processes include policies, procedures, techniques, organization structure, and any other tools used to be successful.

Spendolini and other benchmark experts feel the Baldrige Award stimulated the movement. The award criteria do include a category on competitive comparisons and benchmarks. The theory is that firms can visit the leaders, compare their practices with their own, and then go home to copy and implement the best practices. A word of caution: Do not copy a practice you do not really need or one that does not fit your company's culture, mission, or resources.

The Roles of Purchasing in Quality Assurance

While purchasing personnel do not need the technical depth of knowledge required of the quality engineers, they *do* need to know the terminology and basic mechanics of the statistical tools reviewed in this chapter. It is in the sourcing step and certification process, in which Purchasing prepares the survey questionnaires and organizes the visits to supplier plants, that buyers apply their understanding of quality assurance tools, procedures, and policies. As members of commodity-sourcing teams, they must understand the language of quality but do not need the technical ability of the quality assurance team members. In addition, as purchasing personnel manage the contract, they must be able to help detect the first signs of quality problems and then communicate to the supplier the corrective action to be taken by its quality engineers.

A Challenge

We have reproduced the Deming letter to Pinkerton, Exhibit 12–3, because it is a bit of history but more importantly, it represents a challenge to focus on quality versus price. The letter was written 13 years ago and purchasing has made enormous strides to correct the observations of Dr. Deming. However, both authors still meet buyers who select suppliers based on price alone because of pressure from senior management to lower costs. One more time: Price is just one component of costs. Defects are the major cost drivers up and down the supply chain.

Summary

Quality is fitness for a required use or conformance to correct specifications as defined by the customer. The dimensions of quality run from performance to perceived quality. TQM is the basic platform for all quality, efforts and is best explained by Deming's 14 points. We can't inspect quality in, but we can help prevent defects from being produced by better training, SPC, precontrol, and other methods and techniques. Training and empowering workers to identify and help correct quality problems are the key aspects of TQM. We have to map the progress of TQM. QFD does just that, starting with customer input. TQM strives for CI and this philosophy and system should become a habit, a way of life, and not a one-time project.

SPC and other such control tools do not tell why a process is going out of control—that's the job of investigative tools such as DOE and Pareto analysis. DOE is by far the most powerful tool. *Poka-yoke* systems that shut down machines before they produce defects will become more popular as we keep developing more exotic sensing apparatus.

Exhibit 12-3. Letter from W. Edwards Deming to Richard L. Pinkerton.

W. EDWARDS DEMING, Ph.D.
CONSULTANT IN STATISTICAL STUDIES

WASHINGTON 20016
4924 BUTTERWORTH PLACE

TEL. (202) 363-8552

14 October 1982

Dear Dean Pinkerton,

I thank you for your letter of the 1st October. My statement about purchasing people stems from the fact that, as a rule, they are not educated in statistical evidence of quality, nor do they follow products through various stages of manufacture to know what the problems are. My statement is based on my own observations. I get around and see what is happening. All that you have to do is to talk to a few production workers to find out what some of the problems are with incoming materials and with tools and other supplies bought at a low price. Purchasing managers have a new job, and so does everybody else in the purchasing department. They must learn a lot about statistical evidence of quality. Dependence on the lowest price is no longer acceptable performance. Industry must move into the single supplier with long-term relationships.

If you would follow me around or even look at some of the video tapes that I could show you (were they not confidential) to see what I am talking about, you would see the basis for my statement. I thank you again and remain

Sincerely yours,

W. Edwards Deming

To Dean Richard L. Pinkerton
      Graduate School of Administration
        Capital University
          Columbus, Ohio
            43209-2394

ISO 9000 certification will become even more important as companies around the world demand that their suppliers be registered. ISO 9000 forces a firm into TQM, which is well worth the cost as we strive to eliminate rework and recalls, the real cost drivers. The Malcolm Baldrige Award is a worthy goal but only for a few firms who want marketing recognition beyond ISO 9000. The Baldrige Award does require more customer input but QFD accomplishes the same objective.

Supplier certification programs, which are mini ISO 9000 efforts with individual key suppliers, give precise quality target goals to suppliers, help them achieve these goals, and audit to ensure compliance to criteria for various ratings.

Is quality free? The net savings from TQM and QFD indicate it is. Life cycle costing also gives evidence that if good quality isn't free, it is worth the investment, that is, the payoff is huge.

By now, it should be apparent that the IPS approach to proactive procurement requires teamwork. How are teams developed? How do they function? How do they "improve" themselves? This crucial topic is the subject of our next chapter.

Notes

1. J. M. Juran, *Juran on Planning for Quality* (New York: The Free Press, 1988), p. 5.
2. David A. Garvin, *Managing Quality: The Strategic and Competitive Edge* (New York: The Free Press, 1988), pp. 49–60. Adapted with permission of The Free Press, an imprint of Simon & Schuster.
3. W. E. Deming, *Out of the Crisis* (Cambridge, Mass.: MIT, Center for Advanced Engineering Study, 1986).
4. Howard S. Gitlow and Shelly J. Gitlow, *The Deming Guide to Quality and Competitive Position* (Englewood Cliffs, N.J.: Prentice-Hall, 1987). Reprinted by permission of Prentice-Hall, Upper Saddle River, N.J.
5. John R. Hauser and Don Clausing, "The House of Quality," *Harvard Business Review* (May-June 1988), p. 72.
6. Martin K. Starr, *Operations Management: A Systems Approach,* from the preview of this text to be published in 1996 by Boyd and Fraser Publishing Co., Danvers, Mass., p. 49. We recommend readers buy this exciting and new approach to the study of operations.
7. Ricardo R. Fernandez, *Total Quality in Purchasing and Supply Management* (Delray Beach, Fla.: St. Lucie Press, 1995), pp. 199–202.
8. Keki R. Bhote, *World Class Quality: Using Design of Experiments to Make It Happen* (New York: AMACOM, 1991), p. 181.
9. Ibid. pp. 182–183.
10. Philip B. Crosby, *Quality Is Free: The Art of Making Quality Certain* (New York: McGraw-Hill, 1979).
11. Juran, op. cit., pp. 26–27, 276–278.
12. Kaoru Ishikawa, *What Is Total Quality Control? The Japanese Way,* translated by David J. Lu (Englewood Cliffs, N.J.: Prentice-Hall 1985), pp. 63–64, 203. Used with permission of Prentice-Hall, a division of Simon & Schuster.
13. Ryuji Fukuda, *Managerial Engineering* (Cambridge, Mass.: Productivity, Inc., 1986).
14. Ishikawa, op, cit., pp. 59–71.
15. Shigeo Shingo, *Zero Quality Control: Source Inspection and the Poka-Yoke System* (Cambridge, Mass.: Productivity Press, 1986). Also see by the same author, *Non-Stock Production: The Shingo System for Continuous Improvement* (Cambridge, Mass.: Productivity Press, 1987).

16. Tracy Goings Gorny, "Quality Standards: Meeting on Common Grounds," *NAPM Insights* (November 1991), pp. 22–23. Also see John Nolan, "Understanding ISO 9000," *NAPM Insights* (September 1992), pp. 28–29.
17. John T. Rabbitt and Peter A. Bergh, *The ISO 9000 Book: A Global Competitor's Guide to Compliance and Certification* (White Plains, N.Y.: Quality Resources, 1993), p. 9. *Note:* The American Management Association in New York City (AMACOM) also distributes this book.
18. Jonathan B. Levine, "Want EC Business? You have Two Choices," *Business Week* (Oct. 19, 1992), pp. 58–59. Also see Mary Siegfried, "ISO 9000 Benefits and Concerns," *NAPM Insights* (May 1994), pp. 57–59, and the supplement to the June 1994 issue of the *Management Review: Industry Forum*, "Does the ISO 9000 Need Fixing?"
19. Greg Hutchins, *ISO 9000: A Comprehensive Guide to Registration, Audit Guidelines and Successful Certification* (Essex Junction, Vt.: Oliver Wight Publications, 1993), pp. 164–166. We feel this is the best of the general guide books. ISO 9000 guides and manuals are available directly from ISO, Case Postale 56, CH-1211, Geneve 20, Switzerland. The latest is *ISO 9000 International Standards for Quality Management*, 4th ed., 1994.
20. Francis X. Mahoney and Carl G. Thor, *The TQM Trilogy: Using ISO 9000, the Deming Prize, and the Baldrige Award* (New York: AMACOM, 1994), pp. 71–99.
21. For a fine example of a supplier quality evaluation and audit, see Keki R. Bhote, *Strategic Supply Management: A Blueprint for Revitalizing the Manufacturer-Supplier Partnership* (New York: AMACOM, 1989). This work is an excellent reference on all quality issues.
22. Also see Fernandez, op. cit., pp. 127–138, and the May 1993 issue of *NAPM Insights*, the theme of which is Supplier Certification, pp. 18–39.
23. Michael J. Spendolini, *The Benchmarking Book* (New York: AMACOM, 1992), p. 9. Also see *Benchmarking: A Tool for Continuous Improvement*, by C. J. McNair, CMA, and Kathleen H. J. Leibfried, Omneo, imprint of Oliver Wight Publications, Inc., Essex Junction, Vermont, 1992; and *Benchmarking: The Search for Industry Best Practices That Lead to Superior Performance*, by Robert Camp (White Plains, N.Y.: Quality Resources, 1989).

13
Team Building

Kim Chen, purchasing manager for Medical Test Equipment Company, is frustrated and angry. She has just returned from an electrical component commodity-sourcing team meeting that she considers a waste of time. Two key members sent substitutes who had no idea of what was going on, one engineer wanted to change all the specifications, the representative from Production had no idea of the needed quantities for the next quarter, the Quality Assurance representative read his ISO-9000 manual during the discussion, and the team leader kept asking, "Why are we here?" Kim wonders what to do. She is still uncertain as to top management support for the team concept at Medical Test Equipment.

What Is a Team?

We have stressed the need for and value of forming cross-functional teams to allow the simultaneous integration of necessary inputs from all members of the organization who are and will be affected by incoming materials. This includes design and sourcing or commodity teams. As Ellram and Pearson write, these teams ensure that more in-depth information will make for better decisions as multiple needs and concerns are discussed together, as opposed to the traditional sequential approach that often requires expensive revisions.[1] The advantage of team input is enhanced when suppliers participate (as needed) on these teams. Teams reduce product development time, improve quality, reduce cost, and reduce engineering changes. Chrysler's Cross-Functional Platform teams reduced new auto development from four and a half years to three years. The Honeywell's Building Controls Divisions teams reduced new product development time by 50%.[2] Contrary to early fears, these teams do not diminish Purchasing's authority; they increase Purchasing's involvement in the total decision-making process.[3] The question now becomes, how do we make these teams productive and efficient?

The Team's Charter

Top management must define the purpose of the teams, how they will be staffed, what their authority is, and how they will operate. There will always be resistance by those who historically have made decisions alone, especially if they are senior in rank. Thus, the first step is to issue a written policy and procedure guide to all relevant personnel.

A Recent Case History

One of the authors has installed teams in a high-tech firm, but only after extensive interviews with key management revealed the hazards and waste of sequential decision making by separate departments. This review included the documentation of the excessive costs involved with too many purchase orders, with too many suppliers, and frequent change orders caused by unilateral department action with little advanced supplier involvement. In addition, the purchasing department was relegated to order entry status and a very reactive mode. In fact, orders were often given directly to suppliers by engineering and production personnel prior to the completion of purchase requisitions and purchase orders.

After the review, a list of the critical materials was developed with the goal of consolidating the total volume of each material into long-term contracts with one prime and one backup supplier (when possible and needed). Blanket orders and system contracts are negotiated by teams composed of representatives from Engineering, Production, Purchasing, Quality, and others as needed. The managers of the basic product lines submits names for team membership to the purchasing manager, who is responsible for establishing the teams and their meeting schedules. If the purchasing manager disagrees with the selection, she can appeal up the rank ladder, even to the president if necessary. The buyer most familiar with the product line is always a member of the particular "commodity team" (as it is called). The teams are told to select their own leader and the preferred supplier by voting or consensus. These teams negotiate the final contract subject to the ordinary upper management review.

Prior to actually starting the teams, the author conducted a three-hour meeting on the new team approach and the new supply management system. The new purchasing procedure allows a planner-scheduler to order releases directly via fax from the supplier selected by the team, eliminating the previous waste of repeat requisitions and purchase orders every time material was needed. The cost of this paperwork was estimated to be $50 for each transaction, and it was estimated the new system will save at least $100,000 a year by substantially reducing purchase requisitions and orders.

Another half-day session on the techniques of negotiation including role playing was conducted. In addition, the president arranged for the consultant (one of the authors) to visit once a month to actually "sit in" on team meetings and negotiations. Previously, the consultant and members of the purchasing department had visited several key suppliers to test the validity of the proposed program.

After about five months of operations, the five teams started to become productive and indeed, two teams actually negotiated several consolidated contracts. The consultant met with the teams about once a month for mini training sessions to give advice. In addition, he constantly met with senior management to clarify the objectives and stimulate continued support from the corporate leaders. However, most of the teams experienced great difficulty trying to define objectives and learning to live with one another. The consultant had to jump start the teams many times as they matured.

This case history represents a fairly normal sequence of developments, in particular when commodity and other cross-functional teams are formed at the same time the purchasing department is just starting to evolve from reactive to proactive status. Any major organizational change is traumatic to individuals accustomed to either status quo or "having their own way" in departments "doing their own thing." Nobody likes to give up power or autonomy and it is normal to encounter resistance of various degrees in individuals charged with both instigating and accepting change.

A fair amount of research has produced several guidelines to making teams effective. The characteristics of effective procurement teams as developed by Larson and La Fasto are rather common in most of the literature simply because they are based on real experience and common sense.[4]

How to Have
More Effective Teams

Clearly Defined Objectives, Explicit Goals, and Vision

In our opening case study, we see a group of teams making some progress but not quite sure of their mission. One of the reasons for this confusion was the uncertainty of whether the policy that established the teams was actually in force because the policy was stalled in an ISO 9000 document review committee. This delay was the result of confusion over just who was responsible for the final statement regarding the new supply management policy and the role of teams. Six months elapsed without the official adoption of the policy and procedure statement, (the same period during which the teams were formed and started operation). The president of the firm and key management had all reviewed and approved the basic concepts of the policy and initial training sessions had been held for team members. But the failure to publish the policy led to an initial lack of commitment and confusion over objectives and goals. The teams were formed to pursue the enormous dollar savings by consolidating the supplier base into a few key quality driven suppliers operating under long-term "partnership" agreements.

The early limited success of the teams in our case study did stimulate the final policy adoption. But the general rule is to first adapt, publish, and communicate the goals and rationale for the teams who would operate under a new supply management philosophy and system. Prior to starting detailed agenda preparation, teams must have defined objectives and deadline dates with clarity of purpose supported by the rationale for the policy and endorsement from all senior management.

Team Structure and Mandate

The number of team members, selection procedures, team design, operating procedures, meeting schedules, training, voting methods, focus, and time lines are just a few of the issues to be addressed. Larson and La Fasto identify three basic structures or team types: problem resolution, creative (for new product designs), and tactical.[5] We feel most cross-functional and commodity teams will either be creative (for new product designs) or tactical (for contract negotiation). The dominant feature of a problem-resolution team is trust; for a creative team, autonomy; and for the tactical team, clarity.[6] The tactical team must have a well-defined set of negotiation objectives and tasks based upon analysis of past purchases in terms of volume, price/cost, quality, delivery, and required supplier assistance. To these goals must be added future needs and improvement goals, targets. The four desirable design features common to all teams as identified by Larson and La Fasto are:[7]

1. Clear goals and accountability for each member
2. Effective communication from credible sources, agenda flexibility (we can add topics not on the planned agenda), and documentation
3. Monitoring individual performance and providing constructive feedback for assignments and rewards
4. Decision making based on facts and informed judgment

The key goal of team structure is to facilitate action, accomplishment, movement, and change. These teams cannot be allowed to develop analysis paralysis, pure procrastination, a status quo mentality, a department vs. function focus, or any other disadvantage associated with committees that never come to closure on operational tasks.

Carlisle and Parker use the term *mandate teams* to describe the commodity teams' efforts to prepare the agenda and data for the actual negotiation team. The mandate team must have the authority and responsibility, which actually means a charter and resources from senior management.[8] Although the negotiation team should be selected from the mandate team, its membership may have new members depending on the issue at hand. In effect, the commodity team prepares the RFP. The purchasing manager will have to relinquish total power and authority and learn to accept the team decisions, not an easy behavior change for the autocratic manager.

Competent Team Members

The description "competent team members" refers to a combination of the right technical and personal skills including the desire and ability to work together to achieve the team's objective. Team members should believe in the team mission and give the commitment necessary to contribute. Substitute team members rarely contribute because they may not fully understand the history of the team or the goals and progress to date and they seldom have team loyalty. In fact, substitute members may hinder progress by asking questions on topics already covered. Team members must focus on issues (not positions), share information, listen objectively, and display other such "we" orientation traits vs. "me" or my department first biases. The research by Larson and La Fasto strongly suggests removing team members who cannot collaborate.[9]

Types of Team Members

There are four major types of team members. The best teams are made up of people from each group.

1. *Contributors*. Contributors give the team valuable technical and business advice relative to the task at hand. They know critical information to solve the problem and/or develop good alternatives.
2. *Communicators*. Communicators help produce productive dialogue, defuse angry team members, keep peace, are good listeners, and are empathetic and positive people. Any team must have these sensitive individuals to calm everybody down and reach consensus.
3. *Collaborators*. Collaborators are the integrators; they see the big picture and help to bring the team back to focus when it wanders from the agenda.
4. *Challengers*. All teams need challengers who may appear to be negative but who have the ability, knowledge, and nerve to ask the tough questions, such as "Is it realistic to expect the supplier to ship 100% defect-free parts?" or "Do we really know the exact tolerances for this new part?"

Unified Commitment

Aside from the obvious need for strong team spirit, all members must be willing to invest the time and effort to achieve team goals. Unified commitment means the confidence to disagree without being disagreeable and the need to attack issues, not people. In addition, there must be a productive compromise within a reasonable time frame to prevent analysis paralysis, which is the unrealistic desire to have a perfect solution, plan, or program. Again, self-serving team members are deadly enemies of the common goal for the good of the company. Vote and get on with the business of moving toward goal attainment. The team leader must confront self-serving members outside the meeting and ask for team effort. If the leader does not get it, the "me" oriented team member or "lone ranger" should be replaced.

Collaborative Climate

Team members have to trust one another (another reason for no substitutes). Larson and La Fasto identify honesty, openness, consistency, and respect as the keys to teamwork.[10] If the correct team members have been selected and they agree on a common goal, then involvement, autonomy, and commitment will build trust and the willingness to help one another.

Carlisle and Parker correctly observe that teams have to grow and overcome the normal development stages, which have "crisis periods."[11] These crisis periods include arguments, in-fighting, unproductive sessions, dull meetings, poor time management, uncertainty, confusion, and all the other normal stages of development common to all teams. Effective informal and formal leadership is necessary to overcome these "growing up" problems.

The Four Stages of Team Development

As they develop, teams go through the following four stages:[12]

1. *Formation.* The team is exploring the mission statement, deciding team goals, establishing the criteria for success, learning how to interact with each other, and establishing team procedure.
2. *Storming.* The team is starting to open up with spirited communication, which includes disagreement, self-discovery, and the formation of suballiances and informal leadership. There is a recognition of who will do what, while goals and objectives are debated.
3. *Normalization.* The team now learns how to handle conflict and establishes rules of conduct. Team members come to a common understanding of what they are trying to do and how to do it.
4. *Performance.* As a unit, team members learn to support one another and have a clear sense of purpose. There is trust, shared leadership, support for team decisions, good self-assessment, and objectivity, and they now enjoy working with each other.

Standards of Excellence

This is the level of achievement and it comes from desired external and internal competition. What are the benchmarks? Is it ISO 9000 compliance, getting a supplier to ship faster at higher quality, reducing cycle time by 60%, eliminating non-value-added paperwork, such as 50% fewer purchase orders or what? It is also developing the habit of continuous improvement. We cannot be satisfied with the past: History dictates there is always a better way to do it.

External Support, Recognition, Rewards, and Motivation

Top management must endorse the team's goals and nothing is more destructive than the lack of support. Teams need help and support, not blocking action by others in the organization.

The rewards must be both intrinsic and tangible. Verbal "well done" statements, promotions, certificates, gifts, special trips, and bonus money are the effective tools, in particular financial rewards. Teams require extra effort, and individuals should be rewarded for this kind of performance.

Principled Informal and Formal Leadership

The role of the team leader is critical to the success of the team. Effective team leaders establish a vision, create change, and unleash talent.[13] Leaders of any type of team or endeavor must resolve conflict while avoiding taking on a dictatorial role. They strive for and encourage consensus while keeping the discussion on track toward goal achievement. They must control the agenda while stimulating maximum contribution from each member. Leaders must also encourage calculated risk taking. Having a sense of humor is essential as this helps the leader direct discussion without being belligerent.

Leaders bring out the best performance in those reporting to them. They must also have the courage and sensitive communication skills to remove team members who are counterproductive, dominating, unprepared, and who lack commitment. However, the leader must avoid the pressure to engage in what Kolchin and Trent call "premature closure to the decision-making process."[14] This occurs when a team votes too quickly prior to exploring sufficient alternatives or prior to adequate input from all team members. Finally, successful leaders know how to use the informal leader and all the different types of team members (contributor, challenger, etc.) to accomplish the mission objectives.

We have discussed the issues of motivation and rewarding teams and team members with Purchasing executives at several U.S. and European companies. Our conclusion? There is no one best way! Motivation systems must be tailored to the company—even to the situation. For example, Baxter Health Care employs large teams (15 employees or so) in supply management for significant periods of time. Teams compete annually for team recognition and awards in a manner similar to the competing for the Department of Commerce's Baldrige Award. The winning team members determine how to share the award among themselves.

Lincoln Electric, through its profit-sharing plan, attempts to have all employees see themselves as one big (3,600 employees) team. Each employee, including those temporarily assigned to new product development and sourcing teams, receives an evaluation or rating, which is the basis of determining the employee's portion of the profits shared among all employees.

Honda of America Manufacturing, Inc., also endeavors to have all employees (or associates, as they call themselves) part of the Honda Family. But each family member can earn an individual bonus—all the way up to a Honda Accord. Three successful approaches: As we said, "Motivation systems must be tailored to the situation."

The Special Situation of Cross-Functional Sourcing Teams

We started this book with the role of cross-functional design teams and we are nearing the end with cross-functional sourcing teams. What's the difference? The design team focuses on new product development, and the sourcing team concentrates on the actual supply source determination and contract negotiation.

What we have discussed so far in this chapter is appropriate to both types of teams. Both teams require appropriate input from all affected departments. The team members must drop their department allegiance and think big, think of what's best for the entire company; that is, they must be on *the company team*, not from the departmental staff.

Research by Trent and Monczka supports all of the observations we have made in this book regarding teams. In their study of cross-functional sourcing teams they conclude that the following factors are related to the highest performing teams.[15]

- ◆ Availability of key organizational resources, such as time to pursue team assignments, services, help from others, and budgetary support
- ◆ Participation and involvement of suppliers when required
- ◆ Higher levels of internal and external decision-making authority
- ◆ Effective team leadership
- ◆ Higher levels of effort put forth on team assignments

Notice the time pressure issue, which is a factor that most experts on cross-functional teams cite as a problem. Too much pressure for results too soon will almost always force a team to premature and less effective decisions.[16] This is the old habit of American higher management to act now—prior to good analysis. Our global competitors have the patience to allow time to nurture participative management, and the results are well known. Just ask the U.S. automotive manufacturers the cost of knee-jerk reactions.

We cannot stress enough the need for top management to give the proper mandate for team organization and to give reasonable time for the teams to develop. We seem to forget that great teams have to first practice, then play the game, and they can't play it without good coaches, able players, and team leaders who are a mixture of coach, player, and referee. It takes two to three years to document the real, bottom-line savings of teams, especially when the organization is making a massive change from reactive purchasing to proactive procurement.

Measuring Team Progress

Christopher Meyer is one of the first authorities to point out that teams must be measured on the basis of process of related functions as opposed to single action events.[17] He also suggests that the teams themselves must be the principal designers of their own measurement system (with input from senior management) and that the major purpose of the measurement system should be to help the team track its own progress. Measures include having the correct team members in sufficient time to keep on schedule, identifying key milestones or events with deadline dates, and targeting actual dollar savings, time savings, as well as other goals from the charter or mission statement. It is critical to identify and solve developing problems that will cause delays—problems such as disagreements on criteria for quality, designs, contract terms, lead times, quantities, number of required suppliers and so on.

Process measurement requires the identification of factors that act on the project and then tracing (or "mapping" as it is often called) all the functions that affect that factor: cycle time, costs, process yield, rework, work in process inventory, document control, and the like. The important point to remember is that the team itself must come up with its own measures of progress.

Team minutes give indications of progress. They should include findings, reports, problems, action steps, who is responsible for particular tasks, and time lines. Periodically, the teams should issue formal progress reports.

Final Thoughts and Warnings

Aside from the proper charter from senior management, the key to successful team performance is the selection and training of the team members, in particular, the team leader. This chapter provides the training outline, topics, and resources for team formation and development. Although the initial training session is critical, other training seminars, usually no more than half a day each, will be needed as the team progresses through the early stages of team development. As each teach member is selected, assign background reading including *Teamwork: What Must Go Right/What Can Go Wrong* by Carl E. Larson and Frank M. J. La Fasto (Thousand Oaks, Calif.: Sage, 1989). Another very fine paperback with interesting case histories of business teams is *The Wisdom of Teams* by John R. Katzenbach and Douglas Smith.[18] The National Association of Purchasing Management videotape (PAL 38) on cross-functional teams is excellent and should be viewed at the first team meeting.

Avoid any type of psychoanalytical training as it is unnecessary, risky, too expensive, and in many respects, it is an invasion of privacy and unethical. Many managers know just enough psychology to be dangerous. In addition, many of the psychoanalytical consultants know too much abnormal psychology and far too little about your particular workplace. Individuals with serious behavioral problems should not be on teams, they should be in professional therapy. Normal workers will respond to rational training on how to do something and why they are doing it, without the need to reveal their deep inner feelings and personal value systems. Good communication and team training for adults is reminder training of what reasonable conduct is in a particular company environment. Major behavior modification is well beyond what any business organization can or should do. Use consultants and trainers who are recognized as authorities or leaders and who have good common sense, judgment and experience in the field of endeavor the team is working in. Workers respond to individuals with experience and expertise in their occupations, and this builds credibility for what the trainer and/or leader says plus empathy on both sides of the table.

Finally, do we need one more team? All of us are well aware of the current inclination to establish teams. During a flight to Europe one of the authors conversed with a technical consultant to a large U.S. company. The consultant related that he had just finished an assignment for a company that it could have accomplished itself but all its engineers were too busy attending team meetings. There will be a sorting out of which teams are productive and which are not. Not all buying should go through a team. Teams should only be formed for the "A" items that require interface with numerous functional areas for critical items in terms of dollar value, critically high volume, quality, and significant potential savings. In other words, the payoff must exceed the team cost. (The team cost can be measured in terms of hours expended.) This is another reason teams must quickly learn how to achieve their objectives and not waste that most precious commodity of all, time.

Summary

Teams can provide faster and better decisions by providing simultaneous input from all interested parties. They are designed to tear down department walls and thereby produce an integrated solution to problems or to reduce the time to make something happen with the best payoff. Teams identify more ramifications of increased alternatives than are developed by individual thought. They should substantially reduce rework of any kind while lowering paperwork, time, and costs.

Successful teams focus on an appropriate mission as mandated by senior management. Competent team members who learn to trust each other collaborate and use their technical knowledge with good social-communication skills to produce the best solutions or programs to accomplish their objectives. They recognize that team building goes through stages of development, much like athletic teams. It takes lots of practice to stop fumbling but good leadership, common sense, and training will produce teams that produce profitable results. There is nothing quite like being a member of a winning team who can say, *"We* made a difference."

One of the most fascinating and challenging aspects of procurement is negotiations, the subject of our next chapter.

Notes

1. Lisa M. Ellram and John N. Pearson, "The Role of the Purchasing Function: Toward Team Participation," *International Journal of Purchasing and Materials Management* (Summer 1993), pp. 3–9. Also see Charles O'Neal, "Concurrent Engineering with Early Supplier Involvement: A Cross Functional Challenge," *International Journal of Purchasing and Materials Management* (Spring 1993), pp. 3–9.
2. Robert M. Monczka and Robert J. Trent, "Cross-Functional Teams Reduce New Product Development Times," *NAPM Insights* (February 1994), pp. 64–66.
3. Ellram and Pearson, op. cit., p. 9.
4. See, e.g., Carl E. Larson and Frank M. J. La Fasto, *Teamwork: What Must Go Right/What Can Go Wrong* (Thousand Oaks, Calif.: Sage, 1989). Reprinted by permission of Sage Publications, Inc.
5. Ibid., pp. 42–55.
6. Ibid., p. 43.
7. Ibid., pp. 55–58.
8. John A. Carlisle and Robert C. Parker, *Beyond Negotiation: Redeeming Customer Supplier Relationships* (New York: Wiley, 1989), p. 107.

9. Larson and La Fasto, op. cit., pp. 152–168.
10. Ibid., p. 85.
11. Carlisle and Parker, op. cit., pp. 152–168.
12. "PAL 38," a videotape on Cross-Functional Teams (Tempe, Ariz.: National Association of Purchasing Management, 1992). Reprinted with permission.
13. Larson and La Fasto, op. cit., pp. 118–122.
14. Michael G. Kolchin and Robert J. Trent, "Developing Effective Cross-Functional Teams," *79th Annual International Purchasing Conference Proceedings,* May, 1994. (Tempe, Ariz.: National Association of Purchasing Management), p. 81.
15. Robert J. Trent and Robert M. Monczka, "Effective Cross-Functional Sourcing Teams: Critical Success Factors," *International Journal of Purchasing and Materials Management* (Fall 1994), pp. 3–11.
16. Diane Brown, "Supplier Management Teams," *NAPM Insights* (August 1994), p. 33.
17. Christopher Meyer, "How the Right Measures Help Teams Excel," *Harvard Business Review* (May-June 1994), pp. 95–103.
18. John R. Katzenbach and Douglas K. Smith, *The Wisdom of Teams: Creating the High Performance Organization* (New York: HarperCollins, 1994). Also see Glenn M. Parker, *Cross Functional Teams: Working With Allies, Enemies, and Other Strangers* (San Francisco: Jossey Bass, Inc., 1994); Peter Mears and Frank Voehl, *Team Building: A Structured Learning Approach* (Delray Beach, Fla.: St. Lucie Press, 1994); Landon J. Napoleon, "How Teams Affect Your Suppliers," *NAPM Insights* (September 1994), pp. 14–15; and John M. McKeller and David T. Antonioni, "Don't Burn Out on Teamwork," *NAPM Insights* (July 1994), pp. 69–71.

14

The Winning Way of Negotiating

Larry Smith, purchasing manager for Precision Fabricators of Bridgeport, Connecticut, sits thinking in the boardroom of the Manchester Screw Press Ltd., in Manchester, England. Larry is due to fly out of Manchester to Heathrow the next afternoon. After two days of conducting first a pre-award survey and then discussions that he could not dignify with the term "negotiations," Larry is both frustrated and exhausted. His mind races a mile a minute, or is it a kilometer per 36 seconds? One thing is for sure: Negotiations in the United Kingdom are not the same as negotiations in the United States.

Larry's employer, Precision Fabricators, is a forge shop that employs slightly over 200 employees. The company makes turbine blade forgings of titanium, aluminum, steel, and exotic metals. Recently, Precision entered into discussions with a jet engine producer. The objective of the discussions was Precision's desire to become the supplier of a turbine blade for the new RS-301 jet engine being developed. After an extensive review and more extensive discussions, the jet engine manufacturer agreed to make Precision an approved source, provided that Precision purchases a new 7,000-ton screw press capable of exerting twisting power of 150 metric tons. The screw press had to be installed within 10 months. It was estimated to cost $2 million.

Larry contacted all known domestic and foreign firms capable of manufacturing such a screw press. Only one, Manchester Screw Press Ltd., indicated an ability to meet the required delivery date. In the interest of time, Larry arranged to fly to the United Kingdom. He planned to conduct a site survey and, if appropriate, negotiations with representatives of Manchester Screw. With the possibility of negotiations in mind, Larry sent a fax to Manchester Screw Press requesting that the firm prepare a bid for the 150-ton screw press and be prepared to discuss the cost factors supporting the resulting bid.

Larry then contacted several fellow purchasing managers to develop pricing data on similar equipment. No one whom he contacted had purchased this exact-size screw press, but Larry was able to obtain enough data to develop a parametric cost-estimating model based on twisting power. The model indicated that Precision's screw press should cost $2.7 million plus or minus 10%.

On arriving in Manchester, Larry was met by Malcolm Bresford-West, O.B.E., managing director of the Manchester Screw Press Ltd. After a pleasant lunch at Mr. Bresford-West's club, the two went on to the screw works. Larry was introduced to the chiefs of Sales, Manufacturing, and Engineering and to the controller. Much time then was spent describing the firm's history, World War II and the resulting injustices to Great Britain vis-à-vis the reconstruction aid given to West Germany, and the state of the world economy. The meeting seemed to take forever, but it had lasted only two hours. Then it was time for tea. Following tea, Larry was turned over to Barney Jones, manufacturing manager, who conducted a tour of the plant. Larry was surprised to see highly sophisticated numeric-controlled equipment standing side by side with pre-World War I machines. When asked if the older equipment could hold necessary tolerances, Mr. Jones stated that the machines might be a problem in the wrong hands. But he had many employees with 30 or more years of experience who "could make those old babies get up and dance any tune they desired!" Larry was reasonably satisfied with the plant and equipment. It was apparent that the plant was operating well below capacity. It was past quitting time when Larry and Barney completed their factory tour.

The next morning, Larry met with Mr. Clarence Gibbons, the sales manager, to discuss Manchester's experience with similar screw presses. Mr. Gibbons had prepared a file containing letters from satisfied customers complimenting Manchester on both its quality and ability to meet delivery terms. By this time, Larry felt that he was indeed fortunate. There was no question in his mind that, provided that no unforeseen work stoppage occurred, Manchester would meet or beat Precision's delivery requirement.

Larry then asked Mr. Gibbons if he had received Precision's fax requesting a price for the screw press. Mr. Gibbons responded with a courteous smile and rang for his secretary. In response to Mr. Gibbons's request, the secretary brought in a file containing two sheets of paper. Mr. Gibbons proudly presented the document to Larry. It was a letter, addressed to Precision Fabricators. The letter described the machine in some detail including the fact that it would have a twisting power of 150 metric tons. The press would weigh approximately 190 tons. The screw would be operated by a 350-horsepower reversible direct-circuit motor. The price was FOB Manchester, with freight allowed to Bridgeport. Delivery to Precision's factory would be within nine months after receipt of an order. The delivered price would be £2 million with payment as follows: 10% down and 10% at the end of each of the nine months. Installation could either be accomplished by Precision or Manchester with the details to be negotiated prior to shipment.

Larry sat in a mild state of bewilderment. He had not expected a request for either advance payments, progress payments, or payments in other than dollars. He chose to proceed with discussions with the objective of obtaining cost data in support of Manchester's bid. "There are a few surprises here, but before discussing them, I'd appreciate being able to review the cost data supporting your bid. Could you get them for me, please?"

It was Mr. Gibbons's turn to appear bewildered. He excused himself and returned 15 minutes later with Mr. Angus McFee, the firm's controller. Mr. McFee asked, "Do you find our terms to your liking, Mr. Smith?"

Larry answered that he needed to have all relevant data available before being able to discuss the proposed transaction. "One of the key items of information I require is the cost data in support of your proposal. With this in hand, I'll be a in a position to determine if the price is reasonable."

Mr. McFee responded, "Why, Mr. Smith, we don't do business that way at Manchester Screw! Our price is based on years of experience in the screw press business. Our quality is of the highest order, and our price is totally consistent with our expenses. Ours is not an excessively profitable business."

Larry then spent considerable time attempting to obtain the requisite cost data—to no avail. He began to wonder if Manchester truly did not have any data in support of its bid. He then turned his attention to the price bid by Manchester. In response to Larry's request, Mr. McFee contacted the firm's bankers to obtain the current rate of exchange. The rate quoted was £1 = U.S. $1.7505. This meant that Manchester's delivered price for the screw press would be approximately $3.5 million, some $800,000 over the price Larry had estimated before leaving the United States.

It being lunch time, the three went to a nearby pub for a light meal. On their return, they moved to the firm's oak-paneled boardroom where they were joined by Mr. Bresford-West. Mr. Bresford-West asked if they had a nice lunch and then asked if his firm's proposal was acceptable. Perspiration broke out on Larry's forehead. He mentally clicked off the areas of differences: price, advanced payments, progress payments, payments in sterling, installation, and liability from Manchester to Bridgeport. His biggest concern was the apparent nonexistence of any cost data. Larry thought to himself, "Are these people as honest and simplistic as they appear, or are they sly as foxes?" Even insight into this issue would be helpful in mapping out his strategy. He also thought of his reservations for departure tomorrow.

Having covered the various terms, conditions, and requirements of purchased goods and services in preceding chapters, we are ready to examine how we obtain all these objectives. Negotiation is the method we use to conclude an agreement on critical materials, parts, supplies, and services.

It is important to remember that inadequate lead time is the initial enemy of successful negotiation. Poor or no planning, inaccurate forecasting, and procrastination on any part of the buying organization will preclude the preparation time so essential to the entire negotiation process.

What Is Negotiation?

Negotiation is the *process* of personal give-and-take discussions over desired interests and objectives resulting in a mutually rewarding set of compromises for a win-win agreement for both sides of the contract. Take it or leave it demands are the opposite of negotiation and even the UCC, as well as other contract law principles, stresses the need for both parties to freely enter into a binding relationship without duress, coercion, threat, force, etc.—the key words being *voluntary agreement* by both sides. Of course, unless one can prove illegal coercion or some other mitigating factor and he or she signs a contract that turns "sour," the contract will be upheld in court, should litigation become necessary.

Procurement professionals must avoid a *focus* on what is legal. People perform contracts, not purchase orders. However, if one party of a contract is not in complete agreement or understanding, the actual *performance* will suffer. We want our suppliers to have a 100% commitment to perform because it is to their benefit, not because they will be sued.

For many years, perhaps until the Japanese proved we were wrong, most buyers and sellers in the United States had adversarial relationships and viewed the negotiation process as a type of war. Typically, each session was a distributive bargaining situation where the clever side used trickery, dickering, devious psychological tactics, and even lying to win the larger share of the benefits on the bargaining table. One party had to lose. Just why either side thought the loser would perform to the best of its ability is a mystery. Every chapter in this book cites evidence that if the buyer-seller relationship is to be a partnership, then both sides must bargain for the long-run profit of the partnership throughout the value chain. When you con somebody, the normal response is "I'll get even."

The Best of Fisher, Ury, and Patton's *Getting to Yes*

The landmark work of Fisher, Ury, and Patton of the Harvard Negotiation Project, *Getting to Yes*, is must reading for all buyers and sellers.[1] The method of successful negotiation developed by Fisher, Ury, and Patton includes the following major points.

♦ *Separate the people from the problem.* The word "problem" also means issue, position, or objective. Good communication and perception skills can identify the human interaction/reactions as a separate issue from a position taken by either side. Confront the people or "chemistry" problem directly, then tackle the issues. Empathy is a key skill for any negotiator. Expect emotion, let the other side "ventilate," and control your own reaction. Shouting is not communication and merely escalates the anger.

♦ *Focus on interests, not positions.* Your "interests" are your objectives and a position is what you think will achieve it. Try to develop common interests and options rather than winning on your position or particular way to reach these interests.

♦ *Invent options for mutual gain.* Avoid premature judgment, the tendency to see only one answer. Try to enlarge the benefits instead of dividing up a given option. This may be the heart of developing a long-term relationship with a supplier: Get him or her to think of the total value of the contract over a three- to five-year term versus today's price per unit.

♦ *Insist on using objective criteria.* Fisher, Ury, and Patton call this principled negotiation vs. positional bargaining. In the purchasing field we use benchmarks to establish what is fair and desirable. These benchmarks can be what world class partners do, what an association or society recommends, what the literature suggests, what the law advises, what the government prefers, a going market price, a standard quality measure and so on.

Thus, negotiation, in the context of the procurement system, is the process of preparing, planning for, and conducting discussions on *all* aspects of a proposed agreement between buyer and seller. Except for low-value procurements, a team usually is developed to prepare, plan for, and conduct the negotiation. The team includes the buyer (who may function as the team captain), engineers, technicians, logisticians, and cost analysts, as appropriate.

Problems in Negotiating

Several problems are common in negotiation activities:

- *Lack of formal negotiation training.* Most people think they are good negotiators, but most are not. Negotiators must receive at least one full day of training with a practice case. In addition, team members must read appropriate articles and guide books. Our favorite book is the previously cited Fisher, Ury, and Patton text.
- *Lack of preparation.* Preparation is the key to successful negotiations; however, adequate preparation seems to be the exception rather than the rule. Thorough preparations must be made prior to entering negotiations if the buyer is to achieve his or her planned goals.
- *Failure to establish realistic objectives.* Realistic objectives frequently are not established before entering face-to-face negotiations.
- *Unsound tactics.* Face-to-face negotiations are a four-phased process consisting of fact finding, narrowing the differences, bargaining, and agreement or termination. Sound tactics are required through each phase to achieve the negotiator's objectives. Again, the application of sound tactics is the exception rather than the rule.
- *Cultural misunderstandings.* Negotiations with someone from another culture introduce many new obstacles. Few purchasing personnel take the time and effort required for successful cross-cultural negotiations.

When to Negotiate

Major negotiations are expensive and require a great deal of time and effort, so we use this process when competitive bidding does not work. We negotiate rather than use competitive bidding for custom goods, buys involving high tooling/setup costs, where exact quantities are not known, when the supplier must engage in R&D or special testing, where change orders are anticipated, where supplier input to determine technical specifications is critical, where performance specifications are mandatory, where special terms and conditions must be resolved such as JIT, systems contracts, EDI, construction, unique installation requirements, partnership-alliance arrangements, and so on.

In short, we negotiate when we must have a give-and-take dialogue to determine various needs, alternative solutions, and when the money and or performance value of the contract is large, that is, the stakes are high. The key point is: We negotiate when we need a long-term and ongoing relationship based on interdependence.[2] Of course, when dealing with a sole or single source, we must negotiate. The only possible way to deal with a monopolist is to persuade, *in person.* Although some minor negotiations can be accomplished via the telephone, fax, or mail, person-to-person communication is essential to explore complicated needs and options.

What to Negotiate

Although most buyers concentrate on price, this orientation ignores life cycle costing. Thus, we must explore all performance factors such as delivery, quality, warranty, inventory, postsale service, transportation terms, installation (where applicable), and service life. For example, if poor delivery is the only problem with an otherwise excellent supplier, it is the major agenda item. If yearly price increases by the supplier are the major problem, then supplier cost reduction efforts and plans (such as value analysis) are the major agenda items.

We know of one buyer who always granted price increases as a percentage of the final invoice price based on documented material cost increases. While it may have been proper to grant the supplier a higher price to cover a legitimate material cost increase, the percentage increase should have been granted on the material cost component of the total price, not the invoiced price, which obviously includes labor, overhead, and profit. In this case, the supplier was actually receiving *twice* the price increase that he himself could document, and the price increase request should be a major agenda topic.

The yearly purchasing plan should include a list of suppliers, usually those supplying A items and materials that can shut down your operation, to bring to the negotiation table *before* contract expiration. Plan these sessions with definite future meeting dates to allow both sides time for adequate preparation.

The authors of this book are shocked to discover the large number of buyers who fail to even challenge supplier price increase notices based on rather vague reasons such as "hidden costs." Equally shocking is the number of buyers who overlook many negotiation topics such as supplier plans to receive ISO 9000 certification and the other critical objectives discussed throughout this book.

Most buyers who do negotiate effectively with new suppliers use the two-step method whereby an RFP is used to screen out all but two or three of the best (and interested) suppliers to bring to the negotiation table. Just remember, incumbent suppliers (like politicians) have the inherent advantage because of learning curve and setup experience (he or she may have amortized the cost of tooling), which reduces costs. Unless you *ask* for a price decrease because of past production experience, it will not be offered unless competition dictates such action. This is another way of saying "you get what you ask for."

Preparing for Negotiations

Fact Finding

Almost all negotiation experts state that 90% of the effort should be expended at the fact-finding stage. The following points will be helpful guides:

* *One more time, with the users, what do we need?*, i.e., requirements *not* products. If you need transportation, the truck is just one way to do it. Know the technical ramifications of the product and how it is used. Understand the technical jargon involved with product-service.

* *Who should be on the team?* Do not play technical expert. You may need QC, Inventory, Production Control, Manufacturing, design engineers, logisticians, workers (the actual assemblers), and do not forget Maintenance. Try to have the same number and type of personnel on your team as on the sales team.

While the purchasing manager or buyer is normally the team leader, the best communicator (calm, good listener, analytical, patient, pleasant, etc.) should be the team leader. Somebody from Purchasing should be the recorder (he/she who controls the pen has the power). Before entering face-to-face negotiations, the buyer and leader should remind team members that they are to make input only in their own fields and only when called upon. The team members should be reminded that there can be only one captain and that the leader is *the* captain!

* *Where?* Your place, the buyer's plant. Use the best conference room you have. This avoids travel expense and fatigue, and the buyer has records close at hand.

* *Examine the supplier's record.* Include such topics as delivery, quality, price (especially changes), response time, R&D, value analysis suggestions, personality (do we have a cultural fit?), and responsiveness. If you have no experience with the supplier, a full "sourcing" investigation report must be completed including plant visits, visits to other customers of the supplier, D&B checks, surveys, and perhaps preliminary certification requirements like ISO 9000.

* *Proposal analysis.* Use a matrix form with criteria on one axis and each supplier on the other: What is missing, what is inadequate, what is confusing, what is correct, what is inconsistent, where is the documentation/proof/test results? The buying team must know alternative manufacturing and assembly methods and be prepared to suggest them.

* *Conduct price/cost analysis.* This analysis gives the items you have to discuss. Where do you agree, where do you disagree and what will be your minimum-maximum positions on each issue? How much can you give and what is reasonable to expect?

* *Establish objectives.* What do you need in this contract? Delivery, design help, quality, life cycle costing, performance, JIT, documentation, reporting procedures?

Several basic objectives are common to most negotiations:

- Agreement on the quality to be provided and procedures for ensuring this level of quality
- Agreement on timely delivery (including production schedules)
- A fair and reasonable price and methods to control the costs of the material
- Obtaining adequate control over the manner in which the purchase order or subcontract is performed (especially in the areas of quality, quantity, and service)
- A commitment for necessary cooperation
- A continuing relationship with competent suppliers
- The establishment or growth of trust

Specific negotiation objectives should be established for all items to be discussed during the negotiation including, as applicable:

- All technical and safety requirements
- Types of materials and substitutes
- Purchaser-furnished material or equipment
- The mode of transportation and liability for claims and damage
- FOB point
- General terms and conditions
- Progress reports and personal contacts
- Production control plans
- Labor content and prices
- Cost control methods such as value engineering and value analysis and learning curve
- Overhead rates
- Sales, general and administrative expenses
- Profit
- Incentive arrangements (if other than fixed-price contract)
- Patent infringement protection
- Packaging
- Warranty terms and conditions
- Escalation–de-escalation provisions (if fixed-price with escalation)
- Payment terms (including discount provisions)
- Patents
- Stocking systems
- EDI and other direct communication systems
- Installation details
- Joint design and R&D efforts
- Manuals: operating, installation, maintenance
- Maintenance-service contracts
- Tooling: ownership, transfer provisions, calibration

As appropriate, an acceptable range and target should be established for each item subject to negotiation. The range should be bracketed by a minimum and maximum position. The minimum position should be based on the outcome if everything during production were to work out favorably. The maximum position is based on the premise that virtually every action required by the supplier will work out unsatisfactorily. The target position is the negotiator's estimate of the most likely outcome for any element being negotiated, if accomplished efficiently. It should be the point at which the prospects for overrunning the estimate are substantially the same as for underrunning it.

On critical procurements, the buyer also should establish what he or she believes to be the seller's range and target for any item of discussion. Understanding one's counterpart's needs and objectives can greatly facilitate the ensuing discussions!

Determining Bargaining Strength

This is the time for honesty. Who needs whom the most? You should know at what capacity the supplier is operating. If the supplier has the key patent, be prepared to develop alternate sources using different specifications, if possible. Remember, this is the era of global purchasing and there are very few sole sources and many potential suppliers who could make it for you if the volume were sufficient. We call this *source development*. Many buyers simply believe suppliers who say "you can only get it from us." In a few cases this is true, but the decision to make vs. buy, change specifications, or entice another source are all factors to mention during negotiations with the temporary sole source, unless you are happy with the sole source and this fits your strategy. There are advantages to having a single source such as the long-term commitment it facilitates, consistent quality checks, and having the buyer as a major customer. But, there are also risks. The benefits and risks should be analyzed and weighed.

Several factors affect the buyer's and seller's respective bargaining positions:

• *Urgency.* How urgently does the seller want an order? The more urgently the seller desires a specific order, the weaker is his or her bargaining position. The buyer can gain insight into the seller's position through a review of published data, Dun & Bradstreet reports, and the judicious use of pre-award surveys.

• *Preferred source.* Does the seller perceive that he or she has "the inside track" for a particular order? If the seller realizes that he or she is the only or the preferred source, the seller's bargaining position is greatly enhanced. One of the greatest dangers in the use of a negotiating team is that nonpurchasing team members frequently disclose information on the degree of competition present to the seller's representatives. The seller's gaining of such information can be devastating to the buyer's negotiating position. The existence (or even the appearance) of competition is one of the buyer's major strengths.

• *Lead time.* Inadequate procurement lead time weakens the buyer's bargaining position and results in an inability to obtain adequate competition (a buyer's best friend). It also results in the seller's being able to drag his or her feet during negotiations, secure in the belief that the buyer is under severe pressure to conclude an agreement.

♦ *Cost or price data.* Adequate price or cost data and the time and willingness to analyze them greatly assist the buyer in establishing realistic cost objectives and in obtaining a fair and reasonable price.

♦ *An understanding of your needs and those of your suppliers.* Negotiating skills will help each party to a negotiation. But the buyer who understands his or her needs and those of his or her counterpart and is skilled in the *art* of negotiating is the individual who has the best prospect of achieving success at the negotiating table.

Final Agenda Preparation

Using all of the above possible topics to negotiate, prepare the agenda, starting with the items you both agree on. Discussing easy ones first will establish rapport and comfort zones.

Prepare questions, anticipate questions, research answers, gather documents, and assign roles. Who asks what to whom and who answers questions from the suppliers? Remember, a thorough knowledge of price/cost analysis including industry benchmark costs and ratios by SIC code and other sources is mandatory.

Practice

Negotiation practice is sometimes called a "murder board" or "mock" session. Bring in an independent team of buying company personnel to role play with videotaping. Critique the results, revise and polish tactics, review objectives and interests. Your practice session will reveal what tactics seem to work.

The Negotiation Meetings

The actual meeting involves four phases. The first phase is fact finding using lots of "why" questions regarding the interests of both parties. Be willing to share your interests! Phase 2 is the recess or analysis prior to the next meeting, where the buying team evaluates the strengths and weaknesses of both sides, reviews its objectives, and develops new tactics. Phase 3 involves narrowing the differences by use of problem solving, logic, and persuasion. Phase 4, agreement, is or is not reached by hard bargaining.

There are natural conflicts of interest such as the seller's desire to maximize price and the buyer's desire to minimize cost. As we have previously suggested, one tactic to use is to persuade the seller to think long-term regarding total revenues and profit vs. unit price. The buyer says, "At this price, we can guarantee you a three-year contract worth X amount which should earn you 10% net profit."

Tactics aside, plan to bargain in good faith. This does not mean you reveal confidential information or give away the company store but it does mean using accurate data, telling the truth, and conducting the session with dignity using normal courtesy and ethics.

Terminate an unproductive session and meet another time. Replace a team member who is too abrasive.

The buyer (or buying team) should try to take the offensive. He or she defines each issue; states facts, conditions, and assumptions; and attempts to convince the supplier that the buyer's reasoning is sound. If agreement cannot be reached on an issue, the buyer may choose to state his or her objective and ask the supplier how to meet the objective. If agreement cannot be reached on one issue, it usually is best to move on to another. Frequently, discussions on a subsequent issue will unblock an earlier impasse.

During this phase of negotiations, mutual responsiveness frequently is employed. Mutual responsiveness calls for the buyer and seller to adjust their concessions to the other party's needs and/or to enlarge the pie. Mutual responsiveness avoids many of the problems of pure bargaining. It encourages the creation of new solutions, requires less time, creates less friction, and results in more congenial relations at both the personal and institutional levels than does bargaining. In many negotiations, it is possible to reach a mutually satisfactory agreement at this point. However, if such an agreement is not yet possible, it is necessary to employ hard bargaining.

Bargaining employs persuasion in moving the other side toward one's goal. If persuasion fails, threats may be employed. For example, either party may threaten to break off negotiations. The buyer may threaten to take all his or her business elsewhere if the seller does not yield on a point. Or the buyer may threaten to develop alternative sources of supply or even to incorporate alternative materials if the seller does not capitulate. Before employing threats, one should consider their effect and the credibility of the person issuing the threat if the bluff were called. The experienced negotiator does not make threats unless prepared to follow through. Unsupportable positions should not be taken unless the buyer is willing to give them up if challenged.

Even when bargaining, the buyer and his or her team should conduct themselves in an ethical manner. Distortions and misrepresentations serve no useful purpose. If detected, they can disrupt or terminate the negotiation. Negotiation is not haggling or chiseling. It is an honest effort to arrive at a mutually acceptable agreement. The result of a negotiation should be an agreement that benefits both parties. If either side leaves the negotiating table feeling that it has been unnecessarily abused, the stage has been set for future confrontations. An agreement reached in such a manner generally leads to future arguments, unsatisfactory performance, and the possibility of claims.

Negotiating Techniques

Control and Progress

Avoid any attempts to sidetrack the meeting onto nonessential issues. Show progress. Use summaries to clarify understanding and to demonstrate progress.

Recesses

Recesses should be used as a tactical tool. They should be planned and executed carefully. Recesses may be used to get the members of the buying team back functioning as a team. Use recesses when tempers flare, confusion occurs, or when you need to research an issue. Do *not* call a recess when the supplier has made a strong point that cannot be refuted. Avoid revealing your weakness by proceeding tactfully to the next issue.

Sequential or Package Agreement

Sequential negotiations call for negotiation and agreement on all issues *in turn*. This approach will be much more likely to result in deadlocks than will the package approach.

The package approach calls for discussing individual issues with the objective of reaching agreement on each issue, *if possible*. If agreement on an issue is not feasible *while discussing it in isolation*, the needs of each party become recognized. These needs then can be dealt with in the context of an overall agreement with compromises on one issue receiving offsetting compromises on other issues. When all unresolved issues are negotiated together, such offsetting compromises or concessions are relatively easy to achieve. When a sequential agenda is followed, quid pro quo agreements are not practical.

Tacit Agreements

The process of working through to an overall agreement acceptable to both parties is greatly facilitated through the use of tacit agreements, agreements that are not expressed or openly disclosed but are implied. They are far easier to reach than explicit agreements. Although neither party makes a *formal* commitment, the terms of the tacit agreement are quite clear to each. A tacit agreement is easier to reach than is an explicit one because both parties realize that the "agreement" may be broken without an interpretation or charge of "bad faith." Tacit agreements become binding only in the context of the entire agreement when they are formalized in writing.

Negotiations With a New Supplier

When buyer and seller are entering into negotiations for the first time, it may be desirable to develop an agenda that calls for discussions on the least important issues *first*. This approach allows each party to feel out the other side and make minor concessions in the hope of developing mutual trust. As mutual respect and trust develop, it will be possible to make progress on the more challenging items.

Informal Negotiations

Many agreements are concluded away from the bargaining table. Informal communications conducted over lunch or cocktails may move a negotiation that appears headed for an impasse on to a successful conclusion. Although considerable benefit may be gained from such discussions, the team members *must* recognize the social occasion for what it is: an extension of the bargaining table. The team members must conduct themselves accordingly!

No Agreement Is Better Than a Bad Agreement

Fisher, Ury, and Patton wisely suggest developing your BATNA, your best alternative to a negotiated agreement. Before progressing to phase 3 (problem solving) or phase 4 (hard bargaining),[3] there are instances in which one or both parties are so stubborn or so evenly matched that no amount of persuasion or logic will result in an agreement. If the seller is being totally unreasonable, the buyer should consider terminating the negotiation. Such action may be in the face of demands from the requiring party in the purchasing firm that an agreement be concluded on any terms. Such demands often are the result of failure on the part of the requestor to allow adequate and realistic purchasing lead time and failure to consider the incorporation of competitively procurable materials into the item to be produced. The buyer should *not* enter into an unrealistic agreement in such circumstances and the BATNA is a predetermined plan of action, should negotiations fail.

Several benefits can result from the termination of negotiations. First, open dialogue between buyer and requestor may be essential for the development of realistic discipline within the buying firm and adequate planning for future pro-curements. Thus, although discomfort may be experienced on the initial procure-ment, future procurements will enjoy the benefit of proper planning (lower prices, better services, more timely deliveries, etc.). Second, the break off of negotiations may cause the seller to revise his or her estimate of the buyer's bargaining position and result in greater willingness to enter into the give-and-take of true negotia-tions. Third, such action will move the negotiations to a higher (and, it is hoped, more reasonable) level in the seller's management. Frequently, the seller's repre-sentatives become emotionally involved in *winning.* Higher levels of management will tend to be less emotional and more aware of the implication of the loss of the order on the overall well-being of their firm.

Closure

A seasoned and skilled negotiator knows when to close a negotiation. Prema-ture efforts to close a negotiation are as bad as efforts to close too late. Once a point of agreement has been reached, close; don't keep talking! A timely summary will aid in determining if closure is possible. Nothing should be said that might confuse agreements already made. The agreement reached should be outlined in broad terms. Avoid introducing new issues or any further discussions that might result in reopening issues that have been settled.

How to Handle the Difficult Potential or Current Supplier

The first option is to search for another supplier. If we view the world as our potential supplier pool, there are very few sole sources. If the first option fails, then try to change the specifications—identify substitute materials, a new design, and apply other value analysis methods. Another option is the incentive of a long-term contract, a form of enlarging the pie rather than continual arguments over who gets what piece of it. The buyer can also conduct a make-or-buy analysis.

As Newman writes, when negotiating with a sole source, first determine *why* you have a sole source, what is the annual dollar volume and yearly growth with the source, what has been the price growth (if any), and what is the cost of qualifying another source.[4] Educate the sole source as to the dollar value of the relationship and "hint" at possible make options, value analysis possibilities, and source development options. Stress what it would cost the supplier if it lost the business.[5]

Whatever BATNA is selected, the buying team should confront the selling team with the harmful effects of an unreasonable position and the fact that resentment on either side prevents a partnership approach. This may require the buying firm's executives appealing to higher levels of management in the supplier company regarding the negative effects of a destructive negotiation. After all, suppliers need healthy customers just as the buyer needs healthy suppliers. Stress the total value of the business over a five-year period. The buying firm may have to consolidate all purchases with a single source to improve bargaining clout.

Finally, there are times when the supply and demand situation favors suppliers in an oligopolistic position, an economic description for an industry dominated by two or three suppliers with the largest acting as the price leader. There isn't much even a large buyer can do when the selling power is so concentrated. If such a situation becomes harmful to competition, antitrust laws can be evoked and even a telephone call to the Federal Trade Commission can alarm the giant. The buyer may have to settle in the short run and immediately develop alternative solutions.

Hints for the Negotiator

Now that we have discussed tactics and techniques in some detail, the following pointers will be meaningful:

+ Be yourself.
+ Be persuasive, not cocky.
+ Stress tact for all team members.
+ Stress listening.
+ Avoid being overheard in the hallway, rest room, etc.
+ Prepare questions in writing on four-by-six-inch cards.
+ Use appropriate body language.
+ Take notes as you listen.
+ Avoid talking too much.
+ Be firm but fair.
+ Do not disclose confidential company information "by accident."
+ Have expert assistance on the team.
+ For key negotiations, have top management approve your agenda and objectives.
+ Admit when you make a mistake or don't know; recess and find out.

* Do not have a lawyer present on either side as it sends a negative (untrusting) message.
* Be honest.
* Do *not* give competitor prices.
* Do *not* guess about quantities needed.
* Develop *patience.*
* Recess and review: Change your position when wrong.
* Don't play psychologist or "big man"—"big woman."
* Background data such as cost and production methods are the key. You must know how the product is made and the availability of alternatives to be a good negotiator. You must know the terms. Visit the supplier's plant and other users. Seek appropriate technical advice.
* Learn from your mistakes.
* Do not show anger toward the other person.
* Learn the personalities of the supplier team. Use the knowledge to establish rapport.
* Capitalize on their weakness such as lack of cost data or documentation.
* Try to stay on the offensive yet get them to talk—then *listen!*
* Remember we are *not* negotiating with a mad military dictator—we want the supplier to win also for a long-term mutually rewarding relationship.
* A win/win negotiation is *not* where both parties "win" equally. It is an outcome in which both parties are better off than if there were no agreement.

Terminate and/or Document the Agreement

Even if you have to terminate negotiations, document the details of the negotiation for future reference and as evidence, should key officials of the buyer or seller firm challenge the decision. Agreements must be recorded in detail, and the preliminary "deal" should be reviewed by both sides, a final copy exchanged, and, after revisions, the actual contract should be signed. Some organizations require a pre-award meeting (common in the construction industry) to go over final details, paying particular attention to "sins of omission" such as civil engineering tests, permits, union approval, reporting systems, progress payments, contract liaison personnel assignments, OSHA compliance, and other matters.

Negotiation Post Mortem

Critique the entire negotiation process while it is still fresh in the minds of all team members. What went right? What went wrong? What did we overlook? How could we have been better prepared? We learn the most from our mistakes so this after-action report or summary must be accomplished whether or not an agreement was reached. These reports provide excellent training materials.

The summary highlights such particulars as purchase order number, contract number, price, delivery, quantity, stocking arrangements, essential specifications, start dates, key contact personnel, key negotiators including titles, and so forth.

One final thought. If the negotiation objective is to establish a long-term "partnership," then you need much more preparation. Study works such as *Beyond Negotiation: Redeeming Customer-Supplier Relationships*, by John A. Carlisle and Robert C. Parker (New York: Wiley, 1989), for more information. Mandate teams, as covered in Chapter 13, are a great tool for partnership building as they help to resolve such issues as conflicting policies, procedures, goals, interests, and to establish trust, the heart of any agreement.

Negotiating With Someone From Another Culture

Purchasing from global sources is increasingly common. The negotiating principles that we have discussed apply in virtually all settings, but there are many nuances involved when dealing with people from cultures other than your own.[6]

  ◆ Be sensitive to your opposites' culture. Read about their culture during the preparation phase.[7] Ask questions of others who have experience negotiating with individuals of your opposites' culture. Obtain information on local circumstances in the country. The ability to understand your negotiating opposites' cultural background is of great advantage. It puts the other party off guard. You gain a definite advantage in being able to understand where the other person is coming from. On the other hand, be yourself, as the other side will not expect you to be something you are not. Clumsy attempts at acting will be recognized for what they are.

  ◆ Find out who your opposites are, who their families are, what their education is, their income, and what makes them tick.

  ◆ Attempt to develop a personal rapport, a base of understanding, and a bank of goodwill.

  ◆ In North America negotiations are relatively short in duration. In Europe, they take two or three times as long and in Japan, they take six times as long.

  ◆ Be well prepared on all issues, especially technical ones.

  ◆ Conduct extensive cost and price analyses before the formal negotiation meeting. A European negotiator will probably not have a well-developed cost breakdown, but North American and Asian negotiators tend to use very detailed cost breakdowns.

  ◆ Become familiar with applicable tax laws. Such knowledge can lead to significant price reductions.

  ◆ ROI and dividends vary greatly from country to country. They tend to be lower in many countries than in the United States. Consider this information during the objective-setting process.

  ◆ Obtain guidance from your controller on the issue of exchange rates and the likely costs or advantages of using a particular currency. Then negotiate the exchange rate as you would any other issue.

  ◆ Arrange issues in such a manner that your opposite can win his or her share of issues.

* If possible, ensure that the head of the other team has the authority to reach agreement on behalf of his or her firm. (This is not possible in Japan.)

* The position of recorder is a powerful one. Be the recorder or appoint one from your team.

* Use the package approach of discussing each issue in turn, reaching agreement when possible and then developing an acceptable package addressing all issues.

* Be extremely cautious in being frank and open during discussions. Business people from the United States often speak frankly during negotiations, makings others feel uncomfortable.

* Breaks in the negotiation may be required to allow the other team to gain approval of some proposal. But before such a break, an agreement must be reached on the topic to be discussed immediately following the break. Otherwise, negotiations will become protracted.

* A short working lunch is an effective means of getting your opponent's attention. Such a lunch is not consistent with the normal routine in many countries. The period just after lunch is the best time to introduce important issues but be careful when choosing your beverages! Friday afternoons also are extremely productive times since many people desire to clear things up before leaving for the weekend. This frequently increases the buyer's power!

* When negotiating with Europeans, be prepared for a level of conflict that differs from that experienced when dealing with Americans. Many Europeans, partly because they live in a more closed society with relatively little social mobility, are used to conflict. They do not mind conflict, and sometimes they enjoy it. Such people are not greatly concerned about negative reactions from those with whom they are in conflict. Because most Americans are pragmatic, they think of conflict as a hindrance to achieving goals. It is important for both parties to recognize this as a cultural difference and not to allow the difference to block successful negotiations.

* Negotiating in Japan is a wondrous experience. When negotiating, it is necessary to convince the whole group whose activities will be influenced by the proposed transaction.

* Business people from some other countries, but especially the United States, are uncomfortable with extended silences, whereas others are not. If they feel no compulsion to break a silence, and you are impatient to hammer out an agreement and break extended silences, you will probably end up yielding on the point being discussed. A good negotiator will recognize that such silences indicate doubt or uncertainty and will be content to allow the silence to run its course.

* In some countries a contract is *not* always a contract. Even after signing, negotiators may change their minds the next day. This often happens in China. Be aware of the business practices, laws, and enforcement in the country of the other team.

* When negotiating in Europe, you must be knowledgeable about the Euro-

pean Union (previously called EC) organization, procedures, rules, standards, and philosophy. Also be aware that each EU member has a different interpretation of the European Union.[8]

♦ Be patient. In most countries it is important to first establish relationships, then negotiate. Avoid a "get right down to business" attitude.

Summary

Negotiations should be a cooperative undertaking in which common interests are sought and in which everybody wins or gains something. Negotiating, in the context of procurement, is a process of preparing, planning for, and conducting discussions on *all* aspects of a proposed agreement. The key ingredients of a successful negotiation are preparation, development of realistic objectives, and compliance with sound tactics.

Preparation is the key to successful negotiations. Preparation includes gaining an understanding of what is being bought, conducting price (and possibly cost) analyses, understanding the strengths and weaknesses of the buyer's position, understanding the seller, and the buyer's analysis and understanding of himself or herself.

After completing these preparatory steps, the buyer must develop specific objectives for each variable subject to negotiation (price, schedule, service, quality, etc.).

Face-to-face negotiations normally consist of at least three and sometimes four phases. During the first phase, the buyer investigates any inconsistency between the supplier's proposal and the buyer's target position. During the second phase, the buyer attempts to narrow the difference between his or her and the supplier's position through the use of logic. Agreement frequently is reached during this phase. During the third phase, progress is made through compromise and bargaining, and agreement or termination is the final phase. As Fisher, Ury, and Patton suggest in *Getting to Yes,* separate the people from the problem, focus on interests, not positions, invent options for mutual gain and use objective criteria.

There are instances when it is better to terminate negotiations than to enter into an unsatisfactory agreement. Develop a BATNA, or best alternative to a negotiated agreement as advocated by Fisher, Ury, and Patton. If the supplier's representative is so stubborn that no amount of reason or logic will move him or her to an acceptable position, it may be best to break off negotiations. The buyer will be under considerable pressure from the requestor in his or her firm to consummate a deal at any price. However, several benefits can result from breaking off negotiations. The ensuing confrontation between the buyer and the requestor may be essential to the development of realistic discipline and adequate planning for future procurements. Such action has the potential for significant savings. The halt in negotiations may result in the supplier's representative's revising his or her estimate of the buyer's bargaining position and thus result in greater willingness to negotiate. Further, such action may move the negotiations to a higher and, it is hoped, more reasonable level of management at the selling firm.

A seasoned and skillful negotiator knows when to close a negotiation. Once agreement has been reached, close; don't keep talking! The agreement reached should be outlined in broad terms. Any further discussions that might result in reopening issues that have been settled and the introduction of new issues should be avoided.

Purchasing from nondomestic sources is increasingly common. There are many nuances involved in negotiations with people from other cultures. An awareness of these nuances will greatly aid the negotiator.

In our next chapter, we address 15 attributes of strategic supply management—the ultimate in proactive procurement.

Notes

1. Roger Fisher, William Ury, and Bruce Patton, *Getting to Yes: Negotiating Agreement Without Giving In,* 2nd ed. (New York: Penguin Books, 1991). Copyright ©1981, 1991 by Roger Fisher and William Ury. Reprinted by permission of Houghton Mifflin Co. All rights reserved. Another excellent reference is Ross R. Reck and Brian Long, *The Win-Win Negotiator,* Blanchard Training and Development Inc., 125 State Place, Escondido, Calif. 92025, 1985.
2. Roy J. Lewicki, Joseph A. Litterer, John W. Menthane, and David M. Shunders, *Negotiation,* 2nd ed. (Burr Ridge, Ill.: Irwin, 1994), pp. 24–47.
3. Fisher, Ury, and Patton, op. cit., p. 97.
4. Richard G. Newman, "Negotiating With the Sole Source," *NAPM Insights* (May 1992), pp. 24–25.
5. Ibid.
6. Much of the material contained in this section was developed by David N. Burt under contract F 33 615-80-C-5188, sponsored by the Air Force Business Research Management Center, Wright-Patterson Air Force Base, Ohio, 45433. Also see such works as: Toshihiro Nishiguchi, *Strategic Industrial Sourcing: The Japanese Advantage* (New York: Oxford University Press, 1994); Robert M. March, *The Japanese Negotiator: Subtlety and Strategy Beyond Western Logic* (New York: Kodansha International, 1988).
7. An excellent reference book on culture in Lisa Hoecklin, *Managing Cultural Differences: Strategies for Competitive Advantage* (New York and Workingham, England: Addison-Wesley Publishing and the Economist Intelligence Unit, 1995).
8. Richard L. Pinkerton, "The European Community—'EC 92': Implications for Purchasing Managers," *International Journal of Purchasing and Materials Management* (Spring 1993), pp. 19–26.

15

Strategic Supply Management

Will Irwin, VP of Procurement for Orthopedic Implant, Inc., has just returned from the NAPM International Purchasing Conference where he has heard many of the speakers stress the need for strategic thinking. Will was an ex-U.S. Navy fighter pilot during the Gulf War and had attended many briefings about strategy and tactics during the conflict. He is trying to apply all these concepts to his present job so he could brief the president of his firm: but where to start?

Strategic supply management is the design, development, optimization, and management of the internal and external components of the organization's supply system.* Strategic supply management is the final stage in the evolution of purchasing from a clerical process to a strategic one—a process equal to Marketing, Operations, and Finance in its contribution to the survival and success of the firm. Strategic supply management advances activities begun under proactive procurement such as "measures some cost of ownership" to their logical conclusion such as "optimizes all-in-cost." It also introduces several strategic activities including the development and integration of a supply strategy with other components of the strategic business unit's (SBU) strategy, monitoring of the supply environment, and managing the supply portion of the value chain.

There are 15 attributes of strategic supply management that you need to master to achieve Stage 4—Strategic Supply Management as depicted in Exhibit 15-1.

Supply Is a Competitive Weapon

A few years ago, one of us was having dinner with a senior member of the Japanese Management Association. We said, "We believe that in Japan, supply management is treated as a strategic weapon." Our dinner companion agreed readily, "Ah, so, you very perceptive!"

More recently, one of us was meeting with the vice president of a very successful global corporation that had just invested $7 million studying German and

---

*Much of this chapter is the work of Michael F. Doyle, co-author with David N. Burt, *The American Keiretsu: A Strategic Weapon for Global Competitiveness* (Homewood, Illinois: Business One Irwin, 1993.)

Exhibit 15-1. Self-assessment instrument.

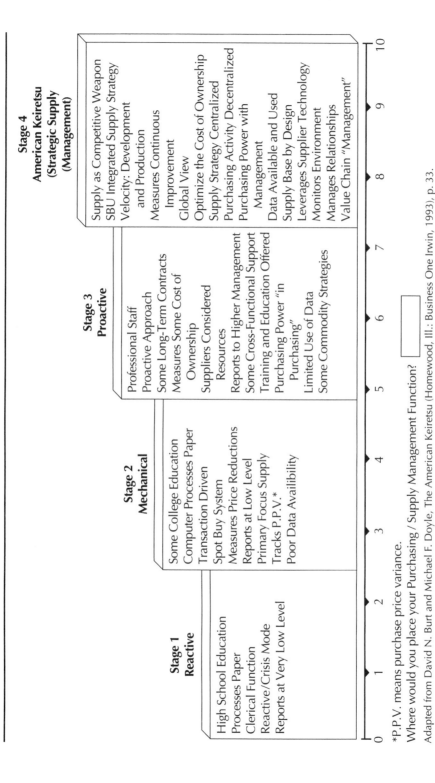

*P.P.V. means purchase price variance.

Where would you place your Purchasing / Supply Management Function? ☐

Adapted from David N. Burt and Michael F. Doyle, The American Keiretsu (Homewood, Ill.: Business One Irwin, 1993), p. 33.

Japanese approaches to supply management. We requested an opportunity to share the insight gained. The response was, "Sorry, but our investment in supply management will give us a strategic competitive advantage." All companies should recognize strategic supply management as a potential competitive edge and try to learn from the companies around the world who are leading the way.

Recently, one of us was working with a cross-functional supply team from a producer of heavy industrial equipment. There are only four major global sources of supply for one key component required in our client's assembly process. Unfortunately, the most attractive of these four potential alliance partners already had entered into a strategic supply alliance with our client's largest competitor. Since technology flow was a major concern to our client, it became obvious that the second (and by far, the second) most attractive supplier would have to be selected. Again: the competition for world class suppliers has already begun! The buyer who establishes the relationship with the best supplier first is ahead of the competition.

Integrate Supply Strategy With the SBU's Strategy

The firm itself (in the case of single division firms) or well run SBUs establish measurable goals and objectives against which their performance can be measured. These goals and objectives must be supported by the various functional plans (e.g., the marketing plan, the financial plan, the production plan, the supply plan). These plans are interdependent, must be consistent with each other, and must support the organization's goals, objectives, and plans.[1]

Supply management must be a member of the planning function. The supply manager has much to contribute to the planning process, especially in the area of threats and opportunities to the organization's supply of purchased materials and services. At the same time, the supply manager must bring back from strategic planning discussions changes to which supply management must be sensitive. Information on new product lines, products to be phased out, changes in time lines, and other such subjects will have major impact on supply plans and actions.

Long-range supply strategy is interdependent with the firm's technology plans. Any organization that plans to be in existence more than a very few years should not attempt to operate without a technology road map for both product and process technologies. These road maps must consider several interdependent issues: likely customer wants and needs, in-house design and manufacturing capabilities (present and projected), personnel and financial constraints, strategic supply alliances (for the outsourcing of products or services at or near the organization's core technologies), and the supply base as a source of new technologies and/or the products of such supplier innovation.

Gain Velocity During Development and Production

In his classic article: "Time—The Next Source of Competitive Advantage," George Stalk, Jr., writes that:

as a strategic weapon, time (velocity) is the equivalent of money, productivity, quality, even motivation. Managing time has enabled top Japanese companies not only to reduce their costs but also to offer broad product lines over more market segments, and upgrade the technological sophistication of their products.[2]

There are two aspects of velocity: the time required to develop an item and the time required to produce it. The ability to compress time (increase velocity) has a major impact on the firm's success.

Market share and profitability are closely related.[3] Ask any new product manager and he or she will tell you, the first producer of a successful new product tends to hold market share. Thus, velocity is a key factor in profitability.

The development and maintenance of collaborative relations with key suppliers is a necessary and indispensable element required to reduce development cycle time and production time significantly. The well-documented experience of Xerox during the 1980s demonstrates the impact of supply management not only on development time, but also on cost, quality, and timeliness of incoming materials.

In 1980, Xerox's Japanese competition was selling copiers for what it cost Xerox just to make comparable machines. Xerox's copier manufacturing costs exceeded those of its Japanese competition by 30–50%. Developing a new product cost Xerox twice as much and took *twice as long* as its Japanese competitors. By 1982, Xerox's share of worldwide copier revenue had shrunk to 41%, half of what it had been in 1976.

At that time, Xerox engineers designed virtually all copier components. Purchased materials represented about 80% of total copier manufacturing costs. Suppliers built to Xerox prints and specs, frequently at excessive costs. The supplier base included over 5,000 companies.

Xerox responded. Management reduced its supplier base to 400. It trained these suppliers in SPC, statistical quality control (SQC), JIT manufacturing, and TQC. Under a program of continuous supplier involvement, it included suppliers in the design of new products, often substituting performance specifications for blueprints, in the expectation that suppliers could better design final parts they were to make themselves.

The new supply approach at Xerox was a key contributor to the improved climate of 1985. From 1981 to 1984, net product cost was reduced by close to 10% per year. Rejects of incoming materials were reduced by 93%. New product development time and cost each were reduced by 50%. Production lead times were reduced 65%, from 52 weeks to 18 weeks.[4] Clearly, Xerox's suppliers and its supply management process represent a strategic advantage.

Measure Continuous Improvement

"Management without measurement is not management."[5] The principle of *kaizen* or continuous improvement (CI) requires an anchor or point against which we can measure progress, metrics (agreed-on units applicable to the situation), and a commitment to improve.

CI can and should be applied to both the internal and external components of the supply system. For example, monitoring the external supply environment may commence with an annual review and progress to a quarterly review, if sufficient additional value results. Today, CI, when applied to supplier relations, normally focuses on cost, quality, and time improvements for items produced by supply alliance partners. In the future, it will also address trust, technology sharing, and flexibility.

The monitoring systems put into place to measure CI have added benefits. They indicate when a supplier has fallen behind in technology, cost control, quality assurance, and/or delivery.

Source Globally

Global sourcing requires the integration and coordination of requirements across worldwide business units, looking at common items, processes, technologies, and suppliers.[6] Such action requires a much closer integration of procurement, design and process engineering, and R&D with the operations of suppliers from around the world.

Optimize the Cost of Ownership

Traditionally, purchasing focused on purchase price and purchase price variance (PPV). During the 1990s, the focus has shifted: Purchasing is to optimize the cost of ownership or all-in-cost. In Stage 3, Proactive Procurement, purchasing personnel are aware of the power and concept of all-in-cost or total cost. Unfortunately, the MIS and professionals in design and manufacturing are unable to provide realistic data on in-house costs associated with different quality levels of incoming materials. As a firm moves to Stage 4, Strategic Supply Management, these data become available, resulting in objective decisions on all-in-cost or total cost.

Centralize the Supply Strategy

The supply strategy must be centralized to be compatible with the goals, objectives, and strategies of the SBU or the firm. At most firms, some 50% of all expenditures for materials and services are purchased without the assistance of the purchasing department. We are *not* advocating that all purchases must be made by the purchasing department, but we do advocate that the firm develop a centralized supply strategy to leverage the clout of its total procurement.

Decentralize Purchasing Activity

Although the firm's supply strategy must be centralized, the order placement activity should be decentralized. This means that the actual placement of orders for materials should be conducted at the operating plant level with production or material control placing orders against contracts awarded by purchasing. Ideally, the plant's MRP should interface with the supplier's MRP so that human intervention is the exception and not the rule. If your current computer program cannot provide for this kind of direct communication, upgrade it to a modern software program that does.

Optimize Purchasing Power

By now, it should be apparent that the power of purchasing is every bit as great as is the power of Marketing, Operations, and Finance. In order to optimize purchasing power, senior management must be as involved in developing and cultivating key suppliers as it is in cultivating key customers and investors! The purchasing manager has his or her work cut out: he or she must educate senior management, both on the power of purchasing to increase profits and the role and responsibilities of senior management in optimizing this power.

Ensure That Data Is Available and Used

Peter Drucker observes that we must see businesses differently—"as links in an economic chain, which managers need to understand as a whole in order to manage their costs. . . ."[7]

There is always a need for data: accurate sales forecasts, accurate forecasts of the price and availability of critical purchased materials, financial data on key suppliers, new technology developments, and data on the estimated or actual in-house costs associated with alternative materials and various levels of quality. The impact of proactive procurement is constrained by the limited availability of data. Under strategic supply management, the purchasing manager works with accounting and MIS personnel to ensure the availability of required data. The data then become the basis of optimized decisions.

Design the Supply Base

"By the year 2000, achieving excellence will no longer be sufficient; success will depend on being a valued member of a successful value chain."[8] In order to achieve world-class status, a firm must have world-class suppliers.

In all but a few U.S. firms, the supply base is the result of happenstance, not design. But such design requires the cooperation and input of marketing, design, engineering, operations, quality, MIS, finance, and accounting. Specific needs to be filled by outside suppliers must be identified, reviewed, and rationalized, taking into account the firm's best interests. These needs then must be matched with the capabilities of outstanding potential suppliers. These suppliers may be "on board" or ones with whom the firm presently has no relations. Supply base plans then must be developed and implemented. In the process, source selection becomes a strategic process. Normally, the supply base will shrink. *Supply base reduction should be a by-product of this process and not an end in itself.* In several situations, the development and nurturing of one or more strategic supply alliance partners may be appropriate.

Once members of the IPS or supply management system have identified the most critical market basket(s) of materials, service, or family of equipment, the supply manager (and his or her key professionals) should develop a plan to identify, cultivate, and select the optimal supply alliance partner(s). This research should include a representative sample of suppliers from all parts of the world, as appropriate. Obviously, present suppliers should be considered, but the potential selection base should not be limited to existing suppliers.

Consider the following issues when selecting an alliance partner.[9]

- Is the potential supplier one with whom a relationship based on trust can be established and maintained?
- Do the potential partners share long-term objectives for their areas of interdependency?
- Will parties respect one another's rights, needs, and opinions? Will discussions be conducted in an atmosphere of respect?
- Are both firms flexible in their time horizons and/or focus?
- Is it likely that both parties will work at understanding issues that arise from the other party's point of view?
- Potential parties to such a supply alliance must examine each other's culture to maximize the probability of a good cultural fit.
- Does it appear likely that it will be possible to establish an atmosphere of cooperation at all levels of the relationship?
- Does it appear likely that all players from both organizations will recognize that "We need them" as much as "They need us?"
- Is it likely that senior management from both sides will fulfill their roles?

When an "attractive" potential supply alliance partner has been identified, the purchasing manager should initiate preliminary discussions on the benefits and implications of a strategic supply alliance. If the discussions lead to a positive conclusion, cross-functional teams from both organizations should meet to conduct further discussions concerning the steps necessary to develop the alliance.

Once the foundation for a strategic supply alliance has been built through these discussions and if a satisfactory approach to pricing can be developed, the two teams should structure a meeting of their respective CEOs/COOs. Just as senior executives consummate key customer accounts, they should be involved in the consummation of key supply accounts!

The outcome of these efforts should be a brief memorandum of agreement (MOA)—an agreement to work together in an open, collaborative mode on projects in a specific area. Specific projects will be conducted under the MOA with more detailed objectives, procedures, and mechanics identified. Once a project has been established, it is necessary for both parties to manage and nurture the relationship.

Several actions must be taken to ensure the success of each partnership including:

* The cross-functional team members (the workers and doers) from both the buying and the selling firms must receive training in being constructive cross-functional team members.
* The interfirm team composed of representatives of both firms must jointly receive training and development in cross-functional team skills.
* The two firms must develop an integrated communication system responsive to the needs of both parties in their area of cooperation.
* Plans to take concrete actions that will enhance trust between the two organizations must be developed and implemented.
* Arrangements for co-location of key technical personnel and for periodic visits to each other's facilities must be developed and implemented.
* Plans must be developed and implemented for training on issues including, but not limited to, designing variance out of products and processes, quality, procurement, value analysis and engineering, strategic cost analysis, and activity-based management.
* Measurable quantifiable objectives must be established in areas including quality, cost, time, technology, and others.

The results of such improvement efforts must be monitored and reported to appropriate management. Finally, it is in the interest of both the buying and supplying firms for the buyer to support the supplier's operations. For example, the purchasing staff at Honda Manufacturing of America—all 300 of them—provides Honda suppliers great support in meeting their quality, cost, and productivity goals.

Leverage Supplier Technology

While developing supply base plans, the buying firm must consider the need for and desirability of acquiring both current and future technologies from the supply base being designed.* No longer should a firm—whether GM, IBM, or a small manufacturer—attempt to develop all of the product and process technologies required to produce its end items. The acquisition of supplier technology should be by design, not by accident.

Under carefully crafted strategic alliances, the supplier should be a key source of technological innovation. If a strategic supply alliance's competitor leapfrogs the supplier's technology, then the supply alliance partner should be given

---

*A firm's supply base includes all suppliers with which it conducts business on an ongoing basis. A supply base plan is a carefully developed action plan that adjusts the firm's supply base to the firm's future technology, quality, capacity, and cost requirements. A strategic supply alliance describes a special type of relationship or alliance emphasizing the critical nature (to both parties) of the relationship. Such relationships normally are reserved for the procurement of critical materials and services where the quality of the relationship is vital to both parties.

a reasonable opportunity to regain the technological lead before considering re-sourcing options.

Whirlpool, McDonnell Douglas, Chrysler, Johnson Controls, and others have contracted large amounts of design work to their key suppliers. There are some disadvantages including: less competition as the supplier base is reduced, union resistance in the buyer firm as jobs are lost to suppliers, and the possibility of giving away key technology and sensitive information to suppliers.[10] The memories of the U.S. television industry giving the TV tube technology to low cost Asian suppliers who later started making and selling the entire TV set still haunts many U.S. industrial leaders. Alliance and partnership agreements must avoid these potential problems and provide adequate safeguards in the resulting agreements.

Monitor the Supply Environment

The SBU or firm must be as aware of its supply environment as it is of its customer environment. The supply environment includes the firm's suppliers, their suppliers, their competition, and the social, legal, and technological environments relevant to the firm's supply base. Under Stage 4, the firm is aware of threats and opportunities in its supply environment and then takes appropriate action.

Manage Relationships

Strategic supply alliances are open ones based on a large element of self-enlightened trust. They substitute the professional management of long-term relationships for the traditional market forces of supply and demand and lengthy contracts that invariably fail in their attempt to address all contingencies. They mesh the buyer's and supplier's operations in an effort to upgrade product quality and performance, appropriate technology development and sharing, and timeliness, while optimizing cost. The downside is that such relationships require the investment by both parties of considerable time and energy. Accordingly, only the most critical relationships evolve into strategic supply alliances.

A variety of forces strain strategic supply alliance relationships: personnel reassignments, the potential for complacency, safeguarding sensitive information, changing priorities at either or both firms, the ebb and flow of business, and the stress associated with demanding projects. Accordingly, we consider it essential that a business relationship manager be assigned at both the buying and supplying firms for all strategic supply alliances. These individuals manage the relationship.

Manage the Value Chain

The firm is not an island unto itself; its survival and success depend on its being a member of a successful value chain. This chain or network is an informal linkage of firms from Mother Earth (the extractors of ores and other natural resources and the growers of grains) through their processors, and on through your firm to the end customer, the source of funds that support the entire value chain. We, in supply management, are primarily concerned with the upstream portion of the value chain, also known as the supply chain. Our task is complicated by the informal (nonequity) nature of this chain. Experience has demonstrated that vertical integration—a very formalized equity approach to supply chain management—seldom works. The Japanese approach to supply—the *keiretsu*—has equity and collusive features, both of which pose legal issues in the Western world. Thus, the purchasing professional in the West must substitute managerial excellence for more formal approaches. Thus, we must persuade our suppliers to adopt a strategic approach to their supply management. In turn this approach must be passed back throughout the supply chain. Our firm, supplier firms, and our economy all will reap a harvest filled with benefits![11]

Summary

Strategic supply management sees supply as a competitive weapon. Supply strategy must be integrated with the corporate and SBU strategy, and supply managers must be part of the planning process. Time is the new competitive advantage. The first to market successful new products will usually achieve the major share of market and higher profits.

Purchasing now takes a global view of technology and supplier availability with constant monitoring of the supply of environment: social, legal, competition, technological and the entire supply chain. Managing relationships to ensure continuous improvement will help achieve the lowest cost of ownership, which is the real cost.

Planning for the progression from reactive to proactive is complex and challenging. Chapter 16 provides useful guidance for the required planning.

Notes

1. Shan Rajagopal and Kenneth N. Bernard, "Strategic Procurement and Competitive Advantage," *International Journal of Purchasing and Materials Management* (Fall 1993), pp. 13–20. Also see T. Scott Graham, Patricia J. Daugherty and William N. Dudley, "The Long-Term Strategic Impact of Purchasing Partnerships," *International Journal of Purchasing and Materials Management* (Fall 1994), pp. 13–18.
2. George Stalk, Jr., "Time—The Next Source of Competitive Advantage," *Harvard Business Review* (July-August 1988), p. 41. Also see Robert B. Handfield, "The Role of Materials Management in Developing Time-Based Competition," *International Journal of Purchasing and Materials Management* (Winter 1993), pp. 2–10, and William M. Bulkeley, "Pushing the Pace: The Latest Big Thing at Many Companies Is Speed, Speed, Speed," *The Wall Street Journal* (December 23, 1994), p. A7.
3. Subhash C. Jain, "Product Impact of Market Strategy," *Market Planning & Strategy,* 4th ed. (Cincinnati, Oh.: South-Western Publishing Company, 1993), pp. 324–328. Also see Robert D. Buzzell and Bradley T. Gale, *The PIMS Principles: Linking Strategy to Performance* (New York: The Free Press, 1987), pp. 70–84 and 103–111.

4. David N. Burt, "Managing Suppliers Up to Speed," *Harvard Business Review* (July-August 1989), pp. 127–135.
5. David N. Burt and Michael F. Doyle, *The American Keiretsu: A Strategic Weapon for Global Competitiveness* (Homewood, Ill.: Business One, Irwin, 1993), p. 185.
6. Robert M. Monczka and Robert J. Trent, "Global Sourcing: A Development Approach," *International Journal of Purchasing and Materials Management* (Spring 1991), p. 3.
7. Peter Drucker, "The Information Executives Truly Need," *Harvard Business Review* (January-February 1995), p. 54.
8. Burt and Doyle, op. cit., p. 109, and see Lisa Ellram, "Total Cost of Ownership: Elements and Implementation," *International Journal of Purchasing and Materials Management* (Fall 1993), pp. 3–11.
9. Burt and Doyle, op. cit., pp. 66–71.
10. Neal Templin and Jeff Cole, "Working Together: Manufacturers Use Supplies to Help Them Develop New Products," *The Wall Street Journal* (December 19, 1994), p. A5. Also see Jordan D. Lewis, *Partnerships for Profit: Structuring and Managing Strategic Alliances* (New York: The Free Press, 1990).
11. See Shawn Tully, "Purchasing's New Muscle," *Fortune*, February 20, 1995, pp. 75–83; and Myron Magnet, "The New Golden Rule of Business," *Fortune* (February 21, 1994), pp. 60–64.

16

Planning for Proactive Procurement

Tucker Marston, newly appointed vice president of Supply Management at Gates Mills Industrial Gas Co., has just returned from the annual procurement forum held at the University of San Diego, a gathering of the top procurement executives from all over the world.[1] In this Think Tank participants spend three days discussing strategic and tactical supply management concepts including integrated procurement operations and policies to achieve partnerships with key suppliers.

Tucker is very excited about what he heard at the forum but is somewhat overwhelmed at where to start. Although his firm has an annual plan, Purchasing was not involved in the formulation. To make matters worse, he discovers there is no procurement plan, audit, or report to senior management. Fortunately, as a former Air Force jet fighter pilot, he had prior experience with the planning process and realizes he would have to install a planning system in order to start the strategic procurement concept at his firm.

Defining Planning

Peter Drucker has the best definition of planning:

> Planning is a continuous process of making present entrepreneurial decisions systematically and with the best possible knowledge of their futurity, organizing systematically the effort needed to carry out these decisions, and measuring the results of these decisions against expectations through organized systematic feedback.[2]

Note the power of the key words: continuous process, entrepreneurial, knowledge of futurity, organizing the efforts to achieve the plan, and measuring results through a systematic feedback. A budget is simply the dollar cost of the resources to be used in a plan, and a forecast is the prediction of the results achieved from the execution of a plan. Far too many executives think a budget or a forecast is a plan and neglect attention to the strategy and tactics behind the numbers. No wonder so many plans fail.

All plans start with the corporate mission or charter with major firms using one or combinations of well-known models such as the Boston Consulting Group (BCG) growth-share matrix and GE's strategic business-planning grid. Eventually, the popular strengths, weaknesses, opportunities and threats (SWOT) analysis finds its way into planning documents. While these approaches and analysis methods are useful at the corporate and SBU level, they must be translated into more detailed operational plans at lower levels. The failure to move from the corporate charter to the selection of specific action steps at lower levels is a major reason for planning failure.

Procurement Planning

Four different types of procurement plans are prepared simultaneously: the internal purchasing department operating plan, the material buy plans for the next operating period, future strategic plans, and special projects. Another common way of designating plans are *strategic* and *tactical*. Strategic plans are usually long range, perhaps five years out, and represent broad objectives. For example, the objective to reduce your supplier base and institute 100% defect-free purchasing is a strategic objective that calls for strategic planning. The detailed steps of *how* this objective is achieved is the tactical plan. Sometimes a third type of planning called the *operational level*, or day-to-day activities, which involves the actual implementation of the plans, is included. The lower level purchasing plans must complement the corporate procurement strategy discussed in Chapter 15.

The installation of an IPS obviously requires a strategic plan. Another example of strategic thinking is the objective to develop an effective supplier management program. One tactic to accomplish this development is a formal supplier qualification screening system, regular supplier-buyer meetings, and formal supplier performance reviews. Another tactic is the use of multiyear contracts. JIT systems, supplier certification programs, TQM, international sourcing, and make-or-buy decisions are all examples of strategic procurement. Technology forecasting for future requirements and suppliers to furnish it is even more "strategic" and sophisticated.

The buy plans for specific items needed for the next operating period are a blend of tactical and operational plans. When we total all the resources needed to achieve all types of purchasing plans, we have the internal purchasing department operating budget and plan to obtain those resources.

However "macro" or "micro" the particular plans, the planning *process* always involves four phases: the current situation analysis, the objective development, the creative-new action steps (new plan), and the implementation-monitoring-revision phase.

The Current Situation Analysis Phase

The current situation analysis phase can be called the audit, the purchasing system review, or the diagnostic phase. Examine the present status of all the items listed in Exhibit 16-1 and any others unique to your organization. Then look for gaps between objectives and results to date. For example, review the records regarding the ability of the supplier to meet delivery dates, quality standards, and costs, and assess whether there is a gap between goals and results. If we want positive partnership relationships with our suppliers, a confidential supplier survey must be conducted to obtain supplier input. Supplier councils, meetings, and performance reports help but there is no substitute for the confidential survey returned to a neutral staff such as the marketing research department. A sample survey, which also includes illustrative questions for internal organization personnel using the services of the purchasing department, is included as Appendix K.

Many other items in the situation analysis are a matter of accurate record keeping and analysis if proper tracking systems are in place such as incoming defect and "late" reports. If you said in last year's plan that the department would set up a value analysis program, you either did it or failed—perhaps with some progress. The key is to be honest at this phase and to determine the reasons why objectives were achieved or neglected.

Also as suggested in the sample, survey your internal customers or the users in Operations-production, Engineering, Finance, Marketing, Quality Control, and others about your *efforts* and *results*. The purchasing plan should address any complaints or service problems identified by the survey. For example, buyers can negotiate price cuts to such a degree they reduce quality and or timely delivery. We must think long term.

Once you have compiled all the information about where you are, prepare the final written report, which compares status to objectives and or the absence of objectives for particular items.

This situation analysis report should also include a SWOT analysis in a final section to stimulate the creative phase of planning. Identify weakness such as an excessive number of purchase orders with particular suppliers, indicating a problem with paper control but also triggering an opportunity to negotiate a long-term contract based on fax or EDI release procedures. Inordinate numbers of suppliers for the same material is a weakness that also presents an opportunity for consolidation. See Exhibit 16-2 for a description of the consolidation procedures, a major creative analysis tool. Each weakness should have a potential opportunity correction action.

The situation analysis also provides the activity data for the Annual Materials Report. This report should be sent to all parties interacting with the purchasing or supply department. Although the manager should omit confidential and/or sensitive data, the annual report is an excellent vehicle to educate all interested parties as to the procurement activity and contribution. Procurement managers must learn to sell their value added activities to the rest of the organization and avoid being a mystery unit in the backroom. In addition, distributing a purchasing

(text continues on page 234)

Exhibit 16-1. The situational analysis: where you are at this time.

A. ABC inventory analysis.
B. Critical commodity list.
C. Key supplier-commodity analysis: dollar volume and percentage of material purchased from individual suppliers.
D. Existing and potential sole source buy situations vs. single source (by design or accident?).
E. Variance + or − from past objectives, goals.
     1. Target price and contract terms.
     2. On time delivery rating.
     3. Quality control-rejection rate.
     4. Supplier development, ratings.
     5. Inventory: average level, number of turns, safety stock.
     6. Stores: receiving and inspection, lost items, delays, damages, material handling capacity.
     7. Value analysis: engineering programs, projects.
     8. Long-term contracting: blanket orders, system contracts, consignment buying, formula pricing, etc.
     9. Make-or-buy projects.
     10. Traffic audit activities.
     11. Surplus analysis- "idle" equipment-material reports.
     12. External trend analysis regarding long-term movement by line item of price, lead time, internal inventory levels, commodity availability, supplier availability, quality rates, and so on.
     13. Internal departmental trend analysis regarding number of purchasing employees, number of purchase orders, number of requisitions, value per purchase order, total purchase dollar vs. total manufacturing cost, buyer training and education, ROI and ROA contribution, etc.
     14. Purchasing policy, procedures, procedure manual, supplier welcome booklet, purchasing newsletter, etc. Consider how they have been working. Identify any weaknesses or needed revisions.
     15. Production control capacity for scheduling and past accuracy record.
     16. Overall material and inventory savings (if any).
     17. Purchasing department budget, especially the trend over several years.
F. Long-term material availability—national and international. Is new technology tracking adequate?
G. Special problems, such as price-in-effect-at-time of delivery.
H. Paperless purchasing progress such as credit card, EDI, and supplier stocking programs.
I. Implementation of IPS.
J. Development and effectiveness of cross-functional teams.
K. Cycle time reduction techniques such as flow tracking studies.
L. Other items unique to your organization.

Exhibit 16-2.   The consolidation procedure, a major planning tool.

1. **Commodity Analysis**
    For all divisions, branches, subsidiaries, offices, plants, etc., obtain computer printouts and look for the same product codes and different descriptions, and the same description but different codes, including slight variations in sizes and other specifications.
2. **Total Last Year's Purchases**
    by product type and specification variations.
3. **Analyze the Volume by Supplier**
    Look for the same product purchases from four or more and in some cases two or three suppliers.
4. **Simplify and Standardize**
    If possible, change the specifications to reduce product variation, and if possible, also change from custom to commercial or standard shelf items. This part of the consolidation process is a type of value analysis procedure using a committee of users with a purchasing manager or buyer as chair.
5. **Forecast the Future Requirements**
    At least one year, two or three if possible.
6. **Prepare Requests for Proposals for Major Consolidated Contracts**
    Either blanket orders, requirement contracts and/or system contracts. Include estimated release schedules, clauses, price warning clauses, inventory control procedures, shipping, master catalogs, supplier stocking programs, and price discounts due to increased volume, etc. Reduce the number of suppliers to one prime, one backup, unless there are good reasons not to do so.
7. **The Distinction Between Blanket Orders and Systems Controls**
    A blanket order is a long-term contract for one class of product with one to three (as a rule) suppliers depending on volume. They are called many names including: international-national contracts, open-end orders, stockless purchasing, corporatewide agreements, evergreen contracts, long-term contracts, multiyear contracts, and so on.
    A *system contract* is a consolidation agreement for an *entire family of products* such as office supplies, tools, forms, repair parts, and general MRO hardware items. Often called stockless purchasing because the supplier usually owns the inventory until issued for use directly to the user (the supplier operated tool room concept). Users have master catalogs and purchasing manages by periodic review. The systems contract is usually issued to one supplier and its use greatly reduces the "small order problem." Direct releases using computer data phone terminals, fax, or EDI are optional features of many system contracts. The term *stockless* purchasing is not accurate as blanket orders and requirement contracts usually have the supplier holding large amounts of inventory. Consignment buys can also be a part of either a blanket order or system contract. Usually, the buying firm must purchase minimum amounts and be responsible for obsolete material held in inventory. The key to all long-term contracts is life cycle cost analysis.

(continues)

Exhibit 16-2.   *(continued)*

8.   **Negotiate the Contracts With as Few Suppliers as Possible**
     This requires more contract instructions regarding delivery, stocking programs, invoicing, and other such issues unique to this form of contracting, but overall costs should be drastically reduced. Don't forget to ask for the price discount. As a rule, this type of negotiation must be conducted in person. Many firms try for one prime and one backup supplier using commodity-sourcing teams to negotiate the contracts.

9.   **Audit the Results**
     Review on a monthly basis for contract performance and issue corrective instructions to the supplier, users, or both if necessary. Remember, the buying company may be at fault, such as unexpected demand, change orders, release error, etc. Watch for price creep. Prepare for the next negotiation cycle.

Note: Steps 1–3 represent the situation phase of planning.
Steps 4–7 represent the objective phase of planning.
Steps 6–8* represent the creative-new action steps phase of planning.
Step 9 represents the implementational phase of planning.
*In most planning, the steps overlap each other.

newsletter on a monthly basis not only helps to inform all the users regarding price trends, material availability, lead time requirements, and other pertinent news, it helps provide a record for the situation summary.

Objective Phase

Objectives are what an organization wants to accomplish. There are many other similar terms such as *mission, aim, target,* and *goal,* but objectives, by whatever definition, mostly deal with change. In fact, it is almost always a desire to improve or correct something that formulates an objective. Most experts state that objectives should be concrete or specific, they should be measurable, and there should be some time limit as to achievement. The mission statement, "to be a world class procurement department" sounds wonderful but it is not operational.

Every chapter in this book contains numerous objectives the authors believe produce "world class procurement departments." They are the programs, policies, and procedures thought to be the most effective and efficient for the present day and the twenty-first century. Rather than repeat all these objectives, we leave it to the reader to select the most appropriate for his or her organization although we will repeat a few in this chapter for illustrations. The term *benchmarking* is a form of objective setting against other organizations described as the "best in their class" or some other industry top rating for a particular attribute. The danger in using benchmarks is that they may not be appropriate for a particular organization's mission or resources.

The situation review will reveal strengths, weaknesses, and opportunities that we translate into objectives, usually corrective action plans to improve some existing situation or status. In addition, we must prepare persuasive and well-

Exhibit 16-3. The great assumptions: examples of environmental considerations.

 1. U.S. energy policy and world oil supply status
 2. U.S. investment credit policy
 3. IRS tax policy
 4. State inventory tax policy
 5. U.S. export-import-tariff position, GATT status
 6. Geo-political climate
 7. U.S. fiscal policy-counsel of economic advisers
 8. U.S. monetary policy, FRB Policy
 9. OSHA, environmental regulations, EEO, government regulation
10. Defense spending
11. Worldwide steel industry position
12. World commodity supply level
13. Currency conversion rates
14. Total gross domestic product (GDP)
15. Productivity level
16. Investment in plant and equipment
17. Administration empathy toward business
18. Population growth
19. Marriage rates
20. Housing starts
21. Auto sales
22. Appliance sales
23. Employment rate
24. Corporate earnings, ROI, ROA
25. Inflation rate
26. Worldwide economic conditions
27. The status of technology in your industry
28. Competitor actions and profiles

Note: There are many sources for the information requirements listed above such as *The Wall Street Journal,* the NAPM's *Report on Business,* published monthly in *NAPM Insights,* Tempe, Ariz., and a multitude of U.S. government documents.

documented staff studies to sell the ideas. Top management must endorse our planning objectives and all members of the team must buy into the new direction.

The Creative-New Action Steps (The New Plan)

Based on the stated objectives, list the *assumptions,* as all plans are based on external environmental conditions such as those listed in Exhibit 16-3. Next, develop the detailed steps and alternatives of how to achieve the planned results. This is the creative step and will call for a forecast of desired results under various alternative procedures or options. A forecast is a prediction of what a plan will accomplish. It is not the plan, just as the budget is the dollar figure for a plan and the

Exhibit 16-4. The materials plan: where do we go and how do we do it?

A. Determine *objectives* from the situation analysis plus new or existing opportunities and *new* or unmet needs (new internal products and new supplier products and technology). For example, we must develop a new source for material X in 1997.
B. How do we do it? List action steps and the environmental (economic, technological, social, legal, and political) assumptions for each action.
C. Who will do it and when? This is the human resource planning and timetable document with start-finish dates, milestones or time line, review-approval dates, etc.
D. Resource allocation: budget for people and dollars. This is the dollar figure for A–C, but it is the area where great oversights occur. Budget for training expenses, supplier survey visits, trade show attendance, equipment, facilities and materials needed to enact the plan.

Note: Your plan must be in writing and it must be completed at least three (3) months in advance of the action year.

pure dollar numbers will never tell you how to execute the plan. The creative phase is the how-to step.

Avoid wishful thinking and programs beyond the reasonable capacity of the organization. Look closely at your assumptions and resources. Exhibit 16-4 summarizes the step-by-step sequence involved in the creative phase. It starts with objectives and ends with the resource allocation necessary to achieve the plan.

The consolidation of industrial fasteners illustrated in Exhibit 16-5 is an example of a new materials plan and is deliberately simple to illustrate tactical planning in detail. It is also a good training example for all personnel. Avoid pure strategic and conceptual plans with no "how to" steps or tactical actions.

Hold a series of retreats away from the office to initiate the creative phase of planning. Everybody should come to the retreat with the situation analysis for the parts or commodities they buy already prepared. The purchasing manager will probably be the individual to work on supplier management programs and more strategic issues with input from all attendees.

Try to draft a five-year strategic plan based on the concepts in Chapter 15 with a rolling one-year tactical/operational plan. For some objectives such as a reduced supplier base, action steps will have to be phased in over a period of years. This entire book contains suggestions that must be converted to detailed planning; some can be accomplished faster than others so the timetable must be realistic. Plans always deal with change and you must determine what *resources* will be required to accomplish your plan. This means an honest and accurate estimate of the number of people, travel funds, training expenses, equipment, facilities, and materials needed for the selected final plan. Certain programs such as the development of a new supplier screening procedure or EDI will require at least some release time for a buyer or manager; they cannot be "added" to the workload of an individual preoccupied with a heavy current workload.

Finally, be aware of the many planning hazards as listed in Exhibit 16-6. Per-

Exhibit 16-5. Procurement planning chart (example is consolidation of industrial fasteners).

Prepared by: _____ Date: _____ Approved by: _____ Date: _____ Date of preparation: _____

Start date: _____ Completion 10%[1]: _____ 50%–75%: _____ 100% Finish date: _____

Current Situation by Priority	Assumptions	Objectives, Creative Phases	Key Steps, Tasks	Budget	Control Responsibility	Scheduling Target Dates, Milestones	Variance Problems, Corrections
EXAMPLE 12 suppliers for industrial fasteners	1. Quantity need will continue for 1996–97 based on past order activity. See attached and forecast 2. Cost analysis as attached indicates too many suppliers	1. Reduce administrative cost by 25% and prices by 20% 2. Negotiate blanket order or systems contract—B/O with 2 suppliers or ONE supplier on a system contract	1. Form commodity team 2. Coordinate with production 3. Analyze past orders 4. Standardize? 5. Supplier meetings 6. Supplier plant visits 7. Other users 8. Legal? 9. Contract terms 10. Negotiate	$2,000[2] for travel	Dick Jones Sr., MRO Buyer	1. Form team 6/25/96 2. Coordinate with production, 7/26/96 3. Supplier meetings, 9/30/96 4. Supplier visits, 9/30/96 5. Final negotiations, 10/15/96 6. Effective start, 11/1/96	1. Complete as planned as execution takes place. 2. Audit: Did the savings really occur?
						Signature of Project Leader	

Notes: [1] The date the project is 10% completed, etc.
[2] In this actual case, the suppliers were all in the same industrial area, hence the small amount.

Exhibit 16-6. Planning hazards: mistakes and attitude problems that must be anticipated, avoided, or corrected.

1. Corporate planning has not been integrated into a firm's total management information system.
2. Lack of understanding of the different dimensions of planning vs. forecasting vs. budgeting, etc.
3. Management at different levels in the organization has not properly engaged in or contributed to planning activities.
4. Planning vested solely in a planning department: The MBAs write it but nobody does it.
5. Many companies do not change plans as the assumptions change.
6. Many companies fail to implement plans: nice studies, but no action.
7. Too much attempted at once.
8. Confusing financing and budgeting with planning and strategy.
9. Inadequate inputs or GIGO! (Garbage in, garbage out.)
10. Failure to see the BIG picture: Hung up on details, computers, printouts, etc.
11. Overemotional commitment. Commitment to a pet project, supplier product, plan.
12. Lack of communication: fear, confusion, poor perception, "I thought."
13. Past success egotism (why change?).
14. What business are we really in (conglomerate confusion or single purpose myopia)?
15. Preoccupation with immediate ROI, ROA vs. long-term payoff.
16. We're too small to plan (but big enough to go bankrupt).
17. Our competition is going out of business (we hope).
18. What new technology?
19. Failure to translate strategy into tactics.
20. Insufficient resources for the plan.
21. Bad timing.
22. Nonexistent or inadequate records.
23. Loose planning structure and lack of marketing research and good forecasting methods.
24. Inability to predict or naive forecasting.
25. Failure to revise in light of new information, poor intelligence.
26. Simple mistakes can lead to big negative results.
27. Blind copying of someone else's plans, no creativity.
28. Poor memory, reinventing the wheel.
29. Failure to integrate plans to all levels.
30. Don't put it in writing, they might check up.
31. Lack of top management interest and support.
32. Wrong assumptions.
33. We cannot think globally, the U.S. market is enough.

haps the number one mistake is failure to implement the plan. Therefore it is essential to have action steps with time lines and assigned responsibility as illustrated in Exhibit 16-5.

Implementation, Monitoring, and Revision

After creating the final written plan, which contains many subplans, make a formal presentation of the new materials plan to the appropriate executive group for endorsement and approval to implement.

Most organizations have a defined planning cycle or timetable to submit annual reports and plans for the next operating period. If this is not the case, use the budget cycle reporting system. Just remember, budget requests without the how and why are not plans. Some organizations are so number oriented they neglect what is behind the numbers and fall into the trap of dreaming, guessing, wishful thinking, and other such games. The oldest game of all is for a senior manager to convince a junior that he or she can do great new things with no increase in resources. This assumes slack in terms of available time and tends to neglect facts concerning expenses and other requirements.

During the year we monitor results, usually on a monthly or quarterly basis. Some industries, such as the automobile industry, track progress and trends on a weekly and even daily basis. The key is to monitor the results in time to take corrective action, that is to revise the objectives, the plan, or both. The assumptions may and probably will change. Such factors as the global exchange rates of the dollar may demand a change in your international sourcing plans. With modern computer MIS programs such as MRPII, CIM, database systems, and Internet, this task is much easier today than a few years ago.

Summary

Planning consists of four phases: the situation analysis or audit, the refinement of objectives, the creative development of strategy and tactics to accomplish your objectives and mission, and the implementation-monitoring phase. It is a continuous process based on economic, social, political, legal, competitive, and technological assumptions that must be periodically monitored. These phases are the same for long-range, strategic, or tactical plans.

Planning is very creative work that requires proactive thinking. It requires input from all the players but it is the primary responsibility of the procurement executive. The need for more planning and strategic activities is another reason why some large purchasing departments are separating the research and planning activities from the day-to-day buying tasks. Good managers have vision and know how to translate vision into operational plans with one eye on strategy for the long term and the other on tactics, for the immediate operational period.

Hopefully, the material in this book will provide a good checklist for the audit or situation analysis and the creative phase of planning. We have advocated what we believe are the leading-edge procurement practices for the twenty-first century. Your first approach to planning should be to compare your present practices with what we advocate or some other benchmark, then see what fits your particular organization.

Most plans require adjustments, and all require the necessary resources to accomplish the tasks. The most precious resource is people. All procurement professionals in your organization should be Certified Purchasing Managers (C.P.M.), a program administered by NAPM in Tempe, Arizona. The only way this will be accomplished is for each individual to write a study plan. The department budget must have a specific dollar amount per person for preparation training and education. Perhaps the illustration just given seems rather insignificant but we believe C.P.M. preparation helps to move individuals from reactive to proactive action. Do not wait to be asked to plan; be proactive and do it.

Notes

1. This forum was originated several years ago by David N. Burt, NAPM Professor of Supply Management at the University of San Diego.
2. Peter F. Drucker, "Long-Range Planning," *Management Science* (vol. 5, April 1959), p. 240. Used with permission. We also recommend reading the classic work on planning, George A. Steiner, *Top Management Planning* (New York: Macmillan (Arkville Press Book), 1969). The first book devoted to procurement planning was David H. Farmer and Bernard Taylor, eds., *Corporate Planning and Procurement* (New York: Wiley, a Halsted Press Book, 1975).

Appendix A
Make-or-Buy Policy and Procedure

by

Kevin C. Beidelman
Director of Supplier Quality
and Purchasing

and

Gary Lenik
Director of Logistics

The Newport Corporation
Irving, California

March, 1994

1.0 Purpose:

   1.1 The purpose of this Newport policy and procedure (NPP) is to standardize the decision-making process to be used in determining if a particular part, subassembly, or finished product should be manufactured by Newport or purchased from an outside source.

2.0 Scope:

   2.1 This procedure is to be used by personnel in Operations, Engineering, Finance, and Marketing for parts and products in the following stages of development: initial design, pre-production phase, major redesign, or value engineering. In accordance with the Product Development Guidelines (NPP-99011) there are two logical points for application where the make-or-buy process should be applied to new products: after optimization phase targets are established and again when reviewing the pilot ECO package.

3.0 Definitions:

Cost:	The total cost of producing a part or product inside Newport or at an outside supplier. This cost should include any set-ups, tooling, nonrecurring costs in addition to the recurring unit costs. The impact of both material and labor overhead is considered as well as investment in new machinery, inspection equipment, processing and maintenance costs. All costs should be evaluated at actual.
Complexity:	Refers to the level of difficulty in manufacturing a part or product. For the basis of evaluation, more complex parts or assemblies with major impact on internal assembly operations favor a make decision.
Design Stability:	Stability refers to the amount of design changes expected during initial production. Less stable designs usually favor a make decision due to design control considerations.
Capacity:	Maintaining a stable manufacturing work force and a high utilization of plant and equipment are company goals. Therefore, products that fill unused capacity, equipment, and personnel skills favor a make decision.
Skill/Knowledge:	Parts or products that require manufacturing skills already existing at Newport tend to favor a make decision. If unique knowledge and skills of suppliers can be utilized, a buy decision is favored.
Sourcing:	If the capabilities, skills, experience, or track records of outside sources is limited or unknown, a make decision is favored.

Specs:	Specifications that are new, limited, or ambiguous and rely on internal awareness and knowledge favor a make decision.
Process/Schedule Control:	Products that require extremely short lead times integral to the scheduling of other products or families made in house would favor a make decision.
Mission/Fit:	A mission of each manufacturing area is to identify its competitive advantages and select parts and products for internal manufacturing that are consistent with this mission. Parts or products aligned with this mission favor a make decision.

4.0 Policy

4.1 Each new product, or a major redesign of an existing product, or major value engineering change, requires a make-or-buy investigation prior to production release. This investigation should take into account all factors that impact the decision for either producing at Newport or buying from an outside source of supply.

4.2 A matrix of nine factors (Exhibit A-1) shall be utilized to conduct this make-or-buy evaluation. Each factor shall be scored on a scale of 1 to 7 points: Scores closer to 1 favor a buy decision, and scores closer to 7 favor a make decision. After determining an individual score for the nine factors, each factor is then multiplied by a weight factor between 1 and 4 points depending upon the importance of the factor in the make-or-buy process. The factor-weighted scores of the nine factors and then divided by 21 (the combined value of the nine weight factors) to create a final index. Index scores over 4 points favor a make decision. Index scores under 4 points favor a buy decision.

4.3 The individual responsible for initiating a make-or-buy investigation is the process assurance engineer. To perform the study, the process assurance engineer should form a team with representation from Purchasing, Manufacturing, Finance, Marketing, and Engineering as appropriate to complete the decision matrix.

4.4 A Make-or-Buy cost comparison (Exhibit A-2) is prepared for each evaluation and is maintained by the process assurance engineer. This document summarizes complete costing information to make the product in-house compared to buying the product outside. The finance department will assist the process assurance engineer by providing appropriate percentages to be applied for determining variable and fixed burden.

5.0 Procedures

5.1 *Preliminary Review.* The initial make-or-buy process is initiated once the Optimization Phase is defined in the Product Development Guidelines (NPP-99011) has been completed. At this point the assigned de-

(text continues on page 246)

Exhibit A-1. Make-or-buy decision matrix.

Production ____________ Date ____________

	Buy Decision Favored			Neutral	Make Decision Favored				
Score Consideration	1	2	3	4	5	6	7	Weight Factor × Score	Total
Cost	1 +20% Less Outside	2 11-20% Less Outside	3 6-10% Less Outside	4 0-5% Difference	5 6-10% Less Inside	6 11-20% Less Inside	7 +20% Less Inside	4	
Complexity	1 Very Simple-1 part end item	2 Simple	3 Somewhat Simple	4 Neutral	5 Somewhat Complex	6 Complex	7 Very Complex multi-interdepart. assemble in house	3	
Design Stability	1 Very Stable No Changes	2 Stable	3 Somewhat Stable	4 Neutral	5 Occasional Changes	6 Frequent Changes	7 Constant Change New/Pilot	2	
Capacity	1 Major Investment in plant, people or equipment	2 Investment in plant, people or equipment	3 Slight Investment in plant, people or equipment	4 Neutral	5 Some overtime required	6 Fills existing capacity	7 Uses significant excess capacity	2	
Skill/ Knowledge	1 Major Investment in training or hiring	2 Some investment in training or hiring	3 Minor skill refinements required	4 Neutral	5 Skill or knowledge resident within organization (not presently available)	6 Skill or knowledge available in existing process	7 Utilize unique knowledge or skills of existing personnel	1	

	1	2	3	4	5	6	7	
Sourcing	Highly reliable proven sources available	Existing sources or manufacturing partners have experience	Known sources available requiring qualification	Neutral	Limited sources available; capability questionable	Capability of known sources inferior to in-house	No known source/ skill/tech not in supplier base	2
Specs	Complete process w/ critical tolerances defined/SPC Tech in place	Process/ inspection available & transferable	Specification complete with critical tolerances defined	Neutral	Specifications complete; official tolerances not defined	Process/ inspection capability in develop-ment	Propose or inspection capability only available internally	2
Process/ Schedule Control	No control required	Standard product available off-the-shelf	Spec product with reasonable lead time	Neutral	Spec procuct integral to assembly & mating parts	Complex spec product reporting to multiple con-figurations	Internal process control mandatory for reasons of quality or performance or schedule	2
Mission/Fit	Contrary to internal manufacturing strategy	Inconsistent with internal manufacturing strategy	Would introduce change to the documented mission	Neutral	Reasonably aligned with mfg. strategy	Consistent with internal mfg. strategy	We do similar product family; mfg. technology part of documented strategy	3

GRAND TOTAL /21

INDEX

Exhibit A-2. Make-or-buy cost comparison.

Elements of Unit Cost	Make	Buy
Material Variable Material Burden (1) Direct Labor Variable Labor Burden (2)	_____ _____ _____ _____	_____ (4) _____
Make or Buy Comparison Price	☐	☐
Fixed Material Burden (1) Fixed Labor Burden (2)	(A) _____ (B) _____	(C) _____
Standard Cost	☐	☐
Unabsorbed Burden (3) D = _____	(D_1) _____	(D_2) _____
Actual Newport Cost	☐	☐
Tooling and other non-recurring expenses	☐	☐
Selling Price Margin @ Std. Cost	_____ _____	_____ _____

Note: The Finance Department will provide fixed and variable labor and material burden percentages for application.

(1) Tabulated as budgeted percentage from the items constituting material burden.
(2) Tabulated as a percentage of the items constituting labor burden.
(3) Unabsorbed burden is the amount of residual fixed burden that remains as a result of changing an existing item from a make to a buy state or a buy to a make state.
(4) Supplier bid price.

Formulas:
$$D = |D| = (A + B) - C$$
If $C < A + B$ insert D into D_2
If $C > A + B$ insert D into D_1

sign engineer will notify the responsible process assurance engineer about the new product. The process assurance engineer will coordinate with purchasing and manufacturing personnel to determine the extent of early design involvement by each group. The purpose of this interface is to ensure that the design takes into account any special capabilities available from either outside suppliers or internal manufacturing operations. It is also to ensure that the design does not inadvertently eliminate internal manufacturing or suppliers from consideration through unique design features outside the capability of either party.

5.2 *Formal Process.* In accordance with the guidelines defined in NPP-99076, "Product Cost Administration," the formal make-or-buy evaluation is conducted as outlined in Section 2.1 above after the product plan has been approved and opinionization targets have been defined. The process assurance engineer is responsible for initiating the make-or-buy process and maintaining any necessary records.

5.3 Exhibit A-2, "Make-or-Buy Cost Comparison," is prepared by the team formed by the process assurance engineer based on information collected and submitted by the purchasing department on supplier costs and by Manufacturing on in-house costs.

5.4 Exhibit A-1, "Make-or-Buy Decision Matrix," is completed by the team incorporating the findings of Exhibit A-2. A decision is then made as to the source of production, in-house or outside supplier.

5.5 Based on the results of the decision matrix, the team should update the current cost field with anticipated production price consistent with the projected first year product demand and submit final pricing to the process assurance engineer. The process assurance engineer will summarize cost information and notify all interested departments in accordance with NPP-99076, "Product Cost Administration" guidelines.

5.6 If a decision is made to "make" the product in house, the process assurance engineer shall identify any of 7 factors that favored a "buy" decision and determine if additional efforts need to be taken to align the item with the "make" decision. Similarly, if a decision is made to "buy" the product outside, the process assurance engineer shall identify any of the 7 factors that favored a "make" decision and determine if additional efforts need to be taken to align the item with the "buy" decision.

Appendix B
Supplier Welcome Booklet

A BRUNSWICK MARINE Company

COMPASS HEADINGS

(Reproduced with permision by Sea Ray Boats, Inc.)

ear Current or Prospective Sea Ray Supplier,

We are pleased to take this opportunity to formalize the procedures and guidelines in conducting business with Sea Ray. This manual will serve to acquaint both new and prospective suppliers to our company's procurement process, as well as familiarize current suppliers to the policies, procedures, and philosophies governing our business relationship.

We view our suppliers as valued assets and extensions of our own business; it is therefore imperative that we share the same goals. The quality, price, and service that we provide our customers can only be as good as what we receive from our suppliers. We strive for continuous improvement in these three critical areas and seek to establish relationships with suppliers that are equally passionate in their quest for better quality, price, and service. By exceeding our requirements and expectations, you'll not only ensure that you will maintain the current business, you will be positioning yourself for more future business.

In fulfilling our obligations to one another as partners, we want and need your input and expertise in the product development process. We also expect our suppliers to be on the leading edge of technology relative to the products they supply to us. We want to be informed of new product designs that may impact our own products and processes. We encourage you to visit our manufacturing facilities to help us ensure we are using your products properly and in the most cost efficient manner possible.

The total pleasure boat market we now serve is substantially less than what it was in the peak year of 1988. There are a number of factors that have contributed to this decline, many out of our control. But within our control is the need to make boating as pleasurable, hassle free, and affordable to the consumer as possible. It will take all of us working together to achieve this goal and we hope you agree, Sea Ray is well positioned to continue and expand our leadership role in the industry.

We believe that the process of continuous improvement is highly dependent upon open and thorough communication. Much of what is contained in this manual is just that, communication of our policies, procedures, and expectations. It is our hope that by providing the following information, a clear understanding of our goals is developed so that we may jointly exceed the needs and expectations of our mutual customer, the boat buyer.

Sincerely,

Michael W. Myers
Vice President - Purchasing

1

PURCHASING POLICY

T he following information is provided to assist suppliers in understanding some of Sea Ray's procedures, policies, and practices that are designed to lend continuity to our supplier/customer relationships. This brief outline is intended to be a general overview and not a complete summary. The purchasing staff is able to provide additional details where necessary.

I. **Product Quality** - - Sea Ray expects suppliers to furnish quality products that conform to specifications and customer demands on a consistent and ongoing basis. This is of absolute necessity in supporting Sea Ray's position as the quality leader in the marine industry.

II. **Product Delivery** - - Leadtime for orders shall be agreed upon between Sea Ray and its supplier. This includes both production orders and warranty/accessory orders. Any changes or anticipated changes to leadtimes must be communicated to Sea Ray's Corporate Purchasing Department.

III. **New Product / Technologies** - - Sea Ray encourages and expects suppliers to introduce new ideas, products, and technologies into our business. Through this creativity, Sea Ray is able to offer the consumer a unique and more advanced product relative to years past and our competition. This premise is a foundation to our long-term supplier relationships.

IV. **Value Analysis** - - Our suppliers, both prospective and current, are encouraged to provide direction and input on Sea Ray value analysis opportunities aimed at enhancing our product value. Conversely, we are eager to work with suppliers in value engineering their products to create mutual benefits. Do not hesitate to present your ideas or ask for assistance in this regard.

V. **Pricing**--Sea Ray desires multiyear agreements that provide an assurance of continuous business. Our preferred suppliers are consequently well positioned to develop long-term strategic plans for their business including R&D, facilities, and equipment investments. In exchange for this volume consideration and long-term agreement, we expect our suppliers to commit to stable pricing and annual price reductions over the term of our agreement. When necessary, any proposed price increases are to be presented for review sixty (60) days prior to the effective date of change. Of course, any price increase must be substantiated and "earned" through performance during the preceding period.

VI. **Warranty** - - Sea Ray warrants its products for a minimum of one year from date of sale to the consumer with an emphasis on ensuring customer satisfaction. Sea Ray's warranty covers both parts and labor. Our suppliers are requested to support this warranty by offering the same warranty on their products. Suppliers will receive a "Warranty Claims Statement" so they can review their current warranties and provide feedback to Customer Service and Corporate Purchasing regarding the disposition and corrective action on defective parts.

2

VII.   **Replacement Parts** - - Sea Ray makes available spare and repair parts for previous model year products. Suppliers are required to support our replacement parts program by making product from past model years readily available. Further, prompt and accurate service to the customer is critical. Sea Ray will periodically send suppliers a "Parts Order Report" that details the number of days it takes to ship each replacement parts order. Our goal is to ship 80% of all replacement parts orders to the customer within three days and 100% within five days of receipt of the order. Suppliers are expected to support Sea Ray in this endeavor.

VIII.   **Return Policy** - - In the event that Sea Ray must return a part to a supplier, regardless of the circumstances, it is our policy to debit the supplier for the cost of that part. "Return Goods Authorization" numbers will be obtained in advance of the return if required by the supplier. Each return will be accompanied by a document that details the reason for the return, the party responsible, and disposition. The supplier may re-invoice Sea Ray for returned parts when repairs/replacements are made. All repair charges must be approved in advance by Sea Ray Purchasing.

IX.   **Product Liability** - - Suppliers are required to maintain general product liability insurance with respect to the products supplied to Sea Ray. This coverage will be a minimum of $1 million and may be more, depending upon the relative liability exposure of the item.

X.   **Confidentiality** - - Insomuch as Sea Ray is continually striving to stay ahead of the competition, it is essential that discussions of any nature be held in the strictest confidence. At times, depending on the circumstances, suppliers will be asked to sign a formal confidentiality agreement.

XI.   **Ethics** - - All purchasing personnel within the Sea Ray organization, and the suppliers they deal with, are expected to conduct their business in accordance with the twelve "Principles and Standards of Purchasing Practice" as defined by the National Association of Purchasing Management (N.A.P.M.). A copy of these principles and standards can be found on page 17 of this document.

XII.   **Supplier Visitation** - - Sea Ray requests that suppliers meet with Corporate Purchasing at least quarterly to review the status of the products supplied. Additionally, suppliers should plan to visit Sea Ray's plants at least quarterly to review the same.

SEA RAY'S MISSION FOR THE 90's

S ea Ray Boats, emphasizing our 30-year history, tradition, and heritage, will continue to lead the marine industry in the manufacture and sale of an extensive line of superior quality fiberglass boats.

Our products will combine innovative styling, design, and advanced engineering concepts with distinct and prestigious brand images. We will promote our growth, market share, and profitability by distributing our products through a worldwide network of exclusive, owner-operated dealerships to whom we will provide appropriate training, support, and development.

Our mission will be accomplished by continuing to attract and develop highly motivated and skilled employees. In support of our mission, the following statements commit us to:

≈ Produce high-quality, cost-efficient boats using superior people, quality materials, state-of-the-art manufacturing equipment, and facilities.

≈ Provide our emloyees with a quality work environment and reward them for superior performances.

≈ Ensure that Sea Ray customers realize superior satisfaction with our products, suppliers, services, dealers, and employees.

≈ Promote a partnership attitude with our suppliers in an effort to improve our products and services.

≈ Designate dealers and sales locations that have the potential to achieve desired market penetration and dealer profitability while better serving the retail customer.

≈ Employ market development strategies in concert with our dealers with the goal of expanding and improving existing and potential dealerships.

≈ Continue our international strategy of addressing foreign competition and opportunities by emphasizing specially-designed, engineered, and manufactured products for international markets.

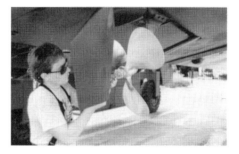

4

SEA RAY PURCHASING MISSION

orporate Purchasing, in support of the Goals and Objectives outlined in Sea Ray's Mission Statement, will strive to enhance Sea Ray's position in the marine industry through development of a world class supplier base that is capable of furnishing a product of superior quality and maximum value.

We will accomplish this through the highest professional standards of business practices and ethics while promoting partnerships with premier suppliers.

We recognize the critical role of our suppliers in the support of our efforts and as such pledge our commitment to:

≈ Establish collaborative relationships with key suppliers in order to infuse new products, practices, and concepts into our industry.

≈ Constantly grow in terms of awareness and knowledge of the marketplace, products, and business practices by maintaining open communications with key parties and partaking in appropriate educational opportunities.

≈ Represent Sea Ray in the highest professional manner while conducting business in an ethical and forthright fashion.

≈ Manage supplier relationships and assume a proactive role in the procurement cycle ensuring that Sea Ray receives the highest value products and services at world class prices.

≈ Promote the concept of value analysis and encourage our supplier base to practice this concept within their organization in order to enhance the value of every purchased product.

≈ Establish and aggressively pursue, on a continuing basis, PACE goals and objectives in order to lower the cost of quality within the Purchasing Organization and throughout Sea Ray.

≈ Produce measurable results favorably impacting Sea Ray's profitability and image.

5

THE PURCHASING PROCESS

Y ou have a product or service and you want to sell it to Sea Ray, but where do you start? The first step is to do your homework!!!

I. Get to know Sea Ray and the Sea Ray product.
    A.   Conduct a literature search.
    B.   Visit a dealer.
    C.   Talk with our customers.
    D.   Visit a marina. They are a great place to meet boat owners and most are eager to tell you what they like and don't like about their boat.

II. Decide which of your products offers the best match for Sea Ray's needs.
    A.   Will it add value to the Sea Ray product?
    B.   Are we presently using a competitors' product or is your product unique and therefore new to Sea Ray?
    C.   From a quality standpoint, how does it stack up to what we are currently using?
    D.   Are colors a consideration? Are you able to color match to our decor?
    E.   How will your product hold up in the marine environment? Extreme heat, high humidity, salt water, suntan oils, etc. are encountered frequently.

You've done your homework and you feel confident that your product or service will provide value to both Sea Ray and Sea Ray customers. It's time to introduce yourself.

I. Schedule a visit with the appropriate "Commodity Purchasing Manager." The individual contacts and phone numbers are contained in this publication. To ensure the best use of both your time and ours, Sea Ray recommends that appointments be made prior to your visit.

II. Develop your presentation to address key products that offer the greatest value to Sea Ray and its customers. Focus on how your products will enhance the value of ours.
    A. Offer factual test results that support your claims.
    B. Make certain that you understand the environment in which your product will be used and be prepared to discuss reliability issues. Again, factual test reports supporting your claims are extremely helpful.

6

C. Most of your time should be spent discussing your key item(s) but don't neglect to make us aware of all your products and especially any unique capabilities your company may have.

D. Pricing is a critical issue and will be discussed from the initial meeting through final approval.

You and your Sea Ray contact agree that there may be some common ground. Where do you go from here?

I. All products used on a Sea Ray craft must be approved by our Product Development & Engineering (P.D.&E.) group and the appropriate manufacturing locations. The appropriate Commodity Purchasing Manager will guide you through this process. Suppliers are expected to have conducted their own product quality evaluations and will be requested to supply a copy of their findings along with the samples submitted for Sea Ray's evaluation. In certain cases, Sea Ray may require industry certifications (i.e. N.M.M.A., A.B.Y.C., U.L., S.A.E.).

II. Prepare your formal quotation. Your Commodity Purchasing Manager will assist you in understanding Sea Ray's volume requirements and will provide you with applicable prints if available. Your quotation should include but not be limited to the following:

A. Your part number, Sea Ray part number, if available, and description.
B. Price. *
C. Shipping and payment terms.
D. F.O.B. point.
E. Your warranty policy. **
F. Term of the quotation.
G. Tooling requirements.
H. Leadtime requirements.

III. Quotations are evaluated on a "total cost" basis. By this, we are referring to all the costs associated with purchasing a particular component including installation labor, freight, payment terms, inventory costs, estimated warranty costs, etc. All quotations are confidential as is Sea Ray's current pricing.

* Pricing: The more detail you provide us in terms of raw material content, labor and overhead, the better we will be able to evaluate your proposal.

** Warranty: Sea Ray warranties its product, parts and labor, for a minimum of one year from the date of sale to the consumer. Suppliers that exceed these guidelines receive more consideration than those that do not. Some key components may require a multi-year warranty. Your Commodity Purchasing Manager will provide you with details.

Sea Ray accepted my bid and approved my product. Now what? Will I be receiving orders? How? When?

I.   Sea Ray utilizes a Material Requirements Plan (M.R.P.) to forecast and plan our requirements. Various planning tools are in place to assist the buyer in scheduling orders in accordance with the suppliers' leadtime requirements. Be reminded that the marine industry is dynamic. Sea Ray takes pride in meeting the customers' requirements and therefore you can expect a certain amount of fluctuation in our long-range forecast. The degree of "nervousness" in this schedule is of course dependent upon the type of product being purchased.

II. Important facts you need to know about Sea Ray Purchase Orders.

    A.   Orders are generated via our in-house computer system and are generally FAXED to the supplier directly from that system. If for some reason you feel that an original is necessary, you and the appropriate Commodity Purchasing Manager and Buyer can work out the details.

    B.   Be advised that orders may come to you from either Corporate Purchasing or the Purchasing department at the individual manufacturing locations.

    C.   If for some reason you are unable to meet the requirements as stated on the purchase order, you are expected to contact the buyer as soon as the discrepancy is discovered. Advance notice of an impending delay is imperative.

    D.   Sea Ray assumes no responsibility for materials purchased or produced in excess of that which is called out on the purchase order. This is done as much for your protection as ours. We strive to keep our inventories low and encourage our suppliers to do the same. Through properly managed inventories, we are better able to meet the needs of our customers. Further, excess inventory increases the likelihood of obsolescence which, in turn, raises the cost of both your product and ours.

III. When invoicing and generating the appropriate packing documents, please be aware of the following requirements:

    A.   All cartons, packing slips, and invoices must be marked with the Sea Ray part number and the purchase order number.

B.   The timing of payment terms becomes effective upon the receipt of the invoice or the material, whichever is later.

C.   When Sea Ray is responsible for the freight charges, it is imperative that shipping instructions on the purchase order are explicitly followed.

IV.   In the event that an item we purchased needs to be returned, the following procedures apply:

A.   We will call for a Return Goods Authorization (RGA) number when required by the supplier. All returns will be accompanied by a Sea Ray return goods form that describes the reason for the return and in most cases the requested disposition (repair and return, apply to next order, issue credit, etc.).

B.   It is a Sea Ray policy that all returns to the original supplier will be debited to that suppliers account upon the return. This procedure ensures that the proper accounting is taking place and that the part disposition is acted upon in a timely manner.

V.   In select cases, Sea Ray may elect to utilize a formal purchasing agreement where the components are either of very high value or unique conditions are present. These contracts are used to protect both Sea Ray and the supplier by documenting key issues associated with a purchasing agreement.

PLEASE UNDERSTAND THAT THESE ARE GENERAL GUIDELINES AND ARE NOT IN-TENDED TO BE A COMPREHENSIVE SUMMARY. YOUR COMMODITY PURCHASING MANAGER WILL PROVIDE MORE DETAILS AS NECESSARY.

9

WHAT IS...

P*eople* A*chieving* C*ustomer* E*xpectations*

P ACE is the name of our continuous improvement process which was implemented in the Spring of 1991. Since the inception of the PACE process, Sea Ray has continued to lower the cost of quality (the cost of doing things over) and improved its efficiency which has resulted in a higher quality product. Employee participation in PACE means that product improvement is no longer the sole domain of engineers and management. Today, thanks to PACE, every employee of Sea Ray can demonstrate their personal commitment to making a better product by suggesting improvements through the PACE Suggestion Process.

And, the best is yet to come!

Total involvement is what PACE is all about. As a supplier of goods or services to Sea Ray, your participation in the PACE process is not only encouraged, but is expected. You can begin right now! After reading the PACE pamphlet, take a moment to fill out a PACE Suggestion Form with your thoughts or ideas as to how we can improve our product or process. With this simple step you can become a part of the Sea Ray Team and join us as we Pick Up The PACE in the marine industry.

No. _____

PACE IMPROVEMENT PLAN
People Achieving Customer Expectations

SUPPLIER PACE SUGGESTION

Submitted By _____ Date _____

Company _____ Phone _____

Boat Models _____

Sea Ray Plants _____

TYPE OF IMPROVEMENT
Check all that apply.

☐ Quality Improvement   ☐ Material Cost Reduction   ☐ Inventory Reduction
☐ Product Innovation   ☐ Labor Cost Reduction   ☐ Safety/Environmental
☐ Product Standardization ☐ Leadtime Reduction   ☐ Energy

Suggestion _____
_____
_____
_____
_____

Sea Ray Response _____
_____
_____
_____

By _____ Date _____

Submit completed suggestion forms to Sea Ray Corporate Purchasing   Revised 12/7/93

SUPPLIER PERFORMANCE RATING

S ea Ray recognizes the valuable role suppliers play in its success. Exceptional suppliers enable Sea Ray to meet and exceed its customers' expectations in everything from product quality and performance all the way down to replacement parts orders. Sea Ray also recognizes that timely and constructive feedback is vital to our suppliers' continuous improvement efforts. To fill this need, Sea Ray has developed a detailed Supplier Rating System.

The objective of this Supplier Rating System is to assist our suppliers in improving the overall quality of their products and services. This is accomplished by providing clear, concise, and user friendly feedback to the supplier in a constructive manner so that appropriate corrective action can be implemented.

The Supplier Rating System addresses fifteen separate performance criteria and assigns each a weight factor based on its relative importance. Ratings, done on a regular basis by a number of Sea Ray departments and functions, ensure a fair and company-wide evaluation. Suppliers are given a rating from one to six on each criteria, with six being the most desirable. The combination of this raw score and the weight factor yields an overall performance rating that is then converted into a scaled score. Suppliers are encouraged to use this performance feedback as a foundation for their continuous improvement efforts.

In addition to the "Supplier Rating," Sea Ray has also developed a "Supplier Representative Rating" that is designed to gauge the value a supplier representative contributes to the Sea Ray - supplier relationship. Here again, there is a defined set of criteria that is given a rating of one to six, with six being the most desirable. Again, these ratings are compiled from input provided by both manufacturing and corporate personnel. Both the representatives and their respective suppliers will be given a copy of the rating and are encouraged to use it as a blueprint for their continuous improvement activities.

Contained on the following pages of this section are samples of both rating forms. If, after reviewing them, you have any questions please contact the appropriate Commodity Purchasing Manager for further discussion.

SUPPLIER
PERFORMANCE APPRAISAL

RATING:		SCALED PERFORMANCE RATING:	
6	Always. Without fail.	92% - 100%	Exemplary
5	Frequently. Most all of the time.	83% - 91%	Acceptable
4	Usually. More cases than not.	67% - 82%	Need Immediate Improvement
3	Occasionally. About half the time.	0% - 66%	Unacceptable
2	Seldom. Once in a while.	**WEIGHT FACTOR:**	
1	Never.	3	Extremely Important
NR	No Rating.	2	Very Important
		1	Important

Appraisal Period May/June/July

Supplier Name XYZ Company Inc.   **Scaled Performance Rating** 90%

1. **5** On Time Deliveries - Shipments are made on the date specified on purchase order when the appropriate leadtime is provided.
WEIGHT FACTOR: 3   WEIGHTED RATING 15

2. **6** Complete Shipments - Quantities shipped are as specified on purchase order.
WEIGHT FACTOR: 2   WEIGHTED RATING 12

3. **6** Accurate Documentation - Documentation (i.e. packing slips, invoices, prints, owners manuals) is accurate, complete and thorough. Written instructions are clear and easy to understand.
WEIGHT FACTOR: 2   WEIGHTED RATING 12

4. **5** Conformance to Specs - Initial engineering and manufacturing requirements are satisfied. Product is initially fit and suitable for its intended use.
WEIGHT FACTOR: 3   WEIGHTED RATING 15

5. **5** Field Reliability/Warranty - The product performs reliably and without issue after installation on the boat and continues to exhibit quality and trouble free characteristics to the user on a long term basis.
WEIGHT FACTOR: 3   WEIGHTED RATING 15

6. **5** Technical Support/Capabilities - Technical and engineering support is readily provided during the product development phase. Thorough instructions and clear explanations in utilizing the product are communicated to the appropriate personnel.
WEIGHT FACTOR: 2   WEIGHTED RATING 10

7. **5** Responsiveness To Issues/Communication - Responses to any issues encountered are prompt and thorough. Communication in general is ongoing, pro-active and informative.
WEIGHT FACTOR: 1   WEIGHTED RATING 5

8. **5** Price competitiveness - Price structure offered is competitive in the industry. The pricing is rational and can be justified from a costing standpoint.
WEIGHT FACTOR: 2   WEIGHTED RATING 10

SUPPLIER PERFORMANCE APPRAISAL
(PAGE 2)

RATING:		SCALED PERFORMANCE RATING:	
6	Always. Without fail.	92% - 100%	Exemplary
5	Frequently. Most all of the time.	83% - 91%	Acceptable
4	Usually. More cases than not.	67% - 82%	Need Immediate Improvement
3	Occasionally. About half the time.	0% - 66%	Unacceptable
2	Seldom. Once in a while.	**WEIGHT FACTOR:**	
1	Never.	3	Extremely Important
NR	No Rating.	2	Very Important
		1	Important

9. __5__ Price Containment - Efforts are clearly visible and demonstrated in holding or reducing prices. When price increases are necessary, they are reasonable and justifiable. Actions are taken to expedite price decreases or delay price increases.
WEIGHT FACTOR: 3   WEIGHTED RATING __15__

10. __6__ Leadtimes - Leadtimes are reasonable and competitive. There is an emphasis on continually reducing leadtimes. A market driven philosophy is evident in leadtimes provided.
WEIGHT FACTOR: 1   WEIGHTED RATING __6__

11. __6__ Parts Order Performance - Accessory orders are filled on a timely basis and support Sea Ray's goals in customer service. Parts and information on noncurrent parts are readily available.
WEIGHT FACTOR: 2   WEIGHTED RATING __12__

12. __5__ Sales Representation/Company Sales - Sales representatives (inside and outside) are professional, responsive, and demonstrate a cooperative attitude in dealing with Sea Ray personnel. They possess a high degree of integrity and work hard for Sea Ray. They are very knowledgeable on both their products and their application to Sea Ray's products.
WEIGHT FACTOR: 1   WEIGHTED RATING __5__

13. __6__ Warranty Support - Warranty and quality issues are addressed in a timely manner. A commitment to warranty support is clearly demonstrated through actions taken in participation in warranty expenses.
WEIGHT FACTOR: 2   WEIGHTED RATING __12__

14. __6__ New Product Support - A high level of support is offered during the design phase and boat development process. This support is considered a valuable resource and brings improvements to both the product and the process.
WEIGHT FACTOR: 2   WEIGHTED RATING __12__

15. __6__ Appropriateness Of Packaging - The packaging utilized offers adequate protection of the product. It is cost efficient and promotes ease of handling.
WEIGHT FACTOR: 1   WEIGHTED RATING __6__

Weighted Rating Total	162
Divided by Sum of Weight Factors	30
Overall Performance Rating	5.4
Divided by 6	6
Equals Scaled Performance Rating	90%

Comments: _____

_____

_____

 **INDEPENDENT MANUFACTURERS REPRESENTATIVES PERFORMANCE APPRAISAL**

Rating Scale:	Scaled Performance Rating:	
6 - Always, without fail.	92% - 100%	Exemplary
5 - Frequently, most all of the time.	83% - 91%	Acceptable
4 - Usually, more cases than not.	67% - 82%	Need Immediate Improvement
3 - Occasionally, about half the time.	0% - 66%	Unacceptable
2 - Seldom - once in a while.		
1 - Never.		

Appraisal Period   6/1/93 - 11/30/93

Representative Name   **ABC Co., Inc.**   **Overall Scaled Performance Rating**   87%

1. **6** Maintains absolute confidentiality at all times regarding Sea Ray's products and business. This includes respect for Sea Ray's intellectual and material property.

2. **5** Provides adequate notification to the appropriate Commodity Manager of planned activities pertaining to specific plant, PD&E, and Corporate Purchasing visits. Follow-up trip report is submitted that details the discussions and results of the visit.

3. **5** Presents new products, ideas, concepts and procedures that assist Sea Ray in producing a high quality and cost efficient product that meets or exceeds our customers expectations.

4. **5** Offers inputs utilizing value engineering and value analysis concepts.

5. **5** Provides assistance with purchase order and invoicing related issues between the supplier and pertinent Sea Ray location, when requested.

6. **5** Reviews product performance issues along with items assigned to second quality (RGA) inventory. Reports conclusions and corrective actions in a timely and responsive manner.

7. **N/A** Reviews the monthly "Supplier Warranty Claims Statement" and supplies feedback to the appropriate Commodity Manager on corrective actions taken along with the suppliers' level of financial participation in those claims.

8. **6** Possesses a thorough knowledge of products represented and their application to the Sea Ray product line.

9. **5** Assumes a proactive role beyond that of solely a liaison while providing a valued service to Sea Ray. Represents the interests of Sea Ray to the supplier ensuring a three way partnership.

Rating Total	42
Divided By	48
Equals Overall Scaled Performance Rating	87%

Comments: _____

_____

_____

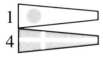

FACILITY GUIDE

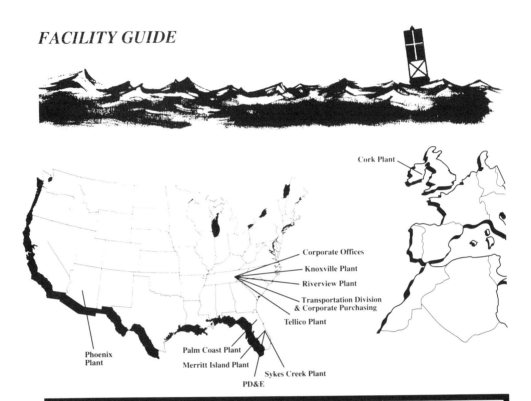

Cork Plant

Corporate Offices
Knoxville Plant
Riverview Plant
Transportation Division
& Corporate Purchasing
Tellico Plant

Phoenix
Plant

Palm Coast Plant
Merritt Island Plant
Sykes Creek Plant
PD&E

CORPORATE OFFICES
2600 Sea Ray Blvd.
Knoxville, TN 37914
615-522-4181; 615-525-5977

CORPORATE PURCHASING
5501 Island River Drive
Knoxville, TN 37914
615-637-3960 (Fax) 637-3727

KNOXVILLE PLANT
2601 Sea Ray Blvd.
Knoxville, TN 37914
615-525-9940 (Fax) 522-4696

PHOENIX PLANT
4140 East Raymond
Phoenix, AZ 85040
602-437-1120 (Fax) 437-0462

**PRODUCT DEVELOPMENT
& ENGINEERING**
200 Sea Ray Drive
P.O. Box 542855 (32954-2855)
Merritt Island, FL 32953
407-452-9876 (Fax) 453-5609

RIVERVIEW PLANT
5502 Island River Drive
Knoxville, TN 37914
615-637-3607 (Fax) 637-2561

TELLICO PLANT
100 Sea Ray Drive
Vonore, TN 37885-9998
615-884-6631 (Fax) 884-6701

SYKES CREEK PLANT
350 Sea Ray Drive
Merritt Island, FL 32953
407-459-2930 (Fax) 452-6158

PALM COAST PLANT
100 Sea Ray Drive
Palm Coast, FL 32037
904-439-3401 (Fax) 439-2060

TRANSPORTATION DIVISION
5501 Island River Drive
Knoxville, TN 37914
615-522-8362 (Fax) 524-8916

CORK, IRELAND
Little Island Ind. Park
Cork, Ireland
011-353-21-354231
(Fax) 011-353-21-354089

MERRITT ISLAND PLANT
100 Sea Ray Drive
Merritt Island, FL 32953
407-452-6710 (Fax) 453-2006

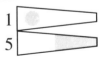

1
5

CORPORATE PURCHASING ORGANIZATION

 Sea Ray Corporate Purchasing
Organization Chart

Phone (615) 637 - 3960

Fax (615) 637 - 3727

VICE PRESIDENT PURCHASING

MIKE MYERS

PURCHASING RECEPTIONIST DONNA CAMERON

EXECUTIVE SECRETARY MARLENE PARKS

COMMODITY PURCHASING MGR. JIM BARCLAY LAMINATES, WOOD, PLASTICS	COMMODITY PURCHASING MGR. JAN MORTON ELECTRICAL, CONTROLS APPLIANCES	COMMODITY PURCHASING MGR. DEAN ELLIS ENGINES, VINYLS, CANVAS, CARPETING	COMMODITY PURCHASING MGR. RUSS NELLIS METAL COMPONENTS
• Laminates, adhesives • Paints • Wood - subassembled • Solvents, fluids, sealants • Lam. - subassembled • Molded parts, plastic/ rubber/FRP • Hoses, thru-hulls • PVC Pipe/fittings/ valves • Plex mirrors/mica/ tambour/drawers	• Elect./Fittings/panels/ wire • Lighting - Int./Ext. • Air conditioning • Appliances • Electronics/navigation/ entertainment • Pumps/blowers • Steering/controls/tabs/ sync. • Head systems/plumb ing fixtures	• Engines and Engine scheduling • Vinyls/canvas/mesh/ screen • Fabrics/carpeting/ blinds/pillows • Upholstery subassemb. • Seating/tables/ hardware • Foam/insulation • Graphics,tape • Emblems/labels/plates • Safety equip./manuals • Engines/generator components/exhaust systems • Generators	• Stainless steel hardware • Fasteners,tape,connec. • Underwater gear/pro- pulsion components • Tanks • Pipe fittings/Valves Strainers BR/SS/AL • Extrusions/tubing/ metals • Metal - subassembled • Window/doors/ windshields • Clamps

Josh Osborne Buyer/Planner	**Rebecca Crews** Buyer/Planner	**Randy Wheeler** Buyer/Planner	**Doug Alexander** Buyer/Planner
Laminates Adhesives Hoses Woods Bottom Paints Tambour	Steering Systems/Wheels Trim Tabs Controls/Control Cables Blowers/Pumps Float Switches Wipers/Windlasses Appliances Head Systems Horns Antennas/Amplifiers Shower/Faucets Stereos/Speakers VHF/TV Compasses	Owners Manuals Generators Fuel Filters Exhaust Collectors Risers Emblems/Graphics Halon Systems Carpet Seating Hardware Safety Equipment	Anchors/ Cleats Deck Plates/ Vents/Bow/Stern Eyes Rod Holders Props/ Tie Bars Rudders/ Shafts/Brass Fittings Stainless Rail Swim Ladders SS Tubing Seacocks

Danny Henry Buyer/Planner	**Don Malburg** Buyer/Planner		**Danny Bivens** Buyer/Planner
Solvents/Sealants Mica/Plex/Lam. Panels Vac Pak Tape Molded Parts Thru Hulls PVC Pipe Shrink Film	Lighting Electrical Panels Harnesses Spotlights Wire/Converters Gauges Shore Power		Sending Units/Hose Clamps PVC/Alum. Angle Windshields Deck Hatches/Screens T - Molding Fuel/Holding Water Tanks Aluminum Frames

PRINCIPLES AND STANDARDS OF PURCHASING PRACTICE

National Association of Purchasing Management

LOYALTY TO YOUR ORGANIZATION JUSTICE TO THOSE WITH WHOM YOU DEAL FAITH IN YOUR PROFESSION

From these principles are derived the NAPM standards of purchasing practice.
(Domestic and International)

1. Avoid the intent and appearance of unethical or compromising practice in relationships, actions and communications.

2. Demonstrate loyalty to the employer by diligently following the lawful instructions of the employer, using reasonable care and only authority granted.

3. Refrain from any private business or professional activity that would create a conflict between personal interests and the interests of the employer.

4. Refrain from soliciting or accepting money, loans, credits or prejudicial discounts, and the acceptance of gifts, entertainment, favors or services from present or potential suppliers that might influence, or appear to influence, purchasing decisions.

5. Handle confidential or proprietary information belonging to employers or suppliers with due care and proper consideration of ethical and legal ramifications and governmental regulations.

6. Promote positive supplier relationships through courtesy and impartiality in all phases of the purchasing cycle.

7. Refrain from reciprocal agreements that restrain competition.

8. Know and obey the letter and spirit of laws governing the purchasing function and remain alert to the legal ramifications of purchasing decisions.

9. Encourage all segments of society to participate by demonstrating support for small, disadvantaged, and minority-owned businesses.

10. Discourage purchasing's involvement in employer-sponsored programs of personal purchases that are not business related.

11. Enhance the proficiency and stature of the purchasing profession by acquiring and maintaining current technical knowledge and the highest standards of ethical behavior.

12. Conduct international purchasing in accordance with the laws, customs and practices of foreign countries, consistent with United States laws, your organization policies and these Ethical Standards and Guidelines.

1
7

THE HISTORY OF SEA RAY

Founded in 1959, Sea Ray Boats, Inc. has become the world leader in the pleasure boat industry by offering the broadest line of boats in the world with over 60 models ranging in size from 13 to 65 feet. Sea Ray's seven families of boats: Sea Rayder, Jet Boats, Sport Boats, Sport Cruisers, Sport Yachts, Yachts, Laguna fishing boats, and Ski Ray tournament approved ski boats are considered to be the highest quality pleasure boats in the world.

In 1986, Sea Ray became part of the Brunswick Corporation, one of the largest corporations in the United States as well as the world's largest marine group. Based in Knoxville, Tennessee, Sea Ray is truly a world class corporation with manufacturing locations in Florida, Tennessee, and Arizona. Internationally, Sea Ray has a Sport Boat and Sport Cruiser manufacturing facility in Cork, Ireland, which serves European markets. A significant portion of Sea Ray's business is generated outside the United States.

Dedication to quality and commitment to customer satisfaction has propelled Sea Ray into the position of industry leader. A tremendous amount of Sea Ray's emphasis has always been placed on researching the customers' needs and expectations. This level of focus and commitment to product development is a hallmark which underlies Sea Ray's respected worldwide reputation.

Sea Ray's extensive dealer network contributes greatly to the buyers satisfaction by offering them experienced service departments and helpful information in selecting the proper boat. These Sea Ray dealers enjoy one of the highest customer satisfaction index ratings in the industry.

It is with great dedication and commitment to quality that each Sea Ray boat is built. The enthusiasm of every Sea Ray employee in making the world's best boats makes the Sea Ray slogan ring true :

"IF IT ISN'T A SEA RAY, YOU'VE MISSED THE BOAT!"

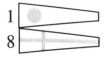

NOTES

Appendix C
The Learning Curve

Many of the estimating methods we have looked at consider the implications of the quantity being produced or purchased when developing the cost estimate. However, when the estimate is for a specific unit or units to be produced or purchased, consideration should be given to the phenomenon that labor and management *learn*—that is, they tend to become more efficient as the number of units produced increases.

Learning occurs in virtually all repetitive operations. The learning curve should be employed when developing estimates, when planning and managing manufacturing operations, and when negotiating prices for purchased materials and components. Typically, learning takes place in two general areas: individual learning and organizational learning. Individual learning occurs when an individual repeats a process and gains efficiency from the experience. Organizational learning results from administrative, equipment, process, and related improvements. The learning reflects the collective efforts of many individuals, both in line and staff positions, with the common objective of accomplishing a task progressively more efficiently. One of the first observations of such learning was in aircraft production when it was observed that the hours required to build an aircraft decreased at a constant rate each time the production quantity doubled over a wide range of production.

Learning curves describe an empirical relationship between the number of units produced and the number of hours required to produce them. The direct labor hours required to produce a unit decrease by a constant percentage each time the quantity produced is doubled. This relationship is very useful in production planning, in estimating costs for make-or-buy analyses, and in preparing for and conducting negotiations with prospective suppliers. Table C-1 shows the labor required to produce the first four units and the two-thousandth unit of an item with a 90% learning curve.

Frequently, a supplier's production capacity may be a constraint on the purchasing firm's production plans. The learning curve is useful in estimating how many units a supplier can produce per unit of time. If progress payments are to be made to suppliers for extended production runs, the learning curve will assist Purchasing in developing a progress payment plan that corresponds with the supplier's incurrence of costs.

Setting aside the effect of inflation, material costs also decrease with experi-

Table C-1.   Ninety percent learning curve.

Unit Produced	Labor Hours Required for Last Item	Cumulative Labor Hours Required	Average Labor Hours Required Per Unit
1st	10.0	10.0	10.0
2nd	9.0	19.0	9.5
3rd	8.5	27.5	9.2
4th	8.1	35.6	8.9
2000th	3.1	7423.0	3.7

ence. Better methods are developed for producing the item, resulting in less scrap and spoilage. Less expensive materials are found to be satisfactory. And Purchasing learns; that is, it locates less expensive sources and is able to negotiate lower unit prices. A learning rate of 95% is typical for material expenses.

Different types of manufacturing operations experience different rates of learning. Typical basic slope percentages for representative activities are:

Job Shop	95
Sheet Metal Stamping	92
Wire Preparation	90
Job Machining	88
Electronics Sheet Metal	87
Electronics Ship Assembly	85
General Subassembly	83
Major Aircraft Assembly	80

Let us assume that a detailed bottom-up estimate is available. This estimate indicates that the first welded forging assembly will require 10 hours. During discussions with the prospective supplier, agreement is reached on this estimate and the expectation that the most likely learning rate will be 90%. It then is possible to estimate the total number of hours required to produce 2,000 units. Using data from the 90% learning rate (Table C-1), the total hours required to produce 2,000 units will be 742.3 times the time required to produce the first unit (10 hours), for a total of 7,423 hours. If likely material cost for the first unit is $60, then the total likely material costs (setting aside the effect of inflation) would be $60 × 1,230, 95% learning rate, 2,000 units, or $7,380. Assume further that delivery of the assemblies paces the production schedule. Based on the cumulative hours available in standard learning curve tables, the buyer and prospective seller should be able to agree on a realistic rate of delivery for each month of the contract period.

The learning experience approximates a straight-line pattern when plotted

Exhibit C-1. Arithmetic 80% learning curve.

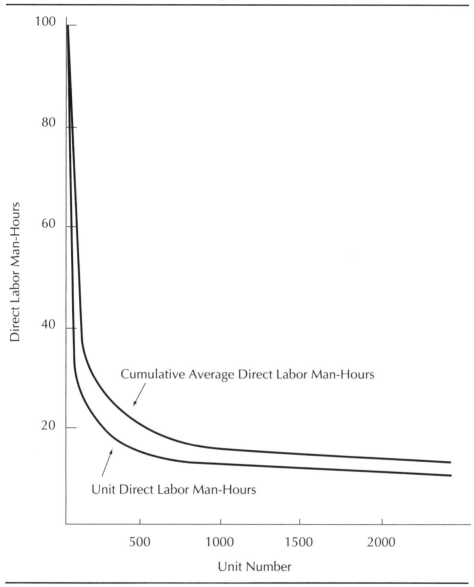

on log-log paper. Exhibit C-1 shows an 80% learning curve utilizing the arithmetic plotting format for an item that requires 100 direct labor hours to produce the first unit. Exhibit C-2 displays the same information utilizing the conventional log-log format.

When producing a new product or initiating a new production process, the assumption of a constant rate of learning or improvement is reasonable for quantities in excess of 50 units. However, for fewer than 50 units, there frequently is a

Exhibit C-2. Log-log 80% learning curve.

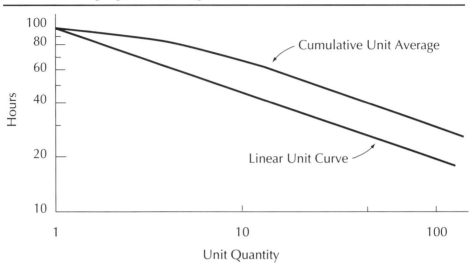

Exhibit C-3. A new product learning curve.

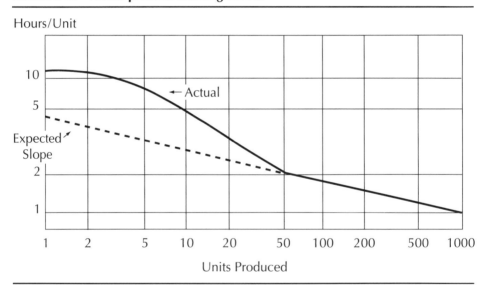

substantial amount of deviation from the linear unit curve portrayed in Exhibit C-2. In many situations, costs run considerably higher for the first units of production. The higher costs incurred during the early stages of production result largely from the time compression that normally occurs when introducing a new product.[1] The amount of excess cost (deviations from the costs that would have been incurred were there no time compression) will vary from product to product and by department. Exhibit C-3 portrays the effect of such time compression on the rate of learning.

Several other problems are associated with the use of learning curves including production interruptions which, if long enough, may change the learning rate and in some cases, require the learning to start over. In addition, nonuniform learning rates, low-labor content items, small payoffs in relation to the time required to develop the rates, and the use of incorrect rates are all potential causes of error.

It has not been the intent of this brief discussion on learning curves to develop the reader into an expert on their use. Rather, the concept and limitations of learning curves have been presented to serve as a way of alerting the estimator, the price analyst, the negotiator, and management alike to the implications of learning on production and purchasing costs and schedules and of the dangers of extrapolating cost estimates from production lots of one size to another.

Note

1. E. B. Cochran, *Planning Production Costs: Using the Improvement Curve* (San Francisco: Chandler, 1968), p. 207. Also see George S. Day and David B. Montgomery, "Diagnosing the Experience Curve," *Journal of Marketing* (Spring 1983), pp. 44–58; Louis E. Yelle, "Common Flaws in Learning Curve Analysis," *Journal of Purchasing and Materials Management* (Fall 1985), pp. 10–15; Pankaj Ghemawat, "Building Strategy on the Experience Curve," *Harvard Business Review* (September-October 1983), pp. 131–141; and David N. Burt, Warren E. Norquist, and Jimmy Anklesaria, *Zero Based Pricing™: Achieving World Class Competitiveness Through Reduced All-in-Costs* (Chicago, Ill.: Probus, 1990), p. 199–212.

Appendix D
Alternative Methods of Contract Pricing

A frequently ignored, but crucial, aspect of procurement is selecting the right method of contract pricing. Historically, over 98% of all purchase orders and contracts have specified a firm fixed price for the product or service purchased. But when such an approach is not appropriate, management must have a sound understanding of the attributes and applicability of alternative methods of contract pricing.

Certainly we can find suppliers willing to provide any good or service at a firm fixed price if that price is high enough. But there is, or should be, a relationship between the amount of cost uncertainty in a given situation and the method of contract pricing. By using the correct approach, the buyer can provide appropriate incentives to the supplier to control costs and avoid excessive or contingency pricing. Thus an understanding of the characteristics of alternative approaches to traditional firm fixed-price pricing and knowledge of when to use the appropriate alternative will result in significant savings by the purchaser.

In addition to the firm fixed-price (FFP) contract, useful alternative contract formats include fixed-price redeterminable (FPR) contracts, fixed-price incentive fee (FPIF) contracts, cost plus incentive fee (CPIF) contracts, cost plus award fee (CPAF) contracts, and cost plus fixed-fee (CPFF) contracts.

Firm Fixed-Price Contracts

From the supplier's point of view, the FFP contract offers maximum incentive to perform effectively. It also contains no (or very few) administrative requirements (such as provisions for cost information) imposed by the purchaser.

Assume, for example, that a supplier has agreed to a unit selling price of $110. If the supplier can reduce costs from $100 (point A in Exhibit D-1) to $90 (point B), profits increase to $20 per unit because the supplier retains as profit each dollar saved below the initial estimated cost. Conversely, any costs over the initial estimate must be borne by the supplier, even to the extent of a loss (if, in

Exhibit D-1. The firm fixed-price contract.

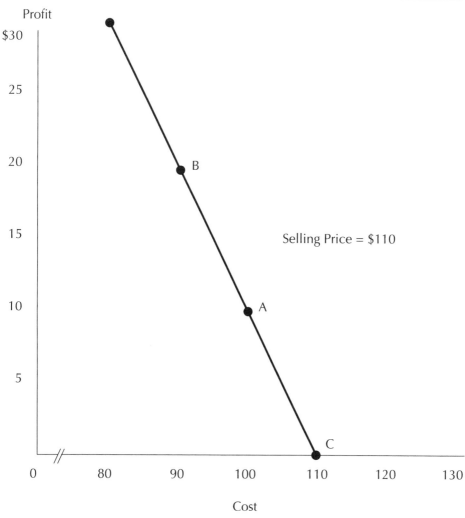

this instance, costs were to exceed $110). Because the supplier receives 100% of all savings below target or incurs 100% of all costs above target, we call this a 0/ 100 sharing relationship.

From the purchaser's point of view, two primary benefits accrue: ease of administration and certainty of purchase price. A potential disadvantage to the buyer stems from the supplier's incentive to control cost—every dollar saved represents a dollar's additional profit. Accordingly, a supplier may be tempted to reduce quality to lower production costs. Little danger of this exists if the buyer is purchasing standard, off-the-shelf items. But if the supplier is producing a non-

Exhibit D-2.   Fixed price with escalation.

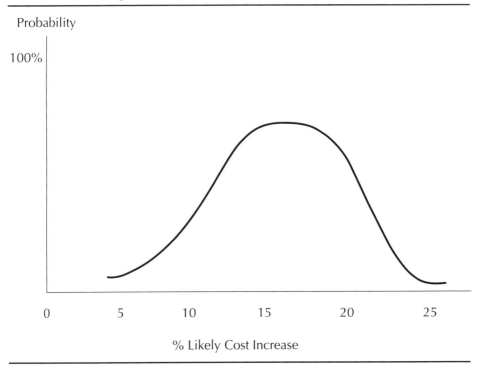

Probability

100%

0   5   10   15   20   25

% Likely Cost Increase

standard item or is providing a nonstandard service, a desire to maximize profit may conflict with the seller's desire to receive the specified level of quality.

A useful variation of the FFP contract involves the introduction of a provision whereby the customer accepts the risk associated with inflation when it is impossible to predict accurately the degree of potential increase (or decrease) in production costs. To illustrate, let us examine a prospective supplier's pricing strategy when it knows, with a high degree of accuracy, the quantity of materials and labor required to provide the product or service, but faces considerable uncertainty as to how much production costs will increase. (The logic for decreasing costs is similar, but will not be carried forward in this discussion.) See Exhibit D-2.

Assume that the seller believes that costs will rise between 5% and 25%, with an advance of 15% most likely. What value, then, will be used in preparing the price?

If the seller is a rational, risk-averse supplier and believes that the competition is similarly risk averse, the pricing quote probably will include a contingency sufficient to protect the firm. Thus the seller in this example will tend to use a value of about 22%.

But if the buyer is willing to assume all risk associated with the uncertainty of the magnitude of cost increases, then the supplier should be able and willing to offer a price containing no contingency for inflation. By assuming this risk, the buyer expects to incur additional costs of about 15%, thereby saving (if expectations prove correct) approximately 7% of the price the supplier would have offered. Obviously, if inflation exceeds 22%, the buyer will pay more than under a firm fixed price containing a 22% contingency for inflation. In most cases, however, the buyer will save money through the use of an escalation–de-escalation provision when the quantity of inputs is known but the effects of inflation are not known.

Fixed-Price Redeterminable Contracts

FPR contracts, which are similar to a letter order or letter contract, should be used with great caution. With this type of contract, the supplier's incentive (assuming it to be a rational profit maximizer) is to increase costs to increase profit.

To illustrate, assume a situation in which a buyer who is contracting for a substantial-dollar-value product has located a supplier with adequate resources and managerial ability but no experience producing the desired product. But because of an urgent need, the buyer is unable or unwilling to take the time to develop a detailed cost estimate. Buyer and seller agree to a ceiling price of $1.10 per item ($1.00 cost plus $0.10 profit), subject to redetermination after the supplier has gained sufficient experience to permit more realistic pricing of the item.

After the seller has gained this experience, the buyer learns that unit costs are running only about half the original estimate of $1.00. What rate of profit should the buyer and seller then negotiate?

Of the several hundred people to whom this question has been posed, only a handful responded that the supplier was entitled to 10 cents or more profit. Most said that, based on a cost of 50 cents, the supplier's profit should be only 4 or 5 cents. But what a strange way to reward a supplier for controlling costs! It does not take a very intelligent supplier long to realize that the greater the production costs (up to the fixed ceiling), the greater the profits (see Exhibit D-3). When a supplier is able to influence costs, doesn't it make good sense to reward good efforts and to penalize poor performance?

Fixed-Price Incentive Fee Contracts

FPIF contracts are appropriate in situations in which a moderate degree of uncertainty exists about the cost outcome and in which the contractor's performance will affect costs. Under this contract, the buyer shares in savings that result when production costs drop below the original target, but also must help to shoulder the added cost if the seller goes above the target cost figure.

An FPIF contract requires buyer-seller agreement on the most likely (target) cost, target fee, ceiling price, and share ratio. Under a share ratio—stated as 75/25, 60/40, 50/50, and so on—the first value indicates the purchaser's share of savings below target cost or of any additional costs above target (but below the point at which the supplier assumes all additional costs—the point of total assumption).

Exhibit D-4 illustrates the effect of different cost levels on a supplier's fee. In

Exhibit D-3.   Fixed-price redeterminable contract.

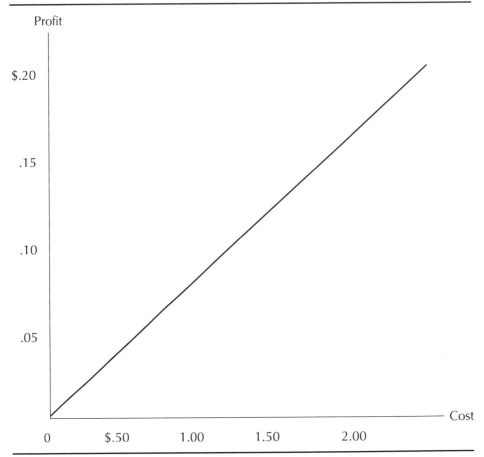

this example, the target cost is $100,000 (point A) and the target fee is $10,000 (point B), making a target price of $110,000; the ceiling price (point C) is $125,000; the point of total assumption is $121,430 (point D),[1] and the share ratio is 70/30.

Thus, in this example, if actual costs are $1.00 less than the target cost of $100,000, the supplier receives the $10,000 target fee plus $0.30 (30% of $1.00) for a total of $10,000.30. Conversely, if actual costs exceed target costs by $1.00, the supplier must pay 30% of the additional cost, resulting in a net fee of $9,999.70.

Although the customer incurs an exposure equal to the ceiling price under the FPIF contract, his or her most likely expenditure is equal to the target price (target cost plus target fee). Thus, as discussed, the supplier has an incentive to control costs because the supplier shares in any savings and must absorb a significant share of cost overruns.

Cost Plus Incentive Fee Contract

The CPIF contract is similar to the fixed price incentive fee contract except that it becomes a cost-plus-fixed-fee (CPFF) contract at two points (A and B in Exhibit

Exhibit D-4.   Fixed price incentive fee contract.

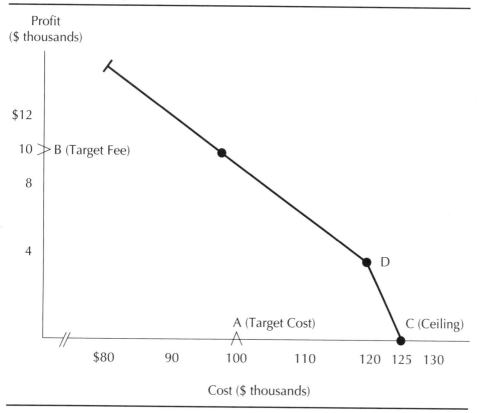

D-5). Point C represents the target cost ($100,000) and point D represents the target fee ($6,000). Under the contract structure portrayed here, there is considerable uncertainty as to exactly what actual costs will be: however, the most likely cost is $100,000, with small possibility of costs going below $70,000 or exceeding $130,000.

Cost Plus Award Fee Contract

The award fee provision of the CPAF contract provides an incentive to the supplier by rewarding superior performance with above-average profits. The award fee is simply a "fee pool" (a specific dollar amount) established by the buyer and awarded in portions to the supplier on a periodic basis as earned.

An award fee pool normally ranges from 2% to 10% of estimated costs. The amount of the pool that the supplier can earn depends on his or her performance—as determined by the buyer—over and above the minimum requirements set down in the contract. The award fee thus gives the buyer's management a flexible tool with which to influence performance. The buyer rewards the sup-

Exhibit D-5. Cost plus incentive fee contract.

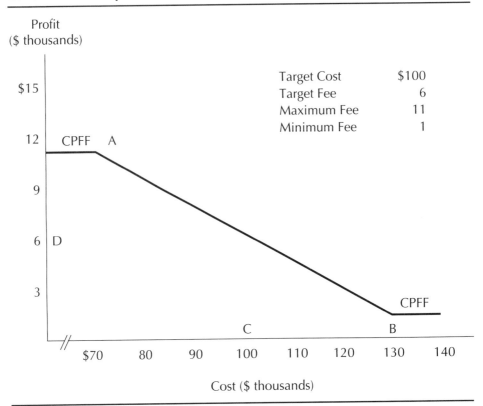

plier in the form of award fee payments based on the buyer's subjective assessment in periodic reviews of how diligently the supplier is applying himself or
herself.

This judgmental aspect of supplier performance evaluations provides an inherent flexibility to contracting situations in an uncertain environment, and the
supplier, as well as the buyer, can benefit from it.

If progress does not meet initial expectations because of unforeseen circumstances, the supplier still can earn the maximum award fee if performance is
judged to be the best possible in the particular situation. While the buyer reserves
the right to make unilateral decisions regarding contractor performance, these
decisions should not be made arbitrarily or capriciously; the supplier has certain safeguards.

All performance evaluations, for example, are subject to review at higher
management levels within the buying organization, and the supplier is given an
opportunity to present its case. But the seller's greatest protection is the buyer's
self-interest. Unfair treatment of a supplier under any contract destroys the har-
monious working relationship that is the key to a successful outcome. Furthermore, a buyer who earns a reputation for unfairness (as opposed to demanding,

but fair) will have difficulty obtaining qualified suppliers at reasonable prices for future contracting requirements.

Cost Plus Fixed-Fee Contract

A CPFF contract requires the purchaser to reimburse the supplier for all allowable costs and to pay a fixed fee regardless of the magnitude of the costs. Such contracts historically have been used to purchase R&D services, exotic defense equipment, and construction when time did not permit the orderly development of plans and specifications. The CPFF contract gives the supplier a set income regardless of performance and how well costs are controlled. In effect, the contractor has no contractual incentive to control costs and turn in a good overall performance.

Under these circumstances, the award fee concept is much more attractive and the CPFF contract should be utilized only where relatively low-dollar-volume purchases are involved or in situations in which there is likely to be little correlation between the contractor's dedication and a successful outcome.

Many factors determine what method of contract pricing should be employed in a given buying situation. Of particular importance in this choice are the magnitude of the expenditure, the willingness of the supplier to make records available to the purchaser, and the relative degree of uncertainty as to costs. The last factor—cost uncertainty—assumes special importance when the value of the contract warrants the effort associated with structuring a realistic fee arrangement, when buyer and seller can agree on what cost elements should be allowed (such as overhead), and when the supplier's costs associated with performance under the contract can be audited.

Note

1. The point of total assumption is determined by solving the following pair of simultaneous linear equations:

$$y = \text{target profit} + \text{share ratio (target cost} - x)$$
$$y = \text{ceiling price} - x$$

where x = cost, y = profit, and share ratio is the contractor's share stated in decimal form—for example, with a 70/30 share, use .3.

Appendix E
Other Approaches to Cost Estimating

Cost estimates are required at several points in the procurement process. There are a number of methods of developing cost estimates. The degree of accuracy of the estimate varies significantly with the approach employed. Those involved in the procurement process must be aware of which estimating approach has been employed so that they know how reliable the estimate is likely to be.

The design process calls for the development of alternative conceptual approaches to manufacturing a product that will meet the needs identified by Marketing or the customer. The estimated cost of these alternatives is one of the criteria used to decide which alternatives to pursue. The degree of realism or *likely* accuracy required of the estimate is a function of the stage of the design process, the number of alternatives available, and the likely cost magnitude of the item whose cost is being estimated. Increased accuracy in the estimate is required as the procurement process moves through the make-or-buy analysis on to price analysis, cost analysis, and negotiations. Many faulty make-or-buy analyses, resulting in unnecessary costs, are the result of inaccurate cost estimates. A realistic cost estimate is a key input to the buyer who is conducting a price analysis. If the buyer enters into detailed negotiations, the ability to negotiate a satisfactory price depends, in large part, on an accurate and specific cost estimate and the ability to use learning curve theory, when applicable.

Preliminary Cost Estimating Approaches

A preliminary estimate is one that is made during the formative stages of design, a time when there is a decided lack of verifiable information. Preliminary cost estimates are used to screen designs and to aid in the formation of *a budget*. They assist management in determining which concepts to pursue and which to cull at an early stage. Mistakes in preliminary estimates can be costly to the firm since they can result in the elimination of potentially attractive designs. We now will look at several preliminary estimating techniques.[1]

The natural estimator. A few individuals are able to combine experience and intuition and predict manufacturing costs with a fair degree of accuracy. Unfortunately, the supply of such individuals is far short of the demand for them. Accordingly, other approaches must be employed when a high degree of accuracy is required.

Conference method. This approach relies on the collective judgment of several individuals from various departments or, possibly, from the cost estimating department alone. These individuals develop the estimate for a new design by comparing known designs and their associated costs with the new design. This could be a key task for a commodity team.

Comparison method. When the estimator has an excessively difficult design and estimating problem—or even an unsolvable one—the principle of analogies can be employed. A simpler design problem for which an estimate is known or can be developed is constructed. The two designs should be as similar as possible. It is then possible to extrapolate from the simpler design and its estimated cost to the more complex one.

Unit method. The unit method approach to cost estimating is very popular. With this method, the cost estimate is a function of one independent variable. This approach underlies the factor estimating method, described in Detailed Approaches below. Examples of unit estimates are (1) the cost of a factory is a function of the number of square feet of production space ($C = a + 40A$, where $C =$ the cost of the factory, $a =$ a constant, and $A =$ the production area in square feet), and (2) conversion cost is a function of the number of machine shop person-hours ($C = 45T$, where $C =$ cost and $T =$ machine shop hours). The constants and the coefficients may be the result of regression analysis or "feel."

Expected value method. The conference, comparison, and unit methods of estimating all rely on a subtle averaging process. Averaging tends to ignore uncertainty and risk. The expected value method assumes that the estimator is able to give a probability point estimate for each of several costs over a realistic range of cost outcomes. The cost estimate derived in this manner is the summation of the product of the likely costs and their associated probabilities: $C = \sum_i p_i c_i$, where $C =$ cost and $p_i =$ the probability of cost outcome c_1 occurring. One of the attractions of the expected value method is that the decision maker has an understanding of the range of likely cost outcomes so that areas of risk are more visible.

Assume that a cost estimating group has provided the probability estimates contained in Table E-1 for a battery in a power supply unit under development as shown in the following list:

Table E-1.   Likely Cost Outcomes

Cost Per Unit ($)	Probability of Event Occurring
15	.10%
16	.60
17	.10
18	.10
19	.10
	1.00 = 100% probability

Expected sales of the power supply unit are 400,000 units per year at a likely selling price of $30. The most likely cost is $16. The expected cost is $C = 0.1(\$15) + 0.6(\$16) + 0.1(\$17) + 0.1(\$18) + 0.1(\$19) = \$16.50$. Of perhaps equal interest to information on the most likely costs is the range of costs. In this situation, we see that there is 1 chance in 10 that costs will be as low as $15 and 1 in 10 that they will be $19.

Cost estimating relationships. Cost estimating relationships, generally referred to as CERs, are used to estimate the cost of an item from one or more of its functions or characteristics. For example, the estimated cost of a jet engine may be predicted as a function of its thrust: $C = a + bT$, where C = cost, a = a constant, b = a mathematically derived coefficient, and T = thrust of the engine in pounds. Ostwald[2] cites an example of a CER as

$$C = 0.13937x_1^{0.74356} x_2^{0.7751}$$

where C = cost in $10,000,000; x_1 = maximum thrust, in pounds; and x_2 = production quantity milestone.

Detailed Approaches

The techniques just described are useful for screening and eliminating unsound proposals without incurring extensive engineering and estimating costs. Additionally, more accurate methods should be employed on those designs the firm desires to pursue. These methods will be useful in preparing estimates for price analysis and in providing detailed cost estimates to the buyer who is preparing for intensive price negotiations and cost analysis. The following detailed cost estimating methods are more quantitative than those just given. Although judgment still plays an important role, emphasis shifts to mathematical models and hard data.

The factor method. We have seen that the unit method of estimating uses only one factor in estimating the cost. This relationship takes the general form of $C = a + bX$, where C = cost, a = a constant, and b = a coefficient of the independent variable or factor, X, which is the number of units in the project whose cost is being estimated. The factor method utilizes the same logic but achieves increased accuracy by incorporating several factors. The cost estimating model takes on the general form of

$$C = a + B_1X_1 + B_2X_2 + \ldots$$

where

C = the dependent variable, the supplier's cost
a = a constant
B_i = net regression coefficients of the independent variables
X_i = independent variables such as labor, material, overhead, square footage

Each coefficient measures the change in C (cost) per unit change in the particular independent variable, holding the other variables constant. The values for the various factors (a, B_1, B_2, . . .) allow us to derive a predictive model based on the firm's own experience.

Power law and sizing model. This approach is useful in estimating equipment costs for designs similar in type to items whose costs are known but are of different sizes. The principle underlying the power law and sizing model is that there frequently is a nondirect relationship between the size of two items of equipment that differ only in size. This relationship takes on the general form of

$$C = C_r \left(\frac{Q_c}{Q_r}\right) m$$

where

    C = total value sought for design size Q_c
    C_r = known cost for a reference size Q_r
    Q_c = design size in engineering units
    Q_r = reference design size
    m = correlating exponent, $0 < m < 1$

Bottom-up estimating. The preceding methods have one element in common: They view an item from the top; that is, they look at the item as a whole or a group of subcomponents *without* analyzing the nuts and the bolts and the sheet metal or bar stock and the amount of direct (and indirect) labor required to build the item up into a "thing" to be sold. Bottom-up estimating starts with the lowest level of materials purchased by the firm and traces the information process through which the materials go in the process of becoming an end item. This method of estimating is especially appropriate for material and/or labor-intensive items. The bottom-up approach requires an operation to be broken down into its basic elements. Time factors are then applied to these elements. Although several approaches are available when applying the time factors, the standard time data method is the most useful in estimating labor requirements. Standard time data provide time requirements for standard tasks within the firm. Standard time data are arranged in a systematic order and are used over and over. An accurate bottom-up estimate requires considerable data:

    Product specifications
    Delivery quantities and rates
    A bill of materials
    Costs of delivered purchased parts and material
    Detailed drawings of parts to be manufactured
    Parts routings
    Manufacturing equipment requirements
    Testing and inspection requirements
    Packing and shipping requirements

Time factors (labor standards)
Overhead rates

Modular pricing. This approach to cost estimating requires the development of a database of information on development and production costs of the modules of a system. A module is defined as a logical work package or subsystem. When estimating the cost of developing and producing a new system, the item is divided into logical modules. Information is obtained from the database on the cost for developing and producing similar modules. A group of engineering and manufacturing personnel then assigns a judgmental complexity factor to the new module. The item's likely cost then can be estimated by comparing its complexity with that of modules whose cost experience is available. This approach to estimating has proven to be much less time consuming and less costly and more accurate than the other approaches described in this appendix. This modular approach to estimating *does* require forward planning and time and effort to establish the requisite data base.

Notes

1. Much of the materials on the various estimating techniques described in this section is discussed in greater detail in Phillip F. Ostwald, *Engineering Cost Estimating*, 3rd ed. (Englewood Cliffs, N.J.: Prentice-Hall, 1992). Refer to this excellent work for additional details.
2. Ostwald, op. cit.

Appendix F
Special Secondary Source Techniques for Estimating Cost Components

Assuming the supplier will not reveal the cost component breakdowns and if the buyer has little or no internal cost accounting help or cost element knowledge, secondary sources can help the buyer derive the individual cost components of a proposed price and do it with an adequate degree of accuracy. Annual reports, 10K SEC Supplements, the *Annual U.S. Industrial Outlook,* Dun & Bradstreet reports and other studies such as *Dun's Financial Record™*, the *Prentice Hall Annual Almanac of Business and Financial Ratios,* Robert Morris Associates annual statement studies in Philadelphia, Moody's Industrials, Standard & Poor Data, Value Line, and the *U.S. Census of Manufacturers,* plus numerous other U.S. documents and documents from the Bureau of Labor Statistics contain cost revealing data. There are a variety of databases such as Dialog in Palo Alto, California; CompuServe in Columbus, Ohio: Nexis (in most libraries); Dow Jones Quick Search; in addition to database directories such as Database Directory and DataBasics.[1]

One such derivative method is the one originated by Newman and Scordo.[2] If the analyst knows the supplier's product Standard Industrial Classification Code (SIC), which is listed in Dun & Bradstreet reports, the 1982 U.S. SIC Directory, all U.S. Census reports, and most industrial directories, he or she can work "backward" as per the following illustration:

Price per unit: $20.00 (from supplier's proposal-quote)
Material to labor ratio: 5 to 1 (from the *U.S. Census of Manufacturers*)
Cost of goods sold (COGS): 76% of sales (from the annual report or *Dun's Financial Record*
SG&A Expenses: 15% of sales (from the annual report or Dun's credit report)
Net income: 9% of sales (from the annual report or Dun's credit report)
Material to sales ratio: 35% of sales (from the *U.S. Census of Manufacturers*)

By converting, we derive the following:

Material costs	=	35% of $20	=	$7.00
Direct labor is 100/5	=	20% of $7	=	1.40
Overhead (76%–35%–7%)	=	34% of $20	=	6.80
SG&A	=	15% of $20	=	3.00
Net income	=	9% of $20	=	1.80
		Total Price		$20.00

Using these figures and other sources such as those already cited plus the buyer's estimates, we can determine which cost elements are out of line when compared to industry benchmarks as well as the total price.

Another such derivative method that produces a "should cost" price or cost model is a type of benchmark method proposed by Burt, Norquist, and Anklesaria.[3] We will use an example of a material intensive electronic component:

Price per unit, $20.00 From the supplier's proposal-quote. Material cost based on 30% of price or sales	=	$ 6.00	From the U.S. Census or Annual Survey of Manufacturers
Direct labor based on a material to labor ratio of 11.31 to 1 or 100/11.31 = 8.8% × $6.00	=	.53	From the U.S. Census or Annual Survey of Manufacturers
Factory overhead at 175% of direct labor	=	.93	From the Annual Statement Studies, Robert Morris Associates
Total Factory Cost	=	$ 7.46	
SG&A at 31.8% of factory cost	=	$ 2.37	From the Annual Statement Studies, Robert Morris Associates
Total Cost	=	9.83	
Profit is 20.00 − 9.83	=	$10.17	

Note that the profit of $10.17 is 103% of total cost v. the normal industry profit rate of 25% (from the annual statement studies). These statement studies indicate that a normal profit should be $2.46 for an expected price per unit of $12.29 (total cost: $9.83 plus profit of 2.46 = $12.29). We now have an excellent agenda item for the negotiation meeting as the profit is way too high unless we have asked for some very special requirement involving very high risk for the supplier. In addition, because we estimated material cost at 30% of the quoted price of $20.00 with this abnormal profit component, the realistic price could be in the $9.00 range as we would now start the process with a much lower price than $20.00.

Presenting our estimate to the supplier team will usually provoke a detailed counter response and, at the least, will stimulate a vigorous debate and possible concession unless the component is unique and in very high demand with unusual terms and conditions. In any event, "should cost" models provide the incentive and documentation to explore cost component breakdowns. One other caution: price is just one part of total cost, which means pure price quotes are actually inadequate indicators of total costs, or total cost of ownership (TCO).

"Should cost" and other derivative type models also identify the key cost drivers and reveal what cost elements are out of line with industry benchmarks. Is it labor, material, overhead, or profit? This analysis also begs the question of "are our specifications too high or is the supplier capability too low?" Do not pay for unnecessary requirements or for services not used or needed. If the supplier is charging high engineering overhead for a part the buyer designed, this cost component should be reduced or eliminated.

Finally, will cost analysis always reduce costs to a reasonable level? "No" is the answer as we always face the supply-demand issue. For example, in the late fall of 1994, several major aluminum producers obtained price increases of approximately 50 percent from large can manufacturers.[4] This price increase resulted from high demand and short supply for can sheet and uniform price increases by all major can sheet suppliers. The price increase was led by Alcoa, which announced that all can customers would have to pay the London Metal Exchange price for aluminum ingot. While such a "peg" could also lower the price in the future, the only actions the can producers have available is to pay the higher price or substitute another material.

Notes

1. See Richard G. Newman, *Supplier Price Analysis: A Guide for Purchasing, Accounting, and Financial Analysts* (Westport, Conn.: Quorum Books, a division of Greenwood Press, 1992), pp. 51–73. Reprinted with permission of Greenwood Publishing Group, Inc., Westport, Conn. Copyright © 1992.
2. Richard G. Newman and J. Scodro, "Price Analysis for Negotiation," *Journal of Purchasing and Materials Management* (Spring 1988), pp. 8–15.
3. David N. Burt, Warren E. Norquist, and Jimmy Anklesaria, *Zero Based Pricing™: Achieving World Class Competitiveness Through Reduced All-in-Costs* (Chicago, Ill.: Probus, 1990), pp. 143–173.
4. Norton, Erle, "Aluminum Makers Pushing Through Price Increases to Can Manufacturers," *The Wall Street Journal* (November 18, 1994), p. A2.

Appendix G
Managing Price Increases

During the inflationary days of the 1980s, Warren E. Norquist, then vice president of Purchasing and Materials Management at Polaroid, developed the well-publicized Zero Base Pricing™ concept that encourages buyers to resist and challenge all price increases. Price increase requests might also indicate that the buyer needs to explore price reduction options. When a price increase is proposed by the supplier, the buyer must review all of the following factors to assess the need for the increase and negotiate a response with the supplier.

The proactive buyer analyzes price increase requests by:

• Asking for documentation and explanation. *Always* ask why price increases are necessary. This may seem obvious, but many buyers fall into the habit of merely accepting price change notices without much of a challenge. Ask for proof, such as a copy of the new labor agreement or materials invoices before and after the increase in the supplier's cost. Be sure that the supplier has correctly calculated and documented the increase as stipulated in the contract.

• Exploring opportunities for cost savings. Can the product be redesigned? Is there a cheaper manufacturing method or substitute raw material? Is the proper freight carrier being used and can the cost of packaging be reduced? Is there a standard part versus the custom one being purchased? Can we reduce the product variation, a form of standardization? Is the produce overengineered? The supplier response may reveal significant cost reduction ideas.

• Considering all-in-costs or total costs. Some price increases due to product quality improvement can reduce the *total cost of ownership,* which means a price increase may result in a total cost decrease.

• Ensuring that appropriate contract terms are employed. Perhaps the buyer should switch to incentive or predetermination type contracts as discussed in Appendix C. Formula pricing contracts may be more appropriate during periods of high inflation and for long lead time products, but in some cases, the firm fixed-price contract is better if the buyer increases its share of business with the supplier.

• Tracking prices. The buyer may not be tracking prices and may be caught off guard with sudden price increases.

• Using the correct prices/indices. Use formula pricing clauses as a basis of comparison with the producer price index (PPI), not the actual change in price. The supplier's cost may have little or nothing in common with the PPI.

◆ Reducing change orders. The buyer's engineering department may be issuing too many change orders, so the supplier feels it must penalize the buyer for the resulting extra costs. This can happen because of either premature buying (the buyer places the order too soon) or indecision on the part of the buyer's engineering or marketing departments.

◆ Using applicable costs. Some suppliers talk in terms of "average," "total," or "high" costs. The buyer must be careful to avoid paying for the maximum possible cost to the supplier. *Only pay for increases that apply to you and your orders.*

◆ Conducting make-or-buy analysis, if appropriate. When the supplier proposes a purchase price increase, conduct a make-or-buy analysis to confirm that it is still financially wise to purchase the product or service.

◆ Considering prenotice price change clauses on a case-by-case basis. During periods of extreme demand and high inflation, suppliers are understandably reluctant to sign long-term agreements and price warning clauses. For example, at the beginning of 1979, the price of copper was 74¢ per pound and at the end of 1978, it was $1.06 per pound. Solvent naphtha prices started at 66¢ per gallon and rose to slightly more than $1.00 per gallon during the same period. Under such conditions, suppliers were unwilling to enter into long-term contracts at fixed prices, unless the prices included significant contingencies.

Using a prenotice price change clause to provide a supplier with the necessary safety valve required in long-term contracts. At the same time, the clause protects the buyer by preventing surprise price increases. Such a clause requires that only written price change requests arriving no later than a specified day each month will be reviewed and then indicates a minimum time, such as 60 days, before a price increase will be granted after approval by the buyer. The clause should include a requirement for a cost breakdown and other justification for the price increase request. In many cases, such a clause can also cover a request by the buyer to lower the price with similar protection terms for the seller.

Analyzing precious metal surcharges clauses is common for products using precious metals such as gold, silver, platinum, or gems such as diamonds. Ordinarily, the material price is pegged to one of the commodity exchanges and prices listed in *The Wall Street Journal* or other recognized publications. It is important for the buyer to know when the material was purchased to confirm the fairness of the price. The buyer should insist on a verified material invoice for the order. In addition, many buyers sign contracts calling only for increases, when, in fact, precious material prices fluctuate up and down. The possibility of a price reduction should be contained in the clause, in addition to the opportunity to reopen negotiations if price swings of a certain percentage take place.

◆ When justified, only granting price increase requests based on the specific cost element. If the supplier documents a legitimate increase in labor, material, or overhead, grant the percentage increase on that component—never on the last total invoice price. Failure to be aware of this tactic results in a change in price based on all the components of price, which seldom, if ever, go up or down all at the same time.

Appendix H
Statistical Process Control

This modified example by Dr. Joseph R. Biggs of California Polytechnic State University in San Luis Obispo is used because it is an excellent and understandable description of SPC. You can try to replicate the results at home because it deals with the manufacture of golf balls.*

We are manufacturing golf balls and assume the PGA states the diameter of golf balls should be 1.500 inches ± one-sixteenth inch (0.0625″) or 1.435″ to 1.5625″. Our firm is going to use SPC because we do not want to scrap any golf balls and 100% inspection is too costly and unnecessary. Exhibit H-1 is a normal or bell-shaped curve and sampling will give us an average value of each sample (not each golf ball but in this case, the average of three balls per sample). This means that if we select each sample of three at random, we will be able to use the average value of each sample to approximate a normal distribution provided each ball has a known and equal chance of being selected, that is, there is no bias such as only selecting balls that "look different." Exhibit H-1 shows that if we will accept only one standard deviation from the grand mean or average, 68.27% of our sample means will fall within these limits and with three standard deviations, 99.73% will fall between the limits. This dispersion will still cause about .27 of the sample to fall outside the tail ends of the distribution. The less deviation, the closer the averages of the samples will be to the grand mean.

To construct an SPC chart, we need three inputs:

1. A normal curve so we can use statistical formulas, tables, and other defined data.
2. The grand mean or average value of all the samples designated as $\bar{\bar{x}}$. Remember, the sample mean, $\bar{x}$, is the average of the sample.
3. The amount of dispersion about the grand mean of the sample means as determined by the standard deviation labeled "S" (or variation among the sample means from the grand mean) and the range, labeled $\bar{R}$, which is the highest value in each sample minus the lowest value.

*Joseph R. Biggs, "3.26, Statistical Process Control (SPC) and Purchasing," *Guide to Purchasing* (Tempe, Ariz.: The National Association of Purchasing Management, 1989). Text, exhibits, and tables used with permission from the publisher.

Exhibit H-1.   Normal or bell-shaped curve.

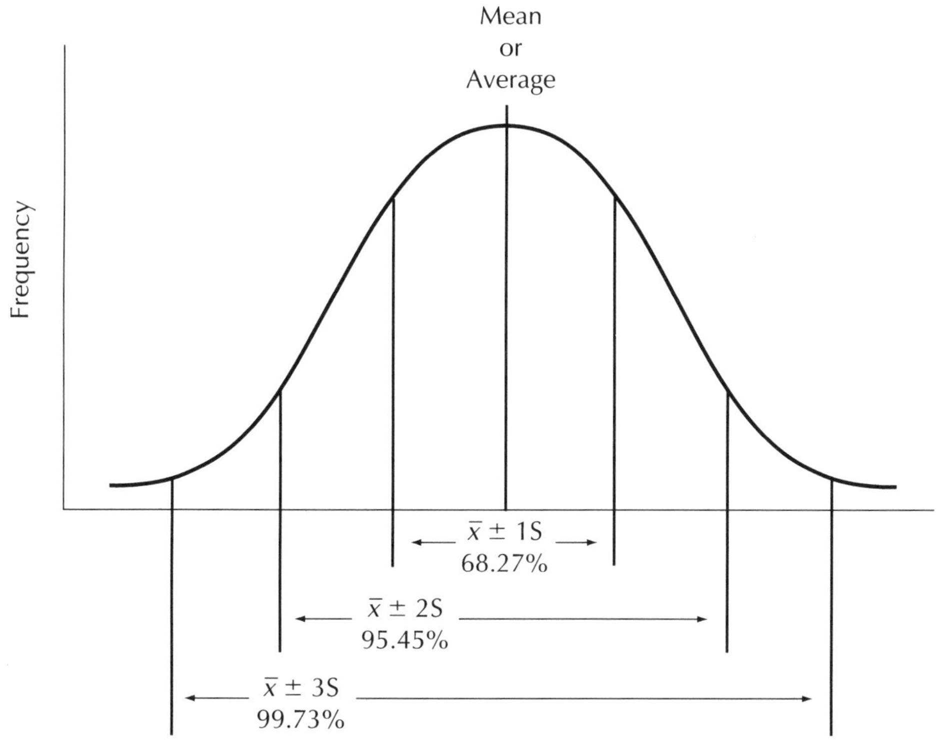

Mean
or
Average

Frequency

$\bar{x} \pm 1S$
68.27%

$\bar{x} \pm 2S$
95.45%

$\bar{x} \pm 3S$
99.73%

Source: Biggs, Joseph R., "3.26 Statistical Process Control (SPC) and Purchasing," *Guide to Purchasing* (Tempe, Ariz., the National Association of Purchasing Management, 1989, p. 4). Reproduced with permission.

Table H-1 gives the results of 15 sample means of 3 balls each and the grand mean of all the samples, the range of all the samples, and the standard deviation of .0051824" derived from a statistical formula based on the square root of the variance.

Table H-2 demonstrates how we use the values from Table H-1 to calculate the upper and lower control limits for both the $\bar{x}$ and $\bar{R}$ charts in Exhibits H-2 and H-3. Remember our observation size is three per sample and we can now use any number of quality control source books (Hayes and Romig; Grant and Leavenworth in this table) to find the factors or math weights of A_2 at 1.023 for the $\bar{x}$ chart and D_4 at 2.57 and D_3 at 0 for the $\bar{R}$ chart. This illustration calculates the upper and lower control limits at ± 3 standard deviations.

Exhibit H-2 now reveals the $\bar{x}$ or dispersion of sample means around target specification of 1.500" and as we can see the process is very much in control from the $\bar{x}$ bar chart data as the machine limits of 1.465" to 1.535" are well within the golf ball specifications of 1.435" to 1.5625". If we see an upper or lower movement trend, the machine should be stopped because it is going out of control. Even if we can wait until the upper or lower control limits are reached and then stop the

(text continues on page 296)

Table H-1. Sample size—diameters: golf ball process.

Sample #	Ball # 1	Ball # 2	Ball # 3	Sample $\bar{x}$	Range $\bar{R}$
1	1.476	1.509	1.512	1.499	.036
2	1.484	1.508	1.490	1.494	.024
3	1.513	1.483	1.489	1.495	.030
4	1.486	1.516	1.477	1.493	.039
5	1.521	1.507	1.481	1.503	.040
6	1.474	1.503	1.511	1.506	.037
7	1.476	1.518	1.506	1.500	.030
8	1.494	1.524	1.488	1.502	.036
9	1.523	1.476	1.513	1.504	.047
10	1.520	1.509	1.486	1.505	.034
11	1.486	1.490	1.412	1.496	.026
12	1.520	1.483	1.406	1.503	.037
13	1.487	1.513	1.515	1.505	.026
14	1.504	1.491	1.475	1.490	.029
15	1.525	1.505	1.485	1.505	.040
			Total	22.500	.511

Grand mean, $\bar{\bar{x}} = \dfrac{22.50}{15} = 1.500''$ $\bar{R} = \dfrac{.511}{15} = .034''$ Sigma $_{n-1}$, S = .0051824''

In this illustration, the grand mean, $\bar{\bar{x}}$, just happens to be the exact number of the desired specification of the golf ball, 1.500."

Source: Joseph R. Biggs, "3.26 Statistical Process Control (SPC) and Purchasing," *Guide to Purchasing* (Tempe, Ariz., the National Association of Purchasing Management, 1989, p. 6). Reproduced with permission.

Table H-2. Factors for calculating statistical process control lines.

No. of Observations in Sample	A_2	D_3	D_4
2	1.88	0.00	3.27
3	1.02	0.00	2.57
4	0.73	0.00	2.28
5	.58	0.00	2.11
6	.48	0.00	2.00
7	.42	.08	1.92
8	.37	.14	1.86
9	.34	.18	1.82
10	.31	.22	1.78

Equations for the $\bar{x}$ Chart:
Upper control limit $= \bar{x} + A_2\bar{R}$
Lower control limit $= \bar{x} - A_2\bar{R}$

Equations for the $\bar{R}$ Chart:
Upper control limit $= D_4\bar{R}$
Lower control limit $= D_3\bar{R}$

Source: Joseph R. Biggs, "3.26 Statistical Process Control (SPC) and Purchasing," *Guide to Purchasing* (Tempe, Ariz., the National Association of Purchasing Management, 1989, p. 6). Reproduced with permission.

Exhibit H-2. x̄ Chart and plot of golf ball diameter means from Table H-1.

| | UCL = 1.500 + 1.023 × .034   LCL = 1.500 − 1.023 × .034 |
| | = 1.535"   = 1.465" |

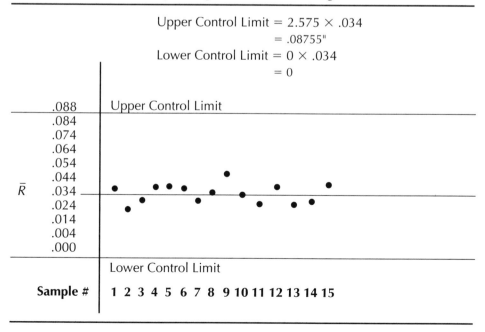

1.563	
1.535	Upper Tolerance
1.530	Upper Control Limit
1.525	
1.520	
1.515	
1.510	
1.505	
1.500	x̄
1.495	
1.490	
1.485	
1.480	
1.475	
1.470	
1.465	Lower Control Limit
1.438	Lower Tolerance

Sample #   1 2 3 4 5 6 7 8 9 10 11 12 13 14 15

Source: Modified from the work of Joseph R. Biggs, "3.26 Statistical Process by Control (SPC) and Purchasing," *Guide to Purchasing* (Tempe, Ariz., the National Association of Purchasing Management, 1989, p. 7). Reproduced with permission.

Exhibit H-3. R̄ Chart and plot of golf ball diameter ranges from Table H-1.

Upper Control Limit = 2.575 × .034
= .08755"
Lower Control Limit = 0 × .034
= 0

	.088	Upper Control Limit
	.084	
	.074	
	.064	
	.054	
	.044	
R̄	.034	
	.024	
	.014	
	.004	
	.000	
		Lower Control Limit

Sample #   1 2 3 4 5 6 7 8 9 10 11 12 13 14 15

machine, no defects will be produced (however, there can be sample error) and the operator in SPC environments can "stop the line."

The reason we also construct $\bar{R}$ charts as illustrated in Exhibit H-3 is that averages can mask what we call *spikes* in the data or erratic operation that means something is wrong but the average would not show it. We must examine both $\bar{x}$ and $\bar{R}$; one may be in control and the other out of control, which indicates a process problem. The range of limits in Exhibit H-3 of 0 to .88" also indicates the process is in control.[1]

Note

1. See Douglas C. Montogmery, *Introduction to Statistical Quality Control*, 3rd ed. (New York: Wiley, 1996); and Ellis R. Ott, *Process Quality Control*, 2nd ed. (New York: McGraw-Hill, 1990).

Appendix I
Design of Experiments*

Bhote's book *World Class Quality* is rather shocking with its indictment of poor quality in the United States and the author's statement "90% of U.S. industry does not know how to solve chronic quality problems." It also dispels the notion that statistical process control (SPC) is the answer and how the Japanese have used design of experiments (DOE) since the early 1970s to solve variation problems.

At Motorola, Bhote used DOE techniques developed by Dorian Shainin, the brilliant 1936 MIT graduate who worked as a quality control engineer at United Aircraft (now United Technologies) and for 23 years as a consultant and vice president of Statistical Engineering for Rath & Strong, a management consulting firm in Lexington, Massachusetts. Shainin now has his own statistical engineering firm with his son, Peter, in Manchester, Connecticut. Although relatively unknown to the business community in general, Dorian Shainin ranks with Deming and Juran among the real professionals in the field of quality control; he received the Shewhart Medal, the most coveted award from the American Society for Quality Control (ASQC).

Part I of the book starts with the need for high quality and the four stages of quality, that is, innocence, awakening, commitment/implementation and, finally, the goal of "World Class." Innocence represents neglect, and Bhote states only 50% of U.S. companies have even reached stage 2 (awakening) by using elementary tools such as SPC and achieving acceptable quality levels (AQL) of 0.1% (1,000 parts per million). Even more alarming, Bhote feels just 10–15% are in stage three and using DOE to achieve AQLs of 100 parts per million and less. Finally, he states there is no U.S. company in stage 4, global class, with AQLs of near zero. Bhote estimates the total cost of poor quality to be 10–25% of the U.S. sales dollar or $100–$200 per day loss by each employee!

Part II: The Design of Experiments (DOE): Key to the Magic Kingdom of Quality is the vital segment of the book. DOE tools discover key variables in process-product design and then find solutions to substantially reduce the variations they cause while reducing tolerances on the lesser variables so as to reduce

* A book review by Richard L. Pinkerton of *World Class Quality* by Keki R. Bhote (New York: AMACOM, 1991) published in *The International Journal of Purchasing and Materials Management*, Summer 1993, vol. 29, no. 3, pp. 51–52. Reprinted with permission of the publisher, The National Association of Purchasing Management.

costs. The DOE tools use many techniques to identify process capability (CP), which is the width of the specification (S) divided by the process width (P); that is, it is a measure of spread. Note that process capability is sometimes written as PC and other times as CP. A more powerful yardstick is CPK, which measures the noncentering of the process relative to the specification limits of a parameter. CPK corrects for the $\bar{x}$ or process average that is too close to the limits at the tail ends of average; that is, the minimum goal of CPK is 2.0, which narrows the process spread within the specification spread to prevent dangerous variation.

As mentioned earlier, we must search out and correct the causes of the variation to achieve a CPK of 2.0 or better. In Chapter 4, Bhote lists "poor management" as close to 95% of the causes of variance by ignoring the total cost impact of quality problems, failure to have a total quality program beyond the slogan phase, the lack of DOE use, no leadership, no training, and the erroneous belief that SPC programs alone improve quality (SPC only monitors variation without regard to the causes of quality problems, let alone solutions). Other sources of variation come from poor product/process specifications, poor component specifications, inadequate quality systems (such as poor instructions, lack of preventive maintenance), poor supplier materials, and operator errors that are the result of poor instructions and inadequate training.

Chapter 5, Three Approaches to DOE: Classical, Taguchi, and Shainin, starts with a brief reminder of the classical and pioneering work of Sir Ronald Fisher who applied DOE techniques to agriculture in the 1930s to isolate and measure variables and interacting variable variation. Except for U.S. chemical process companies and a few enlightened firms in recent years, DOE knowledge was limited to academic statistical researchers such as Box and Hunter.

Dr. Genichi Taguchi of Japan adapted the classical approach for use with the old technique of orthogonal arrays (right angle analysis) and firms such as Nippon Denso, AT&T, Ford, Xerox, I.T.T., United Technologies, and some Ford suppliers have used the Taguchi approach with "marginal success." The reader should review "Evaluating Product Quality: An Application of the Taguchi Quality Loss Concept" by Charles Quigley and Charles McNamara.[1] Bhote credits Dr. Taguchi with "rediscovering" DOE and applying it to industrial production but argues his orthogonal array approach is too costly, too complicated, accepts randomization only if it is convenient, accepts too many variables to study via brainstorming techniques and most critically, Taguchi does not consider variable interaction unless "a severe interaction is suspected." The orthogonal array belongs in the category of fraction factorials and has the same weakness of confounding of interaction effects.

Bhote advocates using the Shainin Diagnostic Tools because they are simple, logical, practical, universal in scope, statistically powerful and excellent in terms of results. The next eight chapters describe in detail the Shainin Techniques.

Chapter 6, Multi-Vari Charts: To Home in on the Red X, he describes Multi-Vari Charting as a stratified experiment to determine whether the major variation pattern (RED X) is *positional*, which means variations within a single unit such as porosity in a metal casting, across a single unit with many parts, by location, from machine to machine, operator to operator, and plant to plant, or *cyclical*, which is variation between consecutive units drawn from a process, variation among groups of units, batch-to-batch variations, lot-to-lot variations, or *temporal* variations from hour-to-hour, shift-to-shift, day-to-day, and so forth. Quoting Bhote, "A few units, generally three to five, are produced consecutively at any given time. Then some time is allowed to elapse before another three to five consecutive units are run off. The process is repeated a third time, and, if need be, a fourth or fifth time, until at least 80% of the out-of-control variation on the process being investigated is captured . . . by plotting the results of the multi-vari run, you can determine if the largest variation is positional (within unit), cyclical (unit to unit) or temporal (time to time)." Note the multi-vari chart technique is *not* a control chart and is the only DOE method in which the selection of units should *not* be randomized as this method gives you a picture of the evolving nature of the variation.

The above description is an excellent definition of DOE or at least an example of one DOE technique. Once we determine the nature of the variation, then we look for the source of the problem. In one case cited by Bhote, as the day progressed, cylindrical motor shafts being produced on an old turret lathe were going out of specification at certain times of the day. The foreman thought temperature might be a Red X and sure enough, the amount of coolant in the lathe tank was low. When the coolant was added, 50% of the allowed variation was eliminated. By the way, this company was all ready to buy a new lathe for $70,000. Unit-to-unit variation only accounted for 5% of the total allowed variation but within-unit positional variation accounted for another 40% of the allowed variation, which was eliminated by a slight adjustment to the guide rail and a new $200 set of bearings guiding the chuck axis.

The remaining eight chapters of Part II discuss other Shainin DOE techniques including components search, paired comparisons, variables search, full factorials, B vs. C scatter plots, and concludes with a full case study encompassing a logical sequence of the seven DOE tools.

Part III covers SPC including the SPC tools, control charts vs. precontrol, positrol, process certification, and operator certification. The concluding Part IV includes, with implementation and an appendix, an excerpt from "Better Than Taguchi Orthogonal Tables" by Dorian Shainin and Peter Shainin. We urge readers to read this book and share it with engineering, production, and quality personnel.

Note

1. Charles Quigley and Charles McNamara, "Evaluating Product Quality: An Application of the Taguchi Quality Loss Concept," *International Journal of Purchasing and Materials Management* (Summer 1992), pp. 19–25.

Appendix J
Supplier Quality Survey Example

APPLE COMPUTER LIMITED, SINGAPORE BRANCH

Supplier Quality Development Program

Supplier Self-Assessment Questionnaire

(TO BE COMPLETED AND RETURNED TO APPLE COMPUTER LIMITED, SINGAPORE BRANCH, FIVE WORKING DAYS UPON RECEIPT OF THIS QUESTIONNAIRE)

Supplier Name: _____
Address: _____
_____
_____
_____

Supplier Representative(s): _____
_____

Form 05.14/1-B

Supplier Quality/Business Systems Qualification Record

Supplier Name: _____   Address (mfg. site): _____
_____   _____
_____   _____

Commodity (Team):_____   Apple Manufacturing Site: Singapore

Quality Requirements	Yes	No	N/A

Documentation Control
• The supplier maintains control of drawings and specifications _____ _____ _____
  that are used in the finished product inspection function

People/Equipment Control
• The supplier has inspection instructions for the finished product _____ _____ _____
  inspection function
• The supplier has instructions for the calibration of inspection _____ _____ _____
  equipment used in the finished product inspection function
• The calibration system is traceable to recognized standards _____ _____ _____

Material Control
• The supplier utilizes in-process controls or a sampling plan for _____ _____ _____
  finished products to insure comformance to customer require-
  ments. In either case, the confidence level for finished products
  is equal to or better than the minimum required as defined by
  the Supplier Quality Engineer.

Business Requirements
Financial Stability
• The supplier has provided the appropriate financial information _____ _____ _____
  and achieved a minimum rating of 'caution' () by Apple as
  defined by the Apple financial evaluation model

Service and Responsiveness
• The supplier has identified the individual(s) within the suppliers _____ _____ _____
  manufacturing site that is responsible for Apple service

Capacity
• The supplier's manufacturing process has the capability to support at least 125% of Apple's forecasted requirements for this
  supplier given standard lead time or as specified in World Wide
  OEM (Original Equipment Manufacturers) contracts.

Authorization (Name & Signature)   *Date*

SQE/Buyer/Procurement Engr. _____   _____
_____   _____

Procurement Engr. Mgr.
(conditional qualification only) _____   _____

Supplier Quality Development Program

Supplier Self-Assessment Questionnaire

Please answer the following questions. For questions that require description, please type your responses on separate sheets of paper. Otherwise, please circle either Yes/No/NA/Description and provide the applicable procedure number(s). You may wish to add comments where necessary.

1. Describe the reporting structure and relationships in your company.
    Yes/No/NA/Description   Procedure No(s):

2. Describe the operating philosophies and the key business processes in your company.
    Yes/No/NA/Description   Procedure No(s):

3. Give a brief description of how you communicate among yourselves regarding the needs and/or requirements of your customers?
    Yes/No/NA/Description   Procedure No(s):

4. Do you have a housekeeping program?
    Yes/No/NA/Description   Procedure No(s):

5. Do you have a contract review process in your company?
    Yes/No/NA/Description   Procedure No(s):

6. Do you have a system that assures customer's needs and expectations?
    Yes/No/NA/Description   Procedure No(s):

7. Are there any documented quality procedures that describe the elements of quality function?
    Yes/No/NA/Description   Procedure No(s):

8. Is there a document control system in the company?
    Yes/No/NA/Description   Procedure No(s):

9. Do you have a system to assure that your operations are provided with and updated on the new operations instructions?
    Yes/No/NA/Description   Procedure No(s):

10. Do you have a system to assure the latest use of blueprints, specifications, and engineering change information?
    Yes/No/NA/Description   Procedure No(s):

Supplier Quality Development Program

Supplier Self-Assessment Questionnaire

Please answer the following questions. For questions that require description, please type your responses on separate sheets of paper. Otherwise, please circle either Yes/No/NA/Description and provide the applicable procedure number(s). You may wish to add comments where necessary.

11. Do you have a system to select suppliers?
    Yes/No/NA/Description   Procedure No(s):

12. Is there any procedure describing the evaluation and development of your suppliers?
    Yes/No/NA/Description   Procedure No(s):

13. Is there any procedure that ensures that all supplier materials meet customer requirements?
    Yes/No/NA/Description   Procedure No(s):

14. Do you have a system for the identification and traceability of your materials?
    Yes/No/NA/Description   Procedure No(s):

15. Are you using any labelling standards?
    Yes/No/NA/Description   Procedure No(s):

16. If you are not using any barcoding system, do you have plans to do so in the future?
    Yes/No/NA/Description   Procedure No(s):

17. Do you have a documented system for identifying and controlling all materials?
    Yes/No/NA/Description   Procedure No(s):

18. Do you have any procedure for process control?
    Yes/No/NA/Description   Procedure No(s):

Supplier Quality Development Program

Supplier Self-Assessment Questionnaire

Please answer the following questions. For questions that require description, please type your responses on separate sheets of paper. Otherwise,
please circle either Yes/No/NA/Description and provide the applicable
procedure number(s). You may wish to add comments where necessary.

19 Do you have any flow chart to show the process flow of your prod-
    ucts? Is there any procedure to identify the key operating characteris-
    tics of your products?
    Yes/No/NA/Description   Procedure No(s):

20. Do you have any procedure that describes the in-process, and final
    process and/or test inspection program?
    Yes/No/NA/Description   Procedure No(s):

21. Is there a system for preventive maintenance and calibration?
    Yes/No/NA/Description   Procedure No(s):

22. Is audit performed on calibration contractors?
    Yes/No/NA/Description   Procedure No(s):

23. Is there any procedure for the inspection and test status of your prod-
    ucts?
    Yes/No/NA/Description   Procedure No(s)?

24. Do you have a system for the control of nonconforming materiel?
    Yes/No/NA/Description   Procedure No(s):

25. Do you have a system that identifies the inspection authority on a
    record?
    Yes/No/NA/Description   Procedure No(s):

Supplier Quality Development Program

Supplier Self-Assessment Questionnaire

Please answer the following questions. For questions that require description, please type your responses on separate sheets of paper. Otherwise, please circle either Yes/No/NA/Description and provide the applicable procedure number(s). You may wish to add comments where necessary.

26. Do you have a plan to reduce nonconforming materiel?
    Yes/No/NA/Description   Procedure No(s):

27. Do you have a system for corrective action that caters for all elements of the quality function in your company?
    Yes/No/NA/Description   Procedure No(s):

28. Is there an inventory control system?
    Yes/No/NA/Description   Procedure No(s):

29. Do you have a system that provides appropriate and timely data to the customer?
    Yes/No/NA/Description   Procedure No(s):

30. Is there a system that assures adequate/appropriate packaging of the product?
    Yes/No/NA/Description   Procedure No(s):

31. Is there a system for the handling of work-in-process goods, between operations, and from final operations to packaging?
    Yes/No/NA/Description   Procedure No(s):

32. Do you have a system for assuring that customer packing and shipping instructions are met?
    Yes/No/NA/Description   Procedure No(s):

Supplier Quality Development Program

Supplier Self-Assessment Questionnaire

Please answer the following questions. For questions that require description, please type your responses on separate sheets of paper. Otherwise, please circle either Yes/No/NA/Description and provide the applicable procedure number(s). You may wish to add comments where necessary.

33. Is there a system for retaining quality records?
    Yes/No/NA/Description   Procedure No(s):

34. Is internal quality auditing performed?
    Yes/No/NA/Description   Procedure No(s):

35. Does the internal quality program assure that all elements of the quality system continue to be implemented?
    Yes/No/NA/Description   Procedure No(s):

36. Do you have a formal training program?
    Yes/No/NA/Description   Procedure No(s):

37. Describe your support system for employee development.
    Yes/No/NA/Description   Procedure No(s):

38. Do you have a formal statistical process control program in the company?
    Yes/No/NA/Description   Procedure No(s):

Appendix K

Sample Audit-Situational Analysis Questionnaire

DOES YOUR PURCHASING DEPARTMENT MEASURE UP?

Here's a quick quiz to help you gauge your purchasing department. Ideally, all questions should be answered "yes." The answers can be tabulated numerically, as follows: Give an absolute "yes" a 5. Give an absolute "no" a zero. Give scores of 1, 2, 3 or 4 as you think appropriate. If you use this system, a total score of 225–250 will indicate an outstanding purchasing group; 200–225 means good performance; 175–200 fair. Anything below 175 will mean that purchasing isn't living up to its profit potential.

PROFIT CONTRIBUTION

☐ Purchasing is active in (preferably leads) a formal value analysis program.

☐ Standards are regularly reviewed for simplification possibilities.

☐ Value analysis studies take place as early as possible in the design cycle.

☐ Suppliers are encouraged to submit design ideas and manufacturing-operation suggestions.

☐ Purchasing rewards suppliers who submit usable ideas.

☐ Purchasing contributes to make-or-buy studies, and make-or-buy decisions are reviewed regularly.

☐ Life cycle costing, not just initial price, enters into buying decisions when appropriate.

☐ Purchasing recognizes that outside suppliers can easily become complacent without the spur of competition and Zero Base Pricing™ philosophy.

☐ Purchasing negotiates firmly with outside suppliers negotiating a win-win result on price, quality, service, delivery, and legal terms.

☐ Purchasing's negotiation includes application of the learning curve where applicable as well as cost/price analysis of supplier's charges.

☐ Purchasing documents cost reductions.

☐ Purchasing has guidelines defining a reportable cost reduction in material expenses.

☐ Purchasing shares the credit for cost reduction achievements with other departments, or suppliers, when appropriate.

☐ Cost-reduction projects chosen by Purchasing reflect an awareness of priorities, payback periods, net present value, etc.

RELATIONS WITH OTHER DEPARTMENTS

☐ Purchasing processes incoming requisitions promptly.

☐ Purchasing is deeply involved in total quality management (TQM).

☐ Purchasing sometimes questions requisitions: the need itself, specifications.

☐ Purchasing works with other departments to test alternative materials or products.

☐ Purchasing regularly supplies pertinent data to Production Planning: lead times, tooling needs, shortages.

☐ Purchasing regularly supplies pertinent information to Marketing: materials availabilities, price trends, new technology.

☐ Purchasing works with Engineering and Production to ensure that suppliers receive clear instructions, readable blueprints, and other data with sufficient lead time.

☐ Purchasing is working with all users and suppliers to reduce cycle time and engineering changes, returns, rejects, rework, etc.

☐ The organization embraces the IPS.

☐ Purchasing has a regular newsletter containing pertinent material news.

☐ Purchasing regularly supplies pertinent information to Engineering: technical data on new products, updates on supplier capabilities, suppliers' R&D projects, supplier literature.

☐ Purchasing regularly supplies pertinent information to management: economic news, marketplace conditions, new technology, new materials.

☐ Purchasing cultivates close contact with other departments involved in the materials cycle: Production/Inventory Control, Traffic, Quality Assurance, Store, Engineering, etc.

☐ Commodity-sourcing teams are efficient and effective.

☐ Cross-functional decision teams are in place.

SUPPLIER RELATIONS

☐ Purchasing has a formal supplier certification program.

☐ Purchasing has adopted the partnership philosophy with key suppliers.

☐ Purchasing is completely honest in its dealings with suppliers.

☐ Purchasing will not overestimate upcoming purchased goods requirements in hopes of getting a lower price.

☐ Purchasing keeps suppliers' confidential data (prices, design developments, proprietary techniques) confidential.

☐ Purchasing interviews supplier salespersons promptly and minimizes interruptions.

☐ Purchasing arranges for supplier interviews by appointment.

☐ Purchasing arranges for salespersons to interview other company personnel such as Engineering, Production, and Quality.

☐ Purchasing insists that salespersons brief buyers on results of such interviews.

☐ Purchasing corroborates what the suppliers say about such interviews by checking the operating staffer involved.

☐ Purchasing visits suppliers' plants regularly.

☐ Purchasing keeps up-to-date records on suppliers' equipment, production/quality systems, labor relations, etc.

☐ Purchasing seeks alternative sources on all commodities, just in case.

☐ Purchasing gives suppliers advance warning on upcoming material requirements and the buying firm enforces schedule stabilization.

☐ Purchasing assists small, new sources to become dependable suppliers.

☐ Purchasing has an equitable method for rating suppliers.

☐ Purchasing ensures that new shortcut buying systems mesh with suppliers' administrative methods.

☐ Purchasing buys from minority-owned firms.

☐ Purchasing resists any and all reciprocal buying pressures.

☐ Purchasing sees that suppliers' invoices are paid promptly.

☐ The relationship between the buying organization and its suppliers is one of cooperation based on open, honest communication, trust, and cultural fit.

☐ Purchasing has reduced the number of suppliers and utilizes long-term contracts in a partnership relationship.

GENERAL

☐ Purchasing provides forecasts on material availability.

☐ Purchasing provides accurate forecasts on price trends.

☐ Purchasing uses scientific management techniques wherever possible, such as PERT/CPM networks for major buys.

☐ Purchasing experiments with new organizational plans: buying by commodity-sourcing teams, establishing planner-schedulers, use of liaison staffers, the possible split of strategic planners from tactical buyers.

☐ Purchasing has a solid training program for its staffers, including tuition-paid night school courses, NAPM and other seminars, and promotes C.P.M. attainment.

☐ Purchasing uses appropriate benchmarks.

☐ Purchasing is actively exploring global buying activities.

☐ Purchasing is actively involved in the organizational planning process and issues an annual materials report.

☐ Traffic audits are conducted on a regular basis.

☐ The buying organization either has or is studying the possibilities of EDI.

☐ The organization uses credit cards under Purchasing's monitoring.

☐ Purchasing has set up systems contracts (where possible) on low-value needs, to gain time for more creative buying on major purchases.

☐ Purchasing has classified inventory with an ABC analysis and is concentrating on big-ticket A items.

☐ Purchasing staffers are knowledgeable in business law and ethics.

☐ Purchasing distributes publications such as a purchasing manual, buying policy booklet, how suppliers can contribute value analysis suggestions, suppliers welcome guide pamphlet, the annual materials report, purchasing newsletter.

☐ Purchasing is proactive and thinks strategically.

Comments:_____

_____

_____

Source: Unknown original document modified by the authors. Thought to be from NAPM Educational
Material.

Note: This sample is intended to stimulate the reader to prepare one tailored to the needs of a particular organization. David N. Burt at the University of San Diego has developed several elaborate
questionnaires including The Dimensions of Supplier Trust.

Index